Towards a Dialogical History of Modern Architecture

The book challenges three perspectives on the modern architectural canon: explanations that disregard impacts and effects beyond the North Atlantic (monologic), superficial modifications that simply add "Other" figures to the canon, and views that reject the canon itself. Instead, it recognizes the canon's significance in comprehending architecture, while seeking to uncover its presumed Western-centric integrity through a shift from a monological to a dialogical approach.

This approach integrates concepts of identity and Otherness as dialectically articulated and mutually interrelated. In essence, the book's main thesis contends that the canon's historiographic construction overlooked the existence of "Otherness", specifically neglecting the world beyond the North Atlantic nucleus of the West. By examining a global context to comprehend the canon formation, the book proposes a more accurate understanding of the history of modern architecture. Recognizing that this task cannot emanate from a single hegemonic center, it presents the prospect of a coral-type architectural history. This narrative should and could encompass voices from diverse cultures to explore the particular circumstances of the world intertwined with each piece or figure transiently integrated into that canon.

As a result, the ideal readers of this book position themselves within multiple settings, keen on engaging in a critical global conversation about modern architectural discourse. It will be of interest to researchers and students of architecture, architectural history, and cultural studies.

Jorge Francisco Liernur, born in Buenos Aires, Argentina, in 1946, is an architect. He graduated from the University of Buenos Aires and pursued postgraduate studies with Manfredo Tafuri at Istituto Universitario di Architettura di Venezia and Tilmann Buddensieg at the University of Bonn's Institute of Art History. Liernur holds an Honorary Doctorate from the Universidad del Litoral (Argentina). He was the founding dean of the School of Architecture and Urban Studies at Torcuato Di Tella University, where he is currently an emeritus professor and the director of the Master's in History and Criticism of Architecture. Liernur has extensively published on the history of architecture in Argentina and Latin America, exploring their connections with international architecture in books and specialized journals. He co-curated the exhibition "Latin America in Construction: 1955–1980" at the Museum of Modern Art in New York and has been a visiting professor in various universities globally, spanning America, Europe, and Asia.

Routledge Research in Architecture

The *Routledge Research in Architecture* series provides the reader with the latest scholarship in the field of architecture. The series publishes research from across the globe and covers areas as diverse as architectural history and theory, technology, digital architecture, structures, materials, details, design, monographs of architects, interior design and much more. By making these studies available to the worldwide academic community, the series aims to promote quality architectural research.

Gated Luxury Condominiums in India
A Socio-Spatial Arena for New Cosmopolitans
Dhara Patel

The Diné Hogan
A Modern History
Lillian Makeda

Architecture's Disability Problem
Wanda Katja Liebermann

Architecture and the Image at the Turn of the 21st Century
After Visibility
Sanja Rodeš

The Architecture and Geography of Sound Studios
Sonic Heritage
Even Smith Wergeland

Towards a Dialogical History of Modern Architecture
Essays on Otherness and Canon
Jorge Francisco Liernur

For more information about this series, please visit: https://www.routledge.com/Routledge-Research-in-Architecture/book-series/RRARCH

Towards a Dialogical History of Modern Architecture
Essays on Otherness and Canon

Jorge Francisco Liernur

LONDON AND NEW YORK

Designed cover image: *Stuttgart, Weissenhofsiedlung, Araberdorf*, altered postcard (1933) 1940, Stadtarchive Stuttgart, Postkartensammlung A 374. Public Domain.

First published 2025
by Routledge
4 Park Square, Milton Park, Abingdon, Oxon OX14 4RN

and by Routledge
605 Third Avenue, New York, NY 10158

Routledge is an imprint of the Taylor & Francis Group, an informa business

© 2025 Jorge Francisco Liernur

The right of Jorge Francisco Liernur to be identified as author of this work has been asserted in accordance with sections 77 and 78 of the Copyright, Designs and Patents Act 1988.

All rights reserved. No part of this book may be reprinted or reproduced or utilised in any form or by any electronic, mechanical, or other means, now known or hereafter invented, including photocopying and recording, or in any information storage or retrieval system, without permission in writing from the publishers.

Trademark notice: Product or corporate names may be trademarks or registered trademarks, and are used only for identification and explanation without intent to infringe.

British Library Cataloguing-in-Publication Data
A catalogue record for this book is available from the British Library

ISBN: 978-1-032-58949-7 (hbk)
ISBN: 978-1-032-58952-7 (pbk)
ISBN: 978-1-003-45226-3 (ebk)

DOI: 10.4324/9781003452263

Typeset in Times New Roman
by codeMantra

To Manfredo Tafuri. In memoriam.

Contents

	List of Figures	*ix*
	Acknowledgments	*xv*
1	Preliminary Words: Introduction to the Book	1
2	Essay 1: Otherness and Canon	12
3	Essay 2: Controversial Positions: The Center–Periphery Tension in the Work of Manfredo Tafuri	39
4	Essay 3: Orientalism and Modern Architecture: The Debate on the Flat Roof	106
5	Essay 4: The Grand Move: How the Smithsons Contributed to the Restoration of Western Europe's Cultural Centrality (1945–1956)	136
	Bibliography	*189*
	Index	*213*

Figures

1.1 "Tableau Comparatif de la Hauteur des Principaux Monuments". By Barbie Du Bocage, J.G.; Dufour, H.; George, F.E.; De Soye Et Bouchet; Vuillemin, A.; Charle, J.B.; Levasseur, V.; Duvotenay, T., Maison Basset, Paris, 1852. An expression of a 19th-century architectural canon comparing the height of its buildings. Public domain. From David Rumsey Map Collection, David Rumsey Map Center, Stanford Libraries   2
1.2 Segment of a page from Bruno Zevi's Historia de la Arquitectura Moderna, Poseidon, 1980, p. 274. The caption reads: "Fig. 144. Diagram on the main relationships between Europe and the United States during the early period of modern architecture". This diagram is one of the clearest expressions of the North Atlantic-centric character of modern architectural historiography   3
2.1 *Delle vite de' piu eccellenti pittori scultori et architettori* (Of the Lives of the Most Excellent Painters, Sculptors, and Architects) by Giorgio Vassari, Apreso i Giunti, Florence, 1568. First page. Alessandrina University Library, Italy. In https://www.europeana.eu/item/446/VIAE000291   13
2.2 *Babylonis Muri* (The Walls of Babylon), from *The Eight Wonders of the World*, 1572, by Philip Galle (artist), Maerten van Heemskerck (artist after), plate 7 (Copy from Herzog August Library, Germany). In https://www.europeana.eu/item/168/item_7XUSQ75RPFWTLEEBHOGAAE66Q4EXOY45   14
2.3 "Allgemeine Landkarte andeütend an welchem Orte jedes von denen in diesem Büche angeführten Gebauden" (General map indicating the location of each of the buildings listed in this book), *Entwurf einer Historischen Architektur* (A draft of historical architecture), by Johann Bernhard Fischer von Erlach, Vienna, 1721 (Copy from Slovak National Gallery, Bratislava, Slovakia). https://www.europeana.eu/item/07101/G_10045_2   18
2.4 "Das Andere", Title page draft by Adolf Loos, 1903. In Albertina, Austria. https://www.europeana.eu/item/15508/ALA692   21

2.5	Motto: "Ein Scheusal Von Einem Haus"; Vortrag Des Architekten Adolf Loos, Mein Haus Am Michaelerplatz; Im Sophiensaal, 1911, design by Urban Janke, 1911, Albertina, Austria. https://www.europeana.eu/item/15508/DG2003_1511	23
3.1	Detail of a photograph taken during an interview with Tomas Dagnino for the Architecture Supplement of the newspaper *Clarin*. Buenos Aires, August 1981. *Clarin* Archive. Photo: Daniel Rodríguez. (Courtesy of *ARQ Revista*)	40
3.2	*San Gregorio da Sassola e Castello Medioevale* (xilography), from *Le cento città d'Italia. Supplemento mensile illustrato del Secolo* (The Hundred Cities of Italy. Illustrated Monthly Supplement of the Century), Milan, Sonzogno, 1894. Unknown author. Wikimedia Commons	44
3.3	Book cover *of L'architettura moderna in Giappone* (*Modern Architecture in Japan*), by Manfredo Tafuri, Capelli, Bologna, 1964	47
3.4	Cover of the magazine *Contropiano* (counter the plan). Year II, N° 1, 1969	53
3.5	Peter Eisenman, Mario Gandelsonas, Jorge Silvetti, Giusi Rapisarda, Manfredo Tafuri, Rodolfo Machado. Terrace of the Institute of Architecture and Urban Studies, New York, c. 1975. Photo by Diana Agrest, other member of the group (courtesy of Jorge Silvetti and Rodolfo Machado)	62
3.6	Book cover of *Vienna Rossa. La politica residenziale nella Vienna socialista, 1919–1933* (Red Vienna. Residential Politics in Socialist Vienna, 1919–1933), Manfredo Tafuri. Electa Editrice, Milan, 1980	65
3.7	Book cover of *Il Dispositivo Foucault* (Foucault's dispositive), by Massimo Cacciari, Franco Rella, Manfredo Tafuri, CLUVA, Venice, 1977	68
3.8	"Pianta di ampio magnifico Collegio formata sopra l'idea dell'antiche Palestre de' Greci, e Terme de' Romani" (Floorplan of a large magnificent college formed on the idea of the ancient Gyms of the Greeks and Baths of the Romans), etching, 600 × 440 mm, from *Opere varie di architettura prospettive grotteschi antichità sul gusto degli antichi romani* by Giovanni Battista Piranesi, Roma, 1761. PD. Getty Research Institute, in https://archive.org/details/gri_33125008448025	73
3.9	Map of Venice, from *Isolario di Benedetto Bordone*, by Benedetto Bordone, Venice, published by Niccolò Zoppino, 1533. From John Carter Brown Library. In https://archive.org/details/isolariodibenede00bord	84

Figures xi

3.10 "Pianta terrena del Palazo Cornaro sul Canal Grande a S. Maurizio", *from Le Fabbriche e i monumenti cospicui di Venezia* (The Buildings and Prominent Monuments of Venice). By Cicognara, L.; Diedo, A.; Selva, G.A. Edited by G. Antonelli, Venice, 1858 (Getty Research Institute). In Tafuri's view, in the layout of the Palazzo Corner, Jacopo Sansovino manages the tension between the Venetian vestibule tradition and the scheme of the central courtyard imported from Rome ... 91

4.1 *Stuttgart, Weissenhofsiedlung, Araberdorf*, photomontage by Kunstverlag Hans Boetticher Stuttgart, 1934, postcard, 1940. (SESAM-Mediathek Stadtmedienzentrum Stuttgart. https://sesam.lmz-bw.de/details/512245.) ... 107

4.2 "Vue d'une partie de la ville de Temboctou ..." (View of a Part of the City of Timbuktu ...), from *Illustrations de Voyage à Temboctou et à Jenné, dans l'Afrique Centrale* ..., by René Caillié, Couché fils, graveurs, Paris, 1830 (Bibliothèque Nationale de France, Gallica) ... 109

4.3 Eugène Delacroix, *Convulsionists of Tangier*, 1838 (Minneapolis Institute of Art) ... 111

4.4 William Holman Hunt, *Nazareth*, 1905, New York, The Macmillan Company London, Macmillan & Co., Ltd. (New York Public Library) ... 112

4.5 Adolf Loos, 1912–1913, Wien, Larochegasse 3, Haus Scheu ... 117

4.6 Tony Garnier, Houses at the *Cité Industrielle*. From the book with the same name and the same author, Vol. 2, Massin & Cie., Paris, 1932, p. 24 (BIbliothèque Municipale de Lyon) ... 118

4.7 Hans Poelzig, House of Friendship, Istanbul, Perspective view, Technische Universität Berlin, Architecture Museum, Inv. Nr. HP 007,005 ... 120

4.8 Villa Allegonda J.P. Oud, c. 1918, Photographer unknown. Instituut Collectie Nederland (inv.nr. AB5055). Katwijk aan Zee ... 121

4.9 Concrete country house. Mies van der Rohe. As presented in *Mies in Berlin*, the catalogue of the exhibition with this name curated by Terence Riley and Barry Bergdoll, The Museum of Modern Art, New York, 2002, p. 191 ... 126

4.10 Magazine cover. "Das neue Frankfurt: internationale Monatsschrift für die Probleme kultureller Neugestaltung", 1.1926/1927. Special Issue: "The Flat Roof". Published by Englert und Schlosser, Frankfurt (Universitätsbibliothek Heidelberg) ... 128

5.1 Second from the left Architect Minnette da Silva (Sri Lanka), the first Asian representative of CIAM. During a session of the World Congress of Intellectuals in Defense of Peace at the Wrocław University of Technology, Poland (August 25 to 28, 1948). To her right Pablo Picasso, to her left Jo Davidson and Mulk Raj Anand ... 139

xii   *Figures*

5.2   From left to right: Josep Lluis Sert, Claudius Petit, Sigfried
      Giedion, and Le Corbusier. VII CIAM, Bergamo, July 22–31,
      1949. The CIAM Collection. (CIAM-D005-0002), photographer
      unknown (courtesy of the Frances Loeb Library, Harvard
      University Graduate School of Design)   142
5.3   A view of the beaches of Rio de Janeiro. Cover of the first issue
      of *The Architectural Review* dedicated to Brazilian architecture.
      Vol. 95, No. 567, March 1945   145
5.4   "The amazing thing for me was the machinery of war – the
      Bailey Bridge, the vehicles, the Jeep" (Peter Smithson to
      Beatriz Colomina. COLOMINA & SMITHSON, 2000, 15). An
      announcement from the War Office published in the *Picture
      Post* on March 13, 1954, and held among Peter Smithson's
      papers in which the demountable bridges reminiscent of those
      used by the Army Corps of Engineers, from which he was a
      part during the war, can be seen. The Alison and Peter Smithson
      Archive. Folder E004 (courtesy of the Frances Loeb Library,
      Harvard University Graduate School of Design)   152
5.5   Axonometric drawing. Coventry Cathedral, 1951. The Alison
      and Peter Smithson Archive. Folder A003. (APS_A003_0001)
      (courtesy of the Frances Loeb Library, Harvard University
      Graduate School of Design)   162
5.6   Alison and Peter Smithson, The School at Hunstanton Norfolk,
      as published by The Architectural Review, London, September
      1954, pp. 134, 135   163
5.7   An image of the exhibition The Family of Man at the Museum
      of Modern Art, New York, as published in the catalog by
      Edward Steichen. Edited by the MoMA with the Maco
      Magazine Corp., c. 1955   167
5.8   Alison and Peter Smithson, Installation of Parallel of Life and
      Art, photos by Nigel Henderson, as published in The Charged
      Void. Architecture by Alison and Peter Smithson, The Monacelli
      Press, New York, 2001, p. 123   169
5.9   Caves of Les Baux de Provence, near St. Remy, 1953.
      Photographer Peter Smithson. The Alison and Peter Smithson
      Archive. Folder BA038 (courtesy of the Frances Loeb Library,
      Harvard University Graduate School of Design)   174
5.10 House of the Future, Section YY HF5518 in which one can see
      the molding of the walls to store the house's equipment. The
      Alison and Peter Smithson Archive. Folder A019 (courtesy of
      the Frances Loeb Library, Harvard University Graduate School
      of Design)   175

5.11 Alison and Peter Smithson, House of the Future. Photography
of the model. See a view of the "theatrical" installation featuring
an elevated perimeter catwalk, from where the audience
observes actors representing future life. From *The Municipal
Journal* (currently "The MJ"), March 2, 1956   176
5.12 Alison and Peter Smithson, Photo of *Patio and Pavilion*
at the exhibition This Is Tomorrow, by Nigel Henderson, as
published in *The Charged Void*. Architecture by Alison and
Peter Smithson, The Monacelli Press, New York, 2001, p. 150   177
5.13 Andrea Mantegna, *Saint Jerome in the Desert* (1448–1451).
Sao Paulo Museum of Art (MASP)   178

Acknowledgments

The essays featured in this book have been presented at esteemed institutions such as Universidad Torcuato Di Tella (UTDT), Harvard University's Graduate School of Design, Berlage Institut, Catholic University of Chile's Doctoral Program of the School of Architecture and Urban Studies, Universidad del Litoral's Master Program of the School of Architecture, the Berlage Institute, Karlsruhe Institute of Technology, Duke University, University of Freiburg, the Technical School of Architecture at the University of Navarra, the and Polytechnic University of Milan. Additionally, apart from Universidad Torcuato Di Tella, funding for the research has been contributed by the National Council for Scientific and Technical Research of Argentina and the Alexander von Humboldt Foundation. Numerous individuals have, in one way or another, provided ideas, critical readings, and support. I extend my sincere gratitude to Ricardo Salvatore, Patricio del Real, Anahí Ballent, Adrián Gorelik, Claudia Shmidt, Beatriz Sarlo, Fernando Aliata, Alejandro Crispiani, Andrés Reggiani, Jorge Silveti, Luis Muller, Werner Oechslin, Victor Perez Escolano, Manuel Plaza, Marco De Michelis, Francesco Dal Co, Gabriel Feld, Fernando Perez Oyarzun, Joaquin Medina Warmburg, Federico Paoloni, Vicente Ballester, Gabriel Feld, Daniele Pisani, Federico Deambrosis, Sarah Williams Goldhagen, George Baird, Emilia Couto, and Diego Goldberg. Their insightful feedback and contributions have been invaluable.

I must thank Ines Zalduendo for her work in correcting my initial and rough English version. In addition, I also relied on the assistance of Patricia Maliar and Fernando Williams for that.

As the reader will discern, this book does not aim to present research on an underexamined topic; rather, its focus is to revisit well-explored subjects from an infrequently employed perspective. Consequently, the materials utilized by the author predominantly derive from secondary sources. Nevertheless, the development of the final essay would have been unattainable without access to primary information gathered from the CIAM collection in the archive of the Institute for the History and Theory of Architecture at the Federal Institute of Technology Zurich. Similarly, invaluable primary data were sourced from the CIAM, Josep Lluis Sert, Ernst Weissmann, and Alison and Peter Smithson archives within the Special Collection at the Harvard Graduate School of Design. In the latter case, the successful completion of this work is attributed to the invaluable collaboration of its director, Mg. Arch. Ines Zalduendo.

The author extends special gratitude to the editors who have authorized the publication (corrected, reedited, and/or expanded) of the following preliminary versions of some of the essays published here, namely:

Essay 2
"Controversial Positions: The Center–Periphery Tension in the Work of Manfredo Tafuri": "Posiciones controversiales: la tension centro-periferia en la obra de Manfredo Tafuri", in PÉREZ ESCOLANO, Victor and PLAZA Carlos (direction and scientific coordination), *Manfredo Tafuri: desde España*, Junta de Andalucía, Granada, 2020; "Para entender la mirada de Tafuri sobre la Arquitectura en América Latina. Un estudio de sus posiciones en torno al paradigma centro-periferia", in TAFURI, ALIATA, BALLENT, CRISPIANI, DAGUERRE, GORELIK, LIERNUR, SILVESTRI, *Tafuri en Argentina*, ARQ Ediciones, Santiago de Chile, 2019.

Essay 3
"Orientalism and Modern Architecture: The Debate on the Flat Roof": "Orientalismo y arquitectura moderna: el debate sobre el techo plano", *Block* (Historiografía), Escuela de Arquitectura y Estudios Urbanos, Universidad Torcuato Di Tella, N° 8, 2011; "Orientalismo y arquitectura moderna: el debate sobre la cubierta plana", *Ra. Revista de Arquitectura*, no. 6, Escuela Técnica Superior de Arquitectura, Universidad de Navarra, 2010.

Essay 4
The Grand Move: How the Smithsons Contributed to the Restoration of Western Europe's Cultural Centrality (1945–1956): "Vanguardistas versus expertos. Reconstrucción europea, expansión norteamericana y emergencia del «Tercer Mundo»: para una relectura del debate arquitectónico en la segunda posguerra (una mirada desde América Latina)", *Block*, N°6 (Tercer Mundo), Escuela de Arquitectura y Estudios Urbanos, Universidad Torcuato Di Tella, 2004; "Descolonización y cultura arquitectónica en la posguerra. El caso de Alison y Peter Smithson (1945–1956)", in SALVATORE Ricardo D. (comp.), *Los lugares del saber. Contextos locales y redes transnacionales en la formación del conocimiento moderno*, Beatriz Viterbo Editora, Rosario, 2007.

Likewise, the author expresses sincere gratitude to Jorge Silvetti, Harvard University GSD Frances Loeb Library, and Humberto Gonzalez Montaner from the Clarin Archive, who have kindly facilitated the publication of several images here included.

This book and the research project it's a part of wouldn't have been possible without the love, support, and encouragement of Bimba Bonardo.

1 Preliminary Words
Introduction to the Book

...es sieht auch nicht das Andere als Wesen, sondern sich selbst im Andern[1]
Friedrich Hegel, *Phaenomenologie des Geistes*

Others, no doubt, will better mold the bronze
To the semblance of soft breathing, draw, from marble, The living countenance, and others plead
With greater eloquence, or learn to measure, Better than we, the pathways of the heaven, The risings of the stars.
Virgil, Aeneid VI.I.847–53

For a Cross-Cultural History

The radical denial of any kind of relationship with the preceding world is a condition of the existence of the avant-gardes. Being modern means, by definition, being Other.

In what would be his first great contribution to the historiography of architecture, Manfredo Tafuri proposed the provocative thesis that the vocation for a conscious rupture was not limited to the artistic movements of the early 20th century. That rupture could be found much earlier in Brunelleschi's works and actions, at the beginning of the great cycle of humanism whose crisis those same movements came to bear witness to.[2]

We know that modernity constitutes itself as a paradoxical double movement: on the one hand, it sets in motion the vehemence of the singular (the bourgeoisie, the new, nations, subjectivities, Romanticism), and on the other it is driven by the iron law of universality and expansion (of capital, of consumption, of political equality, of Reason). However, that constitutive paradox has not guided the studies of the history of architecture of the period. Until relatively recently the idea of a "modern movement", or even "modern architecture", assumed the belief in an international validity of these categories. Furthermore, the hegemonic narratives of the history of modern architecture have been articulated exclusively around "achievements" and "discoveries" produced in a few cities of the territory relatively vaguely referred to as Western Europe and of the Northeast in the United States.[3] In contrast

2 *Preliminary Words: Introduction to the Book*

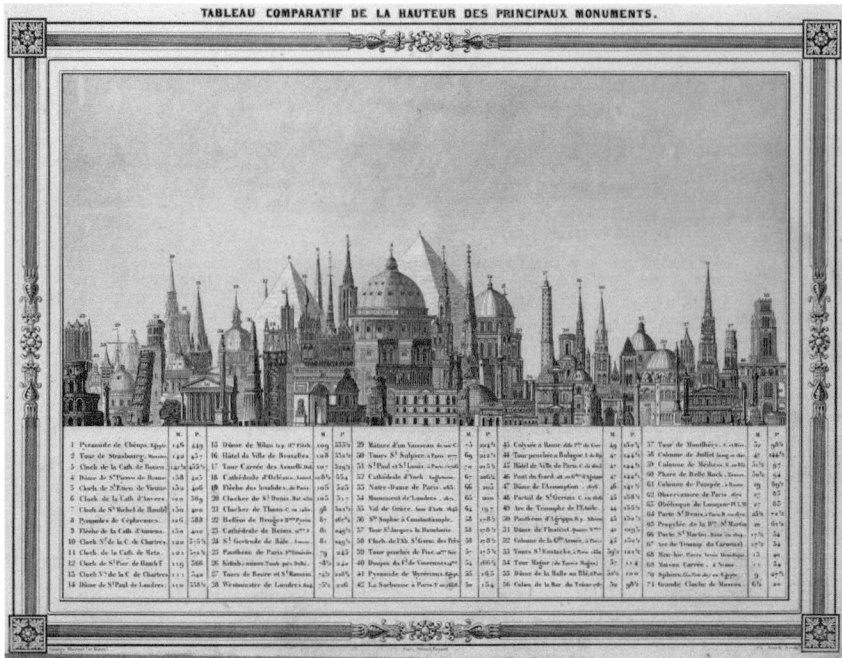

Figure 1.1 "Tableau Comparatif de la Hauteur des Principaux Monuments". By Barbie Du Bocage, J.G.; Dufour, H.; George, F.E.; De Soye Et Bouchet; Vuillemin, A.; Charle, J.B.; Levasseur, V.; Duvotenay, T., Maison Basset, Paris, 1852. An expression of a 19th-century architectural canon comparing the height of its buildings. Public domain. From David Rumsey Map Collection, David Rumsey Map Center, Stanford Libraries.

to what happens in other fields such as art or literature – for whose explanation the expansion of capitalism is a crucial factor[4] – the canonical narrations of the emergence of modern architecture have ignored the existence of imperialism, colonialism, and neocolonialism.

It is true that, in light of the current so-called postcolonial studies, we have witnessed the proliferation of works about modernist expressions of architecture that go beyond the aforementioned geography.[5] In addition, some relatively recent histories of modern architecture have incorporated chapters dedicated to the "expansion" or "dissemination" of canonical modernist ideals in a diversity of areas around the world. However, *when it comes to explaining the factors that determined the fundamental shift in culture and society that occurred sometime between 1890 and 1918*, these narratives ignore the universalizing condition of capitalism, therefore neglecting the existence of a world beyond the "West". Judging by them, it seems one could ignore other stories of humanity during those years: the explanation of the emergence of modern architecture only needs glass, steel, capital, workers, and artists from the great North Atlantic cities. Thus, as an obvious consequence of that gaze, incapable of seeing distant objects (myopic), instead of

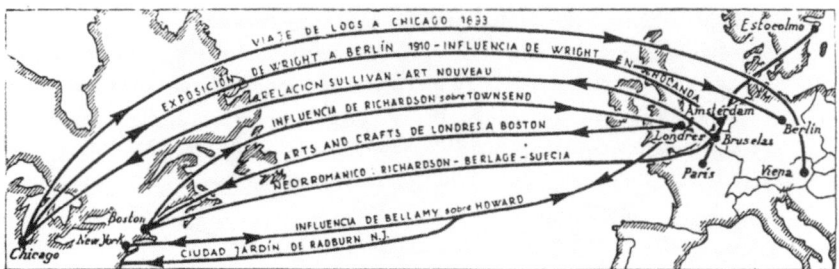

Figure 1.2 Segment of a page from Bruno Zevi's Historia de la Arquitectura Moderna, Poseidon, 1980, p. 274. The caption reads: "Fig. 144. Diagram on the main relationships between Europe and the United States during the early period of modern architecture". This diagram is one of the clearest expressions of the North Atlantic-centric character of modern architectural historiography.

them being determined by processes that installed capitalism *urbi et orbi* – and with it the intricate cultural exchanges that this very process entailed – the formation of the phenomenon of modern architecture is usually attributed exclusively to *provincial*, Western-European, and North American factors.[6]

Following Raymond Williams, the renewal of this canonical narrative, or rather the introduction of a more complex explanation for its foundation, should benefit from the diversity of perspectives outside of the North Atlantic point of view. In *The Politics of Modernism* the British scholar has highlighted the centrality of immigration in the emergence of what he calls the most creative phase of modern culture. To renew that creativity, Williams has proposed the need for new points of view "from outside the metropolis: from the deprived hinterlands (…) and from the poor world which has always been peripheral to the metropolitan systems".[7] For Williams the great theme shared by the intellectuals and artists who are part of the migration of adventurers and foreigners toward metropolises was that of *form* per se, that is to say of *language* – in other words, at the core of modern culture.[8]

Apparently positioned on the other side of the North Atlantic-centered accounts of modern architecture, there is also a consistent interpretation based on nationalist, regionalist, or postcolonial positions. By denouncing that colonial or multinational powers of external origin cause the destruction or deformation of pre-existing cultural fabrics, this interpretation vindicates alternative figures or movements to build local canons, not so much in alleged questioning of the foundations of the North Atlantic canon but rather as its amplification or broadening.

In the climate of the "postmodernist" relativism of the 1980s and 1990s, in the fields of architecture history and architectural criticism, the development of these ideas was greatly stimulated by Edward Said's *Orientalism*, but it also relied on the dissemination and good fortune of the concept of "critical regionalism". In line with Said's initial formulations, this approach conceives the "West" as a homogeneous block or at least as one whose internal contradictions seem to lack a destructuring ability. Instead, they conceive the "colony" as a world equally homogeneous. According to these conceptions, social configurations arise for which the multiplicity of layers, institutions, practices, class or individual interests, languages, imaginaries, and traditions that make up reality need to be cancelled from the analysis. In this way, the "self" and the "other" function in a *complementary* manner.

On the one side, some North Atlantic historians enjoy their material privileges and – stimulated by the demands of the academic and editorial industries– dedicate themselves to studying all the architectures of the earth. Moreover, exploiting these structural conditions, they elaborate and disseminate their point of view at a worldwide scale in the form of "general global narratives". On the other side, presumably to confront these narratives, an alliance between Western "post-colonizer" progressive historians and "de-colonized" native relativists condemns all universalization and self-imposes onto themselves to exclusively focus on local "profound" realities. Their place in the system of Western architectural culture is that of its adjectivized borders: "critical regionalism", "American Tudor", "appropriate modernity", "Asian Art Deco", "American Baroque", "architectures of decolonization", or "tropical modernism".

This is why, since they do not question the premise of an endogenous, exclusively Western constitution of modern architecture, these positions constitute a harmless reversal of the North Atlantic perspective. Furthermore, precisely because such condition is accepted, it is often confronted with the presumed ingenuity or uncontamination of the "colonized". In this way the circle is closed, the original scheme remains intact, and any form of global reconfiguration of the structure of the canon is obliterated. The North Atlantic modernist machine seems to be self-sufficient. It appears to be so powerful that, absolutely consistent and coherent within itself, both sides of the current debate coincide in describing it as immune to any possibility of osmosis with the numerous cultures that it has encountered along its path.

According to Byung-Chul Han, the unlimited amplification of the canon, based on the criteria external to the intrinsic qualities of its components, contributes to the configuration as an infinite series of equals, in a process that he has called "the expulsion of the Other". The canon, by definition, comprises a group of alterities in relation to the conglomerate that it is a reference to. But in a realm without a dynamic tension with "Others", the canon itself loses any reason for existence. On the contrary, for Han, "the negativity of the Other provides form and measure for the Selfsame; without it the Same proliferates. (…) The Selfsame is not identical to the Same; it always appears in tandem with the Other". Without a controversial articulation with the "Other", without "difference", the Same transforms itself into "a formless mass".[9]

The main thesis that has inspired the studies that make up this book consists of a rebuttal, both of the explanation of the canon of modern architecture in disregard to external determinations to the North Atlantic area and of the questionings that are limited to modifying through additions and subtractions, the configuration of that canon. The proposal here is to contribute to removing the veil of the presumed "Western integrity" of the canon itself, or, in other words, to deconstruct the idea that the construction of the western canon is purely self-referential and to replace it with a cross-cultural/dialogical conception, understanding its identity (or Selfsame) as a continuous and changing relationship with Otherness.[10]

What is under discussion here is the allegedly univocal relationship of the canon with the specific places of its gestation. Neglecting for a moment his Swiss nationality, Le Corbusier's architecture was as "French" as "Cubism" could be considered "French", or Picasso could be considered – in the cultural sense – "Spanish"; in the same way that "Suprematism" has not been "Russian", nor "Parametricism" is an "Iranian" invention. The magnitude or greatness of each of these examples does not lie in their relations with the relatively limited conditions of their respective contexts but rather in the exact opposite, that is, in the capacity of Le Corbusier, Pablo Picasso, Vera Ermolaeva, or Zaha Hadid to articulate in the gestation of their creations a vast world of suggestions, knowledge, images, and experiences: precisely the world of modernity, the global world. In the same sense, paradigmatic candidates to represent the peripheries in an amplified canon, such as Geoffrey Bawa, Minette de Silva, Hassan Fathy, or Lina Bo Bardi, should not be reduced to their local contexts as expressions of non-transferable essences beyond their national borders or to the role of the "Others" inside the canon, when in reality they are equally extraordinary personalities sensitive to that same vastness of stimuli provided by modernity.

If we agree that the response to globalization should not be the segmentation but the questioning of any hegemonic center of power – economic, political, ethnic, or cultural – we should not focus our attention on the integration of the canon (by adding or removing some of its components) but rather on the logic and foundation of its constitution. In other words, precisely because they were the product of human efforts that in a way condense the entire past in the line of time, but also the entire planet in the line of space, the achievements of the Japanese Kenzō Tange or the Brazilian Carmen Portinho do not belong to anyone in particular but to all of us who inhabit them. Hence, if we begin with the assumption that modernity's culture is inherently global, we should refrain from pitting the local against the universal. Instead, we should consider incorporating perspectives that naturally stem from specific locales. These localized viewpoints can enrich our understanding of the entirety of the human experience, allowing for a more comprehensive discourse and a new kind of discussion with dominant entities that have historically monopolized these narratives due to their influence and resources.

In appearance the negation of a generalizing "narrative" is an act of resistance to the attempts at domination by the "West", but this is nothing else than a new way of extending that domination. When dealing with the need for broad explanations encompassing various facts and ideas, especially in "grand narratives", we face a choice: either actively contribute to their formation or risk ceding our critical input to the powerful tool of control, as analyzed by Antonio Gramsci, known as "common sense". Even if we insist on sustaining the analysis solely based on "local reality", we can only do so in contrast to some grand narrative.

Therefore, discussing the global dynamics of the constitution of the canon implies at the same time decentralizing the processes of elaboration and construction of criticism and history. Under current conditions, this decentralization is not only possible but indispensable. New historiographical constructions will emerge from it, precisely because globalization provides technical means (from less expensive physical travel to online libraries or digital translation systems) for such constructions to be created, and it also allows (in the intersections and oppositions of an infinity of points of view) for new stories to be consolidated, no less provisional than the previous ones, but surely more truly global and less provincial, regardless of where those provinces are located, whether in Southeast Asia, in the central Andes, or in the North Atlantic.

Michel Foucault allowed us to understand the importance of cultural "dispositifs" of power "without subjects", in which the role of individuals as architects, clients, or politicians is intertwined with the logic of the building industry, with the institutions that regulate and determine architectural production, and with the structures of social control. But that is not enough. We should go deeper into the deconstruction at the very heart of the Western historiographical tradition: the figure of cultural "heroes".

Despite the increasing significance of corporate architecture and specialized consultants and teams, our focus remains centered on those "heroes", with Le Corbusier serving as the quintessential embodiment of originality rooted in the romantic notion of the creative genius. However, in his particular case, a greater acknowledgment should be attributed to the countless young professionals of undeniable talent who, hailing from various parts of the world, played a pivotal role in actively contributing to the creations emanating from Rue de Sèvres. Not to mention his debts to his cousin Pierre, to Eileen Gray, to Charlotte Perriand, to other colleagues, engineers, technical advisors, anonymous craftsmen, and many others that made possible the conception and eventually the construction of his works worldwide.

The setting up of a History of this type is a task that we must carry out from all positions, something that has been happening increasingly in recent decades. However, these investigations still have not reached enough momentum to break the powerful self-centered core of the canonic narratives. To reformulate a new cross-cultural version of these general narratives we should connect, in an alternative network of events, many issues and ideas that until now are being studied in a dispersed manner.

The full construction of these connections cannot be done without readdressing numerous points that are still rather weak. "Colonialism", for example, is one of them. How is it possible that the description of the emergence of modernist ways of living has not accounted for such phenomena? The slow process of passage, transformation, and international dissemination of the "bungalow" model from 18th-century Bengal to post-war California has been brilliantly studied by Anthony King.[11] Many investigations have addressed the prefabrication processes of transportable housing models (and other programs) in wood or cast iron, destined for the vast colonial world. However, how could one not perceive that some of the main myths of the new architecture (transparency, piles, industrialization, fluid interior–exterior relationships, questioning traditional ways of life, uprooting) were already part of the daily reality of that world? The participants of the Conference of Tropical Architecture (London, 1953) were right about the tropical condition of the modernist paradigm: has it not been noted that the Barcelona Pavilion was a *summer* structure, more appropriate – if permanent – for areas of eternal warm weather, than for the long cold spells in Germany?

In this context, the association of Gaudi's "Sagrada Familia" with granary structures in North Africa loses the somewhat extreme "original" character that could be assumed in some studies and is articulated with the relationships established between German expressionist architects and the research by Leo Frobenius – particularly in the environment of Karl Ernst Osthaus – thus building a vast world of representations in which images and intentions of "primitive" purification circulate from one place to another. And the other great modernist cliché, the flat roof, is it is not obviously a structure that is transplanted from the dry North-Saharan climates to the rainy regions of temperate Europe?

Beginning with the debunking "judgment" promoted by *The Architectural Review* in 1954,[12] the flourishing era of Brazilian modernism was isolated and reduced to its "local specificity", transforming it into an "exotic episode". Up until that point, from the influential *Brazil Builds* exhibition at MoMA in 1942, the architectural concepts presented there had ignited the imaginations of architects globally, marking what I term the "tropicalist" phase of modern architecture. What the flourishing Brazilian season demonstrated was that modern architecture had become a new language, capable as such to serve as a *creative means* of expression and communication that allowed local specificities to be accounted for. As the Australian architects would recognize, the *brise-soleil* magnificently used by their Brazilian colleagues was shown as a device that allowed a true internationalization of that language.

The warm world of the great tropical and subtropical zones of the planet awakened and kept open new themes and possibilities brilliantly explored in Brazil, bouncing off new reflections on the part of the canonical masters of the temperate and cold zones of the North Atlantic. The impact of the tropical world on Le Corbusier is not limited to the attraction that his experience in India had on him. It extends to the fascination that Louis Kahn could not escape in Pakistan and Africa; Josep Lluís Sert, Richard Neutra, and Mies van der Rohe in the Caribbean; or Ernst May in Kenya. The passage from "Empire" to "British Commonwealth of Nations" stimulated a phase of infrastructure modernization in overseas territories, which was expressed in the equally "tropicalist" works of Fry, Drew, and Cubbit in Africa or of Seidler and Boyd in Australia.

The emergence of the younger generation organized around Team X in the second post-war period cannot fail to be read as a European *reaction* to the change in conditions at that stage of the global expansion of capitalism, not only because the empires that had constituted the foundation of modern culture in the main countries of the continent were collapsing but also because of the threat of the loss of centrality posed by the simultaneous "socialist" expansion, the flip side of US hegemony. It is in this context that this emergence, in the field that interests us, should be considered. Post-war Congrès Internationaux d'Architecture Moderne (CIAM) was characterized by the unfulfilled hope of integration with a North American environment that was hostile to modernist radicalism, the added rejection to a relative self-exclusion from the "socialist" camp, and the enthusiastic disposition of several Latin American groups on which the old pre-war leaders relied on. It is not by chance that it was Josep Lluís Sert, with his complex connections to these diverse directions, who occupied a position of balance in that scheme. Team X didn't aim for balance but sought to demonstrate that brise soleils were practical solutions for developing countries lacking the resources and technology for air conditioning. Simultaneously, they characterized US-Americans, much like Le Corbusier did with the engineers, as a sort of new "primitives" (powerful but childish) because they didn't fully understand the cultural consequences of the technological advancements they were pioneering.

But the contempt and abandonment of that brief "tropical" season did not occur on the sidelines of another return to the "purity" of the "Others": only that this time it happened in the form of a fascination with an urban vivacity and intensity that the "West" seemed to have lost. The "casbah" model replaced that of the "huts" and "caves" of the 1920s.

Parallel to the European recovery of centrality in the reconstruction of the "canon", the new nations, the majority of them poor, that emerged out of the colonial world constituted what for several decades was known as the "Third World". For the "Free World" (as the new central space of the post-war period liked to call itself, and that extended to Japan) the peoples whose cultures had been seen in their presumed uncontaminated state as reservoirs of "primitive" purities, since then came to be considered under the new denomination of "underdevelopment".

When considering the arguments of these debates, the processes of Independence, the raid of masses of immigrants into Western countries, the international dissemination of cultural forms and projects that had until then been silenced, the new symbolic demands, the gigantic infrastructural demands, the distortions and bitterness of enormous defeats that made the colonial world collapse – including its cultural values – and the no less enormous hopes opened by those defeats usually occupy an irrelevant place in the canonical narratives of the history of architecture and of cities in the 20th century. Or at least they do not seem to have been components to be considered to explain the crises, the discoveries, the cultural regroupings, the technical solutions, and the experiments that characterized architecture and urban studies in that period. Similarly, how was one to approach the extended saga of the experiences of prefabrication in construction without considering the global dimension of the competition/dialogue that took place between the protagonists of the Cold War?

In the decades that followed World War II, the consumerist optimism of the newly expanded West had in its immediate horizon the threatening presence of nuclear catastrophe and the more than certain possibility of a generalized state of rebellion. So, from the tribal huts or from "cubism" and other vernacular solutions that Rudofsky belatedly vindicated, from the "casbah" that excited Candilis and the Smithsons, and from the "Pueblos" of Arizona or the Dogon villages that inspired van Eyck, attention shifted to the extraordinary self-generative capability that was now no longer discovered in remote and ancient villages in sub-Saharan Africa, or in the American desert, but in the very heart of the same geographies now considered *more* economically – and as of a distorted "development".

The "villas miseria", "callampas", "favelas", "bidonvilles", or "shantytowns" constituted in the 1970s a demonstration, in the mere fact of their existence, of the possibility of equally questioning the disorderly commercialized city and the authoritarian modernist notion of the plan. In a cultural climate seeded by the situationists, as well as by the anarchists in favor of the "no plan" or an "after the planners" urbanism, but also by the tumultuous holding of two Union International des Architectes congresses – in revolutionary Havana (1963) and Buenos Aires (1969) – the campaigns of John Turner and Leonardo Benevolo culminated in the PREVI experience in Peru. This time it was in Lima that the renewed enthusiasm of the main figures of those years was concentrated, from Christopher Alexander to James Stirling, passing through Aldo van Eyck or the Atelier 5 group.

It should not be necessary to clarify that a story built exclusively around "Otherness" is not being postulated here. Instead, what is being proposed is the adoption of a cross-cultural point of view for the construction of *new* great narratives. If its elimination of these great narratives is not only detrimental but also impossible, what must be overcome then is their monological constitution. It is not in the alleged shattering of history into infinite splinters but in the coexistence of *numerous projects* of great histories – coming from different, global dissemination centers, where the richness of this dialogical history that we are postulating here could or should be sought.

Presented in two parts, four essays make up the book.

The first part starts with an essay that delves into the theoretical approach to the main concepts that inspire what we call a cross-cultural/dialogic way of thinking about the history of architecture. It begins with a reflection on the idea of canon and its role in the organization of the field of values that define the specificity of architectural practice. It follows with an examination of the tensions and dynamics that characterize the relation identity/alterity and ends with a consideration of the expression of that relation in the arc that ties together the ideas of "originality" and "influence" through the instrument of "hegemony". The second essay studies the intellectual trajectory of one of the most important architectural historians of the 20th century: Manfredo Tafuri. Studying the development of his ideas, we will try to understand how the bias of his gaze, focused exclusively on the history of a certain Western production during its maturation period, was disinterested almost to the point of contempt in the many and extraordinarily rich contributions generated in other latitudes. The conceptual framework that will guide this study will be the center/periphery paradigm as a spatial manifestation of the coupling identity/alterity. The tension between both poles enables the understanding of a good part of the changes and the emphasis of his own studies throughout his intellectual journey. As a consequence of this study, it will become evident that the privileged role that critics (especially Anglo-Saxon) assigned to his "Project and Utopia" is far from being proven in a detailed analysis of his career.

10 *Preliminary Words: Introduction to the Book*

The second part of the book presents two case studies. The first was conceived within the framework introduced by Edward Said with his "Orientalism". Said's approach was applied to different expressions of "East" and has been widely explored in recent years but in general without overcoming the unidirectional colonizer (dominant)/colonized (dominated) equation that was considered in previous paragraphs. The study of this case was based on the need to verify a movement in the opposite direction, whereby it is the "dominated" culture that actively modifies the "dominant" culture. For this reason, in this section of the book we study the way in which the typical flat roof of buildings in the Middle East and North Africa acted as an object of desire for modern Western architects and helped them reinforce the trend that, hand in hand with the consolidation of abstraction, required the elimination of all figurative references in buildings. And if there was a formal key that identified a construction as such, this one is like a *manufactum* designed to solve a certain program in a certain place: that is the use of the pitched roof. On the contrary, the flat roof presumably made it possible to solve these problems and at the same time maintain the *manufactum* as a pure geometric form, *devoid of meaning*. In the last essay, we will present a new inversion of the scheme. The question that organizes it is the following. It is evident that as part of the construction of global processes of hegemony, the metropolises underwent fundamental changes in their culture, but what happens as a consequence of the gradual *disintegration* of these conditions of hegemony? The book ends with an analysis of the impact of the result of World War II on the configuration of architecture culture, which determined the loss of centrality of CIAM and its *European* leaders, followed by the revision of the ideas of Alison and Peter Smithson as an attempt to recover that centrality in the context of the extraordinary identity crisis generated by the fall of the British Empire.

Notes

1 *It does not see the other as an essential being, but in the other sees its own self.* Trad A. V. Miller, Oxford University Press, 1977.
2 TAFURI, 1980, 16.
3 I refer to the 20th-century main narratives of the History of Modern Architecture like: HITCHCOCK & JOHNSON, 1932; HITCHCOCK, 1951, 237–255; PEVSNER, 1936; ZEVI, 1950; BENEVOLO, 1960; BANHAM, 1960; TAFURI & DAL CO, 1976, 1979.
4 This can be seen in countless presentations on modern art like: BOWNESS, 1972; MEECHAM, 2018; COTTINGTON, 2008; GOMPERTZ, 2012; ACTON, 2004. All of them record in one way or another the impact of the globalized political and commercial relations, and the nascent mass tourism in the imagination of the artists of Northeast Europe, as well as the emerging appreciation of the indigenous past in the United States.
5 As, for example, CURTIS, 1983; COHEN, 2012; FRAMPTON, 1980; GLANCEY, 1998, without mentioning the numerous studies on local or regional histories of modern architecture.
6 In this book I will use the word "America" to designate the whole American Continent with its northern, central, and southern sectors. I will designate the State located between Canada in the north and Mexico as the United States of America (USA), and I will use US-American as an adjective to qualify what refers to the United States of America.
7 WILLIAMS, 1994, 49.

8 Ibid., 45.
9 HAN, 2018, 9.
10 The concept of dialogism was coined by BAKHTIN, 1981. For a summary and expansion: HOLQUIST, 2002 (1990); LINELL, 2009; ZAPPEN, 2004.
11 KING, 1995.
12 I am referring to the October 1954 issue of *The Architectural Review* with a special section organized under the title of "Report on Brazil", with texts by some of the participants in the recent São Paulo Biennial.

2 Essay 1: Otherness and Canon

Canon and Architecture[1]

With his *Vite* (*The Lives of the Most Current Painters, Sculptors, and Architects*, 1550), characterized by Julius von Schlosser as "the true church and the grandfather of the history of art",[2] Giorgio Vasari becomes the author of the canonical construction that served as the basis for the Western history of art and architecture.[3] Nevertheless, although the importance of the *Vite* is indisputable, it seems that the consideration of two other books published shortly after can contribute to better understand the foundation of the canonical grid. In 1572 Philips Galle's printing press in Antwerp presented the engravings of Maarten Jacobsz Heemskerck van Veen in a book titled *De acht wereldwonderen* (*The Eight Wonders of the World*), and, inspired by Vasari, in 1604 Karel van Mander tried to shift the axis of the canon toward northern Europe – "an entire region that Vasari largely ignored" – with his book *Het Schilder-Boeck*, that had the addition of a section dedicated to "The Lives of the Illustrious Dutch and High-End Painters".[4]

Van Mander's book makes evident that the centrality of Florence in the canonical system of the Vasarian *Vite* was questioned very early on from the other side of the Alps. But that questioning had already taken place in Florence and throughout Italy (Bandinelli, Varchi, Cellini, Scardeone, Dolce), with particular emphasis in the second half of the 17th century (Malvasia, Bellori). The questioning of Vasari's canon was expressed, for example, in the *postille* of the addition of the "Vite" attributed to the Carracci, where Vasari was accused of not even considering the northern Italian masters, in particular, the Venetian masters.[5]

In the expansive France of Louis XVII the *Entretiens sur les vies et sur les ouvrages des plus excellents peintres anciens et modernes* by André Felibien (1619–1695), he harbored one of the most aggressive criticisms of the Vasarian canon by replacing Michelangelo for Raphael at the center of the system, and thus opening the way to a classicism embodied in the figure of Poussin as a pillar of the Académie Royale.[6] On this basis, the critic would later support the transfer of the center to France itself, given that "there is little that remains of it today in Italy and that after all this Art seems to (…) have ended in France after the King established the Academies for those who practice it".[7] The nationalization of the Vasarian canon

DOI: 10.4324/9781003452263-2

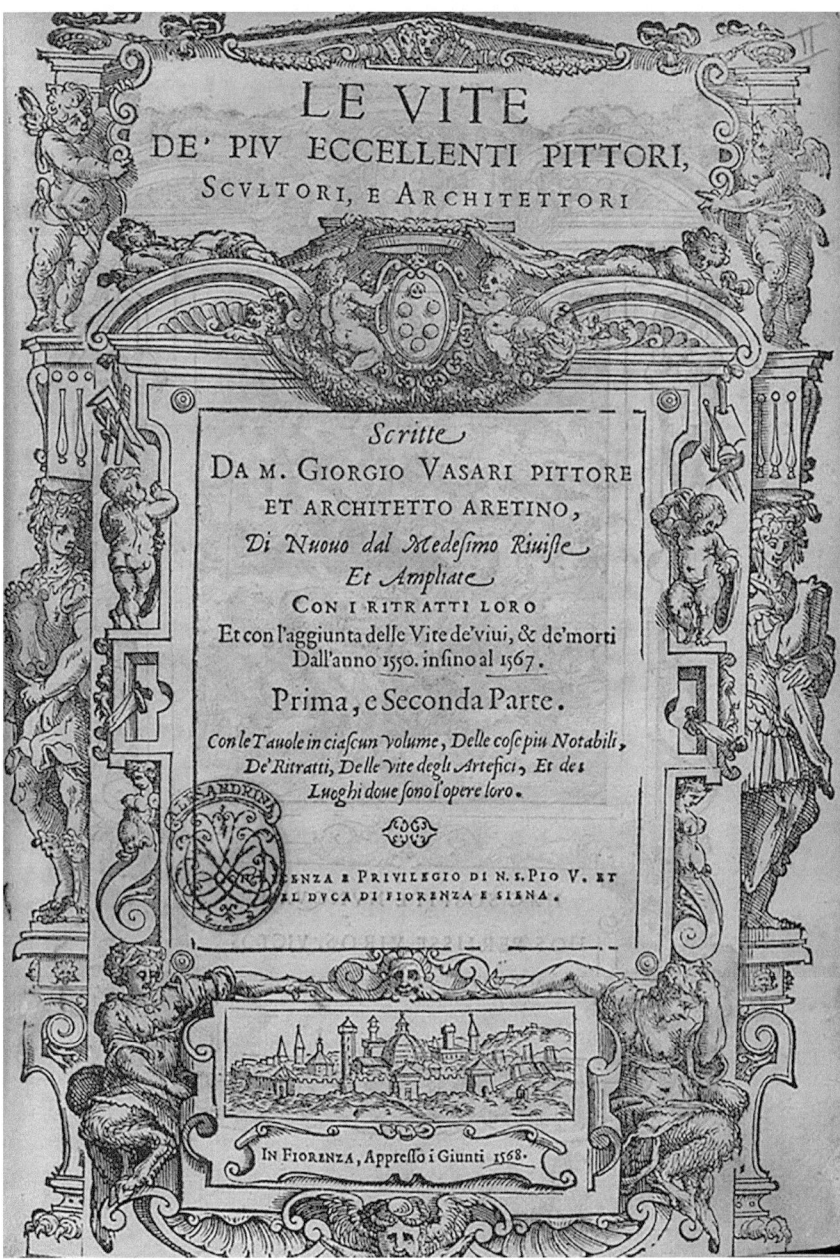

Figure 2.1 Delle vite de' piu eccellenti pittori scultori et architettori (Of the Lives of the Most Excellent Painters, Sculptors, and Architects) by Giorgio Vassari, Apreso i Giunti, Florence, 1568. First page. Alessandrina University Library, Italy. In https://www.europeana.eu/item/446/VIAE000291.

14 Essay 1: Otherness and Canon

Figure 2.2 Babylonis Muri (The Walls of Babylon), from *The Eight Wonders of the World*, 1572, by Philip Galle (artist), Maerten van Heemskerck (artist after), plate 7 (Copy from Herzog August Library, Germany). In https://www.europeana.eu/item/168/item_7XUSQ75RPFWTLEEBHOGAAE66Q4EXOY45.

took place in England as well. Its construction started there in 1686 with *Painting Illustrated in Three Dialogues* by William Aglionby and was embodied in *An Essay towards an English School*, the book that Bainbrigg Buckeridge published in 1706.[8] Similarly, in Spain in his 1675 manuscript (published in 1853) *Discursos practicables del nobilísimo arte de la pintura*, Jusepe Martínez is critical of El Greco and Vicente Carducho.[9] In short, these reveal that the Vasarian canon functions as a narrative structure, whose central pieces may change their relative positions, and many of them may even disappear, while others replace them.[10]

Instead of focusing on notable *individuals* like Vasari's canon, Heemskerck's *De acht wereldwonderen* comprises *works*. Equally remarkable is that seven of these works belong to the Hellenistic period and are located in the current territories of Italy, Greece, Turkey, Egypt, and Iraq, that is to say, forming part of a cultural geography in which "East" and "West" are integrated.[11] As of the invention of the printing press that could reproduce engravings, Heemskerck's canon benefited from an enormous dissemination in the 16th century. But the interest of humanist architects in these ancient models was registered long before their publication, as the continuation of a phase of reflection that started in the Middle

Ages. For example, in 1521 Cesare Cesariano included and illustrated a list of the "wonders" in a note in his comments on the book of Vitruvius.[12] Similarly during the 17th century Juan Caramuel y Lobkowitz referred to "wonders" in his treatise, highlighting as its best exemplar the Temple of Solomon.[13] The humanists were seeking a bridge between the tradition of the Seven Wonders and that of ancient Rome whose architecture – they considered – could overcome the Eastern/Western mix of the Hellenistic world. Heemskerck considered the Colosseum (Colossus) as the eighth wonder as Cassiodorus had already done with the city of Rome itself in the 6th century.[14]

In all of these cases, the idea of "wonder" in constructions was associated with beauty. But the original Greek sense had to do with the word "theamata" associated with "sight" (things to be seen), equivalent to the Latin "mirabilia", mirare (look at), ad-mirare (to admire). In short, the "wonders" were a selection of human artifacts that world travelers had to see.[15] In the Middle Ages, the list of wonders drawn up by Saint Gregory of Tours used to be included in the "guides" for travelers to Rome and Jerusalem.[16]

In recent decades, especially in the field of literature, and with greater intensity in Anglo-Saxon academic circles, the necessity of a canon has been questioned *tout-court*, mostly because its existence was considered an instrument of domination by the established powers. The relation between any and all cultural manifestations in wielding power is not under discussion here. It is obvious. But there are other considerations that need to be thought about.

With a similar criterion in regard to the previously examined versions of the canon, for Harold Bloom "the Canon's true question remains: at this point in history, what shall the individual who still desires to read attempt to read".[17] Or, in the context of this book: what works should an architect "see" today? This question confronts us with a dramatic problem, because while the works of visual arts are protected in museums, and literary works or even musical works in libraries, architecture works are part of the ever-changing dynamics of everyday life, urban or rural. Therefore the problem is: which works should be preserved to be seen for future generations?[18]

In the field of art history, Ernst Gombrich argued that the function of the canon is "(to offer) reference points, standards of excellence which we cannot level down without losing direction".[19] As demonstrated by authors such as Charles Altieri, Georg Langfeld, Barbara Vinken, or John Guillory, the disregard of the canonical reference presupposes the striking out of a corpus of values (historically constructed, of course) that, because they are not the product of current tensions, allow precisely that the differences of that present be outlined against them.[20] If, on the contrary, we accept the *objective* necessity for the existence of the canon, what follows is the establishment of parameters of value.

Gombrich's vindication of the Western canon as a quality-based system was a consequence of his defense of Western values such as individualism and liberalism. It is true that his position is not in consonance with politically correct contemporary ideas. Nevertheless, his critique was rooted in rejecting the metaphysical elements present in positions derived from Hegelian idealism, anchored on the belief in the superhuman existence of unifying "spirits" within culture, whether at the individual, national, or historical level. It was this anti-idealism that determined his approximation to its objects of analysis precisely in their *difference*, which is to say in their unique and concrete conditions of existence. The qualitative approach to the canon is currently rejected, because of its intrinsic dependence on the function of the selected works as a part of the power systems in which they were forged. With a legitimate concern in defense of the sectors ignored by these power systems, criteria of inclusion based on identity or representational values are being adopted. But let us consider this point.

In *Cultural Capital*, Guillory cites a paragraph by Peter Osborne that is worth remembering here:

> (By) claiming an "identity" on the basis of the experience of a specific oppression (…) oppressed social identities are transformed directly into oppositional political identities through a celebration of difference which inverts the prevailing structure of value but leaves the structure of difference untouched.[21]

On the contaray, the defense of internal determinations as the main standard in the recognition of canonical works is not limited to "conservative" positions. The ability of certain works to constitute themselves as "summits" and to "endure the test of time", in Gombrich's sense, constitutes a hard point in the Marxist aesthetic debate. It should suffice to remember that Karl Marx himself raised this problem in the *Grundisse*: "The difficulty we are confronted with (Greek art) is (…) that (it) still gives us artistic pleasure and that in certain respects is regarded [by us] as a norm and unattainable model".[22] Of course, Marx's vindication of the aesthetic pleasure of Greek art was not immune to the "invention of Greece" in Prussia as part of the construction of modern German "national" identity. Nonetheless, for Marx, the central question wasn't why Greek art could still captivate us as "pinnacle achievements".[23] His problem was the abyss between the relatively primitive (social) development of Greece and the high aesthetic quality it had achieved, that is – in his terms – a contradictory relation between "structure" and "superstructure". His response, as is known, was the association of classical Greece with the infancy of humanity: in other words, its unrepeatable "innocence".[24]

It is worth remembering that, as the excellent pianist and extraordinary musicologist that he was, Edward Said built his own canon based on quality concepts. In this regard Colin Symes has observed that

> Said most admired (composers like) Bach, Busoni, or Webern, (because) for him, the contrapuntal method, the capacity to hold many voices together, was (…) an "exemplary" way of (…) thinking (…) analyzing (…) conflicting (…) strands of history and culture. (This) style of thinking (…) was also a metaphor for democracy, which permitted different voices to be heard and represented, as opposed to the concerto, in which one voice attempts to dominate others. (…) The contrapuntal approach enabled Said to see cultures not

as monolithic (…) entities, but as (…) interdependent, in which the patterns of power and domination are never expressed completely, but are accompanied by resistance and subversion, by point and counterpoint.[25]

Said was no exception in postulating a progressive assessment of the canon. In the 20th century, Walter Benjamin and Theodor Adorno raised the need for an "immanent critique", that is, one that emerged from the very premises of the work itself. An "immanent critique" means the consideration of the ability – or not – of the work to respond to its internal premises and to its external conditions of existence. In the words of Thijs Lijster, for Adorno, "immanent criticism could be described as evaluating what something is as compared to what something pretends to be, given its own goals and norms, or with what that something could be, given its historical possibilities".[26] Both authors employed these premises as fundamentals of their canonical constructions. Nevertheless, this does not negate that those same "historical possibilities" could constitute an obstacle to the inclusion in the canon of other individuals or social groups equally able to overcome scrutiny through "immanent criticism".[27]

A detailed quantitative study of Victor Ginsburgh and Sheila Weyers proves the idea of "immanent valuation" of the works and, with this, of their persistence over time. As we previously mentioned, Vasari's selection of canonical figures has been questioned since the publication of his book. What is surprising is, as Ginsburgh and Weyers proved by analyzing reference texts of art history up to the present,[28] that 25 of these figures have maintained their canonical role *despite* the changes in power relations and cultural projects throughout history.[29]

We can certainly add to the analysis of single works the study of projects within creators' life paths, their physical and cultural contexts, and their contingent production processes. Nevertheless, in a world where the concept of artistic progress has been banished, these artistic experiences hold an enduring, timeless reference.[30] For this reason, unlike what happens with other professions or disciplines with a dominant scientific and technical base such as dentistry or genetic engineering, for which history itself has less importance, in the case of the arts, the study of the legacy of the cultural heritage of past generations constitutes an unavoidable reference. The contact with that legacy determines in all arts a tension or what Bloom calls "anxiety of influences". But, in the case of architecture, we also have to consider the constructive, tactile, spatial, and even functional experiences that this legacy proposes. This is the reason why that legacy provokes or challenges us in our daily experience. Young literature students may refuse to read books written several centuries ago and cancel them from their canon, but young architecture students cannot avoid seeing nor making use of the buildings of the past.

As Barbara Vinken warned, in any case, it would be

> not on reading other (subjects) [Anderes], but on reading in another way [anders] – and that means reading something other than the repeated assertion of an "other" – identity; to read differently because it not only becomes fairer to the texts in order not to understand the canon as a sluggish confirmation of

auctoritas, but to brush it against the canonicity fixed in it. From this perspective, the canon conveys neither positive values nor norms and identities, nor does it bring any heteronomy to the individual or the collective experience to be expressed. Rather, it makes it possible to read identity and historical memory as ideologically coagulated constructs that may be asserted in texts, but that at the same time are repeatedly willfully thwarted by them. If something is "expressed" in them, it is at best the failure of "experience". Perhaps this warning is what enables the real strength and the actual reason for their canonical status, which is suppressed in humanistic reading. It may otherwise be empirically necessary to read something other in order to understand this learning to read others. What one would learn from reading the canon would be consequently not the assertion of one's own identity, but the difficult and not always peaceful dealing with difference.[31]

The Western Canon was the object of harsh criticism, supported by the provocative conservatism of its author and coming particularly from the area of postcolonial studies and the different expressions of ethnic, regional, national, or gender sectors discriminated against in the book. In the case of architecture, it is true that, until the

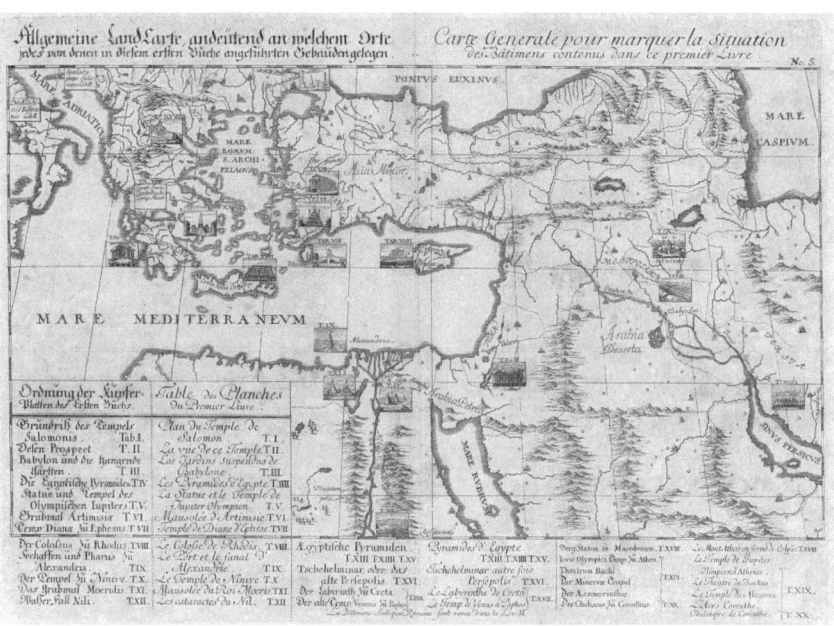

Figure 2.3 "Allgemeine Landkarte andeütend an welchem Orte jedes von denen in diesem Büche angeführten Gebauden" (General map indicating the location of each of the buildings listed in this book), *Entwurf einer Historischen Architektur* (A draft of historical architecture), by Johann Bernhard Fischer von Erlach, Vienna, 1721 (Copy from Slovak National Gallery, Bratislava, Slovakia). https://www.europeana.eu/item/07101/G_10045_2.

last decades of the 20th century, numerous experiences and figures of great value were also ignored in the formation of the canon of modern architecture and that the production of white men from North Atlantic regions had almost absolute priority. In the following paragraphs, we will analyze this topic in particular. However, in more recent accounts of this history, there is a clear inclination to encompass global experiences and to emphasize the previously overlooked contributions of women like Eileen Gray, Lina Bo Bardi, Jane Drew, Minette de Silva, or Beverly L. Greene, among many others, who have gained well-deserved recognition.

Although architects were considered by Giorgio Vasari's *Lives* (1550), the first Western attempt to set a canon exclusively dedicated to architecture was Johann Bernhard Fischer von Erlach's *Entwurf einer Historischen Architektur* (1721). As Heemskerck did two centuries ahead of time, Tempesta in his engravings in 1608, and Athanasius Kircher in his *Turris Babel, sive Archontologia* in 1679, Fischer's canon included Eastern and Western examples but without distinguishing between existing or imaginary buildings.

The first modern presentation of a "universal" canon of really existing architecture was Jean-Nicolas-Louis Durand and Jacques Guillaume Legrand's *Recueil et Parallele des Edifices de Tout Genre Anciens et Modernes Remarquables par Leur Beaute, Par Leur Grandeur ou Par Leur Singularite*, published in 1800. From then onward, numerous canonical constructions were produced, mainly in the United Kingdom, France, Germany, Spain, and the United States that, culminating in the works of James Ferguson, Banister Fletcher, and Auguste Choisy, included everything from pre- and post-Columbian American examples to Asian and Eastern European examples and also included African huts and other adobe constructions.

In the midst of the emergence of modern architecture, the modernist canon was established with *Internationale Architektur*, published by Walter Gropius in 1925. As happened in the Renaissance, this canon, which continues to shape architectural history and thought today, was once again created around a set of examples located in the North Atlantic area. As in the Renaissance as well, it radically broke with all architectural precedents.

What has been said thus far is only a description and does not constitute anything new. In any case, a critique with postcolonial and/or gender roots shall strive to contribute to the expansion of the canon and reorder what we could call its general economy, displacing some pre-existing works and filling in the still-empty boxes that will allow it to claim a broader global reach. After all, as we have seen, the canon is not a stable and permanent system but a field of historical forces with a limited area or, as Homi Bhabha recalls paraphrasing Bernard Williams, a field "continually being modified by all sorts of shifting social forces".[32] We also know that its constitution and its ability to position itself in a hegemonic manner for a certain period of time depend on the relative intensity of those forces. The canon is articulated according to what Hans Robert Jauss calls the "horizon of expectations" of each moment and is the product of a struggle of those "social forces" that have a material base. For such a struggle, powerful apparatuses of construction, legitimation, and dissemination are put into play, for whose operation gigantic economic and political resources are available: educational institutions in a position to hire the best teachers, to finance the most sophisticated research and international meetings, and to grant scholarships to the best students, in addition to biennials and festivals of architecture, significant publishing houses, and journals with the capability of international circulation. To this is added, at least in the past century, a not minor factor of imbalance: the "natural" supremacy of the English language over the rest of the planet's linguistic conglomerates.

There is no doubt that the numerous works that are being carried out throughout the world with such purpose of questioning, expanding, and reordering constitute a great contribution to a renewal of the historiography of architecture ostensibly centered on the production of the North Atlantic area of the West. Nevertheless, it is a limited movement that, although it may not currently seem so, as has also been warned by other authors such as Osborne or Vinken, does not carry out a truly radical transformation of the *foundations* of the canon.

Loos's "Das Andere" (the Other): The Impossible Synthesis

That Adolf Loos had titled *Das Andere* the brochure he edited in 1903 is another manifestation of his extraordinary brilliance. But what did that Otherness consist of for Loos? Rigorously speaking, was his position an avant-garde position?[33]

The first answer is obvious and emerges from the subtitle of the brochure: "a brochure for the introduction of Western culture in Austria" where Austria represents the self, and the West represents the Other. However, the definition of both poles is not as simple as it appears. In the first place because the identification of Loos with "Austria" is ambiguous: he himself was not Austrian but Moravian and was therefore foreign to Viennese culture. Moreover, his ideas were critical, external to that culture. Yet he liked to use the first-person plural to refer to the citizens of the city. To understand this ambiguity we need to remember that "the West" was for Loos neither the source of Greco-Roman tradition and values nor the seat of the great political and economic transformation, emblematic of the articulation of the French Revolution with the Industrial Revolution. For Janet Stewart

> In Das Andere, Loos's choice of title is predicated on the binary opposition between the Self and the Other. Implicit in the title itself, this opposition is highlighted by the fact that before settling on Das Andere as the title for his journal, Loos played with the idea of Das Eigene (The one's own), as well as Das Äussere (The External) and others.[34]

Stewart's observation reinforces the consideration of Loos's "outsider" condition as a determining factor of his own interest in Otherness. Loos was part of a circle of intellectuals and artists like Karl Kraus or Peter Altenberg who, like him, were "Others" in relation to Viennese official culture.[35] Kraus himself expressed it this way: "No doubt, the artist is other. (…) The more the artist is other, the more necessary it becomes that he uses common clothing as a mask".[36] As another trait of this ambiguity, Loos was alien – in spite of his radical criticism of the Viennese culture – to the gestures of radical alterity of artists such as those of his friend and

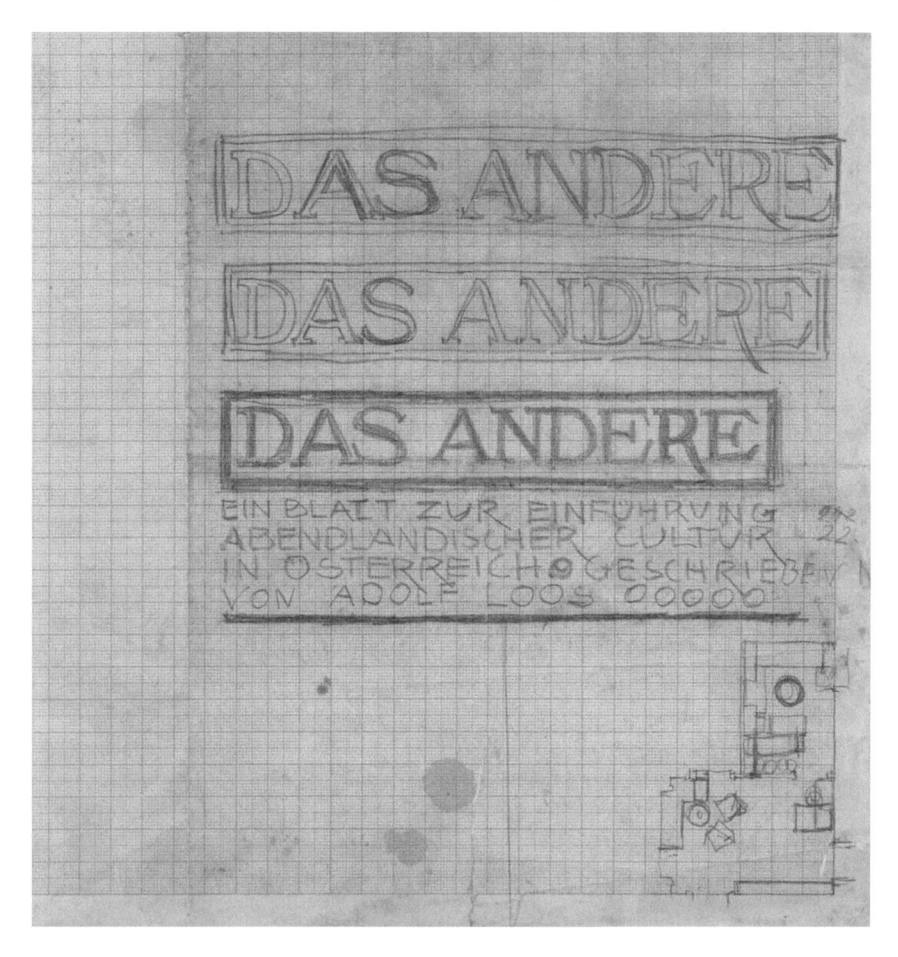

Figure 2.4 "Das Andere", Title page draft by Adolf Loos, 1903. In Albertina, Austria. https://www.europeana.eu/item/15508/ALA692.

protégé Kokoschka, or the nudist anarcho-naturists of Monte Verità, or from the Kirchner circle,[37] nothing more alien than nudism for Loos, a great admirer of the importance of being well-dressed.

It was not by chance that the two issues of the brochure were published as a supplement to a journal where, together with Altenberg, he was one of the editors on at least those two occasions. The magazine was called *Kunst. Monatsschrift für Kunst und alles andere* (*Art Monthly* magazine for art and everything else). This title expresses that the program of *Das Andere* was intended to deal with a wide variety of "Western" topics, with the exception of any that had anything to do with art. Some examples are the vindication of children as paper carriers, the use of capital letters in nouns, the use of teaspoons to serve salt, or, as provocatively highlighted in the posters advertising the second edition of the magazine, reflections on the use of toilet paper or on the option intercourse versus masturbation.

This program was not presented autonomously but rather in an explicit differentiation from the main content of the magazine, that is, in contrast to *Die Kunst*. Although at first reading one could think that in a functionalist way *Das Andere* sought to vindicate the world of simple things and everyday use *in contrast* with the mystery of Art, it is possible to consider an interpretation in reverse, that is, *Das Andere* tried to speak of the ungraspable multiplicity (in-formality) of life in its radical alterity to highlight form as a constitutive condition of artistic creation.

Massimo Cacciari has shown that for Loos

> The particular (…) linguistic game that we call art (…) lies in the manifestation of the utopian form as a form and a condition of otherness and difference. (…) But all of this has meaning only in relation to other specific premises: without their inherent limit there could be no presence of "das Andere". And this limit is the condition of the form of otherness. (…). The artistic act reveals an otherness, a conflict. But it does not resolve it, nor give consolation for it.[38]

In the sense that Cacciari proposes, Loos does not rule out art but rather the idea of an integration of art with the production of objects for use, the house being the most important of those objects. Furthermore, following Cacciari Loos does not rule out the reference to the "Greek" world either. On the contrary, his opinion was that our culture is built on the knowledge of what stood out in classical antiquity.[39] Loos was aware of the implicit error in the search for a synthetic solution of the art-life polarity or, what is the same, the opposition identity-alterity. Any attempt at dialectical synthesis would be nothing else than the forced elimination of what constitutes an immanent *difference* in that polarity.

The project for *The Chicago Tribune* is not a joke, much less an irony.

> A work of art is brought into the world without there being a need for it, a building meets a need. A work of art has no responsibility to anyone, a building to everyone. The aim of the work of art is to make us feel uncomfortable, a building is there for our comfort. (…) So the building has nothing to do with art and is architecture not one of the arts? That is so. Only a tiny part of architecture comes under art: monuments. Everything else, everything that serves some practical purpose, should be ejected from the realm of art.[40]

The Doric column of *The Chicago Tribune* is just that: a monument. And the Michaelertplatz building expresses the Loosian rejection of synthesis between art and pure use, self and other: the segment of the building that is "house" appears naked and without any quality *in contrast* to the ground floor that provides the gesture (*monumentum*, from *monere/to remember*) where what wants to be highlighted in the memory of the passer-by is a *differentiated* presence. It is about the same coexistence of two opposite universes anticipated by the *Das Andere/Die Kunst* pair. As Cacciari would say, here "the artistic act reveals an otherness, a conflict. But it does not resolve it, nor give consolation for it".

Figure 2.5 Motto: "Ein Scheusal Von Einem Haus"; Vortrag Des Architekten Adolf Loos, Mein Haus Am Michaelerplatz; Im Sophiensaal, 1911, design by Urban Janke, 1911, Albertina, Austria. https://www.europeana.eu/item/15508/DG2003_1511.

The recognition of that duality, of that coexistence of opposites in tension that we observe in Loos's personal life as well – Anglophile and Austrian, liberal and aristocratic, modern and classic – is of crucial importance. Unlike other cases in which the underscoring of identity is the result of a radical separation in relation to alterity, in Loos the tension (tragic, Cacciari would call it) becomes evident between those two forms that coexist in human behavior. That is why his work has been linked so many times to the work of other Moravians such as Mahler and Freud, with whom he shared the special intellectual climate of the Habsburg capital.

In reference to the work of Freud – another Moravian in Vienna – on this subject, Silvia Hernández has pointed out that

> far from a conception derived from the Cartesian cogito, psychoanalysis places us before a split or double subject. (…) The unconscious (…) establishes an alienness within each member of the human species; if the unconscious is the discourse of the Other, it will be in the discourse where the subject is spoken, where the Other speaks in its place. (…) The presence of the other in the self is evidence of the impossibility of closure of subjectivity.[41]

Hernández alludes to the theme of the split self in her analysis of a short story by Jorge Luis Borges entitled "There Are More Things", but her reasoning applies to much of Borges's work. The title of one of them is precisely "The Other, The Same".[42] In this story the narrator is an elderly Jorge Luis Borges who, resting on a bench in Cambridge, Massachusetts, in 1972, while contemplating the Charles River during a break from his university classes, initiates a dialogue with Jorge Luis Borges, a young man who sits by his side and claims to be in 1918 watching the River Rhône in the city of Geneva. The horror that this "other/same" causes the narrator by questioning his own monolithic identity was described by Freud in "the Uncanny", a concept that Julia Kristeva analyzed in *Étrangers a nous memes*, for Kristeva Freud's work invites us "to discover our own disturbing otherness (…), that threat (…) generated by the projective apparition of the other at the heart of what we persist in maintaining as a proper, solid "us". (…) The foreigner is within me".[43]

The acknowledgment of Otherness as a constitutive presence, evident not only within the artistic avant-garde but also within our individual identities, compels us to reconsider this dualism. It encourages us, above all, to definitively discard the centrality of the Cartesian "Ego" upon which much of modern civilization has been built. Any effort to emphasize the significance of this disregarded Otherness should transition from a monological narrative—representative of a single speaking subject, the West—to a cross-cultural/dialogical narrative. This shift involves considering a dialogue between diverse subjects and, by choral extension, encompasses the history of human creations. Contemporary philosophy offers a fundamental examination of the change to a paradigm in which the Other appears as an inseparable component in the definition of identity. In relation to the self-referentiality of the historiography of modern architecture, supported by the belief that the emission of a message generates only changes on the receiver but not on the sender, the point of view that we are trying to propose is largely indebted to authors such as Levinas or Bakhtin. As David Patterson has observed, basing himself on the ideas of the Russian scholar,

> signification is not a static set of points or an organization of signs but a movement, a shifting, from one to the other. (…) The movement Bakhtin describes is from mouth to mouth, not from mouth to ear; speaking and listening are simultaneous, not mutually exclusive. The organ by which we hear is the tongue; whether we are in the position of speaker or listener, we hear by responding (…) there is no understanding without speaking.[44]

Against "Originality"[45]

In the June 1954 issue of *The Architectural Review* Nikolaus Pevsner published a brief yet significant essay simply titled "Originality". His intent was to argue against the views that Harry Stuart Goodhart-Rendel had formulated the previous year in his book *English Architecture since the Regency*. Pevsner reacted against Goodhart-Rendel's equating "modern architecture" with other "styles" of the past ("one [new] string of the [architect's] lyre"). Pevsner proposed a parallel between what architects did in the period 1900–1920, with what was done by architects in Florence in the period 1420–1520. For him both groups had been able to express themselves and their "time" with great "originality". "Originality of style – wrote Pevsner – is distinct from originality in individuals […] style is what ties together the aesthetic achievements of the creative individuals of one age". In our age, for the architect, it is not anymore about deciding "between borrowed forms but between borrowed forms on the one hand and on the other forms created afresh if not by him at least by his age".[46]

Three main ideas determined Pevsner's way of thinking. The first was his rejection of the disintegration of the value system, and consequently of its expressions, in human production. The urgent need to reconstruct an integrated world was the driving force that organized his famous 1936 text. For Pevsner

> the campaign of William Morris's lifetime was directed against the complete lack of feeling for the essential unity of architecture (… because) almost all contemporary building which surrounded him (…), and practically all industrial art was crude, vulgar, and overloaded with ornament.[47]

The second was that what would allow that reconstruction would be the awareness of and subordination to a "spirit of the age", a "spirit" that, beyond the singular will of individuals, presumably governs human action. Moreover, Pevsner linked the "spirit of the age" to a "spirit of the place". The third was the idea of "Progress". In short, the style of the age was the style produced by the "men of original genius" of the most advanced countries in the capitalist world who have been able to detect that "spirit".

The desire to correct the going astray of present society through a new beginning, or what is the same, the search for a pure and uncontaminated origin, was not a new drive in the West. It was preceded by the "discovery" or rather the invention of ancient Greece by the Prussian culture of the late 18th and early 19th centuries. It is a topic that has received the attention of numerous scholars, who have linked this invention to the configuration of a pure and uncontaminated German nationality that was promoted, among others, by the works of Wilhelm von Humboldt in the footsteps of the initial preaching of Johann Joachim Winckelmann.[48] But that first vindication of the need for a return to the "origin" already had, especially in Winckelmann's formulations, a melancholic content: that Greek purity was an ineffable result so that at present it was only possible to aspire to the imitation of its ways of thinking and acting. For Jan Blanc, among the explanations of romanticism one must include that of a reaction to the melancholic attitude of neo-Hellenic originalism.[49] That is why romantic originality, its form of rejection of the prosaic and bourgeois present, sought to express itself not by means of the "purity" of "Greece" but by the uncontaminated "authenticity" of individual feelings and of the anonymous, and therefore not less genuine "popular culture".

In the context of modernization and modernity, the requirement of "originality" is a consequence of deeper and more general factors. Jürgen Habermas postulated that

> With the modern empirical sciences, autonomous arts, and theories of morality and law grounded on principles, cultural spheres of value took shape which made possible learning processes in accordance with the respective inner logics of theoretical, aesthetic, and moral-practical problems.[50]

That is, "modernity can and will no longer borrow the criteria by which it takes its orientation from the models supplied by another epoch; it has to create its normativity out of itself".[51] Peter Weiss had expressed it with a masterful phrase: "The important thing is to pull yourself up by your own hair to turn yourself inside out and see the whole world with fresh eyes".[52] The other factor derives from the expansion of the possibilities provided by what Walter Benjamin characterized as "mechanical reproduction". As we know, he detected that reproducibility through mechanical means meant putting into crisis the meaning of painting as a copy or simulation of the "Idea" and gave rise to what he called the "loss of aura", the loss of the value of uniqueness in a work of art. The entire system of Art that we call modern has not ceased to revolve around this fundamental conflict.

Thus, whether as an unavoidable requirement if we follow Habermas, or to dodge the question of reproducibility raised by Benjamin, whoever proposes the creation of a work of art in our time has to confront the demand for originality. By definition, in modern art, repetition is forbidden. According to Rosalind Krauss:

> The self as origin is safe from contamination by tradition because it possesses a kind of originary naiveté. (…) With his own self as the origin of his work, that production [of the avant-garde artist] will have the same uniqueness as he; the condition of his own singularity will guarantee the originality of what it makes.[53]

But what is the search for absolute originality by the artistic avant-garde based on, if not a superstition coming from the religious belief in the ex-nihilo creation of the world? The awareness of originality as an illusion acquired consistency with Nietzsche's criticism of the idea of "origin" – recovered in recent decades by Michel Foucault.[54]

For the argument I am trying to develop, the legitimacy of this criticism of the idea of "origin" itself, and therefore the possibility of "originality", is a condition of fundamental importance, for Foucault Nietzsche rejected the idea of origin

> because it is an attempt to capture the exact essence of things. (…) We tend to think that this is the moment of their greatest perfection, when they emerged dazzling from the hands of the creator or in the shadowless light of first morning.[55]

Manfredo Tafuri asked himself:

> And why a beginning? Is it not more "productive" to multiply the "beginnings", recognizing that where everything conspires to make one recognize the transparency of a unitary cycle, there lies hidden an intertwining of phenomena that demands to be recognized as such?[56]

The Dada Manifesto postulated that "the new artist protests: he no longer paints (symbolic and illusionistic reproduction) but creates directly in stone, wood, iron, tin, boulders, locomotive organisms capable of being turned in all directions by the limpid wind of momentary sensation".[57] Despite its radical appearance, the idea of "creation" that organizes the preceding paragraph contains the religiously based superstition criticized by Nietzsche. Aware of this initial heavy load, Russian constructivists replaced the idea of "creation" with that of "invention", a "materialist" shortcut to achieve the desired originality without the metaphysical halo that they also glimpsed in the foundations of Suprematism. As did the surrealists, they used preexisting materials to achieve their aesthetic purposes. Therefore, it is not strange that other groups of the avant-garde sought originality by going back to the very beginning of humanity, paradoxically situating themselves at a "primitive" ground zero in history, transforming that primeval past into an omen of the future.

In his work on the difference between originality and copying, or plagiarism, George Steiner explained that "creators bring entirely new matter into being. Inventors, however, permute preexisting material into novel combinations. According to one paradigm the work of art is an addition to what exists; according to the other, it is an edition of it".[58] With regard to repetition, copying, and plagiarism, Edward Said has observed that

> the best way to consider originality is to look not for first instances of a phenomenon, but rather to see duplication, parallelism, symmetry, parody, repetition, echoes of it – the way, for example, literature has made itself into a topos of writing. (…) The writer thinks less of writing originally, and

more of rewriting. The image for writing changes from original inscription to parallel script, from tumbled-out confidence to deliberate fathering-forth (…), from melody to fugue.[59]

Plato established two forms of repetition: the copy and the simulacrum. The philosopher postulated that the primordial thing was the Idea, while what we perceive as tangible reality was a somewhat degraded version of that Idea. In the artistic field, the copy was a version of that Idea, while the simulacrum was a version of the copy. For Giles Deleuze, "the copy just looks like something insofar as it resembles the Idea of the thing", while the simulacrum "is a copy of a copy, an infinitely degraded icon, an infinitely diminished resemblance".[60] In this Deleuzian version of the copy as "degradation" or "diminution", we can read a valuation that inherits a-historical prejudice: Greece as the copy, Rome as the simulacrum. But, by undervaluing Roman sculptures because they are very often reproductions of Greek pieces, the conditions of the singular, complex, and multifaceted Roman history, *with their own evaluation systems*, are not considered. Within that specific historical roman framework, the question of "originality" does not occupy the same place that the culture of modernity attributes to it.

An extraordinary example of this mistake is provided by Jorge Luis Borges's text "Pierre Menard, Author of Quixote" in which a 19th-century individual proposes and succeeds in writing Don Quixote without copying it but "thinking" like Cervantes. To undertake this feat, he must manage not only to situate himself exactly within the conditions that determined it and actually re-live in his mind the life of the Spanish author and the smallest details of his circumstances in the 16th century, but he also has to manage to eliminate from his mind his own knowledge subsequent to the publication of the book. In spite of these enormous difficulties, Menard achieves a version exactly the same as Cervantes's Quixote. However, read in the context of his own time, it results in an extraordinary "original" work. Repetition in this case has become creation. As viewed by Ivan Soll, "it must be recognized that the two Quixotes can be considered apart from their etiologies, and when this happens, they become identical".[61] Considered instead within their own etiologies they are absolutely different. One of the features that characterize what we call the classical Greco-Roman system of architecture – despite the aspects that differentiate the societies that generated it – is that it sought to be based on a set of socially accepted norms or conventions. And as happens in other civilizations as well, in this system the emphasis on the means of production of a work is placed on the repetition of those norms or conventions.

Said proposed a brilliant assessment of repetition based on his analysis of Giambattista Vico's *Scienza Nuova*. In his interpretation of that work, the recurrence of the "corsi" and "ricorsi" presupposes the survival of a set of norms or conventions on which the very existence of humanity is based on. On Vico's "ricorsi", Said observes that

> repetition is useful as a way of showing that history and actuality are all about human persistence, and not about divine originality. It is most nearly true to

say, I think, that whatever else it is, repetition for Vico is something that takes place inside actuality. (…) Indeed, repetition connects reason with raw experience. First, on the level of meaning, experience accumulates meaning as the weight of past and similar experiences returns. Men are always afraid of their fathers; they bury their dead; they invariably worship a divinity fashioned in their image. These repetitions are what human society is based on. Second, repetition contains experience in a way; repetition is the frame within which man represents himself to himself and for others. (…) Finally, repetition restores the past to the scholar, illuminating his research by an inexhaustible constancy. (…) For Vico then, whether as the beginning of sense, as representation, as archeological reconstruction, repetition is a principle of economy, giving facts their historical factuality and reality its existential sense.[62]

In terms of our argument, Said-Vico's position suggests understanding the canon as a referential set of what is considered the most accurate expression of those norms or conventions repeated over time. As Colin Symes has very well warned, Said placed himself at the antipodes of those who, attributing a transhistorical condition to those norms or conventions,

> have argued that the canon continues to provide a repository of incomparable values; that its abandonment by educational institutions has created a condition of cultural lawlessness that poses a threat, no less, to the axiological bedrock of Western civilization. Said took a contrary view, that the strengths of the canon derive, paradoxically, from its failings, in the degree to which the supposedly great literary (and also political) works of the West are infected with hubris. (…) Said thus recasts humanism not as a vehicle of human perfectibility via "withdrawal and exclusion" but as one to "make more things available to critical scrutiny as the product of human labor, human energies for emancipation and enlightenment, and, just as importantly, human misreadings and misinterpretations of the collective past and present".[63]

A beautiful consideration by Thomas Stearns Eliot allows us to reconnect the theme of repetition with the question of the canon. In his opinion,

> if we approach a poet without this prejudice we shall often find that not only the best, but the most individual parts of his work may be those in which the dead poets, his ancestors, assert their immortality most vigorously [… Tradition] involves, in the first place, the historical sense, […] and the historical sense involves a perception, not only of the pastness of the past, but of its presence; the historical sense compels a man to write not merely with his own generation in his bones, but with a feeling that the whole of the literature of Europe from Homer and within it the whole of the literature of his own country has a simultaneous existence and composes a simultaneous order. (…) The existing monuments form an ideal order among themselves, which is modified by the introduction of the new (the really new) work of art among them.[64]

For several decades now, the historiography of architecture has been showing the controversial nature of the alleged radical originality of the protagonists of modernist transformation. At this point, it is difficult to understand the work of leaders such as Frank Lloyd Wright, Le Corbusier, or Mies van der Rohe neglecting a study of their subscription to a complex network of genealogical relationships. Post-classical architecture lacks "Ideas" in the sense of the platonic statement. Its history is presented as a succession and articulation of mutual references between singular proposals that are unrepeatable by definition. For a cross-cultural/dialogical view like the one presented here, uncritically sharing the belief in the need for radical originality entails not only reiterating an anachronistic and irrelevant approach but also ignoring that; on the contrary, that belief carries with it the stigma of influence.

Influence and Hegemony

The word "influence" is repeated like a catchphrase in the historiography of architecture. So evident, so legitimized and crystallized in its condition of truth, that its use seems to us absolutely natural in stories with the power of the obvious.[65] The word "influence" comes from the Latin "in-fluens", and according to the *Oxford English Dictionary*, its basic meaning (currently out of use) is "the action or fact of flowing in; inflowing, inflow, influx: said of the action of water and other fluids, and of immaterial things conceived of as flowing in. Also, concrete flowing matter". The third (also considered out of use) and last meanings suggested by the same source are more specifically relevant to our subject. The third is "the inflowing, immersion, or infusion (into a person or thing) of any kind of divine, spiritual, moral, immaterial, or secret power or principle; that which thus flows in or is infused". The last is:

> The capacity or faculty of producing effects by insensible or invisible means, without the employment of material force, or the exercise of formal authority; ascendancy of a person or social group; moral power over or with a person; ascendancy, sway, control, or authority, not formally or overtly expressed.[66]

According to these definitions, in all cases, the action takes place between two poles, one of which is active and exercises some kind of dominance over the other, which experiences it passively. The meanings that are out of use are especially interesting since they not only corroborate the idea of the "immersion" of an entity within "another" but also because they reveal the mystical nature of the idea.

From philosophy as in Emmanuel Levinas, Jacques Derrida, Paul Ricoeur, Chul-Han, or Franco Rella; from psychology as in Jacques Lacan; or from linguistics as in Mikhail Bakhtin or Julia Kristeva, an immense amount of reflections have shown us that, even on the level of interpersonal relationships, it is controversial to suppose that the speaker, or the "Self" if you prefer, is immune to the presence of the "Other".[67] From this point of view, exercising power – as referred to in the definition – is not possible without the acceptance of a set of conditions or of a certain action on the part of the presumably passive pole. We would not speak of "influence" but of the simple exercise of force where the conditions of reception are not considered by the pole that is considered active. For this reason, influence should not be thought of as a unidirectional process but, rather, at least as a bidirectional process between the two poles of the equation.[68]

At the level of political ideas, this condition of power where one pole acts and is conditioned precisely by the pole on which that action is intended has been introduced by the writings of Antonio Gramsci and – as is known – is expressed in the concept of "hegemony".[69] For Gramsci, a social class does not become dominant through the simple exercise of force but through the extent that it has managed to install a "common sense" within the social sectors that are the basis of its own position of power.[70] "Common sense" consists in transforming the values of a certain sector of society into values shared by all groups of society. It is this expansion that allows that sector to exercise its "hegemony" (or its "influence" when we refer to the issue we are dealing with here). Gramscian thought that "hegemony" cannot be made effective without what he calls "consent", that is to say: without the active acceptance by the rest of society. To obtain this "consent", the "hegemonic" sector must modify its own ultimate objectives, adapting them to the conditions that characterize that society or, in other words, that that society imposes on it. In one of his letters, he put it this way:

> The proletariat cannot become the dominant class if it does not overcome this contradiction through the sacrifice of its corporate interests. It cannot maintain its hegemony and its dictatorship if, even when it has become dominant, it does not sacrifice these immediate interests for the general and permanent interests of the class.[71]

It is to this "sacrifice of its own interests" that we refer to when we say that it is not possible to think of "influence" as simply unidirectional or that it does not have an effect on *both* poles of the process.

And this finding is not limited to political theory. In the theory of art, we owe to Hans Joseph Jauss the introduction of what he called the "reception theory".[72] Just as Gramsci does not deny the existence (historical, that is: momentary) of a hegemonic pole, neither does Jauss ignore the existence of processes of influence. Only that, in his opinion, these processes are bidirectional: paraphrasing Karl Kosik, he recalls that "the work lives to the extent that it has influence. Included within the influence of a work is what is achieved both in the consumption of that work, as in the work itself".[73] Jauss has provided us with a dynamic idea of the relationships between author, work, and public, and among works and authors themselves. In his opinion,

> If the life of the work results not from its autonomous existence but rather from its reciprocal interaction of work and mankind, this perpetual labor of understanding and of active reproduction of the past cannot remain limited to the single work. On the contrary, the relationship of work to work must now be brought into this interaction between the work and mankind, and

the historical coherence of the works among themselves must be seen in the interrelations of production and reception.[74]

However, not only does the "producing" pole affect the "receiving" pole, but it is also far from being passive. And it is not passive in the first place because, at least on a cultural level, there is always a set of alternatives, for example, like those that we have indicated in the case of architecture, which presupposes choosing one or the other, or a combination of them. But also because even if the "receiving" pole decides to reproduce exactly a piece created by the "producing" pole, the context of reproduction makes that piece take on an absolutely new dimension.

To understand the former, we can rely on the distinction proposed by Edward Said between "filiation" and "affiliation". As Conor McCarthy sums it up,

> By filiation, Said means that relation which seems to be natural or given to a writer or a critic by birth, by tradition, by nature, by inherited location. By affiliation Said means that network of relationships which human beings make consciously and deliberately for themselves.[75]

This link between filiation and affiliation determines the device referred to as "influences", which are articulated in complex networks of relationships.

Even when observing exclusively the effects in the presumably passive pole, the filiation/affiliation nexus is complex and dynamic and gives rise to works with a strong identity and innovative content. The impressive resulting intersections that are unleashed by a context of repetition in art are accounted for in an uneasy reflection by the Argentine poet Macedonio Fernandez, who in one of his autobiographies wrote:

> I was born porteño in the very year 1874. Not right away, but very shortly afterwards, I began to be cited by Jorge Luis Borges with so little restraint of praise that – through the terrible risk to which he exposed himself with this vehemence – I started to become the author of the best of what he had produced. I was a de facto talent, by overpowering him, by usurping his work.[76]

Macedonio and Borges even discussed the possibility of authorship in opposition to the "avant-garde aesthetic of the radically new".[77] As we have already mentioned, Borges claimed the effect of the context of repetition in "Pierre Menard author of Don Quixote",[78] and that claim, against the radical originality of the avant-garde, cut across all his work. In "The Theologians", for example, the same text that is orthodox in one historical context is heterodox in another and can have the author condemned to the stake. Moreover, on the occasion of his eulogy to Macedonio he confessed:

> In those years I imitated him to the point of transcription, to the point of devout and passionate plagiarism. I felt: Macedonio is literature. Those who preceded him may shine in history, but they were drafts of Macedonio,

imperfect and preliminary versions. Not to imitate that canon would have been incredibly negligent.[79]

For these reasons, when applied to architecture, the words "original" or "influence" have not always been used. They do not seem to have been part of the lexicon or mentality that characterizes discourse in the 16th, 17th, and 18th centuries. It is because the treaties that built the architecture of humanism did not promote originality but "progress". And progress was based on the experience of solutions to new problems, examining the limits of the classical orders. Donato Bramante was the one who tried to apply them with the utmost rigor, particularly in his works with either the smallest or the most gigantic of dimensions. This led him to admit that they did not survive their application to new demands without introducing "inventions"[80] that were farthest from those that had determined their initial foundation. Faced with this finding, Michelangelo's freedom for creation emerges. It is the *creative* path that Francesco Borromini will follow later.

But Michelangelo is a "miracle", that which is *beyond* language.[81] Giorgio Vasari literally refers to this "miracle" in his biography of the artist:

> The great Ruler of Heaven looked down and, seeing these vain and fruitless efforts and the presumptuous opinion of man more removed from truth than light from darkness, resolved, in order to rid him of these errors, to send to earth a genius, universal in each art.[82]

It is not by chance that Vasari uses two different words to refer to the processes of the origin of architecture: "invenzione" and "creazione". The first refers to the production of artifacts through logical procedures applying readily available knowledge, while the second indicates acts dependent on the acts of divinity: the world, life, the appointment of popes, Adam and Eve. Not coincidentally, the French classicists' rigor of the 17th century, and their staunch defense of the application of the classical orders, struggled with Borromini,[83] not so much because of Borromini's openness to Gothic "barbarism" but because of his penchant for originality as a self-confessed follower of Michelangelo. And it is also no coincidence that the re-evaluation of Michelangelo promoted by Joshua Reynolds at the dawn of the 19th century was a prelude to the new romantic demand for "genius" and "originality".[84]

In a future global history of choral authorship of modern architecture, the canon will not disappear. But it will be supported by new lines of meaning. In such a future narrative it would have been learned that behind the presumed original creations there is, and has always been, an intricate global network of human values, discoveries, and protagonists worldwide. Let's conclude by saying with Roland Barthes:

> We know now that a text is not a line of words releasing a single "theological" meaning (the "message" of the Author-God) but a multi-dimensional space in which a variety of writings, none of them original, blend and clash.

The text is a tissue of quotations drawn from the innumerable centers of culture. Similar to Bouvard and Pécuchet, those eternal copyists, at once sublime and comic and whose profound ridiculousness precisely indicates the truth of writing, the writer can only imitate a gesture that is always anterior, never original.[85]

Notes

1 The debate on the canon has a very extensive bibliography, and it is not my intention to try to deal with it in this brief paragraph that only aspires, like the rest of this essay, to provide a brief statement of the premises that have guided the selection and the type of analysis of the studies illustrated in this book. Although in the architecture of humanism there is a specific field of debate about the canon in reference to the number and characteristics of the orders (THOENES, 2017, 296–311), in this work we are interested in reflecting on the canon as comprised of works and/or authors.
2 VASARI, 1991 (1550).
3 ROWLAND, 2017; VINKEN Barbara, "Auf Leben und Tod: Vasaris Kanon", in HEYDEBRAND, 1998.
4 ROWLAND, op. cit., 347. The following phrase by van Mander serves as an example: "for what the ingenious Greeks and Romans, as well as other folk, were not privileged to find (…) has finally been brought to light by the admired Netherlander Jan Van Eyck, born in Maseyck, on the illustrious river Maas, which can now compete in honor against the Arno, the Po, and the brave Tiber". VAN MANDER, 2001 (1604), 9–10, cited in GALLEY Nicolas, "Between fascination and exasperation, la réception des Vite chez Karel van Mander", in LUCAS-FIORATO & DUBUS, 2017, 373.
5 DEMPSEY Charles, "The Carracci Postille to Vasari's Lives", *The Art Bulletin*, Vol. 68, No. 1, March 1986, p. 75. On the reception of the *Vite* cf. in LUCAS-FIORATO & DUBUS, op. cit. For the role of Aglionby, particularly in his intention to compete with France for the inheritance of the canon initiated by Vasari cf. HURLEY Cecilia, "Englishing Vasari", in LUCAS-FIORATO & DUBUS, op. cit., 415–418. In the same volume on the work of VAN MANDER cf. AURIGEMA Maria Giulia, "Ricezione Europea delle Vite (van Mander et von Sandrart) e fonti antiche", 209–232, and GALLEY, op. cit., 373–388. In BAROCCHI, 1997, the author even notes that the first edition of the book (Torrentiniana) "provocò lla dubbiosa ironia di Michelangelo e il vivo risentimento dei raffaeleschi".
6 SAUDRAIS, 2021/1, 13–20, and FRANGENBERG, 2012, 223–260. In the cited text Paola Barocchi reports an anti-Vasarian offensive by Fréart in France, as a continuation of the one already started in Italy by the Veneti Ridolfi and Boschini and the Bolognese Malvasia.
7 FELIBIEN, 1697, 287.
8 SICCA, 2013.
9 CIVIL Pierre, "Sur les commentaires, traductions et adaptations des *Vite* de Vasari en Espagne (fin XVIe-XVIIe si è clés", in LUCAS-FIORATO & DUBUS, op. cit., 331–346.
10 The detailed work by GINSBURGH & WEYERS, 2010, 37–72.
11 RODRIGUEZ-MOYA & MÍNGUEZ, 2018. On the importance of the destruction of the ancient "wonders" in Heemskerck's text, cf. SAMMUT, 2022, 27–49. On the literary origin of his representations cf. SPRONK Ron, "Maarten van Heemskerck's use of literary sources from antiquity for his Wonders of the World series of 1572", in FENOULHET & GILBERT, 2016, 125–131.
12 CESARIANO, 1521, books Second, Seventh, and Tenth.
13 CARAMUEL Y LOBKOWITZ, 1687.
14 CASSIODORUS, *Variae*, c. 525, in MADONNA, 1976, 56.

15 CLAYTON, 1988.
16 RODRIGUEZ-MOYA & MÍNGUEZ, op. cit., 4.
17 BLOOM, 2017, 23.
18 The preservation of the architecture legacy of the past depends not only on natural processes, human violence, or the political/cultural variations of valuation but also on the purely economic dynamics linked to the ownership of the land and the interests linked to it.
19 GOMBRICH Ernst, "Lecture Romanes 1973", delivered at the Sheldonian Theater in Oxford, 22.11.1973. In GOMBRICH, 1979, 163.
20 LANGFELD, 2018, 1–18.
21 OSBORNE Peter, "Radicalism without Limit? Discourse, Democracy, and the Politics of Identity", in OSBORNE, 1991, 216–217, cit. in GUILLORY, 1993, 12.
22 MARX, 1993, 215–216, cit. in VON STADEN, 1976, 82.
23 Marx uses that term precisely to refer to Greek art: "As regards art, it is well known that some of its **peaks** (e.a.) by no means correspond to the general development of society, nor do they therefore to the material substructure, the skeleton as it were of its organization. For example, the Greeks compared with modern [nations]"; in MARX Karl, "Appendix to A Contribution to the Critique of Political Economy", in MARX, op. cit., 109–111.
24 MARX, op. cit., 110 ff. Marx refers on different occasions to permanent or essential human values; cf. MARX Karl, *Economic and Philosophic manuscripts*, and *The Holy Family*, in MARX & ENGELS, 1973, 131, 133.
25 SYMES, 2006, 317.
26 LIJSTER, 2017, 259.
27 For an enriching debate about the place of "internal" (aesthetic) evaluation in the formation of the canon, cf. VAN PEER, 1996, 97–108, and (reply) RAJAGOPALAN, 1997, 75–83.
28 The books examined were Vasari (1550), Félibien (1650), Lanzi (1775), Burckhardt (1850), Berenson (1900), Chastel (1950), and Grove (2000). Cfr. GINSBURGH & WEYERS, 2006.
29 GINSBURGH & WEYERS, 2006, 24. Ginsburgh and Weyers deepened their study observing in parallel the formation of the canon of Italian and Flemish artists and concluded that "though criteria such as invention, originality, newness, and progress, and their relative weights and importance in evaluating artists change over time, it is surprising that half of the canon was there almost from the beginning. This appears to be in contradiction with the suggestions made by Junod (1976), Genette (1994), for instance, that canons are continuously moving and that no artist can survive forever". GINSBURGH & WEYERS, 2010, 63.
30 Particularly suggestive in this sense is the reflection of T.S. Eliot, for whom the poet "must be quite aware of the obvious fact that art never improves, but that the material of art is never quite the same. He must be aware that the mind of Europe – the mind of his own country – a mind which he learns in time to be much more important than his own private mind – is a mind which changes, and that this change is a development which abandons nothing on route, which does not superannuate either Shakespeare, or Homer, or the rock drawing of the Magdalenian draftsmen. That this development, refinement perhaps, complication certainly, is not, from the point of view of the artist, any improvement". ELIOT, T.S., "Tradition and the Individual Talent", in ELIOT, 2014, 107.
31 VINKEN, 1998, 202.
32 BHABHA Homi, "Introduction", in SORENSEN, 2018, 10. On the flexible condition of the canon cf. also WESTPHAL, 1993, 436–449. Also GORAK Jan, "More Than Just a Rule: The Early History of the Canon", in GORAK, 2014, 10, we read: "almost from the very start of its history writers on the canon [in Classic Greece] have regarded it as an inherited set of rules and practices to be broadened, sophisticated, and generally loosened up".

33 The meaning of "Das Andere" has been discussed among others by PURDY, 2006, 41–62; DAMISCH, 2000, 26–41; and KRAVAGNA Christian, "Adolf Loos and the Colonial Imaginary" in AVERMAETE et al., 2010, 245–261.
34 STEWART, 2000, 38.
35 KLAWITER, 1968, 1–55. Also RIECKMANN, 1985, 39–49.
36 KRAUS, 1965, 67, cited in COLOMINA, 2012, 6.
37 I am referring to the libertarian cultural movement of Monte Veritá, closely linked to the emergence of radical European avant-gardes. VOSWINCKEL, 2009; BOLLMAN, 2017. On the development of nudism in the German-speaking world: GRISKO, 1999; WEDEMEYER-KOLWE, 2004.
38 CACCIARI, 1993 (1975), 116.
39 LOOS Adolf, "Architektur", in *Sämtliche Schriften*, Herold, Wien, München, 1962 . [*On Architecture: Studies in Austrian Literature, Culture and Thought*, Ariadne Press, Riverside, 2007, pp. 73–85].
40 Ibid., p. 229.
41 HERNÁNDEZ, 2011, 91.
42 RODRÍGUEZ MARTÍN, 2008, 277–291; ARROJO, 2004, 31–53; JAMES, 1999; MUALEM, 2017, 315–343.
43 KRISTEVA, 1991, 192.
44 PATTERSON, 1991, 35. The paragraph refers to M. Bakhtin, "Problems of Dostoevsky's Poetics".
45 "'Genug der Originalgenies! Wiederholen wir uns unaufhörlich selbst!' ("'Enough of the Original Geniuses! Let Us Repeat Ourselves Unceasingly!)':The slogan was expressed by Loos (in LOOS, 1962, 341). LOCHER, 1994, 76–85; HARE, 1964–1965, 139–142; MCFARLAND, 1974, 447–476. In a quite different dimension, the issue of "originality" is crucial in terms of economic valuation not only of cultural and artistic production but, especially, of the products of science and technology (intellectual property): GUETZKOW et al., 2004, 190–212. On the debates about originality and copy in the history of Western culture: GAZDA, 2002. The same theme in the 19th century: MACFARLANE, 2007.
46 PEVSNER, 1954, 369.
47 PEVSNER, 1977; PEVSNER, 1954, 368. The best expression of his belief in the existence of a "spirit of the place" was his well-known series of lectures for the BBC on the "Englishness of the English Art", 20.
48 For Humboldt "knowledge of the Greeks is not merely pleasant, useful or necessary to us – no, in the Greeks alone we find the ideal of that which we should like to be and produce. If every part of history enriched us with its human wisdom and human experience, then from the Greeks we take something more than earthly – almost godlike", in VON HUMBOLDT, 1963, 79, cited in BERNAL, 1987, 287. Cf. especially the chapter "Hellenomania I", pp. 281–316.
49 BLANC, 2018.
50 HABERMAS, 1998 (1985), 1.
51 Ibidem, 7.
52 WEISS, 1965 (1964), 27.
53 KRAUSS, 1985, 157.
54 ZUCKERT, 1983, 48–71.
55 FOUCAULT Michel, "Nietzsche, Genealogy, History", in BOUCHARD, 1977, 142–143 [VV.AA, 1971, 145–172].
56 TAFURI, 1990 (1980), 3.
57 TZARA, 1918.
58 STEINER, 2002, 13–53, cited in MCFAIRLANE, 2007, 1.
59 SAID, 1983, 135.

60 DELEUZE, 1990 (1969), 257. See also HUDSON HICK & SCHMÜCKER, 2016; SCHWARTZ, 1996.
61 SOLL, 2000.
62 SAID, op. cit., 113–114.
63 SYMES, 2006, 311.
64 ELIOT, op. cit., 106.
65 The concept of "influence" has been especially developed in political science. In the cultural field, the work of BLOOM, 2007.
66 Online edition. https://www.oed.com.
67 I am referring to works such as LEVINAS, 2000 (1967), —45–74; LEVINAS, 1972; DERRIDA, 1996; MELMAN, 2007; LACAN, 1955; LAPLANCHE, 1999; RELLA, 1978; RICOEUR, 1990.
68 A clear example is the well-known difference between the exercise of force on the Native Americans by the Conquistadors and its complement with the intervention of religious organizations, especially that of the Jesuits, with their learning of the languages and customs of the communities under their control, in some cases, even verging on heresy.
69 JOSEPH, 2002; MOUFFE, 1979; WILLIAMS, 1960, 586–599; BATES, 1975, 351–366; DI BIAGIO, 2008, 29–54; COSPITO, 2016, 49–88.
70 The bibliography on the subject is extensive. Cf. among others LIGUORI, 2005; FILIPPINI, 2012, 89–106.
71 GRAMSCI Antonio, Letter of October 1926 to the Central Committee of the CPSU, in GRAMSCI, 1971, 128–129, cit. in COSPITO, op. cit., 58.
72 JAUSS, 2005 (1982).
73 Ibidem, 39.
74 Ibidem, 83.
75 MCCARTHY, 2010, 100.
76 FERNANDEZ, 1989, 90, cit. in GARTH, 2005, 32. The inhabitants of the city of Buenos Aires are called "porteños".
77 On the aesthetic of repetition in Borges MARFÈ, 2017, 227–239.
78 DAPÍA, 1996, 100–113; GRACIA, 2001, 45–57.
79 IVARS, 1999, 306.
80 BRUSCHI, 1969.
81 It is worth remembering here Said's words in this regard: "never mind if epistemologically the status of repetition itself is uncertain: repetition is useful as a way of showing that history and actuality are all about human persistence, and not about divine originality". SAID, 1983, 113. I'm referring to the famous last sentence of Ludwig Wittgenstein's *Tractatus Logico-Philosophicus: "Whereof one cannot speak, thereof one must be silent".* As Massimo Cacciari argued: "Wittgenstein does not at all deny that for some, after long doubt, 'the problem of life' has become clear – he does not at all declare the impossibility of the miracle. Instead, he simply asserts that they couldn't say it. Likewise, for Augustine, the ineffable is that which you cannot express or say, but which you must not be silent about in any sense" (a.t.), in CACCIARI, 2005, 136.
82 VASARI, 1991 (1550), 414.
83 CONNORS, 2000, 191–204.
84 "The idea of genius became a cornerstone of the Romantic movement in the arts. The genius, especially in poetry, drama, sculpture, painting, and music was seen by many Romantics as endowed with semi-divine forces of creation, thaumaturgical in his miraculous yield. Closely allied with the Romantic idea of genius, especially in the German states, was the idea of peoples or races endowed with special hereditary, creative powers and forming the necessary genetic sources of individual geniuses". NISBET, 1982, 441. The mystical/religious content of the idea of "genius" has even been admitted by Harold

Bloom: "I am aware that I transfer to genius what Scholem and Idel follow Kabbalah in attributing to God, but I merely extend the ancient Roman tradition that first established the ideas of genius and of authority. In Plutarch, Mark Antony's genius is the god Bacchus or Dionysus […] The emperor Augustus, who defeated Antony, proclaimed that the god Apollo was his genius, according to Suetonius", In BLOOM, 2002, 1.
85 BARTHES, 1984 (1968), 65.

3 Essay 2: Controversial Positions

The Center–Periphery Tension in the Work of Manfredo Tafuri

> Oltre e per conseguenza rinforzate, che gli gran corpi sieno gravi o lievi non è possibile, essendo l'universo infinito; e per tanto non hanno raggione di lontananza o propinquità dalla o alla circonferenza o centro.
>
> Giordano Bruno[1]

Introduction[2]

The onomastic index of *Architettura Contemporanea*,[3] the book published by Manfredo Tafuri, with Francesco Dal Co in 1976, mentions 1,268 names of architects, artists, writers, politicians, intellectuals, and groups with relevant roles in the history of a period that spans from the mid-19th century to the date of its publication. Of those 1,268, only 8 are figures coming from Latin America: the Brazilian film director Alberto Cavalcanti; the Argentine architect César Pelli, who shows up as an "American architect" (that is, from the United States); the Spaniard Félix Candela, known for his work in Mexico; the artist, theoretician, and designer Tomás Maldonado, identified as a participant in the experience of the Ulm School of Design; the Mexican Mario Pani; the Venezuelan Carlos Raone (sic) Villanueva; Lucio Costa and Oscar Niemeyer. Only the latter two receive a significant analysis where, also in passing, the name of Affonso Eduardo Reidy is mentioned.

What draws our attention is that the contribution of the Latin Americans in the construction of *Architettura Contemporanea* seems to have been judged by the authors as less than meager. This is particularly evident when Tafuri, in one of his chapters, although dedicating a large space to Costa and Niemeyer, does so to unload onto them a decidedly negative critique, bordering on contempt. Niemeyer's creations are described as "unexpected events, spectacles of the absurd, euphoric fragments of nature crystallized", stating in addition that his work in Brasilia reached "the limits of his approach, used in Brazil ad nauseam", and that in them "the gratuitous is tinged with sophistication; although they make a fine show, it is one of superfluous velleities".[4] The undertaking of Brasilia is described as "born out of demagogic intentions", and the plan by Lucio Costa is "laid out on a puerile allegorical ground plan – that of an airplane". The superblocks, on their part, had only tried to "reinterpret the urbanistic model tried out in the Soviet Union beginning in the 1930s".

40   *Essay 2: Controversial Positions*

Figure 3.1 Detail of a photograph taken during an interview with Tomas Dagnino for the Architecture Supplement of the newspaper *Clarin*. Buenos Aires, August 1981. *Clarin* Archive. Photo: Daniel Rodríguez. (Courtesy of *ARQ Revista*).

This cursory and arbitrary way of treating the topic of Latin American architecture did not remain unnoticed by critics. In the review published by the US-American *Journal of the Society of Architectural Historians*, William Curtis pointed out that "little or nothing is said about either industrial or rural vernaculars, and next to nothing about the crucial problems of 'developing countries.'"[5] Curtis argued that these were curious omissions for historians who were happy to announce their Marxist affiliations.

How was it possible that a scholar that had been defined by James Ackerman as

> the most dynamic and innovative force in architectural history and theory of our times, a scholar whose formidable production, which included some twenty-three books, was complemented by continuous engagement with the issues and controversies in contemporary architecture, planning, and conservation,[6]

could fall into such a damaging approach to the topic?

In the trajectory of such a brilliant intellectual like Manfredo Tafuri this lack of consideration could not be the consequence of a mistake, isolated and insignificant but, on the contrary, an expression of his theoretical construction. This study was stimulated by this intriguing incongruence. Within the conceptual framework of this book, our hypothesis reads as follows: the lack of interest, and even the disdain in the approach to Latin American architecture (and in general that of the "third world"), in *Architettura Contemporanea* is the result of a construction where the absences and presences, the intensities with which each piece or protagonist is studied, are determined by the place they occupy in the field of Tafuri's historical vision, or what we could call the geography of the author's point of view. We will try to show that during an especially important part of his career, Tafuri's thought was organized around a classic scheme of the "center–periphery" relationship. *Architettura Contemporanea* was probably the last expression of this North-Atlantic-centered viewpoint as a spatial manifestation of the self/other structure of the canon.

Aesthetic Cycles: The Geographical Dimension of History

Probably given his interest in the work of Giulio Carlo Argan or as a consequence of the direct reading of Giambattista Vico's *Principii di scienza nuova* and/or of its reinterpretation by Benedetto Croce. Tafuri's studies were organized since the start of his career by the belief in the existence of grand aesthetic cycles. One of his most recognized contributions was the notion of the emergence of the 20th-century avant-garde and modern architecture as a result of the crisis of the overarching cycle of "Humanism".

Already in his master's thesis, presented in 1960 and published two years later, he claimed that the works analyzed there had to be understood as a product of local "cultural humus".[7] However, in the manner of Argan, he believed that those buildings belonged as well to "entire cultural cycles" that affected geography at least at the "European" scale. Based on the specific case of the Federician works that were the object of his analysis, he concluded that this particular "cultural humus" enabled the evolution of a "process that is closely related to the implicit developments of (…) the particular Italian interpretation of that aesthetic cycle".[8]

The idea of an "aesthetic cycle" gains significance for our analysis as far as what he outlined in the mentioned text was an articulation of the temporal and spatial dimensions of the phenomenon. The "aesthetic cycle" crosses throughout a specific time that stretches within an equally specific space (Europe, in this case). In the manner of the processes that had been explained by the Prague Linguistic Circle, the *center–periphery* dynamic underlies this historic/geographic scheme, as far as it consists in the deployment of a nucleus that originates in a certain point of space and expands toward other areas of the territory where it experiments changes.[9] Further along, in his studies on "Mannerism" the young Tafuri would prove that Humanism's crisis was reached as the result of a process of expansion from the original Florentine/Roman nucleus to other areas, where it had encountered different types of resistance or adaptations determined by their specific historical conditions.[10]

His observation was not limited to the classical cycle: indeed, in relation to Gothic architecture he refers to a "European artistic language, which (…) expands, articulating itself in semantic experiences (…) finally breaking up into (…) antinomic components that express the definitive crisis of the first, great European artistic experience".[11] Furthermore, in the case of the "Gothic" Tafuri understood the European space as a

> dialectical unity of artistic-cultural exchanges, whose crisis coincides with the rise of (…) Italian Humanism, which in turn takes on the task of catalyzing the disintegrating cultural ferments, to redirect them to a new synthesis of a secular and universalistic value.[12]

Throughout the 1960s his interest in semiotics increased, and in *Theories and History of Architecture*, the "cycles" came to be identified as "linguistic units". "The great linguistic systems in the history of architecture can be defined" – he wrote –

> as, somehow, unitary systems. It is sufficient, in fact, to measure their integrity with the yardstick of a dynamic conception, keeping in mind (…) that every artistic code can only be defined based on the contributions that transgress, offend, and marginally contest that very same code. The problem is, then, in the criteria to be used in order to distinguish among the linguistic units in the history of architecture.[13]

The similarity of this approach with that of the Prague Circle is surprising. Tafuri was perceiving here the aporias of the idea of a cycle, or rather of the "linguistic units" understood synchronically as structure. The problem was the explanation of changes or modifications, so these should be attributed to the fact of the "geographic" expansion. In this sense, in reference to the task of Brunelleschi he argued that

> we have a true linguistic revolution when the enrichment of a given code – particularly the Gothic– is carried so far as to cause a crisis in the dynamic system of the relations that, in spite of inversions and contestations from within, sees its universe of discourse as unitary.[14]

All in all, and even when he could intuitively and progressively understand the reciprocal interrelation of both poles of the *center/periphery* system, this first phase of Tafuri's research was characterized by the insistence on an understanding that we could denote a simple duality. A duality that was key to the dynamic of creation, expansion, and crisis of the cycles or linguistic units. As expected here, that understanding would reach its most schematic and mono-directional expression coordinated with his "anti-operative" radicalization in the first half of the 1970s. In that new context, his purpose was to understand the role of the avant-garde and architecture in the "modern" cycle. But, in this phase of his intellectual history, the explanation of its dynamics would be attributed exclusively to the contradictions and aporias within the system itself, with no attention to the geographic dimension and to the crisis produced through the process of expansion.

To understand this process, we will delve into other dimensions of the center/periphery problem.

At the Beginning, the Periphery

During the initial stages of his intellectual production, Tafuri's point of view in relation to the topic we are discussing was expressed most clearly in his master's thesis, and in his first three books. One can recognize in this period an inherent contradictory attitude. On the one hand, the traditionally self-centered tendency of the history of European and US-American art, and in an opposite direction the specific situation of post-war Italian culture, which was itself considered as minor or peripheral in relation to contemporary Anglo-Saxon currents. In those preliminary years, this inherently contradictory condition seems to have stimulated in him an open attitude, expressed through the intuitive explorations of the expansion of cycles or cultural units, as explained above. Taking into account this specific historical condition, we cannot overlook that in his first work – his thesis mentioned above – the young Tafuri concentrated on two buildings of the Sicilian city of Taormina, seemingly peripheral both because of their relative scarce value in the history of architecture and because of their geographic location.

During the last years of his graduate studies, he was impressed by the texts of Giulio Carlo Argan about Brunelleschi (1956) and Borromini (1952), and by Argan's *Walter Gropius and the Bauhaus* (1951). Moreover, Tafuri attended Argan's History of Modern Art course at the University of Rome upon his return from the University of Palermo, where Argan had overseen the courses in History of Medieval and Modern Art since 1955. According to Maria Giulia Aurigemma "Argan rejects the center/periphery formula, because (for him) art is true in every place, and this also applies to his art studies in Sicily. (…) The geography-style-nation theme (…) is not Argan's approach".[15] Aurigemma argues that in his *Storia dell'Arte* (1969), Argan had forcefully returned to the topic of Latin/German pluri-centrality in the Renaissance (Dürer/Masaccio/Van Eyck). In that essay, he explains that the assumed Florentine centrality

> would not serve to explain the work of the Flemish Jan van Eyck or Rogier van del Weyden or the Frenchman Jean Fouquet, who also, in the context of European painting of the first half of the fifteenth century, are no less important than the great Florentine masters.[16]

Tafuri's *Problemi di Critica* ... seems to work in harmony with that position of Argan. For him, the Badia Vecchia reveals

> a recovery of the traditional eclecticism of Sicilian art, (…) and a particularly interesting aspect of a moment of crisis in the history of architecture that is anything but provincial, and in many ways complex and problematic, despite the superficial simplicity of its figurative qualities.[17]

Figure 3.2 San Gregorio da Sassola e Castello Medioevale (xilography), from *Le cento città d'Italia. Supplemento mensile illustrato del Secolo* (The Hundred Cities of Italy. Illustrated Monthly Supplement of the Century), Milan, Sonzogno, 1894. Unknown author. Wikimedia Commons.

During those formative years Tafuri also analyzed the Baroque reform of the town of San Gregorio da Sassola, an intervention that was generally considered "peripheral" and therefore of lesser value because it supposedly lacked a creative attitude regarding the "high" Baroque system.[18]

In the manner of Argan, this denial of a simplistic application of the *center/periphery* paradigm was also expressed in his early intuitions about Borromini. "What is truly revolutionary (in Borromini's work) – he wrote – (was) the demonstration of the inexistence of a center and a periphery, in art as in life, which makes his architecture related to the new truths of a Galileo".[19]

In 1964 Tafuri published his two first books *Ludovico Quaroni e lo sviluppo dell'architettura moderna in Italia* and *L'architettura moderna in Giappone*. In the first he started to organize his ideas in relation to his own contemporary reality. While, in the second, in what was his first opening to an international dimension of the architectural debate, he presented Japan as a mirror of his own reality.

In the framework of the *center/periphery* paradigm, *Ludovico Quaroni ...* was primarily oriented toward his own questioning of the peripheral condition into which he was immersed within the context of the immediate post-war Italian culture. Furthermore, one could interpret the book as a presentation of a counter-figure in response to Argan's *Walter Gropius e la Bauhaus*: Quaroni as an anti-hero expressive of the mix, confusion, and difficulties of an "Italian" interpretation of modernism, in the manner of the anonymous Federician builders studied in Taormina.

According to Tafuri,

> Quaroni was struck by an article of mine on the political developments of Rome (…) after the war up to 1961 in order to see how architects were (…) "engaged" with the situation, and I had mentioned him in this context.[20]

This text impressed Quaroni to the point of proposing his young critic be his teaching assistant in his course at the University of Rome, and "to edit an anthology of his writings".[21] To write such a book was for Tafuri an opportunity to study

> an architect who had participated in the whole trajectory of Italian history. (…) He had posed the same questions I would pose for myself in the 1960s and 1970s: "Where are we coming from?" and, "Where are we?" –not so much "Where are we going?".[22]

For Tafuri, the problems of architecture in Italy derived fundamentally not only from political and material limitations but, above all, from the ideological constraints imposed by Fascism.

> Over the years between the 1920s and the 1930s (…) those shy and little pregnant attempts of cultural opening came suffocated by an involution that had its roots in the nationalist rhetoric, in the closing towards Europe caused by fascist chauvinism, and by the complex of inferiority in comparison with the most industrial developed nations.[23]

Those limitations had disconnected Italian architecture from the international culture in a process with roots that could be found, following Edoardo Persico, at the beginning of the 19th century. Since then, "the problem and the drama of architecture, as of the whole of our culture was therefore that of the lack of a European "historicity"".[24]

Tafuri argued that once Fascism was defeated, Italian culture was unable to rediscover itself in a dimension beyond its stringent borders. "In Italy" – he stated –

> it was (…) a controversy between continuity and crisis (…) without having established within which limits the Italian experience of the modern movement could take a margin of validity in the context of the European international culture. (…) The Italian attempts at "overcoming" demonstrated the unrealistic and provincial origin of its entire cultural world.[25]

Throughout the 1960s Italy was characterized by what the increasingly radical expressions of different social sectors understood as a failure of the "center-left" administration, where many intellectuals had put their hopes.[26] As a manifestation of the increasingly tense political and social climate, they closely related the "poverty" of Italian culture to the "incapable" traditional political forces that were unable to situate Italy at the level of other European nations. This is why, in reference to the failure of urban policies as one of the most strident consequences of that lack of capability, and introducing a Marxist tone not noticed in previous works, Tafuri argued that

> the ideological emphasis of urban activity and prevalent spatial expression of planning are phenomena to put in relationship with the low degree of global development in our Country (…) the Italian economic structure has not admitted thus far different possibilities.[27]

Ludovico Quaroni … registers a second nuance that anticipates the direction that Tafuri's later works would take: for him, the Italian crisis could no longer be attributed exclusively to internal causes, but to the "peripheral" and "underdeveloped" condition of the country. By the end of the 1950s, recovering the view toward Europe was not enough, because Europe's own architectural culture was itself in crisis. "The fair indifference of the Hansaviertel – he wrote – (…) was the more obvious sign (…) of a crisis that extended primarily to the roots of an operative model and to the entire culture".[28]

The thought about a "European", or rather an international dimension, occupied a much more relevant place in his work on Japan.[29]

As mentioned above, to look toward Japan meant to create a reflective surface where to mirror the critical Italian situation. Japan had been equally defeated in the war, devastated, and occupied by a foreign power; and Japan, like Italy, had to face an accelerated process of modernization within a dense traditional culture. According to Tafuri, architects in both countries, albeit employing different approaches, were dedicated to fostering an architecture intended to function as an "instrument for the continual advancement and self-renewal of society".[30] Indeed, we can observe this reflective intention on various occasions, such as when referencing Kenzō Tange's Hiroshima Peace Memorial, where he emphasizes that

> the degree of maturity with which the experiment is conducted should be noted, especially in relation to the series of failed attempts of Italian architectural culture (…) in which the problem of historicity and "tradition" end up exhausted in populism or in deplorable evasions.[31]

When studying contemporary architecture in Japan, it became clear to Tafuri that it was the "Modern Movement" that was going through a crisis. Not only was the crisis not limited to the Italian context, nor did it originate exclusively within architecture itself: for Tafuri, in post-World War II years, the crisis affected Western culture *tout court.*

Tafuri's most significant sources evident in *Modern Architecture in Japan* seem to have been his readings of Jean-Paul Sartre and Edmund Husserl. His interest in the former began in 1951, but it would be years later, when – according to himself – he was amid the "battle" of the master plan for Rome when "Sartre's litérature engagée became a reality".[32] As is known, Sartre's position in relation

Figure 3.3 Book cover *of L'architettura moderna in Giappone* (*Modern Architecture in Japan*), by Manfredo Tafuri, Capelli, Bologna, 1964.

to international politics took an important turn in 1956 when, confronted with the repression of Russian tanks during the upheavals in Hungary, he decided to abandon his position as a "fellow traveler" of French communists. In addition, at the time, the Algerian Revolution expanded, and Sartre published in 1961 his famous foreword to Frantz Fanon's book *The Wretched of the Earth*, published in Italian in 1962.

Tafuri paraphrases in his text a statement by Sartre, which expresses commitment to the third world: "For the first time with the struggle for independence and sovereignty conducted by the 'underdeveloped' nations, history has become truly universal. (...). Based on the real unity of history, the contradictory unity of culture must be achieved".[33] *Modern Architecture in Japan* denotes the purpose of bringing awareness to the "contradictory unity of culture". For Tafuri, "the contradictory unity of cultures of different origin and history, in particular of Western and Eastern cultures, is (...) a profound instance that has been acting for a long time in all sectors of European culture".[34]

Tafuri's interest in the "Orient" was linked to the conviction of the state of cultural "crisis" that we have mentioned. Furthermore, it is not strange that such a crisis be read from a Husserlian viewpoint. In his interview with Passerini, Tafuri recalled that "another influence on my thinking at the time was Enzo Paci, who insisted on the trajectory of Husserl, and on the other hand, the trajectory of Heidegger".[35] In that interview he remembered his interest in the courses of Saverio Muratori who also referred to Husserl's *The Crisis of European Sciences and Transcendental Phenomenology*. Giorgio Ciucci, one of his closest colleagues during his first years in the Roman athenaeum, has also supplied testimony of Tafuri's close interest in the ideas of Husserl.[36] As has been discussed by several scholars,[37] in the face of the tragic and wrenching conditions of the first European post-war, Husserl had initiated an opening toward "Oriental" thought, and this inspired his disciple, Martin Heidegger. One can then understand that Tafuri decides to finish his book referencing a conference by Giulio Carlo Argan where he underlined the figure of Paul Klee because of his ability to take from the "Orient" those elements that contributed to the revitalization of his own culture:

> By substituting image with form as the supreme value of art – writes Tafuri citing his Roman master – Klee has reopened, as in philosophy Husserl and Heidegger, that conversation with non-European culture, in a historical moment in which this conversation appears, to those who are not blind, indispensable for the very survival of European culture.[38]

The result of that "conversation" between both cultures could not be other than mutual enrichment. On the one hand, in reference to the European exoticism of the 18th and 19th centuries, we read that "the need to broaden the European cultural horizon merged with the very common starting point of contact with Asian civilizations".[39] On the other, he argued that in contemporary Japan "The synthesis between Eastern and Western culture (...) was pursued (...) from the mid-nineteenth century onwards (...). The relations of exchange between the two different cultures (...) do not have an indifferent place in the genesis of the present experiences".[40]

Tafuri sought clues in Japan as an exit strategy from the crisis he perceived within the architectural culture of his time. He pointed out that if

> one can see in the plurality of motives and in the contradictions of the new Japan itself the possibility of a crisis, that can also indicate to Europe a new

way to solve problems that are now common to civilizations whose crises are becoming more and more analogous.[41]

According to him Japanese architecture had been able to find "methodologies and stimuli capable of offering alternatives or solutions to the problems that the European or American modern movement was struggling to respond to".[42]

"Mannerism" is one of the central concepts used to understand and judge the topics analyzed in *Modern Architecture in Japan*. Much later, Tafuri reminded us about that Italian – but also European – "present" time of 1964. A present that in his later course of 1985 on Giulio Romano he would define as that of "el desengaño" (disillusionment).[43] In reference to the above-mentioned reaction of "progressive" intellectuals to the failure of the "center-left" government. In those lectures Tafuri explained that in that context the concept of "Mannerism" had acquired an extraordinary currency thrust forward by the preaching of Bruno Zevi and Paolo Portoghesi, and by the memorial exhibition of the fifth centenary of Michelangelo's death.

In broad terms Tafuri considered that the Japanese metabolists "remained entangled in a too generic avant-garde mannerism".[44] But the category was also useful to explain figures of the intermediate generation such as Tange, whose search "will almost require setting a new mannerism understood in the best meaning of the term (…) historically rooted in oriental culture".[45] Precisely,

> Japan provides its own contribution to the question of mannerism, and here the significance that this phenomenon can have, when considered in relation to the kind of tradition from which the whole of modern Japanese culture originates, must be emphasized.[46]

To Occupy the Center: The Leap to Europe

In 1966 Tafuri published his third book, specifically dedicated to the topic of "L'Architettura del Manierismo nel Cinquecento Europeo" (*The Architecture of Mannerism in European 16th Century*), a work he qualified later as "a horrible thing that weighed heavily on my conscience".[47] This essay was conceived as part of his application as Professor of the History of Art at the Politecnico di Milano, for which he had to participate in a competition backed by Ernesto Rogers.

Christoph Frommel – who at the time was librarian of the Hertziana Library in Rome – remembers that the book followed "Argan's abstract method",[48] as opposed to the opinions of the scholars of German institutions that confessed "to be in love with Raphael and to be tired of the cult of Mannerism". According to Frommel

> Tafuri (did not doubt) that there was a Mannerist style in architecture, a definable and circumscribable phenomenon between the Renaissance and Baroque. (…) The interest in Mannerism became almost a cult and reached its peak in the 1955 exhibition in Amsterdam.

For the German historian, "Tafuri's youthful book reacts to the intellectual chaos and confusion in the discussion of Mannerism and looks at the phenomena with the rationality and methodological clarity of his master Argan".[49]

From the very start the book makes clear Tafuri's position in relation to his contemporary situation. For him "the reasons that moved us to undertake our research on Mannerist architecture are not exempt from an interest (about) the consciousness of the tragic present condition – artistic but, even more, human".[50]

In opposition to the main currents at the time, he understood "Mannerism" because of an openness to the new scientific attitude toward the world that characterized the 16th century. Adopting the interpretation of Ernst Cassirer in *Individuum und Kosmos in der Philosophie der Renaissance* he believed that

> (the) connection with nature, anti-naturalism, unrealism, and anti-structuralism, characteristic of the architects of Mannerism, are precisely in the atmosphere of a new search for the enlargement of man's cognitive power, (…) with its faith in experiment as research and not taken for granted a priori.[51]

The analysis of "Mannerism" enables Tafuri to revert his point of view in relation to the topic we are considering. If in his first works he was confronting the problem of the peripheral ("provincial") condition of Italy, or of the "Italian interpretations" of the European course, with *The Architecture of Mannerism* …, probably coordinated with the international celebration of the "Italian miracle" and the accelerated inclusion of the country in the circle of developed nations, the phenomenon to be looked at adopts the opposite direction. The study of "Mannerism" was, in the end, the study of the expansion of the Italian "High Renaissance" toward Europe. In the 16th century, the problem was not the Italian difficulty in sharing the "European" destiny, but vice versa, the obstacles of Europe itself to assimilate

> the rediscovery of man and history (…), which from the Florence of Salutati and Bruni to the declarations of human rights to the present day, constitute the structure of the modern search for the meaning of reality and the tools to transform it.

Furthermore, he believed that with the diverse forms of "resistance" to the forms of that "Florentine discovery",

> Rome and Italy were paying for the cultural, economic, and political exploitation imposed on Europe (…) now the barbarians and Goths (…) almost seem to claim revenge, inserting themselves precisely (…) as corrupters and destroyers (…) within the vast crisis of Renaissance classicism.[52]

He analyzed three expressions of these "resistances" to the Italian "accomplished classicist experience".

In the first case, he presented Philibert de l'Orme as the most representative figure, and Sebastiano Serlio and his treatise as the communication venues of that experience. France, we are told, holds the powerful technical and figurative tradition that has been signaled in Gothic architecture. "What French architects welcomed most in Serlio's teaching – Tafuri argued – was his recklessness in interpreting the classicist repertoire".[53]

Lacking the consistent French heritage, presumably determined by different spiritual impulses, and being the main protagonists of the confrontation with the papal Roman version of Christianity, Nordic societies are considered structurally external to the "accomplished classical experience". For Tafuri "the Nordic disposition for themes connected to the fantastic (… were) thus soon introduced into architecture, (…) giving rise to a Flemish Mannerism".[54] Moreover, "it is precisely that eccentricity that enables the birth of an autonomous Nordic Mannerist attitude that will help undermine the international primacy of Italian art".[55]

The English experience is presented as the weakest among the three main forms of expressions of "resistance" to the Italian "accomplished classical experience". He considered that from the *prodigy houses* to the work of Wren, Vanbrough, and Hawksmoor the English interpretation of that "classical experience" was not more than an "unscrupulous empiricism in support of a programmatic eclecticism".[56] The determining factors of this "empiricism" were, according to him, the

> new political and civic climate created by the novel anti-feudal aristocracy because of Henry VIII's separation from the Roman church, (and therefore the) readiness to accept absolutely external classicist premises (in order) to be in sync with continental culture.[57]

The research and ideas that Tafuri examined during the early 1960s also permeate his *Theories and History of Architecture* (1968), published two years after *The Architecture of Mannerism* …. Here the conflicts between both "cultural cycles" – classicist and modern – comprise one of his most incisive arguments. With this stance Tafuri detects that "the European Borrominism (…) develops a problematic relationship with the non-classical and anti-classical historical cultures",[58] and in a geographic synchronic dimension he furthers the idea of a blind "resistance" to classicism, maintaining that it is even necessary to understand that "in the misunderstanding of Classicism in the Middle-European countries a 'historical' revenge was carried out by 'popular', empirical and anti-Roman cultures".[59]

In relation to our topic another of the intuitions of *Theories and History* … is the discovery of the transformative effect produced by the insertion of external elements within the "linguistic units". Indeed, Tafuri warns us here that one of the "typical "instruments of architectural experimentalism" (is) the introduction of a theme, deeply rooted in a certain context", into another totally different one.[60] Moreover, he understands the consequences that these operations bring to the works themselves by corroding their presumed purity, and at the same time destroying the alleged self-referentiality of the systems or cycles. Analyzing the way in which Borromini includes, in the tomb of Cardinal Giussano, "mosaics, gothic mullioned windows with twin lights, sculptures and headstones" he concludes that here the ancient fragments are inserted (…) in ideal spaces achieved through elastic perspective deformations: as if to demonstrate, from the inside of these unnatural windows open onto an "autre" universe, the problematic of an existential condition that cannot reject history.[61]

Theories and History … constitutes his first great attempt at a synthesis of the totality of construction processes, expansion, and the crisis of the humanist cycle starting with the Bruneleschian discoveries. Given his coupling with the Gothic universe on the one end and the modernist universe on the other, Tafuri must take charge, incipiently, of the need to broaden both the geographic dimension of his reasoning to the entire globe and the temporal dimension to the totality of human expression. In this way, the world beyond European frontiers, a world highlighted by the background of the colonialist expansion over Africa, Asia, and America, and the encounter with other "peripheral" cultures rises in complexity with consequences that cannot go unnoticed.

Architecture, from absolute object, – he writes – becomes in the landscaped context a relative value. (… In this way) the Gothic, Chinese, classical, and eclectic pavilions inserted in the texture of a "nature trained to be natural", are ambiguous objects. They allude to something other than themselves, losing their semantic autonomy.[62]

If with Tafuri's study about Japan, the bold leap toward the Pacific and the encounter with "Orient" had been facilitated by the referential mooring to the Italian situation itself, this first leap beyond the Atlantic confronted him with the need to explain some intersections – even more complex and unexpected – such as those related to the figure of Frank Lloyd Wright. This new dimension of his construction led him to notice that

today we can see Wright's anti-historicism as richer than Gropius's, because of its capacity to absorb fragments of anti-European historical memories: the Mayan, Aztec, and Toltec architecture of the Barnsdall and Ennis houses, or the North American Indian tepees in the Lake Tahoe huts and floats.[63]

Similarly, the analysis of the avant-garde required stretching to its limits the diachronic dimension. In one direction taking on the issue of "futurisms", and in the opposite the unavoidable topic of "primitivism". "Alexander Dorner –he argued – recognizes in primitive art a counterpart, or at least a direct precedent, of the Modern Movement".[64]

Paradoxically, at the same time that the international reach of his thought and his own positioning in the "center" of the historiographical debate was being consolidated (by overcoming the relatively "peripheral" condition in which he found himself in the first years of his career), in his 1960s publications the static spatial scheme of a unilateral center/periphery radiation lost the relative flexibility that had characterized his initial works. As we anticipated, the course of his ideas during the 1960s leads us to attribute the greater rigidity of the scheme to his political radicalization as part of the so-called workerist ideology and negative critique. The following paragraphs analyze this argument in more detail.

The "Third World" as Insignificant Agent

As a consequence of *Theories and History* ..., and of his other publications of the same years such as his *Jacopo Sansovino*, or of his essays in the journal *Contropiano* (deployed later in a more definitive manner in *Project and Utopia*) along the 1960s and early 1970s the prestige of Tafuri reached an unexpected local and international dimension representing a neo-Marxist criticism of architecture.[65]

Figure 3.4 Cover of the magazine *Contropiano* (counter the plan). Year II, N° 1, 1969.

54 *Essay 2: Controversial Positions*

Here Tafuri published his first version of *Per una critica dell'ideologia architettonica* (Toward a critique of Architectural Ideology).

This was a time marked by his political commitment but, notably, Karl Marx was mentioned barely twice in *Theories and History* …. Certainly, this does not mean that Marx was not a figure of reference at the time of the writing of the book. But this observation helps us understand that, even when among his most important referents many Marxist authors such as Walter Benjamin are present, and even when important sections of the book allude to a Marxist relationship between artistic and socio-economic phenomena, the theoretical horizon that preside his intricate argument owes much more to semiotic contributions of structuralism, to Argan, and even to closer interpretations such as that of Leonardo Benevolo. In a certain way, "*Theories and history…*" is bracketed between two different moments, clearly expressed in both of its introductions. In the Note to the second Italian edition of the book (1970) Tafuri introduced the famous paragraph where, in opposition to the idea of a "class architecture" (a class political economy in Marx's original) he proposed, as Marx had done, a "class criticism of architecture". It was in that "Note" where the "Marxist" Tafuri, the one that would seduce "left-wing" readers worldwide, started to be constructed.

However, we must consider that even when the second edition was re-published and was translated and circulated worldwide mainly in the 1970s, the book was published in 1968, and it was conceived and written in the second half of the 1960s, before the immersion of its author into the roaring context of the Istituto Universitario di Architettura di Venezia.

Until then Tafuri had a relevant role in the student movement in Rome, but his direct involvement with politics was reduced to two brief affiliations, one to the Socialist Party (1962) and the other to the Partito Socialista Italiano di Unitá Operaia (PSIUP, 1964). As he himself reminds us in Passerini's interview, he was a reader of leftist journals such as *Quaderni Rossi*. And he was probably in touch with some PSIUP cadres, like Mario Tronti, active in university politics.[66] As was the case for many young Italian intellectuals of the 1960s, Marxism – and in particular its critical revision after the events of Hungary in the late 1950s and of the Khrushchevian "auto-critique" of 1956 – was a part of the cultural and theoretical universe of Tafuri. Furthermore, his first encounter with these ideas took place during his adolescence. But it was only in the 1970s when, as he said to Passerini "in a certain sense I **returned** to my origins and to the philosophical teachings of Bruno Widmar".

His first contacts with the Istituto Universitario di Architettura di Venezia's (IUAV) intellectual and political milieu happened in 1966 when, invited by the new director Giuseppe Samonà, he participated with Guido Canella, Vittorio Gregotti, Luciano Semerani, and Aldo Rossi in the seminar "Teoria della progettazione architettonica". In 1967 Samonà offered Tafuri a position as full professor to dictate his first course. Massimo Cacciari was one of the most radical young leftist figures in Venice and one of the leaders of the "workerist" movement, active and prestigious among the workers of the petrochemical complex of Puerto Marghera. When Tafuri arrived to the city Cacciari, with Tronti and Antonio Negri, among others, edited a local leftist journal called *Classe Operaia*. In 1968 the same group created an intellectual journal called *Contropiano*, where Tafuri published two contributions.

But according to Marco De Michelis Tafuri's contact with Massimo Cacciari didn't happen until 1968, something that reinforces our interpretation: his process of radicalization in "workerist" terms came *after* the publication of *Theories and History* ....[67]

Tafuri was one of the thousands of young people who participated in an epochal historical wave. As part of the extraordinary Italian intellectual history, the interest in the revision of Marxism had been increasing since the beginning of the 1960s. This was due to the emergence of the accelerated development of capitalism in the country, particularly in the northern "industrial triangle", the motor of the "Italian miracle". With this "miraculous" growth a new and dynamic player emerged in the Italian social and cultural scene, shaking up the theoretical structures of the Left: the new working class made up of young migrants from the more depressed southern regions without any ties to the old Italian leftist parties.

The publication of *Quaderni Rossi* since 1962 and the figure of Raniero Panzieri constituted the pivot around which the big debates of those years took place.[68] For Panzieri the fundamental task was "to restore Marxism to its natural terrain, which is that of permanent critique".[69] Given that this argument has already been widely studied by Marco Biraghi, it is not necessary to further here the importance of this demand for "permanent critique" as a "revolutionary" instrument in Tafuri's thought.[70]

However, the intellectual space constructed by Panzieri and *Quaderni Rossi* was not homogeneous, and the "re-reading" of Marx led to different conclusions that brought about the dismantling of the original group in 1963, and of the foundations of the previously mentioned publication *Classe Operaia*. In synthesis, we can say, with Steve Wright, that the keys to "workerism" expressed in *Classe Operaia* founded by Tronti were:

> the identification of the working class with the labor subsumed to the immediate process of production; an emphasis upon the wage struggle as a key terrain of political conflict, and the insistence that the working class was the driving force within capitalist society.[71]

This journal promoted a radical interpretation of the ideas of Marx, an interpretation that would carry on to become one of the theoretical lines of thought of *Contropiano* and of Tafuri himself. Steve Wright has pointed out that "writing in 1958, Lucio Colletti insisted that Marx's mature work was concerned not with 'general laws, nonsensical truisms valid for all epochs', but 'with one society only, modern capitalist society'".[72] And indeed, the idea of focusing the analysis and politics in the "modern capitalist society", already predicted by the followers of Galvano Della Volpe by the end of the 1950s, dominated the construction of the new groups. According to Giuseppe Bedeschi,

Essay 2: Controversial Positions

> by making Marxism a materialist sociology, that is a science of the modern bourgeois social-economic formation, "dellavolpism" insisted more on the features **common to various advanced capitalist societies than on the "particular" and "national" features** that distinguished one country from another.[73]
>
> (a.e.: author's emphasis)

It is on this concept that the construction of a new excluding "centrality" is based: the "workers centrality".[74]

Tafuri would later recognize that

> two points made by Raniero Panzieri remained important to us: first, to return to Marx meant to negate Marx himself, that is, to understand today's world and to try to understand that which seems to be its nemesis: the capitalist system.[75]

Furthermore, in line with Bedeschi, his conviction in relation to that excluding centrality led him to abandon his militancy in the socialist Partito Socialista di Unita Operaia "**almost immediately because they were talking about Cuba, China, and the Third World, and I was irritated because my problem was the suburb**"[76] (a.e.).

In January 1966, the first Tricontinental Conference took place in Havana. It gathered revolutionary leaders of Asia, Africa, and Latin America, and in a 1967 special edition of *Tricontinental*, the organization's journal, the famous call by Ernesto Guevara was published: "Create, Two, Three, Many Vietnams". In July 1967, the journal *Quaderni Piacentini* edited its 31st issue, dedicated to "Imperialism and Revolution in Latin America", in conjunction with the group that had continued publishing *Quaderni Rossi* after the death of Panzieri. As a result of a research seminar, the editors of the journal analyzed in detail the development of the armed struggle in the region, profiled against a strong critique of the politics of "peaceful coexistence" and "reformism" promoted by the USSR (and defended by the Italian Communist Party). They lamented the "years-long lull of class struggle development in capitalistic countries as ours", and supported the idea of the centrality of the "anti-imperialist struggle" at the time, as well as the fundamental role and even the leadership of the movements in favor of armed struggle in the "third world".[77]

In January 1968, the first Congreso de la Cultura took place in Havana. It brought together over 500 intellectuals from 70 countries, among them Eric Hobsbawm, Ralph Miliband, Jorge Semprún, Rossana Rossanda, Hans Magnus Enzensberger, Aimé Césaire, and Julio Cortázar. The atmosphere of the Congress was hopeful of the role of the "peripheries" in the development of the "class struggle", and at the same time of the subjacent critique in recognition of the "belated" European workers' movements.[78]

At the start of the construction of "workerism" with which Tafuri would identify during those years, Massimo Cacciari published in the first number of *Contropiano*, also in 1968, a bibliographic note where he distanced himself from that "third-worldism" that seduced left-wing intellectuals all over the world. In this note he analyzed recent texts by Jules Regis Debray, Fidel Castro, Ernesto Guevara, and Andre Gunder Frank. A fundamental preoccupation in Cacciari's commentary was that the proposals for the Tricontinental by Guevara could be valid in the specific conditions of the "third world" but "they don't respond to the fundamental requests of whom addresses himself to the analysis of anti-imperialist struggle from the point of view of the working class in the countries of advanced capitalism".[79] To advance in the resolution of the problem (which was the role of the Italian working class in the evident heyday of the process of international struggles) the young Venetian philosopher had to question the Leninist approach to the issue of imperialism, which was until then the dominant interpretation of Italian communists. "It's about seeing – he maintained – what does this term mean today, if it matches or not past Marxists theories".

The main point was the Leninist idea (and its translation and adoption particularly on the part of the increasing expansion of Maoism) of the "centrality" of the issue of "imperialism". For Cacciari "to rely on a historical-political imperialist prospect as a superior phase is extremely dangerous today". On the contrary, it was a matter of being able to locate the insurgent movements in Vietnam and Latin America in a global analysis to define "the relationship between them and the clash of classes in countries of advanced capitalism",[80] and to warn about "the urgency of a specific discourse of the workforce today, on the rapport workers-proletariat within the capitalistic international plan".[81]

One of the most referential expressions of "Workerism" was *Operai e Capitale [Workers and Capital]*, by Mario Tronti. In relation to our topic Tronti postulated in that text that the analysis should focus on those places where capitalism found itself in its most advanced phases of development and particularly where the working class was most prepared to defeat it thanks to the quality of its organization and development of ideas. According to him, "it is the most advanced point which explains the least developed and not vice-versa".[82]

The annoyance inflicted on Tafuri by the interest in the "Third World" on the part of the PSIUP and other expressions of the new left such as "Lotta Continua", had its origins in these ideas. For Tronti

> to watch underdeveloped countries as being at the epicenter of the revolution, because Lenin has said that the chain will be broken in the weakest of its links, is a concrete way to be in the practice which coincides with the highest form of contemporary opportunism. (…) We prefer the thesis that the chain goes broken today not where capital is weaker, but where the working class is stronger. (…) Not by chance Italy offers today an ideal ground for theoretical research on the working class.[83]

In relation to this, Tronti's argument had its most incisive moment of formalization in an essay published in *Classe Operaia* in 1964.[84] There the Italian intellectual gave a 180-degree turn to the reasoning by which the leader of the Russian Revolution had justified that the Communist Party – that he directed – could take over power in an "underdeveloped" country, in opposition to the Marxist tenet that saw that possibility mainly where capitalism had its greatest level of development. For Tronti,

> With a masterly stroke, the Leninist strategy brought Marx to St Petersburg. (…) What we call "Lenin in England" is a project to search for a new Marxist practice of the working-class party: it is the theme of the struggle and organization at the highest level for the political development of the working class.[85]

The rejection of "Third World-ism" constituted one of the main aspects of "workerism". For Wright "according to the youth-oriented journal "Classe e Partito" (…) the peasant struggle in Vietnam could serve working-class internationalism, so long as the two were not to be confused".[86]

From an opposite position of critical militancy, Giangiacomo Feltrinelli thought that for the "workerist group"

> the condition of underdevelopment of southern Italy and its islands would be a transient fact. (…) From that condition derives the thesis that the problem of underdevelopment, the problem of the South basically does not exist or that in the end it is so transient that it is not even worth lingering on.[87]

For "workerism" the "Third World" was a gigantic "reserve army" where the unstoppable expansion of capitalism would be based. In what constituted a paradoxical inverted version of Walt Rostow's theories, "underdevelopment" –and even the underdevelopment of southern Italy – was understood simply as a belated area of that process of expansion. According to Wright

> Tronti was to deny that the recent (1965) round of contractual struggles posed any serious threat to capitalism. The social system based upon the accumulation of value for its own sake was young and vibrant, with most of the "Third World's" population yet to be conquered by the wage relation.[88]

The essay that catapulted Tafuri into a position of worldwide fame was "Toward a Critique of Architectural Ideology". We will analyze it in relation to another essay, also published in *Contropiano*, but not frequently remembered: "Lavoro intellettuale e sviluppo capitalistico" (Intellectual Work and Capitalist Development, 1970),[89] which was proposed as an instrument of "combat" to demolish the "bourgeois" versions of the architectural discipline as a whole.

The following will help us understand his reasoning.

Like his "workerist" comrades, Tafuri believed at the time that capital's tendency toward its expansion had no limits of class, of ideas, or of space. The working class had been its only real antagonist until 1929, and it was the working-class struggle that had pushed Capital to make big transformations in production to maintain a gain in the rate of income. But, since the Big Crisis, Capital had discovered the key to completely controlling the cycle of its infinite reproduction: the

Plan. In this way worker organizations had become an instrument of Capital as far as they accepted negotiation as an agreement for the increase in salaries and, given the introduction of technological change, that of productivity. The accelerated development of broader and stronger cybernetic systems contributed to achieving a maximum expression of that totalizing capability of control. The pre-1929 artistic avant-gardes had played a fundamental role. Some of them, as sectors of a "negative" destruction of the bourgeois "Kultur" that (with its values) balked at the expansion of Capital to transform every aspect of human existence into commodities; others, the "positive" avant-gardes, as anticipatory of the logic of the Plan.[90]

However, as of 1929, while "positivity" was absorbed by the plan, "negativity" could only take the form, irrelevant, of "utopia". In each case the possibility of a relevant role for any kind of avant-garde was null, and their contemporary expressions could be nothing but pathetic ideological pantomimes with no value at all. No new synthesis was either possible, or even worse, desirable. The main enemy intervening in the peremptory need for the "critique of ideology" in all its destructive capacity, was the "dialectic synthesis" of Hegelian overtones, a synthesis that had precisely been the key to the relentless machine of Capital. According to Tafuri

> at the beginning of the twentieth century, the unmasking of the ideals that obstructed the path to a global rationalization of the productive universe and its social dominion, became the new historical task of the intellectual. (…) For Weber, Keynes, Schumpeter, and Mannheim, the problem lies in the means capable of making positive and negative (capital and the working-class side of work) function together, of prohibiting a separation of the two terms and realizing their complementary relationship.[91]

Matteo Mandarini has synthesized this state of the ideas of the *Contropiano* group in the following manner:

> for Cacciari (and Negri) the Hegelian dialectic represents the highpoint in the victorious and expansive cycle of capitalist development, in which all contradictions, all conflicts are turned directly into productive moments of capital's advance as the self-realization of Spirit.[92]

For the "workerists" the only real "negativity" was inscribed in the vital, corporeal reality of factory workers, where the development of capital was most advanced. In line with the already analyzed ideas of Tronti, Tafuri argued that "the 'radical' opposition (…) has avoided a confrontation with the highest levels attained by capitalist development. It has instead inherited the ideologies which capital used in the first phases of its development but has since rejected".[93]

Therefore, intellectual work only has ahead of itself the task of demolishing or deeply integrating into that expansive logic:

> Even in its most elevated form, the one made manifest in utopia, ideology is in contradiction with the developed capitalist system. It is no longer of

any use to simply establish that the negative is inherent in the system. The problem posed is completely "technical", completely concerned with identifying, within the economic-productive base, the real, concrete factors which actually make this "negativity" (the negative of the working class) function as a "necessity" intrinsic to the processes of the system.[94]

Having adopted this extreme position, where the focus had to be on the most "advanced" developments of Capital, and in the struggles of the working class in the cities of the "industrial triangle" of northern Italy, there was little space for the shades of tone, contradictions, and intuitions expressed in the texts of the previous period. The "geographic" construction was in this way reduced to *a center* in continuous infinite expansion, and to *a periphery* purely receptive, or at most reduced to rearguard interests and skirmishes.

In effect, in Tafuri's judgment

> It may even be that many marginal and rearguard roles exist for architecture and planning. Of primary interest to us, however, is the question of why until now, Marxist-oriented culture has very carefully, and with an obstinacy worthy of better causes, denied or concealed the simple truth that, just as there can be no such thing as a political economic class, but only a class critique of political economics, likewise there can never be an aesthetics, art or architecture of class, but only a class critique of aesthetics, art, architecture and the city.[95]

Within this context of ideas, in 1970 Tafuri became a member of the Communist Party, where he was a militant until 1976. As part of the "revolutionary" atmosphere of the time, his provocative texts of the early 1970s were translated into French, Spanish, German, and English, and his figure inspired the work of young people with Marxist sympathies in different countries of Europe, such as Matko Maestrovic in the former Yugoslavia, Jean-Louis Cohen in France, and the Spaniards Victor Pérez Escolano, José Quetglas and Carlos Sambricio. But at the same time his success contributed, especially in the Anglo-Saxon sphere, to prevent a more nuanced reading of his polyhedral work that continues today.

Testament to this dramatic theoretical imprisonment is the way in which in 1973 he concluded his course on "Antiurban Ideology" (formidable, in many ways) where literally all his laborious analysis was resolved in a specific expression of the workers' struggles.

> Traditional urban planning regionalist ideologies of re-equilibrium – he explained to his students – reveal themselves as out of place instruments with respect to such new shifted levels of capitalist development. (…) The national strike of 1969 for housing, transportation and services, read as inseparable elements and as part of the salary, or the claims of metalworkers (…) should be seen as new facts within class movement, to be

translated into articulated political struggles to which the political forces and the technicians will have to reply without anchoring themselves in myths as aged as inoperative.[96]

During the 1970s Tafuri decreased his interest in the "humanist cycle" and focused his attention on the construction of the Department of History of Architecture at the IUAV, researching and publishing his writings about modern architecture. This period ended with a study of the work of Vittorio Gregotti in 1982.[97] A clear expression of his focus on the themes of modern architecture where he saw an expression of the system of ideas strongly marked by "workerism" is the sequence of courses taught as a professor at IUAV, that included "Avant-Gardes, Architecture and the City in Germany (1905–1933)", "The Social-Democratic Administration of the City (1923–1933)" (1970); "Avantgarde, City and Planning in the Soviet Union (1917–1937)" (1972); "The History of Anti-urban Ideology" (1973); "Structure and Architecture in the Tertiary City in America (1850–1973)" (1974); "Urban Development in the United States and the Problem of Housing (1780–1974)" (1975); "The Skyscraper and the Structure of the Tertiary City in America and Europe (1850–1975)" (1976); "Avant-Garde and Architecture: The Adventures of Language in the Contemporary City" (1977); "Great Vienna: The Formation of the Habsburgic Myth and the Crisis of Austro-Marxism" (1978); "The Adventures of the Avant-Garde" (1980), only interrupted by "Francesco Borromini and the Crisis of the Humanist Universe" (1979). Contrarywise, from 1980 onward he only taught courses related to the Renaissance. The main publications that reveal his preoccupations during the 1970s were two books that include essays by different authors – one about architecture in the Soviet Union, the other about the American city – and a work of synthesis of his construction about modern architecture, the volume on *Architettura Contemporanea*, written in co-authorship with Francesco Dal Co.

In parallel to Massimo Cacciari's analysis of the European "Krisis" of the grand bourgeois "Kultur" Tafuri set himself to observe the case of the United States as the most unquestionable example of "advanced capitalism" and, on the other, the Soviet Union as the most conclusive example of the intent of dominating the Plan on the part of the "State of the working class". His study of the "American city" was oriented to understanding, in a process of expansion of the Plan, the articulations and conflicts between public and private forms of resource mobilization characteristic of North American capitalism. Not by chance, his essay begins with the "skyscraper" and advances toward the mega-interventions of the Rockefeller Center, the Regional Plan of New York, and the urban renewal processes in Pittsburgh. Thus, the big interventions immediately following 1929 are seen as "a shift of interest from the city as a place of autonomous production and a source of capital accumulation to the region as a coordinated whole".[98] The study of the mechanisms of production of the "American city" proved the idea of the dynamics of conflict between Capital and the working class that was at the base of "workerism". He argued for example that "the renewal of Pittsburgh (…) was revealed at

62 Essay 2: Controversial Positions

its completion to be a wholly uncompromising instrument of class".[99] Within the framework of capitalism, good intentions and struggles seem to derive inevitably from Capital itself always being a step ahead.

Of equal importance was his intention to observe the "inefficient" role of intellectuals in such process. Indeed, in the premise of the book one can read that

> our efforts have been directed at demonstrating how the levels of integration of cultural products and ideologies is based not only on an implicit vocation but also on a well-defined complex of techniques, which, in turn, is even partly shaped by the intellectual production as a whole.[100]

Within that context, he highlights the inevitable transformation of Architecture purely into technique – "architecture and city planning turned into agents of the ponderous process of transformation set in motion by the American capitalist system".

The study on the "American city" started in 1969, and in 1970 he was invited by Rudolf Wittkower to visit the United States, where he returned in 1973 and in 1976, to deliver lectures at conferences at Princeton University, Carnegie Mellon, and at the Institute for Architecture and Urban Studies in New York, whose journal "Oppositions" published Tafuri's work. He established connections with many of

Figure 3.5 Peter Eisenman, Mario Gandelsonas, Jorge Silvetti, Giusi Rapisarda, Manfredo Tafuri, Rodolfo Machado. Terrace of the Institute of Architecture and Urban Studies, New York, c. 1975. Photo by Diana Agrest, other member of the group (courtesy of Jorge Silvetti and Rodolfo Machado).

its members, and particularly with Peter Eisenman. This relationship was perfectly consistent with the development of Tafuri's ideas at the time, and it explains his contribution to the catalog of the exhibition *Five Architects NY*, held at the Facoltà di Architettura di Napoli with his essay "Les bijoux indiscrets". The "Five" served for Tafuri as "emblems of a generalized unease (…) fruit of a 'desengaño'",[101] and to prove the definitive cancellation of any semantic content in contemporary architecture, to show that the total absence of meaning or – better yet – that the separation between signifier and signified – "frivolous" in Derrida's terms –, was the only way out for those who discarded the iron clad demand for "Technique" and the futility, in his view pathetic, demand for "Utopia".

On the opposite side of the political spectrum, the study on the USSR was part of his attack on the hegemonic politics within the Italian Communist Party, making sure to demonstrate that the presumed representatives of the working class did nothing but play a functional role in Capital. A functional role as main supporters of the "Synthesis" and the "Plan", either as ideologues of utopia or as an uncritical apotheosis of the proletariat.

> Instead of class, – Tafuri states in his essay – the proletariat is the unique arbiter of its own destiny (…); rather than the revelation of the objective operation of Soviet Russia at the moment of crisis of international Capital, we have the assumption of the proletariat's October as a moment of universal palingenesis, of ethical epiphany.[102]

In this manner, seen from a "workerist" Italy, the whole experience of Soviet intellectuals was that of a single block incapable of understanding the operative logic of Capital and the Plan. This is (thanks to the measures baptized by Lenin as the New Economic Policy (NEP)) from the moment that it was deployed at the outset of the war economy. According to Tafuri, the soviet intellectuals

> did not grasp that the dialectic inherent in the NEP and to choose as their own field of work the organization of modes of production was the same thing – as pure ideology for formalists or, for the members of the Organization of Contemporary Architects, as an ambiguous compromise between ideology and technique for sectorial intervention – (…) with the misrepresentation of the Leninist project they were confronted not with canceling class nor the plan, (but) to free, indeed, the potential struggle from within the working class itself.[103]

In the same way that the North American case showed architecture as one of the main agents for the processes of expansion of capitalism, the Soviet case made evident the "incapacity" of Russian intellectuals, immersed in ineffectual ideological clouds, to comprehend the dialectic of capital. According to Tafuri

> the unbridgeable distance between intellectuals and the revolutionary process remains precisely in their (…) inability to (…) discover the role of capital as

64   Essay 2: Controversial Positions

instrument for the enhancement of the organization of the plan (…) to refuse to unveil the mythology once the disappearance of the social division of work was reached.[104]

This is why, in completing a game of mirrors and reflections, while in the case of the United States the only lucid attitude for those who discarded their transformation into pure "technicians" of the Plan, and decided to remain in the field of language, was that of a frivolous decoupling of signifier and signified, in the case of the USSR that recognition was replicated in Russian formalism, also dedicated, half a century before, to "Investigate, with absolute autonomy from the internal evolutionary structure, the ways of operation of linguistic units".[105]

Together with Francesco Dal Co, Tafuri published *Architettura Contemporanea* (*Modern Architecture*) in 1976, as part of the series "Storia Universale dell'Architettura" directed by Pier Luigi Nervi. Despite its title and forced by a pre-existing volume by Robin Middleton and David Watkin dedicated specifically to *Architettura Moderna*, the text covers from the mid-19th century to the date of its publication and constitutes Tafuri's most ambitious intent of broadening his reasoning at the time, and of the construction of a new narrative about modern architecture.

With the undertaking of this book, we return to the initial question of our work, and the answer appears evident. In other words, at the moment of writing *Architettura Contemporanea* Tafuri fully embraced the "workerist" thinking. Therefore, for Tafuri the main task was to study the most "advanced" processes, considering the logic of expansion of Capital as that of a homogeneous and unstoppable imposition of the Plan throughout the whole world and throughout all areas of human experience. Thus, with a simplistic conception of the center/periphery dialectic he could not but consider the latter as a marginal phenomenon. In addition, within the framework of this reductionist opposition, he also incorporated what was a geographical characterization to a temporal one, in which the "periphery" represented the past and the "center" its future.

The "workerist" attempt to apply the "workers/capital" scheme to the analysis of contemporary architecture made this book one of the weakest of Tafuri's contributions. Forced by a long-standing commitment to the admired Wittkower,[106] the authors were caught in an unsolvable contradiction: the book had to respond simultaneously to two different logics. On the one hand the authors believed that the history of modern architecture was that of the places where the conflict "workers/capital" was most intense; but on the other hand, the editorial demand was that of describing "contemporary architecture" as a global phenomenon.

The result could not but be unsatisfactory given the difference in the treatment of the themes; or, rather, by the superficial approach to most of them. Thus, the text is a patchwork of affirmations coming from the works completed at the time within the investigations of the IUAV, focused on the United States, the USSR, Le Corbusier, Weimar Germany, Austro-Marxist Vienna, and Italy, with the addition of quick descriptions, and strong but superficial value judgements on the rest of the broader architectural scene of 20th century architecture.

Figure 3.6 Book cover of *Vienna Rossa. La politica residenziale nella Vienna socialista, 1919–1933* (Red Vienna. Residential Politics in Socialist Vienna, 1919–1933), Manfredo Tafuri. Electa Editrice, Milan, 1980.

Within this framework, the geography of the peripheries presented is not limited to the so-called Third World. To refer to northern European "peripheries" it was enough for the authors to affirm that "the romantic tendency flourished in countries seeking their native roots: in Germany (…) and in Switzerland".[107] For those of the south of Europe one could celebrate that "(In Barcelona) Domenech attempted to make order out of a mixture of architectural languages (…) explode into a visual fiesta in which (…) the urban collectivity is summoned to recognize its own image",[108] and to criticize that "the will to power of intellectuals frustrated by the technological backwardness of a static Italy unloaded itself in the idolatry of the machine, (…) with the city masses transformed into things and, for that reason, in revolt".[109]

The reception of the work by the Anglo-Saxon academics was harsh and, to a great degree, from what were clearly anti-communist positions:

> The interpretation (the authors) clamp on the material does not persuade, and all too frequently they recite it in the arcane tongue of a Marxist litany,[110] (…) with the historians posing as wizards in that Marxist game of "unmasking the true ideological kernel of events". (The book) turns out to have the complexion of what one might call standard left-wing despair.[111]

Due to the cryptic language, to the improbability of many of its affirmations, to the uneven degrees of knowledge of the arguments, and to the excessively arbitrary selection of themes analyzed, Christian Otto categorically pointed out what he called the

> weakness in the text: 1) purpose and methodology emphatically adhered to, although not easily comprehensible to the non-Marxist reader; 2) stimulating interpretations of architectural events and personalities, but 3) interpretations that are often problematic; and 4) a use of evidence that raises too many questions.[112]

Crisis

The meager enthusiasm generated by *Architettura Contemporanea* and the critiques received, particularly if contrasted to the explosive effect of the support that Tafuri's previous publications had generated, must have constituted one of the elements of a crisis that he described as follows:[113] "In 1977 I embarked on a series of ferocious auto-critiques of everything I had done, which were repeated in a violently self-destructive manner".[114]

As an expression of this crisis, in 1980 Tafuri delivered his last course on modern architecture, and in 1982 he published his last significant critical work on the same topic.[115] This moment of internal commotion led him to begin a different period of his intellectual trajectory.

But by the late 1970s his state of shock was not just an individual experience. The totality of Italian political life was going through a serious crisis that was accompanied by no less serious problems in the country's economy. On one side, the period of the "economic miracle" that had been started with US-American support and had expanded with the participation in the European Coal and Steel Community seemed to have definitely come to an end with the 1973 oil crisis. On the other side, the workers' movement boom that had started in the 1960s had declined by the end of the 1970s until reaching a brutal defeat of the FIAT workers union in 1980. In parallel, the broadening of ideas and the questioning of the old theoretical constructions that were at the origin of the student and popular movements of 1968 and 1969, reached their highest point with the "NO" triumph in the referendum that sought to have divorce repealed in 1974, and with the emergence – related to this repeal – of new players such as feminism and ecology. But even if these continued to represent a positive and driving force, in the opposite direction the emergence of extreme alternatives such as the left Red Brigades (connected to an extreme version of "workerism"), and the fascist actions known as the "strategy of tension", ended in the political earthquake that led to the assassination of the former prime minister Aldo Moro in 1978.

After a lengthy process of uninterrupted growth in voter preferences that had pushed them increasingly closer to actual power, in 1978 the Communist Party suffered a brutal loss in the voting ballot.

The social and political crisis contributed to Tafuri's radical change, given the big failures of the militant political struggles of the previous years that he concludes ended "with the fading away of the dream of knowledge as a means to power". Thus, he decided to fold the critical apparatus onto itself. As he wrote in *The Sphere and the Labyrinth*, what remains is "the constant struggle between the analysis and its objects – their irreducible tension".[116]

Toward the end of the 1970s, the crisis of the radical totalizing and dualist aspirations went far beyond "workerism" and affected every theoretical system that was being discussed in the Western world ever since the end of WWII. One of the outcomes of this crisis was the idea of the end of modernity, understanding it in the words of Jean-François Lyotard as "incredulity toward metanarratives. (…) The narrative function is losing its functors, its great heroes, its great dangers, its great voyages, its great goals".[117]

During those same years, as an alternative to the crisis of the meta-narratives in Italy emerged the new historiographic wave of "microhistory", represented by the investigations of Carlo Ginzburg, Carlo Cipolla, Piero Camporesi, and Giovanni Levi, which attracted the attention of Tafuri.[118] Although these studies still maintained certain Marxist matrix inspired in the works of E. P. Thompson, they were intended to push aside the generalizing approaches of "class" in favor of an observation of individual behaviors within the framework of social history. Even when Tafuri cited Michel Foucaut's *The Archaeology of Knowledge* in his *Theories and History*, Foucault's publications of the late 1970s such as *The History of Sexuality: The Will to Knowledge* and *Discipline and Punish: The Birth of the Prison* contributed during the following years to changes in Tafuri's research and to the important shedding of positions that he had maintained until then.

The text where the impact of French post-structuralism was revealed with greater force was "The Historical Project", first published in *Casabella*, in its issue no. 429 of October 1977, and that was later included as the introduction in *La Sfera e il Labirinto* (*The Sphere and the Labyrinth*) of 1980, one of Tafuri's most successful books. The significance of Foucault's ideas within the context of IUAV at the time was well recounted in a 1976 symposium titled precisely "Il Dispositivo Foucault" with the participation of Franco Rella, Massimo Cacciari, Georges Teyssot, and Tafuri himself. In relation to our topic, the most important issue that Tafuri deals with in "The Historical Project" is a new way of understanding Power. Even though here, and in the work presented in the mentioned symposium, he criticized the purely deconstructivist function attributed to the Foucaultian point of view. What has definitively fallen apart at this stage of Tafuri's thought was

Figure 3.7 Book cover of *Il Dispositivo Foucault* (Foucault's dispositive), by Massimo Cacciari, Franco Rella, Manfredo Tafuri, CLUVA, Venice, 1977.

the localization of power in *one* determined place or center. As he admitted in "Il Dispositivo Foucault": "In synthesis, **a** place of power does not exist" (a.e.).[119]

Tafuri said some years later in an interview in Buenos Aires:

> In relation to Power I believe I can accept (...) Michel Foucault's formulations on the topic. In the sense that, in effect (...) power concentrated in a single space never existed, not in the 1500s, not in the 1400s, not even in Medieval times.[120]

Revising his own claims in previous works, guided both by the most strictly Adornoian *Critique of Reason* and in a polemic with Deleuze and Guattari's *Politics of Desire*, in "The Historical Project", which was also presented as essential was the explosion of the context itself into planes or layers of what he called "technical incidents" (subterranean ideologies, diverse techniques of domination, and so forth). The consequence of this work would be the generation not of one, but of multiple meanings. It was not "Power" and its institutions that had to be "unveiled" by critical analysis, but the confrontation between the multiple "dialects" spoken by power, because when traversing the real in multiple directions, that confrontation revealed at the same time ruins, margins, the expendable.

However, once the idea of "one" place of power fell apart, not only was the Marxist class-based understanding of the functioning of society become diluted, but also the belief in any type of centrality. Precisely, when considered in a Foucaultian manner, power is embedded in space in all directions: here places of privilege or of differences of intensity do not exist. Power is stronger in as much as it is less apparent, less solid, less visible. For Tafuri,

> There is no point in identifying these barriers within the Great institutions. Power is itself plural: it runs through and cuts across social classes, ideologies, and institutions. On this we can still agree with Foucault: a single locus of Great Refusal does not exist; only from within systems of power can the mechanisms of power be known.[121]

Foucault developed his concept of "heterotopia" in an article published in 1984. He argued that our present epoch was an epoch of space, in opposition to the 19th-century epoch centered on time. In its "spatial" condition, our epoch would be defined by juxtapositions, co-existences, and simultaneities. In a "spatial" epoch place would be made up of a group of relationships and structured by grids and coordinates. Nevertheless, Foucault recognizes certain continued existence of ancient modalities for defining space, and understands that even the medieval modality, which he refers to as "emplacement" (given the fixed condition within which the totality of space is articulated) still has a partial currency, a sort of remnant. In his judgement "perhaps our life is still governed by a certain number of oppositions that remain inviolable, that our institutions and practices have not yet dared to break down".[122]

The need to critically abandon the "hallowed oppositions" (and with them all imprint of the "sacred") is what also requires questioning the paradigm of the organization of space, of thought, and of a culture frozen within the simple center/periphery polarity. That is why one of the breaks that is perceived in "The Historical Project" affects this paradigm, and in the following years and works Tafuri will insist on the reorganization of "historical space". In "The Historical Project" this important change is expressed in a rhetorical question: "How much longer must we remind those that cling nostalgically to 'centrality' that there is no other alternative, at present, than to trace the history that leads to the divorce between the signifier and the signified?".[123]

Heterotopia: The Disintegration of Centered Space[124]

Throughout Tafuri's career one can notice a growing consciousness about the articulation between the concept of space and worldviews, as well as about concepts that coincided with the Foucaultian system. In a conference in the United States in 1976, he put forward an idea seemingly contradictory to the rigid *center/periphery* opposition that dominated his thought at the time. That it was just apparently contradictory is clear if one notices that he went deeper into the "workerist" argument: the *center/periphery* opposition was reduced to a transitory problem. Unless the working class could make it melt into thin air, the world entirely dominated by the Plan of capital could not be but a thick homogeneous matter, only characterized "spatially" by contingent explosions of worker counterattacks. Indeed, for Tafuri "it is the increasing rationalization of the capitalist universe what has removed every 'center' to the world".[125]

Already in his lecture of 1973 in the United States, published the following year in *Oppositions 3*, his intuition of the gradual disappearance of a single center in modern culture had emerged, and with it the need to re-think the *center/periphery* paradigm. In relation to Rossi's operation, he had confirmed there that it proved

> that his removal of form from the sphere of the quotidian is forced continually to circumnavigate the central point from which communication springs forth, without being able to draw from that primary source. This is not so because of any incapacity on the part of the architect, but rather because that "center" has been historically destroyed, because that "source" has been dispersed into multiple streams, each without beginning or end.[126]

The fact is that Tafuri's process of change in his understanding of the *center/periphery* paradigm did not originate exclusively in the logical development of his *political* assumptions; it also had a parallel development in his *specifically architectural* research since the very start of his career.

The center/periphery paradigm manifested itself in two distinct levels: in one case the paradigm was applied to the construction and dissemination of ideas, while in the other it was concerned with the physical world. What both levels had in common was the theme of space.

One of the most innovative contributions in his book on Mannerism was the importance he gave to the complexity of spatial articulations of several of its main characters, and in particular the experimentations of Giovanni Battista Montano: "manneristic disfavor for the unity of space, of which the 'inventions' of Montano" – he wrote – "are a typical example".[127] In these experimentations Tafuri noticed the beginnings of a slow process of questioning the humanist mandate of *concinnitas*. Once the existence of a single center as an organizing space was put into question, the opposition center/periphery tended to lose consistency.

> The analytical insistence and the deteriorating spirit act like tools of confirmation "per absurdum" (…) the absoluteness of the image (…) as is shown in the inventions of Montano (in which) the aggregate spaces do not act anymore as peripheral reaffirmations of additional value but as programmatic negations of every perspective of unity of space.[128]

Although they were not able to completely destroy the homogenizing nature of the classic structure, in Montano's experimentations Tafuri observed "the multiplication of the organizing schemes, based on the composition of central and longitudinal formations, of central formations solved through untold gimmicks with a spatial decorative character of centric formations with crowns of supplementary radial (…) spaces".[129]

In 1968 Tafuri delivered a lecture showing the importance of this theme in the ideas of Guarino Guarini. For him architects such as Giulio Romano, those of the School of Fontainebleau, or those of the Nordic Rollwerk "giving up identifying the space of visual communication with the space of scientific research, put in crisis the unity of the concept of space, discovering on the other hand the virtual values of the polycentric perspective". Choosing a "collection of objects that contest Brunelleschi's and Alberti's scientific traditions" were operations that led to a break in the center/periphery relationship in the classical spatial system.[130]

The "clash of antithetical formal arrays" and the "paratactic and discontinuous aggregation of complex geometric spaces" that were common in the work of Guarini could find precedents in studies such as those of San Domenico in Siena by Baldassare Peruzzi,[131] but the most baffling work by Guarini according to this approach was, for Tafuri, the project for the Santuario della Consolata in Torino. In harmony with his earlier discoveries, Guarini's project confirmed a long-held crisis related to the existence of a space subordinate to a single organizing nucleus.

> Surely, (…) – Tafuri pointed out – Guarini had the opportunity to study those spaces of the late 16th century that Wolfgang Lotz calls "geometric games": the inventions of Montano (…) and the compositional paradoxes attributed to Smeraldo Smeraldi. (…) But what in Peruzzi was strictly research becomes, for Smeraldi in particular, (…) an evasive pretext, a scenographic exploitation of the uneasiness in the discovery of the polycentrality of space.[132]

72 *Essay 2: Controversial Positions*

This preoccupation was also present in the compendium of earlier works by Tafuri that became *L'Architettura dell'Umanesimo*. Here, the crisis of a homogeneous conception of space was articulated with the crisis of the humanistic identification of architecture and science. Tafuri could now start to confirm that the problem of centrality went far beyond architecture. Thus, he wrote: "if beyond the measurable and intellectual space of mathematical-geometric laws and of harmonic coordinates, there exists an empirical space, irreducible within them, the postulate of an absolute homogeneity of space itself falls apart".[133]

This line of research led to one of Tafuri's most extraordinary contributions to the understanding of the construction of modern space: his analysis of the Piranesian production. Even in the apparently "normal" buildings of his first published works, Piranesi refers to a crisis of the classicist spatial order. "It has already been pointed out" – Tafuri writes – "that, as far back as the perspective compositions of the Prima parte di Architetture e Prospettive (1743) Piranesi presents organisms that appear to have a centrality, but that never actually achieve one".[134]

A more alarming conclusion emerges from his observation of what accounts for an operation of over-saturation: classical centrality disintegrates at the moment that the dimension of expansion (or at the moment of trying to control peripheral structures) goes beyond a certain limit. From that limit onward not only do the peripheral structures acquire an increasing autonomy, but – in addition – they start to impose themselves onto the central structure. This is the case of the *Pianta di ampio magnifico Collegio*. Tafuri initially warns us that:

> Piranesi's engravings offer us not merely a set designer's whim, but rather a systematic criticism of the concept of "center", this is clearly shown in the Pianta di ampio magnifico Collegio inserted in the 1750 edition of the Opere varie di architettura.[135]

He further explains how in the Collegio "The centrality of the composition (…) is, significantly, one of the smaller spaces. As one proceeds gradually from the center toward the periphery of the composition, the dimension of the rooms seems to grow progressively larger".[136]

The study of Campo Marzio allowed him to expand the "critique of the concept of center" to the city, here conceived as an uncontrollable multiplication of organizations desperately tied to their own individuality and consistency as a unit. But it is the analysis of Piranesi's *Carceri* that allows him to discover the magnitude of the Piranesian destruction of all *concinnitas*, of all possibility of control, and with it the emergence of a new disarticulated space, with no limits nor dominant hierarchies. "In Carceri – he writes – the indefinite opening up of spaces, one fitted within the other, their multiplication, their metamorphoses, and their disarticulations arguably supersede the sources of Carceri itself".[137]

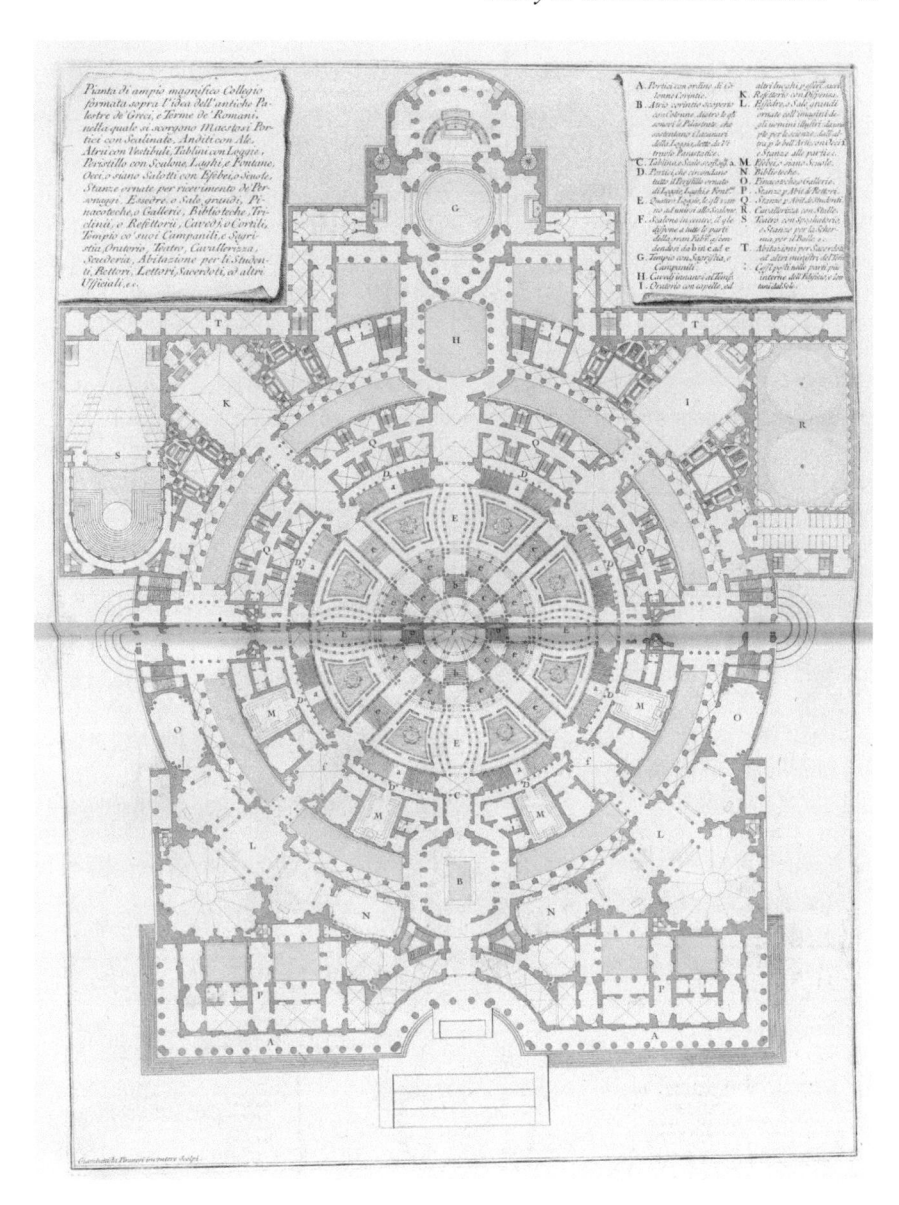

Figure 3.8 "Pianta di ampio magnifico Collegio formata sopra l'idea dell'antiche Palestre de' Greci, e Terme de' Romani" (Floorplan of a large magnificent college formed on the idea of the ancient Gyms of the Greeks and Baths of the Romans), etching, 600 × 440 mm, from *Opere varie di architettura prospettive grotteschi antichità sul gusto degli antichi romani* by Giovanni Battista Piranesi, Roma, 1761. PD. Getty Research Institute, in https://archive.org/details/gri_33125008448025.

The "Modern Movement" as "Delirious Representation": Toward a Plural History

Before analyzing the changes experienced in Tafuri's ideas after the crisis of the 1970s, in relation to our topic let us analyze one of his most valuable contributions to the historiography of modern architecture: his critique of the concept of the "Modern Movement". Tafuri's contribution is essential for our approach given that for the traditional explanations of "modern architecture" the use of the binary unidirectional construction "center/periphery" is based on the idea of a system made up of "one" center of emission/transmission, surrounded by several receptors/translators of the ideas coming from that "center". Thus, there was a clear division of functions and values between that single creative center where those core themes and expressions of modernity were constructed, and a passive periphery limited to their reproduction, at most conditioned to a re-elaboration of what was emitted from that center. Very early on, Tafuri had expressed doubts about an idea that supports this simple system: the notion of "influence". In his graduation thesis, one can read that "in that synthetic taste, beyond the frequently invoked French influence, **the concept of 'influence' in the history of art is devoid of any critical value**"[138] (a.e.).

The collapse of the idea of "one" "Modern Movement" requires re-thinking the binary and unidirectional scheme center/periphery, compelling us to imagine more complex ways of understanding the space of creation of architectural culture. Indeed, the disintegration of that paradigm took many years to consolidate and manifest itself. Furthermore, one could say that Tafuri himself was not able to grasp the full ramifications of his discovery.

One of the first moments where one can glean a preliminary outline of this questioning of the idea of the "Modern Movement" in Tafuri's intellectual history was his debate with Carlo Melograni, in a meeting with young architects organized by *Casabella* in 1964.[139] He still did not completely discard the idea of a "Modern Movement" which was "born as a conscious attempt to transform the world through design".[140] He preferred to designate this new architecture as "constructivist" as long as "all the avant-garde currents of the first half of the twentieth century that proposed the creation of an art that was interpreted as an instrument for the continuous development and self-creation of society".[141] However, Tafuri understood that, in line with the interpretation of Benevolo and Pevsner, Melograni had put forward "an interpretation that I would define as unidirectional in the development of the modern movement itself".[142] According to Tafuri, this unidirectional interpretation was mistakenly based in the existence of "a single development cycle" and, therefore, the present task was "to update and solve (the) reasons of the break down".[143] This is why he considered that "the identification of the Modern Movement with rationalist architecture is arbitrary", and that it was necessary to recognize the "extremely composite character of the whole story of the architecture of the last two centuries, recalling, for example, the double origin of the new experiences, (…) that are a testimony of that complexity, that can show as simplistic Benevolo's interpretation".[144]

Toward the end of the 1960s and because of his understanding of the "Modern Movement" as comprised of at least two different tendencies, his following step was to recognize that the problem was even more complex. In *Theories and History* ..., he concludes that confronted with "so many explosions of intricate movements, agitations, new questions, and the resulting multiform and chaotic panorama of international architectural culture in the 1970s" what was necessary was

> a courageous and honest scrutiny of the very foundations of the Modern Movement: in fact, a thorough investigation of whether it is still legitimate to speak of a Modern Movement as a monolithic corpus of ideas, poetics, and linguistic traditions.[145]

In Tafuri's following works he continued to use the term,[146] but ten years after *Theories and History* ..., the critique became mandatory: in *Architettura Contemporanea* he considers the construction of the concept as "an attempt to credit the new architecture with a collective and teleological doctrine, and that it is itself the product of a reassuring, but entirely inoperative fable"[147]; in *Il Progetto Storico* ("The Historical Project") he even notes that its use leads to "sinking in quicksand, comprised of a sublime mystification".[148] The demolition of this "obstinate, hard word" continued throughout the writings that followed. In the introduction of the second edition of his *Storia dell'Architettura Italiana, 1944–1985* he wrote:

> In this book you will not find terms such as modern movement, rationalism, neo-rationalism, and tendency; the term postmodern has also been redefined. As our most informed historiography demonstrates, such formulas in fact conceal deep ambiguities and reflect historical considerations that that have since become useless.[149]

In the same text Tafuri recognized his debt to the work of Mario Manieri-Elia, who in his works on William Morris and Louis Sullivan conducted systematic research immersing himself into the origins of the idea of "Modern Movement". Following Manieri's and Tafuri's steps, Maria Luisa Scalvini studied the process of that historiographic construction, offering a definitive argumentation for the destruction of the myth.[150]

Tafuri returned to the topic even in his last work, dedicated to the Renaissance. There he criticized the

> recent claims concerning history and memory. (...) In this case the "evil" seems to be a kind of elective and collective amnesia. (...) The revision of the "roots" ascribed to the historical avant-gardes or to a mythical "Modern Movement" can be healed only by a sort of "mnemic therapy".[151]

The Option for the Renaissance and *The Question Concerning Technology*

After Tafuri's crisis of the late 1970s, it appears that his "workerism" – and in particular, his belief in the centrality of the workers/capital conflict as the main characteristic of modernity– fell apart. Even when he did not stop referencing

Marxist thought, his interest moved toward other authors who identified the causes of contemporary problems as the product of a longer historical process, mainly analyzed through Nietzsche and Heidegger.

Although Nietzsche's ideas had been part of the "critique of ideology", the radically anti-modern character of his positions would affect with greater strength the research that Tafuri conducted during the last period of his life. During his interview in Buenos Aires in 1983, the magnitude of that long process became evident in one of his most surprising responses:

> The critique to the concept of foundation – he argued – is already present in "The Birth of Tragedy" and has been developed throughout his life by Martin Heidegger. (…) All his work is a critique of "foundation", and therefore a critique of "method". It is Nietzsche who in "The Birth of Tragedy", identifies Socrates and Euripides as current enemies. Socrates for his philosophy; and Euripedes for his destruction of Greek tragedy, (…) It is evident that the stance completely based on reason is the one that becomes an accomplice, for example, of the age of technique, and this is precisely the central objective of our critique.[152]

This renewed interest on Nietzsche and Heidegger, as well as on Foucault and Derrida, determined shifts also in his own position in relation to the topics we are discussing. "Otherness", "difference", the crisis of European logocentrism, and with them the abandoning of a teleological vision of history came into play. The new place allocated to such themes that until then were considered "minor", opened the space for a new approach to the *center/periphery* issue.

Although Tafuri's work at the time did not necessarily cover Heidegger's corpus, and even if other referents such as Benjamin, Wittgenstein, or Marx himself, continued to be important guides for his thought, Heidegger's *The Question Concerning Technology* and *The Age of the World Picture* contributed during those years to the whole reorganization of his research program. In the interview with Passerini, he maintained that

> while I was studying the Renaissance (…) the relationships between that period and our present situation became increasingly clear. I began to connect many threads around this time, in the late 1970s and early 1980s. For example, Heidegger came back as a fundamental problem, which is: what is the function of art in the age of technology? (…) The other question was life in the age of representation. (…) Thus, the dominance of calculable grids, which translate everything into mathematical terms. There were also architects, painters, and sculptors who (…) had the humility to make manifest a concept that is contrary to the violence of the age of representation, the age in which the world was subsumed to a representational grid.[153]

Tafuri's studies about Venice played an extraordinarily significant role in this new stage. The Heideggerian inspiration was expressed in *Venezia e il Rinascimento*, his most ambitious publication dedicated to this city. He explained there that the Renaissance can be considered as the moment in modern history of "repraesentatio". In "Off the Beaten Track" Heidegger speaks of the "era of the image of the world": an era in which man carries before him "simple presence like a contrary thing" (…). Heidegger sees the essence of the "modern" in the world becoming an image and in man's becoming "subjectum".[154]

Tafuri stated his debt to that Heideggerian essay on many other occasions. For example, in his understanding of irony on the part of Giulio Romano: "It seems to have been his very own culture –he wrote– that he observed with benevolent disenchantment, as if to emphasize that the world of representation and what had become common behavior had simulation as its limit".[155] In the introduction of his last book, one reads: "The reflections that have guided the basis for this book (…) attempt a dialogue with the 'era of representation'".[156]

In line with Heidegger's idea, Venetian studies depict the repressive character of the construction of a single "image of the world", or of an idea of the world conceived in a logocentric manner. Analyzing Daniele Barbaro's *Comentarii Vitruviani* Tafuri observes how in them "the 'machinatio', the 'planning rationality' (…) readies itself to shape the natural environment according to human concerns".[157] At the same time, he shows that, going against the complex Venetian cultural stratification, in San Salvador "a reticulated, mathematical, and perspective space, modularly arranged and based on the organization of the classical orders, forced the neo-Byzantine program to speak a humanistic language".[158]

Following "The Age of the World Picture" and "The Question Concerning Technology", the need to examine the submission of the totality of the existing – minerals, vegetables, animals, cosmos, and man himself – to the condition of "assets" (Bestand) to be incorporated into the logic of production was one of his structural preoccupations during these years. Particularly since his publication of *Krisis* in 1976, Massimo Cacciari intensified a critique of "planning rationality" and became a privileged interlocutor and source of encouragement for Tafuri, with whom he shared a close friendship.

In *Storia de l'architettura italiana. 1944–1985* Tafuri recognized that

> Cacciari's reasoning pursues the problem of architecture to its roots. Identifying nihilism as the motivating force of the "age of technique" and formulating the idea of its completion. (…) The tradition of thinking that links Nietzsche to Heidegger and beyond is interpreted seriously (in Cacciari's text).[159]

Heidegger's "The Question Concerning Technology" occupied a prominent place in Tafuri's studies on Alberti. One of his sharpest observations refers to the doubts of the author of *De Re Aedificatoria* in relation to this theme. Analyzing Brunelleschi's dome of Santa Maria del Fiore and his *Novella del Grasso Legnaivolo*, Tafuri writes:

> Alberti is known to have admired the first: however, the gratuitous, anti-naturalistic character of the second is completely un-Albertian. These two

concrete results of Brunelleschi's "ingenium" might be described, then, as Janus Bifrons: an apt figure for the moment of ethical decision implied by the modern "techne".[160]

It is not a surprise then that the second paragraph of the chapter dedicated to the relationship between Nicholas V and Alberti is titled "Leon Battista Alberti: The Limits of Techné".

Through the analysis of the *Theogenius*, where the humanist condemns the "pitiless violence of homo faber" against nature, Tafuri shows Alberti's doubt in relation to "modern techné".[161] "There can be no doubt" – he adds further along – "that technology is assigned a 'civilizing' mission in De re aedificatoria". But

> this approach can be refined by plumbing the depths of Alberti's mentality. Indeed, the Theogenius reflects a profound meditation on the myth of Prometheus. (…) His theft of fire, achieved at the expense of the gods, can be seen only as compromising the gift he offers to man. As Massimo Cacciari has profoundly written, Promethean theft and deception have a specific meaning: "the foundation of techne is not in techne itself". In other words, this foundation has itself been stolen. To make "techne" into an absolute is, therefore, an authentic "dolos": an act that lays claim to the power to dissolve divine "nomos".

According to Tafuri, for Alberti

> the heir of Prometheus "recognizes the culpability of technology": he knows that it is simultaneously criminal and "unfounded". Precisely this recognition allows for a conscious use of "techne". (…) Technology, which alleviates human suffering, is at the same time an implacable instrument of violence.[162]

Tafuri's already mentioned study about Venice revolves around the confrontation between the technological "ratio" with one of the strongest "organic" forms of government and communal life in the 16th century. For Tafuri, in Venice, "already, in the earliest phase of the modern conception of technology there was the mythical root of the presupposition that conditions the concept of 'planning'".[163] And it will be in relation to the Arsenale where "the interpretation given by opposing parties of the role of sciences and technical practices"[164] would become evident. Therefore, without being able to articulate itself with the traditional, organic corpus of the Lagoon City, Palladio's architecture, which Tafuri characterizes by "its programmatic refusal of 'abuses' and its Olympian adherence to a universe guided by the 'proud wind of reason'"[165] was pushed aside. In one of his last lectures, Tafuri did consider Venice as embodying the place of defiance to that terrifying homogenized universe denounced by Heidegger's "Question …".

Tafuri concluded that lecture arguing

> that Venice, even as cadaveric as it is today, projects an unbearable provocation to the world of modernity. What Venice manages to propel are whispers,

but they are unbearable for the world of technique, for that era of technique that was not able to launch bridges between an immobile time and the various accelerated times that Le Corbusier had thought in a genial way, being even him one of the defeated within our civilization.[166]

Tafuri's Heidegger: The Importance of the Apparently Insignificant

Tafuri's interest on Heidegger was not an isolated case. Toni Negri has coined the phrase: "left-wing Heideggerianism" to describe a shift in the debate in favor of the German philosopher. The significance of this change of direction on the part of several Italian intellectuals after the failure of the positions taken in the "roaring 1970s" has been analyzed by several scholars such as Matteo Mandarini, Carlo Scilironi, Marco Assennato, and Francesco Fistetti.[167]

In what constitutes a critique of the theoretical repositioning of those intellectuals, Diego Fusaro argues that

> for some years now the old Marxist expression "capitalism" has been replaced in the public debate by a new expression, apparently analogous, but in fact secretly very different. (…) I am referring to the expression "Technique", with which nowadays (…) philosophers that are in fashion refer to capitalism, precisely qualifying it as "Technique". The passage of the Marxist lexicon of "capitalism" to the Heideggerian lexicon of "Technique" is anything but innocent. (…) Capital as thought by Marx (…) is a product of human action that is historically determined, or in other words a product of the objectification of human praxis. (…) As product of human praxis (capitalism) can be eliminated by such praxis itself. (…) On the other hand, "Technique" as thought of by Heidegger is not a product of historical human action. (…) Heidegger's "Technique", as an impersonal device (Gestell) used by man/woman in terms of his/her "will of power" (…) cannot be transformed by man/woman, cannot be changed by a Revolution.[168]

Supporting these ideas required a reorganization of several key concepts. Once the conditions of "Gestell", of "Technique", were admitted as an impersonal tool that even takes over the rational attempts of bringing it into question, what should be the attitude of one who, like Tafuri, conceived the legitimacy of his work in terms of productivity? Assuming a Heideggerian position, he adhered to the idea of "truth" as a process. "Truth" was for him the result of a critical historical work that had to be measured in terms of the ability of such work to insert itself in a determined dynamic, in the sense that it could be identified with the Freudian *Analysis Terminable and Interminable* (1937),[169] but at the same time within Heidegger's hermeneutic circle.

To the question of who decides on the validity of critical historical constructions, Tafuri said in the interview in Buenos Aires: "We construct upon a productive base. The arbiter is the productivity of our critique. (…) (Those) constructions can only be verifiable with distance; that is, over long periods".

Essay 2: Controversial Positions

This position relates to Heidegger's concept of *Gelassenheit*, defined as "releasement":

> I would call this demeanor (…) which expresses "yes" and at the same time "no", by an old word "releasement". (…) I call the demeanor which enables us to remain open to the hidden meaning (…) "openness to the mystery". Releasement and openness to the mystery belong together.[170]

"Gelassenheit", a term that is often translated to English as "detachment" is translated differently to Spanish by Yves Zimmermann,[171] who prefers to understand it as "serenidad" ("serenity" or "disaffection"), although in both cases the implicit sense of the verb "lassen" ("to let be")[172] is lost. That allowing for the process to develop or mature to enable the emergence of an alternative seems to be in tune with Tafuri's position during those years.

In the previously cited interview in Buenos Aires, this was exactly the content of another of his answers

> whatever changes while I am alive does not interest me at all, because the change I profoundly desire, is so strong that I hope that there will not even remain a breeze of Buenos Aires, of Rome, of Manhattan left on the surface of the earth. Therefore, because I know that the cities of the enemy will remain standing during my lifetime, my soul remains calm, serene, and I live as a stoic, epicurean.

Nevertheless, Tafuri himself criticized what he considered a mistaken interpretation of the concept. In his *Storia dell'Architettura Italiana*, he wrote: "But what is one to make of the current vogue for partial and 'pensiero debole' (weak thought), of the temptations to give in to mystical 'abandon' –perhaps Gianni Vattimo's 'starting again' is a lay version of Heidegger's Gelassenheit?".[173]

Beyond his position as a historian, Tafuri never abandoned his commitment to Italian contemporary reality, as expressed in his political administration of IUAV, or in his militant attitude in cases such as his collaboration with the journal *Rinascita*, of the Italian Communist Party, or in his activism against the realization of the Fair of Venice. Furthermore, even though in the notion of "productivity" there was a certain "resignation" ("Gelassenheit" can also be translated as such) in the sense of a sort of letting oneself flow forward in the river of history awaiting unknown future results ("Erwahrtung", another Heideggerian concept). It is no less true that what was thrown into that river was the result of an action with a transformative purpose. And through reading Heidegger, paths to develop that purpose could also be implied.

The whole work of the German philosopher was the result of an attempt to provide an alert, a warning in the face of what he considered to be the biggest threat assumed in the capitulation of the "Dasein" (human Being there) in relation to the logic of modern Technique and to what he called the "forgetfulness of Being"

Heidegger conceived the need and possibility of resistance to that "forgetfulness", and that resistance was rooted in "thinking".

For that "thinking" not to be absorbed by the "Gestell", Heidegger had to astutely make use of areas foreign to his domain: language (and particularly words in their primary form), art, and simple or apparently insignificant things. It seems that this critical expectation was shared by Tafuri. In relation to our theme, we must pay attention to the third possibility. The philosopher began some of his essays with the observation of quite simple things. It is there where he would dig deeper into them extracting unexpected meanings, "revealing" them: the boots of the farmer in *The Origin of the Work of Art*, the old stone bridge in *Building, Dwelling, Thinking*.

This oblique method of thinking seeking to avoid the instrumentality of Gestell was more fully explicit in *Der Feldweg*, the short work where he developed with greater density the metaphor of the country path. There he argued:

> Perhaps the enigmatic character of the simple conceals itself behind the appearance of an indeterminate tangle. (…) In releasement there could be an endurance concealing itself, one which rests purely in the fact that releasement enters ever more purely into an intimate awareness of its essence and, enduring it, stands within it.[174]

Recalling Foucault, Tafuri writes in "The Historical Project": "Not by chance does Foucault base on Nietzsche his 'The Archaeology of Knowledge' which, like Nietzsche's genealogy, is 'made up of small, not obvious truths, arrived at by a rigorous method'".[175] Further along he would say: "We don't believe in 'grand narrations' anymore, however we do believe that in the extra small (…), as in any Zen tale, there is an instant where redemption is possible".[176]

According to this idea the apparently insignificant, imperceptible, the (yet) unsaid, transforms itself into a way of shedding light onto the significant.

Isn't it possible, and even necessary, to broaden it? Isn't this the way where the peripheral becomes central and vice versa? With great insistence and detail Hubert Dreyfus has paid attention to this aspect of Heidegger's thinking. In his judgment:

> Heidegger sees that all our marginal practices are in danger of being taken over and normalized. (…) (He) sees in these marginal practices the only possibility of resistance to technology. Greek practices such as friendship and the cultivation of the erotic are not efficient. When friendship becomes efficient networking, it is no longer the mutual trust and respect the Greeks admired. Likewise, the mystical merging power of the erotic is lost when we turn to private sexual experience. Similarly, Greek respect for the irrational in the form of music and Dionysian frenzy do not fit into an efficiently ordered technological world.[177] (…) Heidegger holds that we must learn to appreciate marginal practices – what Heidegger calls the saving power of insignificant things. (…) All these practices remain marginal precisely because they resist efficiency.[178]

In "The Historical Project" Tafuri referred explicitly to the importance of this calling attention to the marginal: "For how often – he wrote there – when probing what is on the fringes of a given problem, do we discover the most useful keys for dealing with the problem itself".[179]

Furthermore, in the same text Tafuri even vindicated – and here surely in debt with Freud – the attention to accidents, involuntary minutiae:

> A failed work, an unrealized attempt, a fragment: do they not, perhaps, raise problems hidden by the completeness of works that have attained the status of "texts"? Do not Alberti's "errors" in perspective or Peruzzi's excessive "geometric games" speak more clearly of the difficulties intrinsic to the humanist utopia than do those monuments that appease the anxiety appearing in these incomplete attempts?[180]

In addition, the understanding of the value of "marginal practices", or what amounts to "the saving power of insignificant things" would feed, at a different level, into the interest in microhistory defended by Carlo Ginzburg and Giovanni Levi, a theme we have referred to above.

We can then return to the organizing outline of this study and try to observe how this potential inversion of values in the *center/periphery* paradigm presumed a modification in the role of both poles.

Having taken on this new perspective tinted by Nietzschean and Heideggerian thought, and understood in a broad sense, modernity became the main target of the Tafurian critique. Furthermore, while questioning what he considered an authoritarian and homogenizing core, it was from that same critique that a radical revision of the concept of "center" emerged.

> How much longer must we remind those who cling nostalgically to "centrality" –he asked himself in "The Historical Project"– that there is no other alternative, at present, than to trace the history that leads to the divorce between the signifier and the signified?[181]
>
> The world – he stated – has tried to recuperate the concept of center, and many intellectuals of exceptional integrity have become fascinated with forms that are Fascist, Nazi. (…) These figures are for me very strongly connected with this abstraction: the center. That is, I don't accept the labyrinth that Benjamin saw as the only viable path. Therefore, **it is necessary to invert the center**.[182]

(a.e.)

Center–Periphery; 16th Century

In 1980 Tafuri approached the German research institute of the Bibliotheca Hertziana to organize an exhibition on the architecture of Raphael on the occasion of the 500th anniversary of his birth in 1983. The essay published in the exhibition catalogue discussed specifically the re-construction of Rome as the capital of the

Essay 2: Controversial Positions 83

world – "Roma Caput Mundi" – particularly under the papacy of Julius II. It was an attempt in the end reduced to a "provincial" tone by the first Medici Pope that resulted in a complete failure in the context of the new European political condition given the Sack of Rome in 1527.

Tafuri argued that with the policies of Julius II "a new universalism would be opposed to that of the ancient. A war was unleashed (…) against everything that hindered **the centralizing role** of the Pontiff and the structures of the new State".[183] A good part of that essay is dedicated to analyzing the urban policies of Julius II and his complex relationships with the Roman aristocracy and the Roman people. The Pope's restructuring projects for the city expressed the same centralist purpose. Thus, "If Raphael's frescoes in the Stanza della Signatura start an unpublished conversation between ancient and modern, the four 'great works' from Bramante seems to carry out multiple functions for a global reconfiguration of the 'earthly Jerusalem'".[184]

Tafuri continued to treat the issue of Roman "centrality" years later with the publication of his last book *Ricerca del Rinascimento*. Highlighted as part of the research was, again, the centralizing purpose of Pope Julius II, which was reinforced by an atmosphere of highly favorable and hopeful ideas. In that context Tafuri notes that

> Dante's "De Monarchia" a text whose precepts Mercurino di Gattinara (the counselor and tutor of Charles V) attempted to realize, established the doctrine of the equality of the Pope and the Emperor as persons called upon to provide "mesura aliorum" (measure for all)). The metaphor of the center was valid for both – a **radiant** universal harmony.[185]
>
> (a.e.)

But as I indicated before, the purpose of this research was not limited to describing the papal project. More important, in relation to the theme we are analyzing, are the internal and external aporias of that project. Tafuri proves in his essay on Raphael that

> (the) alliance established between Pope Della Rovere (Pope Julius II) and his intellectuals (…) only in first instance is functional to the conquest of an ideological hegemony and to an "imperial" universalism' (…) from the network of relationships (…) derive dissatisfied instances and oblique directives which often join demands for reform, frequently distant from the interests of the Pope.[186]

Julius II program continued in force until the Sack of Rome of 1527, when that perceived centrality, the "radiant universal harmony", – fell apart: "Roma coda mundi". "The Sack of Rome: Rupture and Continuity" is the title of the fifth chapter of this last book. Tafuri tells us there that "the Sack (…) destroyed the image of Rome as "communis patria" –ideal locus of the confluence of cultures and symbol of possible European cohesion".[187]

84 Essay 2: Controversial Positions

Once the crisis of a stable centrality in the "time of the image of the world" was verified, the history examined by Tafuri became a history of the multiplication of centers, of the emergence of difference, of the development of a culture of mix, of forms of resistance to homogenization, of an increasing importance of the marginal and the peripheral, and of the discovery of the dialogical notion of cultural construction. We will now investigate these themes one by one.

The studies of 15th and 16th century Venice constitute by themselves a sign of the interest in understanding a pluri-central space. Not only because of the *Nova Roma* vocation that at least since the *impresa* of 1204[188] characterized the Serenissima (Venice), be it as inheritor of Constantinople – Rome of the Orient[189] or as the primal Rome celebrated with emphasis in the era of the Doge Andrea Gritti as studied in-depth by Tafuri. While analyzing the 1528 map of Benedetto Bordone, during his interview in Buenos Aires, Tafuri puts forth the idea of Venice as "umbilicus mundi", or center of the world. Presenting the city at the center of a lagoon/lake alluded to that condition. That lagoon/lake with a regular perimeter was a reference to the first edition of Thomas More's *Utopia*, published in 1526. In Tafuri's words:

> twelve years after the disaster of Agnadello (…) Venice begins to represent itself in a lake, which is to say that the island of Utopia, is a place that does not need to be searched for in Thomas More's book because it already exists. It is called Venice.[190]

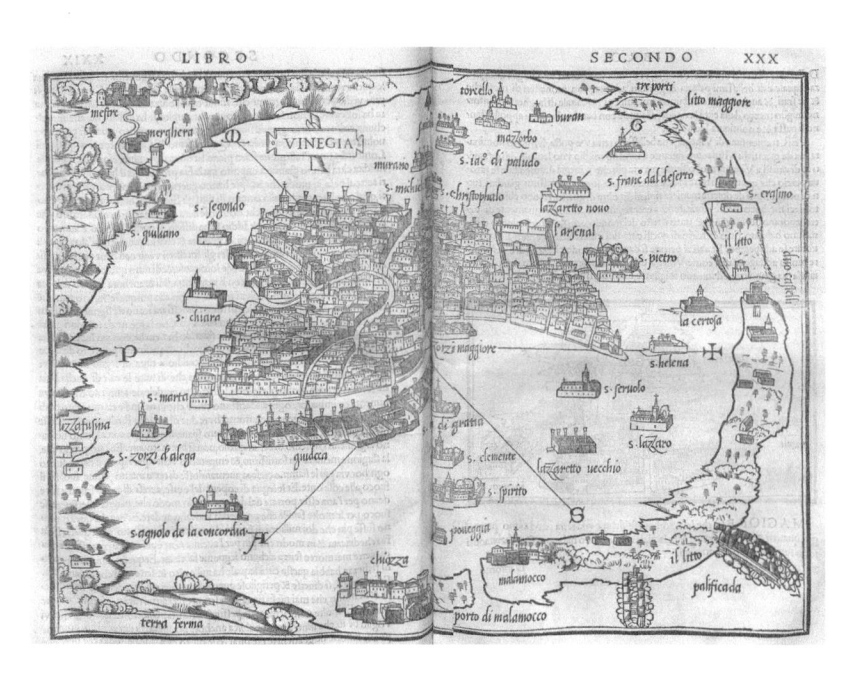

Figure 3.9 Map of Venice, from *Isolario di Benedetto Bordone*, by Benedetto Bordone, Venice, published by Niccolò Zoppino, 1533. From John Carter Brown Library. In https://archive.org/details/isolariodibenede00bord.

The situation of Venice, in and throughout the century that starts with the defeat of Agnadello in 1509 up to the 1606 Interdict, was that of a declining power as the product of the emergence of other powers and national states, favored by the grand opening toward the Atlantic of 1492. The buildings, the urban proposals, and the projects that Tafuri analyzes in his book are to a great degree determined by the world pressures derived from such event, and from the increasing multiplication of centralities at the core of the *Res Publica Christiana*, which would be officially recognized through the Peace of Westphalia in 1648.

Venice must confront not only the internal Italian dispute, particularly with Genoa, Florence, and Rome, but also the pressures coming from the north, sometimes through Milan and on other occasions from Paris, Amsterdam, Madrid, London, or the Empire. "The new Venice – Tafuri tells us – resurrected after the dark years of the war against the League of Cambrai, renewed its own 'myth' opening itself simultaneously to new organizational structures and new cultures".[191] And he emphasizes further along: "behind the obstinate will to safeguard Venice's particularity, one could often find voices advocating independence from Rome and openness toward Europe".[192] The projects of the end of the 16th century (Rialto, Arsenale, San Marco) expressed the contrast between the "papalisti" and the "giovanni", a conflict that crosses every study of the city: "the policy opened to Europe and to new political, religious, and economic outlets was opposed by the policy of rhetoric or of straightforward conservation proposed by Jacopo Foscarini and Marcantonio Barbaro".[193]

In theoretical terms, in his last book Tafuri sought to articulate this dissolution of all stable centrality with the main ideas he had been working on for many years. He admits there that "adopting a different kind of tragic outlook (alta tragicità) Hans Sedlmayr formulated a critique –reactionary in every sense– organized around concepts such as the 'loss of the center' and the 'death of light'". Despite the conservative sign that permeates the Austro-Hungarian art historian's thought, Tafuri recognized the validity of his conclusion and proposes a "close affinity between Sedlmayr's intuition of loss, with Benjamin's concept of the 'decline of the aura' and Robert Klein's reflections on the 'anguish of the referent'".[194]

He described his own methodology in *L'Armonia e i Conflitti*, with the term, precisely, of "polycentric research". "Polycentric research – he wrote – will be that which is capable of making the various systems react, that in a variety of ways produce the visible form of a historical structure".[195]

The usual *concentration* on the object of analysis in historical research, here had been converted into a dispersed group of thematic cores or nuclei to be researched in relation to that object, which therefore was defined through the intersections of directions and data. Furthermore, those nuclei were not fixed or stable, but a dynamic group of data, everchanging because of the organization of the totality of the system. "The plurality of the centers that the analysis must take into account – Tafuri concluded– presupposes the capacity to change the ways to approach each one of them departing from the problem of their intersections"[196] (a.e.). In these conditions "historical space appears to dissolve, to disintegrate, to become a justification for a disordered and elusive multiplicity, a space of domination".[197]

86 Essay 2: Controversial Positions

To verify that the historical space is comprised of a plurality of centers that coexist at diverse levels, interacting among each other, and being in continuous transformation, went hand in hand with Tafuri's interest in the subject of the multiplicity of languages. The conception of historical research as the study of confrontations, fissures, contradictions, voluntary and involuntary junctions, the non-translatability, and the relative autonomy of the "languages of Power" constituted one of the clearest "obsessions" of Tafuri, particularly as of the publication of "The Historical Project", where he wrote: "if Power –like the institutions in which it incarnates itself – 'speaks many dialects', the analysis of the 'collision' among these dialects must then be the object of historiography".[198]

Once again, Venice was the most paradigmatic place for that plurality.

> Venice, sacred city, does not have her own language, and how could she have it? She has the language of Babel. She can assume all of them because she hides, as Simmel intuited (…), that what is preserved, what is our most intimate, what is hidden, (…) what counts (…) is the ability of Venice to absorb any language. Venice does not have any other language than its own unrepeatable structure and organicity.[199]

The Venetian Babel replicated the contemporary condition but without the "unrepeatable organicity" of the Serenissima. With a certain melancholic tone, Tafuri published in 1986 the second edition of his "Storia dell'Architettura Italiana". In this opportunity the direct attack on a large part of the Italian architectural production, which had characterized his 1982 edition, was somewhat tempered, as if assuming "serenity": the Heideggerian "Gelassenheit". Faced with the dissolution of all expectations of the existence or of the recovery of some constitutive axis of the "Modern Movement" and faced with its explosion into a myriad of "dialects", Tafuri admitted the phenomenon of "post-modernism" as an auspicious experimental exploration that would demand expectation ("Erwartung") for it to mature.

> The processes mentioned – he wrote at the end of the earlier edition – are proliferating in a variegated and articulate fashion. (…) (It) is a collective attempt –albeit still confused– to shuffle the cards fairly in order to extract from the hybrid (…) a series of experiments emphasizing the problems of time, of permanence and uprooting, and of continuity and discontinuity.[200]

The melancholic celebration of a "fair shuffling" of cards was not limited to contemporary architecture. If Raphael had been selected to examine the limits of a homogeneous architectural language with a universal purpose, the study of Giulio Romano allowed Tafuri to explore the intellectual adventure derived from an active and dynamic relationship with language, where rules changed in the exercise of speech itself. Furthermore, the research about the rhythmic disturbances of Giulio Romano Pippi allowed him to go deeper into the effects of "cross-contamination" of different languages.

The same principle of imitation from diverse models –he writes – was the one adopted by Baldassare Castiglione who denies the absolute authority of the Tuscan language. He instead recommends collecting the "most splendid and elegant words from every part of Italy" and even "French and Spanish words, which we have already accepted through usage".[201]

When referring to the program of Abbot Giovanni Andrea Cortese for the Abbey of San Benedetto in Polirone, in what Tafuri calls the "strategy of 'contaminatio'",[202] he shows the ensuing tension as a consequence of the discovery on the part of Giulio Romano of *imitation*. No longer the language of the ancients, but of their own ability to break the rules. "It was truly the infinite field of ancient license and variation that became the authentic exemplum: 'to be imitated'. Once this road had been taken, the precariousness of a universe that wished to be perfectly grounded was inescapable".[203]

At this point a focus of immense importance for our theme was introduced. When referring to the issue of *mixture* in Giulio Romano's work, Tafuri asks himself,

> Should one be surprised by the persistence of a medieval mentality in humanist culture? The fact that Bakhtin speaks of the medieval carnival in his book on Rabelais should make us reflect. Certainly, we can make no generalizations here; but the specificity of artistic creations does not float in a void.[204]

Even when Bakhtin's *Rabelais and his World*, cited by Tafuri, had been published in 1963, it was known in Italian only in 1979. Bakhtin showed there how in the Renaissance **the themes of popular culture entered the sphere of great literature**, referring to Rabelais, Boccacio, Cervantes, and Shakespeare to illustrate his point. Carnival and laughter were presented by the Russian linguist as mediums for the critique of dogma, authority, and hegemony through procedures of torsion, transmutation, inversion, profanation, and degradation of the common themes of the dominant social composition.[205] It was about a series of procedures that, although in an obviously different context and level, Giulio Romano had also resorted to. For Tafuri,

> In recognizing values as relative, the internalizing of the concept of authority found limits: the rapport with the real met the measure of the subject. As this analysis has demonstrated, Giulio exaggerated Bramante's great intuition of a language which is regularized but without rules, the virtual foundation for the multiplication (and consequent fragmentation) of the concept of "the model".[206]

Desiderius Erasmus, a figure Tafuri mentions several times as the incarnation of a critical spirit, is a guide to this new mentality that refuses the imperative of single models. His book *Ciceronianus*, where the Dutch humanist critiques Cicero's use of Latin in a "normative" fashion, noted that

> Ruminatio vindicated the liberty of the interpreter and opposed the primacy of the question to the assertions of dogma. (…) The invocation of multiple models implied the assumption of a mode of responsibility on the reader's part that went far beyond the "question of speech". (…) Cicero thus becomes another model to surpass implying that the greatness of achievement must be equaled.[207]

Ruminatio returns to the individual the ability of judgment and autonomy for the appreciation of reality, and with it opens the possibility of plurality. Thus, in relation to anti-Ciceronianism, Tafuri argued that

> from a theoretical standpoint, the refusal to rely on a single model seems to originate in the same impulses that animated Erasmian thought as well as Giovanni Pico's thought. The "concordia philosophorum" (espoused by both) implied a form of truth capable of being known and transmitted only when mediated by interpretations, thereby opening a space for the principle of tolerance. Thus, in this conception, tradition –the "delivery" (tradere) of knowledge – was inevitably bound up with its own betrayal (tradire).[208]

During the years of Tafuri's crisis at the end of the 1970s, some events and ideas that stimulated and enriched the construction of a new historiographic focus were disseminated in Italy. This new focus sought a pluralistic space with an increased interest in questioning homogeneous versions of history. The discussion on "difference" flowed from the libraries to the streets. In 1971 the most important theorizations of the French debate on the theme were known: "Différence et répétition" by Gilles Deleuze, and "L'écriture et la différence" by Jacques Derrida, to which in 1975 was added the translation of the famous essay "La Différence", and in 1980 Gianni Vattimo's "Le aventure della differenza".[209]

Furthermore, while the crisis of ideologies and policies that had led to the "Storming of the Winter Palace" became more than evident, and the Communist Party initiated a decline toward its dissolution in 1981, the new expressive movements of minorities, of those that were "different", grew and consolidated. Two examples follow. One was the development of the movement of gender choice, having important milestones in the foundation of FUORI[210] (Fronte Unitario Omosessuale Rivoluzionario Italiano) in 1971, the debates and mobilizations aroused by the assassination of Pier Paolo Pasolini in 1975, and the addition of the "homosexual issue" to the agenda of the Communist Party in 1978. The other is the feminist movement, with an ascending trajectory that went from the creation of the group "Rivolta Femminile" in 1970, to the approval of abortion laws in 1978.

Interested in the ideas of Nietzsche and Heidegger, neither these facts nor those debates went unnoticed for Tafuri. In the end, as noted by Vattimo, "The new thinking envisaged by Nietzsche [and to which Heidegger also related to] with his proclamation of the superman may also be regarded as a kind of 'adventure of difference'".[211] To a certain extent, Tafuri must have shared with Vattimo the "adventure of difference" in as much as it was a key topic for the appreciation of new social and political phenomena, but also for the construction of a critical point of view about the history of architecture. He believed that "the apexes of modern thought are nevertheless moving toward a threshold limit animating a "**profane attention to difference**" regarding nihilism"[212] (a.e.). And with "difference" a new path was opened for more radical considerations.

Already in "The Historical Project", Tafuri recognized that from de Saussure onward we know that "language itself is a 'system of differences'".[213] But the topic did not affect only language. The strength of "difference" penetrated research methodology as well: for Tafuri "To question the will to design is to carry to its limits the arythmos of the calculating intellect, in order **to encompass both differences and unity**, and to break the historicist continuum"[214] (a.e.). It is true that, with Franco Rella, by the end of the 1970s Tafuri resisted searching in the "Other" for a full alternative for his own uncertainty when faced with the failure of the research lines he had followed until then. In a time when he shared courses with the Italian thinker, he strongly maintained that reading into that Otherness

> the immediate, true expression of a natural totality "beyond contradictions" means thinking, illusorily, that certain subjects exist which are immune (or redeemed) from contradiction, subjects which precisely because of their "purity" (or "impurity" –the insane, the marginal, etc.) are other from the society and the history in which we live, bearers of needs and values that are inevitably incomprehensible to any form of reason.[215]

In synthesis, it meant "to destroy the metaphysics of alterity and difference".[216]

In this sense, his approach to the topic of "difference" was gradual and careful, seeking not to fall into a simple inversion of values that, in the end, would maintain unchanged the terms of the game under consideration. For Rella the partisans of "difference" faced what seemed to be "the reversal of this reality that we live in: to the machine of technology, they oppose the machines of desire; to history, oblivion; to progress, underdevelopment, and nomadism".[217] Tafuri was far from favoring "difference" to the point of making disappear all possibility of what he called the "historical project". He recognized that "the frustration experienced in dealing with large-scale solutions, which were as global as they were ineffectual, had accelerated this new realism. Furthermore, the demarcation of experimental fields was accompanied by a progressive reevaluation of local differences and dialects".[218] But in his judgment, the difference had to be given another type of function: "to lend a voice to the tragic (…) without lapsing into comical bricolage or mixture".[219] That function seems to have been to provide a base for "resistance".

Venice as Place of Resistance

We can then come back again to the axis of our work and say that, based on the recognition of the role of "difference" as the basis for "resistance", Tafuri was during the last part of his work in a position to approach the *center/periphery* paradigm in a dynamic manner, that is to say where both poles have an active role. The first

90 *Essay 2: Controversial Positions*

phase of this novel approach seems to have enabled him to recognize that the "periphery" did not have an inert role when faced with the hegemonic and dominant impulses coming from the "center", and that its reaction was manifest in different forms of "resistance". The place he chose to study and reveal them was Venice. His book *Venezia e il Rinascimento*, Tafuri tells us, was written to show "the way in which Venice tries to endure within its own origin".[220] That is why Venice appears as an anti-dialectic place, as a place where opposites coexist. Here, "tradition and innovation, development and memories, continuity and renewal, sacred and worldly, public and private are not in contradiction".[221]

To attribute that condition to the Serenissima allows Tafuri to explain complex positions particularly in relation to the center/periphery conflict. As already mentioned, during the 16th century and a good part of the 17th century, Venice experienced multiple pressures coming from a pluri-centric world. Until a certain moment, these multiple pressures cross each other in a complex manner in institutions and individuals. They can combine, for example, aspects seemingly opposed such as tradition, continuity, sacred spirit, defense of public interests, openness to Europe, and integration into the new landscape of the world. That complex multiplicity of pressures was contained or articulated among each other thanks to the particular political constitution of the Republic within the European panorama. And that political constitution was based on the defense of "difference", of the singularity of its own myth.

Jacopo Sansovino was the figure selected by Tafuri to show the way in which, based on that original myth, Venice established ways to resist, to remove itself from the overwhelming gaze of "humanism" that was raised as a cultural flag of the Roman papacy. In his judgment, "Sansovino is (…) the figure who interprets, in Venice, an antiquarian manner informed of the novelty of the Roman debate".[222]

As is true for Serlio, Sansovino stands out in a background of Venetian religious upheaval that was averse to Rome; and the austerity his architecture embodies toward the 1550s and 1560s is interpreted as an expression of the reformist and anti-Roman attitude that characterizes the Serenissima. In this manner "Venice, as a State of divine origin dedicated to Christ, also seemed to be setting itself against Roman eloquence through this 'simplicitas'. (…) Christus pauper is contrasted with Christus dives".[223]

> In the Serenissima, – Tafuri will write in another of his books – the "new" is accepted on the condition that it gives up its claims to the absolute. (…) Venice's resistance to absolute systems of thought makes her diffidence toward the harmonic "artificium" anything but surprising.[224]

Tafuri dedicated significant effort to the study of Doge Andrea Gritti's main attempt at introducing the language of the "image of the world". According to Tafuri that introduction had severe limits, in many cases unbreachable, and in others had to deal with realism given the talent of Jacopo. The introduction of a new language was possible in very concentrated doses, particularly around San Marco; "their basic presuppositions encountered symptomatic resistances; indeed, a state of overt

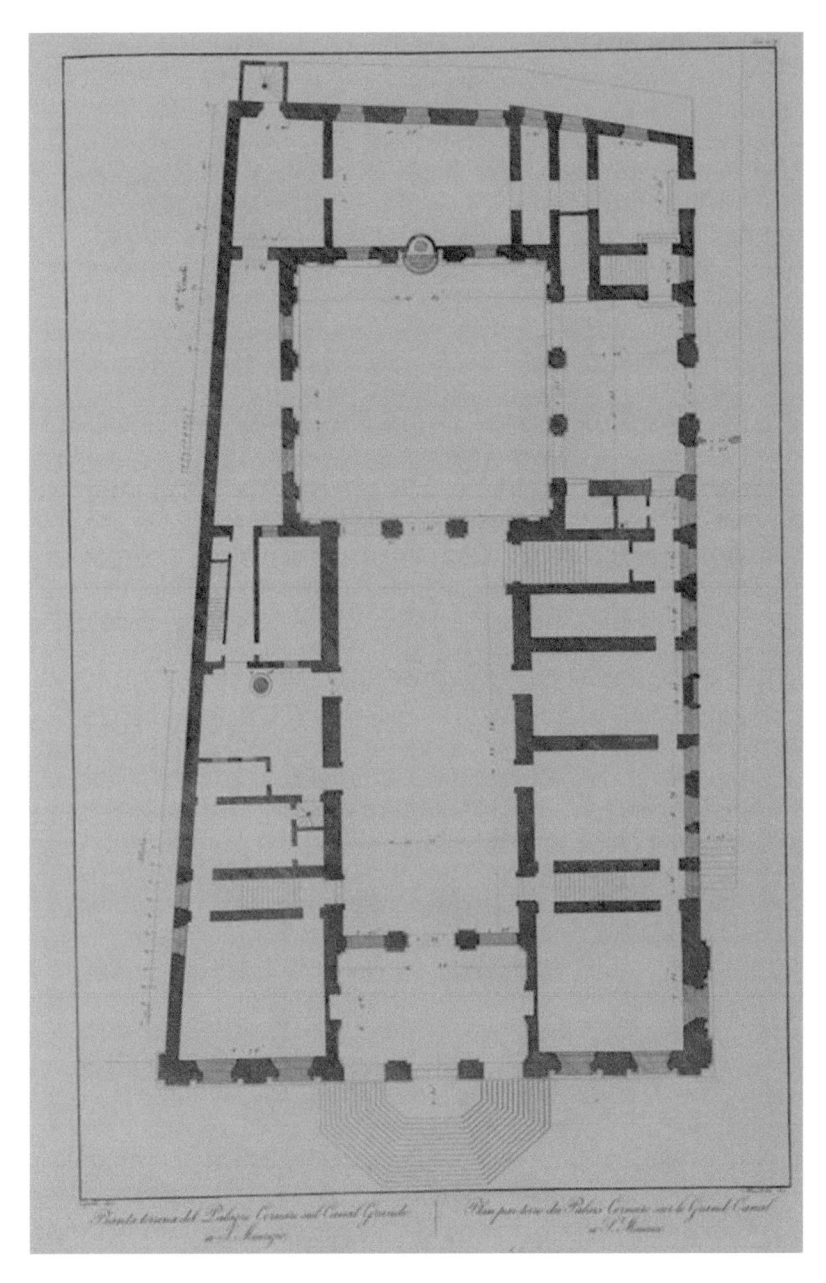

Figure 3.10 "Pianta terrena del Palazo Cornaro sul Canal Grande a S. Maurizio", *from Le Fabbriche e i monumenti cospicui di Venezia* (The Buildings and Prominent Monuments of Venice). By Cicognara, L.; Diedo, A.; Selva, G.A. Edited by G. Antonelli, Venice, 1858 (Getty Research Institute). In Tafuri's view, in the layout of the Palazzo Corner, Jacopo Sansovino manages the tension between the Venetian vestibule tradition and the scheme of the central courtyard imported from Rome.

conflict between Rome and Venice persisted on the architectural front".[225] In relation to the refusal of Fra Giocondo's project for Rialto after the fire of 1514 he wrote:

> That language (…) speaks in fact of the primacy of the classical ratio, of a triumphant Romanity, of "heroic" ideals that were not welcomed in the Serenissima, maybe it also speaks of the explicit rejection of any ideological character: the "New Constantinople" (or the "New Jerusalem"), (…) expresses ideals that are antithetical to those of "Venice, the other Rome".[226]

To a certain degree it seems that, for Tafuri, Venice is proof of the existence of a historic entity that must be attributed to an autonomous force, capable of allowing the conviviality of immediate interests, sectors, individuals, or even of class: "Was the Venetian mentality, therefore, resisting the Renaissance?"[227] he will ask. That historical entity is the "mentality", a fundamental category that Tafuri introduced in the construction of his ideas.[228]

Tafuri assumed that in Venice an incredibly special "mentality" maintained that multiplicity in equilibrium. And, paradoxically, it was even that force that led to its tragic destiny. Within that multiplicity in equilibrium, the extreme of a "primacy of classic reason" was as unacceptable as the positions that in the opposite extreme looked to question it. Venice's was

> an "analogical" (or metaphorical) culture based on the historical memory, on the cult, on the "memory of the origin". Foreign to such a tradition is the intervention by transformation of the urban fabric: also, for this reason, in Venice urban renewal will never be able to follow "Roman" models (… nor to) provide space for neo-feudal ostentation.[229]

Paradoxically, the most fervent supporters of the Roman linguistic renovation were on the opposite sidewalk of those who supported a decisive entrance of Venice into the world scene (opened by the American enterprise), and into scientific and technological renovation. Two figures should be noted among those selected by Tafuri as examples of the ambiguous way in which Venice resists the attempt at penetration on the part of the "ratio clásica" with support from the papacy. One is Nicolo Zen, of whom he highlights his actions while directing the construction of the Arsenale:

> Zen – he writes – did not identify renovatio with the cult of pure and absolute novitas. Renewal, on the contrary, was a goal that could be realized through a "progression" that was also a "return": the original could guarantee, legitimize, and confirm the "new".[230]

The other is Leonardo Donà, who, as Doge, opposed Rome, causing the papal interdict of 1606–1607.

> Leonardo Donà is the one that wants to open Venice to Europe, but Leonardo Donà is the young man that (…) knows that change, novitas, is not an

ephemeral change of dress, but it is very much about changing such structures that involve the whole of Venice with Europe, with those Western exchanges.[231]

When analyzing the process of renovation of the Arsenale, by allowing the inclusion in his administration of new technical proposals and Dutch capital, Tafuri highlights that Leonardo Donà became an emblem to those who rejected that option together with the consequences it would have introduced into Venice by breaking with local traditions. With a Heideggerian tone, Tafuri understood this episode as an example of a clear rejection of modern "technique".

The refusal to admit the English and Dutch "new men" into Venetian trade was certainly a way of fending off the danger of disruptions in the areas of religion and tradition: "deterioration" was in some way accepted in favor of the "conservation" of a State as it was. Was this a rejection against "modernity"? In a certain sense, it was.[232]

In a later work, Tafuri will interpret the rejection of Donà to the hegemony of the papacy in an even more radical fashion: "Exactly at the end of the significant episode of the Interdict (…) Venice decides (…) her own will of a slow death in the modern world, of a total rejection of modernity".[233]

The Periphery in the Center

According to a report prepared by Caritas di Roma, 148,838 immigrants lived in Rome in 1970; 61.3% of them came from Europe, 25.7% from the American continent, 3.3% from Africa, 7.8% from Asia, and 1.9% from Oceania. In the 24 years that passed between then and up until 1994, these numbers underwent significant changes. By 1994 immigrant numbers jumped to 677,791, 28% coming from Africa, 16% from Asia, 14.5% from America, and 0.3% from Oceania. The proportion of European origin had decreased to 41%.[234] The "extra-community", the "other" non-whites, had become the majority. Unexpectedly, the "periphery" had been transformed into a problem **within** the "center" itself (a.e.).

In addition, the crumbling of the Soviet Union not only affected the field of ideas that Tafuri still related to. The cataclysm experienced by the "first workers state" affected all countries of the Warsaw Pact and the ex-centric cases of Romania, former Yugoslavia, and Albania. Consequently, on March 7, 1991, 27,000 people arrived at the port of Brindisi in what would be only the first wave of an unexpected and unforeseen immigration stream. In April 1992 war broke out in Bosnia and highlighted the real drama of the situation. In addition, from China to Argentina, from the United States to India, from Mexico to Russia, during the 1980s the entire world was affected by a wave of "neoliberalism". In 1981 an article by Theodore Levitt began to use the new term "globalization" to designate what was happening. While an unexpected war shook the heart of Europe, nations with poor economies two decades earlier, such as those called "Asian tigers" began to have similar indicators as those of Western powers (the GDP in Singapore in 1994 was equal to 90% of the GDP in the United States). The designation of "Third World" had lost currency given the numerous political changes experienced in countries that were once members of the "Tricontinental" and seemed a concept as obsolete as a static representation of the concepts of "center" and "periphery" in use since the end of World War II.

Very close to Tafuri, Giacomo Marramao and Massimo Cacciari sought new answers to this new panorama. On the opposite side of the coin of homogenizing globalization, "difference" in the form of mandatory conviviality with peripheral cultures or of defensive local reactions, started to occupy a place of relevance in their thinking. Marramao wrote: "Today, the West is an exploded cultural sphere (… but that explosion), occurred not despite but as a consequence of the apparent global victory of its model".[235] Or, as Cacciari would argue in reference to the homogenization produced by "Technique" to the "Earth" as its expanded area ("Missionsgebiet"):

> (From) Istanbul, (…) Alexandria, (…) Damascus, (…) Urfa, the great cities of the Maghreb (…) from all these places –and lastly Sarajevo– there arrive no more armies but refugees, exiles. And they find no more hosts, but defense, obstacles, or at best the tolerant search for assimilation, in the end they find "dumb" individuals that in no way "remember" having been foreigners themselves as well.[236]

Following Emmanuel Levinas, Cacciari welcomed the new attention on "difference", as far as it meant a significant contribution to the own identity of the West. On his side, Marramao recognized that it was not a matter "of thinking in accordance with an ethnocentric and colonial model of Reason". It was therefore necessary to recognize that what was being faced was "not only a confrontation between Western culture and other cultures but a conflict of values that traverse the very heart of (…) the Western metropolitan life". Furthermore, "the problem of cultural alterity does not exist only as a clash with the outside, but as an aporia internal to the functioning of Western society itself".[237]

Tafuri was also affected by this new global condition and found himself profoundly troubled by the corruption of the Italian political system that would come to an end with the beginning of the process of "Mani Pulite" in February 1992. On numerous occasions, he warned that we were "on the verge of an abyss: not only in Italy, but it is also modernity that is on the brink of the abyss, and we don't have any way out".[238] By then he was far from limiting his preoccupation to the "centers" that were most "advanced".

As alluded to above, the "world" was at the time forcing its way into Europe and into Italy in a particularly desperate way, simply trying to survive. Tafuri shared and suffered this tragedy and its burdensome dilemma. In the mentioned course he warned that in the 19th century the West could envision the democratic and egalitarian functioning of its societies, but that that desideratum was limited to "a third of humanity, presupposing that the other two-thirds should be subjected to it, if not slaves". He admitted that at the end of the 20th century that cynical possibility was not possible. Even more so because

> if the entire world becomes democratic, we will all die of hunger. But before dying of hunger those of us who can eat two and a half times a day, faced with the invasion of millions and millions of people that will want to eat at least once every three days, we would kill them. (…) Today, when we understand the food deficit figures, while reason tells us that we should send them back rather than die of hunger, the pietà instead tells us that we should welcome them.[239]

It is in this context that we should interpret the fact that – in the second edition of *Storia dell'Architettura Italiana* in 1986 – for the first time in his work Tafuri recognizes the need to take into account the impact of the production generated in areas that were until then marginal to his intellectual geography. "The same process –he wrote there – (…) of homogenization generated by mass media and computers gave rise to new needs for self-identification, **a new awareness of peripheral identities**"[240] (a.e.). Of course, one should not understand that this recognition happened in a linear fashion. He did not carry out any research directed to contribute to the understanding of those "peripheral identities". His attitude was even more ambiguous because even at the time that he noticed the need for a new approach to the *center/periphery* paradigm, his rejection of the invention of "postmodernism" (and particularly the Italian formula defended by Paolo Portoghesi), led him to approach the subject with a critical and cautious attitude.[241]

Tafuri believed that what he called the "week moves" of Portoghesian postmodernist pluralism provided "life to forms of interrogation related to 'difference' and singularity: places, historical periods, traditions, peripheral truths, memories, modifications, expressions of 'pietà' for what has been vanquished, and transformations avoiding the hubris of the 'novum' in favor of 'letting be'".[242]

In a certain way Cacciari joined the formulations of the Prague Circle and of Emmanuel Wallerstein in relation to the importance of intermediary and mobile spaces between centers and peripheries.[243] This can be noticed when in his *Geophilosophy of Europe* he refers to the unique position of Ionia between the Hellenes and the Persians. For Cacciari, in the 7th and 8th centuries BCE "the power of limiting has not asserted itself yet. (…) In the manifold Ionia, East and West meet immediately, almost without having to meet".[244]

That same consciousness of the porosity of intermediate zones was already understood at a theoretical level in Tafuri's "The Historical Project". But in the new context of the early 1990s this understanding allowed him to adjust his reading of the problem. In that essay he wrote that "on the basis of a partial reading of Nietzsche, Simmel recognizes in his 'Metaphysics of Death'" that

> the secret of form relies in the fact that it is a boundary; it is the thing itself and at the same time the cessation of the thing, the circumscribed territory

96   *Essay 2: Controversial Positions*

> in which the Being and the no-longer-being of the thing are one and the same. If form is a boundary, there then arises the problem of the plurality of boundaries.[245]

It will be in Wallerstein's sense that Tafuri's research on humanist architecture in Spain will lead him to conclude that

> (the Alhambra of Granada) reads as an example of a "rigorist" attitude that appears in this light only if we consider Spain to be a periphery. Nonetheless, it is also important to recall that the palace registers a programmatic intention whose purpose is to overturn the existing relation between center and periphery, in favor of Spain in general and of Granada in particular.[246]

He will warn then that, even in that frontier field, a creative potential of unexpected richness is housed:

> it is possible to consider the "case" of Venice by adopting interpretive criteria that do not differ substantially from the ones already used to study Spain. Even more so than in the case of Spain, however, in (the) Venice (of the second half of the 15th century) **interactions between centers and peripheries** become legible.[247]

L'arcipelago (*The Archipelago*) a book published by Massimo Cacciari in 1996 – two years after Tafuri's death – was dedicated, precisely, to examining a human organization in equilibrium, based on the full recognition of differences. That organization is built on the basis of

> a universal sympatheia without confusion, a relationship between entities where none is the privileged center, a place of definition-explanation, but where each in its own distinction, as clearest as possible, seeks to reflect the other and be reflected as well.[248]

Furthermore, for Cacciari "no island is a fixed axis", and "none has within itself the own Center".[249] In the space of the archipelago

> as in Bruno's cosmology, the center is everywhere, even better: we could say that here the image of the center is the place at one time occupied by the theorós, at another by the hístor. Nevertheless, the nostalgia or the seduction of the Center always inevitably appears, the will to "cure" the European illness of rebuilding its space around a visible, stable axis.[250]

At the same time, if the issue of the "disintegration of the center" had been pre-announced in Tafuri's studies on post-humanist architectural composition, especially in his Piranesian studies, in the final years of his life he stated, already in a fully geographic-cultural sense, that

Venice is not the center of the world because the world has no centers, therefore we need to know everything (...) Venice should become a place where (in groups, together with us) we have outside experiences, in which the world beats.[251]

Most moving of this affirmation is the conclusion derived from questioning the idea of "centrality" as an unavoidable organizing factor: "therefore we need to know everything". In these words, expressed almost at the end of his life, Tafuri was opening the possibility of a radically different focus for history, and not only of the history of architecture.

According to Alessandro Carrera, for Cacciari

difference, not harmony, is what keeps us together, in peace as well as in war. But how do we think the essential differences, differences supposed to remain different, without despairing about the actual possibility of living together with them? Ramon Llull and Nicholas of Cusa may have been among the few Europeans who happened to "think of difference" in a way that it did not minimize its otherness.[252]

Cacciari's interest for such authors is not limited to this last study. In *Europe and Empire* he referred to the *Book of the Gentile and the Three Wise Men* by Ramon Llull. He highlights there the stubborn dialogical purpose of the three wise men described in this book, who in a religious dispute trying to convince a gentile they disregard the possibility of knowing which was to be the final decision of the latter:

an unheard of and unexpected suspension brings the great dialogue to an end: only in this are the three wise men truly in agreement, in knowing that they have to continue debating, trying to understand, and that this is their way of loving and honoring God (...) they decide to meet again more times and continue arguing with the power of reason, without negligence or indifference or empty tolerance.[253]

Toward the end of his work Tafuri noticed that "difference" and its ability of "resistance" did not constitute a static condition, but a dynamic and transformative force that referred to the importance of "dialogue", of controversy, as a creative tool of incredible value. As he recognized in his last book, *Venice and the Renaissance*, he had sought to show that "resistance and contradiction do not represent trivial residues of a fatal process. They are productive phenomena that simultaneously condition and question this process. (...) A complex intersection of spatial and temporal images that problematize unilinear concepts of historical understanding".[254] Furthermore, the whole 16th century could be understood as a period of

an essentially dialogic culture. (...) While dialoguing, that culture sustains a battle with ways of life, consolidated mentalities, everyday behaviors, structures of the imaginary: the analysis of sixteenth and seventeenth-century architecture in European countries or in the Americas has much to teach in this regard.[255]

In his *Geophilosophy of Europe* Massimo Cacciari presented the conflict between the West (Europe) and the East ("Orient") in its paradigmatic form through the battle between two women in the dream of the Queen Mother Atossa in *The Persians* by Aeschylus. The whole book is a test of that fundamental conflict within the construction of Western identity. For Tafuri that "terra incognita" to discover also started through an "Orient" that had already "invaded" his studies on Venice. An "Orient" that he had already encountered in that frontier space of the Danubian Empire of the Habsburgs when he was delivering his 1978 course in Vienna. An "Orient" that he would relate to again in his research on Spain. It is not by chance that the analysis of the Palace of Charles V in the Alhambra of Granada makes up the last chapter of his later book. In the same way, if little or no attention to the "Orient" was necessary for him when studying the architecture of Guarino Guarini, in the late 1960s – a quarter century later – he would respond to a question from one of his students:

> I like your question in the sense that fortunately you became curious about non-Western architecture: Arabic, Mozarabic; furthermore, you have caught (…) one fleeting sentence in which I asserted that Guarini looks and takes an interest in them. All of this, however, is worthy of two university courses: one that should explain the genesis and rationale of non-Western architecture (Arabic or Islamic); the other about how was it that a philosopher-mathematician from a religious order (Theatine), at the end of the 17th century passing through Spain in his way to Portugal (Lisbon) to build a church (…), becomes evidently fixated by something that he had never seen in Western architecture (…), to the point of using it in his architecture in Bohemia, and that afterwards it gave rise to its wide circulation there.[256]

The implicit leap and productivity of this idea was extraordinary. It was no longer only about recognizing the creative potential of the controversy, but of the articulation of cultures, of a dynamic reading of the center–periphery paradigm. Nor did Tafuri limit himself here to recognize, as he had done in *Ricerca del Rinascimento* inspired by Peter Burke, that "an entire artistic geography dealing with modes of reception still awaits exploration".[257] In the paragraph quoted, what is highlighted is not the reception in the "periphery" – creative but derived – of ideas generated in the "center", but a movement in the opposite direction: this is a "central" figure, and the consequent creativity that derives from the experience of his contact with a "peripheric" culture. "You cannot walk among palm trees with impunity". Nothing better than the powerful Goethean metaphor as an expression of this point of an intellectual journey prematurely interrupted: "You cannot walk among palm trees with impunity".

Tafuri had abandoned for more than a decade his studies about the architecture of our time, and there is no way of knowing how he would have continued to advance based on this mature state of his ideas. For those pursuing a truly global approach to the history of modern architecture, a perspective not restricted by the provincial North Atlantic view, these intuitions illuminate an aspect of Tafuri's remarkable legacy previously underappreciated, an aspect that this new approach cannot continue to ignore.[258]

Notes

1 BRUNO, 1584.
2 For the most complete bibliography of Tafuri's publications see PEREZ ESCOLANO & PLAZA, 2020.
3 TAFURI & DAL CO, 1976. a.t. (author's translation)
4 TAFURI & DAL CO, 1976, 379. Many years later, almost at the end of his life, when asked for the reason of those derogative references to Niemeyer and Brasilia in *Archittetura Contemporanea*, Tafuri responded: "Niemeyer was one of the first to be aware of a regional reality. By the end of the 1930s, the allegory of his architecture is that of a very exuberant and sensual Latin country, with vague references to an unreal nature, and exaggeratedly vigorous. He later follows a surreal path such as in Brasilia, where the buildings try to prove a non-logic, emerging as a big unexpected mushroom. But I think that experience has a significant importance when recovering the concept of "wonder" absent in our daily reality". VV.AA., 1993, 68.
5 CURTIS, 1981, 168–170.
6 ACKERMAN, 1994, 137.
7 TAFURI & SOPRANI, 1962, 6. a.t.
8 Ibidem.
9 I have conducted a more detailed analysis of the center-periphery paradigm in the most comprehensive Spanish version of this work, which is currently in press as of the date of this publication. Among others, the primary texts from the bibliography that I have utilized for this study are as follows: VON THÜNEN, 1850; Stefan Müller attributes to Noam Chomsky a fundamental reflection on the C-P system in MÜLLER Stefan, "Kernigkeits: Anmerkungen zur Kern-Peripherie-Unterscheidung", in MACHICAO Y PROEMER et al., 2014. Particularly relevant to our analysis are the works of the so-called "Prague School", such as KOCOUREK, 2010, 21; and KISS, 2010, 70. In addition LANGHOLM, 1971, 273; LOVE Joseph L., "The Latin American Contribution to Center-Periphery perspectives: History and Prospect", in REILL & SZELÉNYI, 2011; PINTO et al., 1973; WALLERSTEIN, 1974; and GINZBURG & CASTELNUOVO, 1979.
10 TAFURI, 1966, 260. a.t.
11 Ibidem, 257.
12 Ibidem.
13 TAFURI, 1980, 208.
14 Ibidem, 208.
15 AURIGEMMA Maria Giulia, "Geografia dell'arte e periodi dell'arte secondo Argan" in DI NATALE & GUTTILLA, 2011, 113. a.t.
16 ARGAN & FAGIOLO, 1974, 29–30.
17 TAFURI & SOPRANI, op. cit., 8.
18 TAFURI et al., 1961, 369. a.t.
19 TAFURI Manfredo, "Borromini e il problema della storia", *Comunità*, No. 129, 1965, in TAFURI, 1979, 24. a.t.

20 PASSERINI, 2000, 29.
21 TAFURI, 1962. a.t.
22 PASSERINI, op. cit., 29–30.
23 TAFURI, 1964 (LQ), 24. a.t.
24 Ibidem, 9.
25 Ibidem, 7.
26 Since 1963 an organic center-left coalition between the Christian Democratic Party, the Italian Republican Party, the Italian Social-Democratic Party, and the Italian Socialist Party was in charge of the Italian government. This meant that for the first time after the creation of the Italian Republic, members of the ISP integrated the cabinet.
27 Ibidem, 172.
28 Ibidem, 155.
29 TAFURI, 1964.
30 *Casabella* No. 289, 9.
31 TAFURI, 1964 (J), 57.
32 PASSERINI, op. cit., 18.
33 TAFURI, 1964 (J), 12.
34 Ibidem, 12.
35 PASSERINI, op. cit., 14.
36 CIUCCI, 1995, 12–13. a.t.
37 LAU Kwok-Ying, "Husserl, Buddhism and the Problematic of the Crisis of European Sciences", in LAU et al., 2010, 221–233. Lau highlights here in particular "Über die Reden Gotamo Buddhos", the article by Husserl published in *Der Piperbote für Kunst und Literatur*, Vol. 2, No. 1 in 1925. See also Pushpakumara Saman "Edmund Husserl's Transcendence of Early Buddhust Theory of Consciousness". One of the most appreciated texts about the relationship of Heidegger with the Orient is MAY, 1996.
38 ARGAN Giulio Carlo, "I grandi problema dell'arte contemporánea" (conference, Galleria d'Arte Moderna di Roma, April 12, 1960), in TAFURI, 1964 (J), 154.
39 TAFURI, 1964, 15.
40 Ibidem, 13.
41 Ibidem, 49.
42 Ibidem, 66.
43 Spanish in the original.
44 TAFURI, 1964, 137.
45 Ibidem, 73.
46 Ibidem, 9.
47 Indeed, the book had a negative reception in the specialized press, where what was noted was the lack of analysis of works, the difficult read, and the generalizing approach. See WHITFIELD, 1968, 414.
48 "Manfredo Tafuri" text of a lecture delivered by Prof. Dr. Frommel in the symposium "Manfredo Tafuri. Seus leituras e seus leitores" (Sao Paulo, FAUUSP, February 2015). The author is grateful to the generosity of Prof. Frommel for access to the manuscript text.
49 Tafuri was aware of the differences of his own tradition with German historiography, that – in the figures of Dvoráz, Friedländer, Curtius, Hocke and Hauser – he criticizes for forcing the line of argumentation. TAFURI, 1966, 20.
50 TAFURI, 1966, 6.
51 Ibidem, 121.
52 Ibidem, 309.
53 Ibidem, 265.
54 Ibidem, 296.
55 Ibidem, 309.

56 Ibidem, 320.
57 Ibidem, 320.
58 TAFURI, 1980, 22.
59 Ibidem, 229.
60 Ibidem, 110.
61 Ibidem, 20.
62 Ibidem, 82.
63 Ibidem, 41.
64 Ibidem, 45.
65 The reference is related to TAFURI, 1969; TAFURI, 1969 (C), 31–79; TAFURI, 1971, 257–311; TAFURI, 1971 (C), 257–312; TAFURI, 1973.
66 PASSERINI, op. cit., 32.
67 Testimony of Marco de Michelis to the author, 06.18.2023.
68 For Tafuri "In 1962 and 1963, Quaderni Rossi had already started to come out, and a problem arose that was entirely new in political terms [...] I remember the slogan we used, that is, to return to Marx means to do what he has done, that is, to start all over again". PASSERINI, op. cit., 27.
69 PANZIERI, 1973, 47. a.t.
70 BIRAGHI, 2005. About the work of Tafuri during this period there is an extensive bibliography that includes: the pioneering work of COHEN, 1984; AURELI, 2008; LEACH, 2006; ÖZYETIŞ, 2013; DAY, 2012, 31–77; HEYNEN, 1999; HOEKSTRA, 2005; MOMETTI, 2012, 107–133; LLORENS, 1981, 83–95; SHERER, 1996, 32–56.
71 WRIGHT, 2002, 63.
72 Ibidem, 27. The quote is from COLLETTI, 1974, 23.
73 BEDESCHI, 1983, 90. a.t.
74 TRONTI et al., 1978.
75 PASSERINI, op. cit., 32.
76 Ibidem, 33.
77 VV.AA., 1967, 4.
78 POSADAS, 1959, 8. a.t.
79 CACCIARI, 1968, 203. a.t.
80 Ibidem, 205.
81 Ibidem, 206.
82 TRONTI, 1966, 32.
83 Ibidem, 23.
84 Ibidem, 89–95.
85 Ibidem, 95.
86 WRIGHT, op. cit., 66. Refers to da, 1988, 23.
87 FELTRINELLI, 2012. a.t.
88 WRIGHT, op. cit., 86. The citation is related to TRONTI, 1967, 28.
89 TAFURI, 1970, 241–284. a.t.
90 Ibidem, 246.
91 Ibidem, 50–52.
92 MANDARINI Matteo, "Beyond Nihilism: Notes towards a Critique of Left-Heideggerianism in Italian Philosophy of the 1970s", in CHIESA & TOSCANO, 2009, 58.
93 TAFURI, 1969 (C), 31–79. [Also published in English in TAFURI, 1994, 170–171].
94 TAFURI, 1970 (C), 247. [English version p. 61].
95 TAFURI, 1969 (C), 31–79. [English version p. 32].
96 TAFURI, 1972–1973, 183. a.t.
97 TAFURI, 1982.
98 TAFURI, 1980 (CA), 432.
99 Ibidem, 491.

102   *Essay 2: Controversial Positions*

100 Ibidem (Preface, p. xi).
101 TAFURI, 1976, 11. Spanish in the original: disillusion
102 TAFURI Manfredo, "Il socialismo realizzato e la crisi delle avanguardie", in VV.AA., 1972, 57. a.t.
103 Ibidem, 60.
104 Ibidem, 71.
105 Ibidem, 43. The enthusiasm for Russian formalism had its height in Italy at the end of the 1960s as a result of the translation to Italian of texts such as that of Victor Erlich (1966), and the publication of essays such as those of Ignazio Ambrogio (1968), Galvano Della Volpe (1967), and Tzvetan Todorov (1968) among others.
106 PASSERINI, op. cit., 60.
107 TAFURI & DAL CO, 1979, 87.
108 Ibidem, 89.
109 Ibidem, 120.
110 OTTO, 1980, 423.
111 CURTIS, op. cit., 169.
112 OTTO, op. cit., 424.
113 PASSERINI, op. cit., 59–61.
114 Ibidem, 59–61.
115 TAFURI, 1982.
116 TAFURI Manfredo, "The Historical Project", in TAFURI, 1990 (1980), 3.
117 LYOTARD, 1984 (1979), XXIV.
118 GINZBURG, 1976; CIPOLLA, 1977; CAMPORESSI, 1980; LEVI, 1985.
119 TAFURI Manfredo, "Lettura del testo e pratiche discorsive", in CACCIARI et al., 1977. a.t.
120 VV.AA., 2018, 48.
121 TAFURI, 1990, 5.
122 FOUCAULT, 1986 (1984), 23.
123 TAFURI, 1990 (1980), 6.
124 TEYSSOT & HENNINGER, 2000, 13.
125 TAFURI, 1976, 10.
126 TAFURI Manfredo, "L'architecture dans le boudoir", in TAFURI, 1990 (1980), 274.
127 TAFURI, 1966, 253.
128 Ibidem, 246.
129 Ibidem, 250.
130 TAFURI, 1968, 669. a.t.
131 Ibidem, 675.
132 Ibidem, 677.
133 TAFURI, 1978 (1969), 126.
134 TAFURI Manfredo, "The Wicked Architect: G.B. Piranesi, Heterotopia and the Voyage", in TAFURI, 1990 (1980), 27.
135 Ibidem, 27.
136 Ibidem, 30.
137 Ibidem, 26.
138 TAFURI & SOPRANI, op. cit., 9.
139 VV.AA., 1964. Debate with Carlo Aymonino, Pietro Barucci, Alberto Samonà, Carlo Melograni, Manfredo Tafuri, Ugo Sacco, Carlo Chiarini, Giuseppina Marcialis, Stefano Ray.
140 Ibidem.
141 Ibidem.
142 Ibidem.
143 Ibidem.
144 Ibidem.

145 TAFURI, 1980 (1970), 2.
146 TAFURI & DAL CO, 1979 (1976), 11. In "The Historical Project" (Ibidem, 14), he refers to "the *forms* of the architecture of the Modern Movement".
147 TAFURI & DAL CO, Ibidem, 9.
148 Ibidem, 14.
149 TAFURI, 1989 (1986), IX.
150 SCALVINI, 1984.
151 TAFURI, 2006 (1992) xxvii.
152 VV.AA., 2018, 29.
153 PASSERINI, op. cit., 61.
154 TAFURI, 1989 (1986), X.
155 TAFURI, 1998, 41.
156 TAFURI, 2006 (1992), XXIX.
157 TAFURI, 1989 (1986), 124.
158 Ibidem, 31.
159 TAFURI, 1989 (1982), 198–199.
160 TAFURI, 2006 (1992), 20.
161 Ibidem, 43.
162 Ibidem, 50–51.
163 TAFURI, 1989 (1986), 126.
164 Ibidem, 191.
165 Ibidem, 136.
166 TAFURI, 1994, 30.
167 MANDARINI, 2009; SCILIRONI, 1991, FISTETTI, 2007/4 , 159–183; ASSENNATO, 2017.
168 FUSARO, 2016.
169 FREUD, 1964 (1937), 216–253.
170 HEIDEGGER, 1959 (1966), 54–55.
171 HEIDEGGER Martin (ZIMMERMANN Yves trans.), *Serenidad*, Ediciones del Serbal, Barcelona, 1994.
172 Heidegger uses the verb at the same time to comprise different words, such as einlassen, or loslassen.
173 TAFURI, 1989 (1986), 197.
174 HEIDEGGER, 2010 (1989), 89.
175 TAFURI, 1990 (1980), 4.
176 TAFURI, 2014 (1993), 181.
177 DREYFUS, 1993, 303.
178 Ibidem.
179 TAFURI, 1990 (1980), 2.
180 Ibidem, 13.
181 Ibidem, 6.
182 PASSERINI, op. cit., 62.
183 TAFURI et al., 1984, 60.
184 Ibidem, 63.
185 TAFURI, 2006 (1992), 182.
186 TAFURI et al., 1984, 74.
187 TAFURI, 2006 (1992), 157.
188 We are referring to the defeat of the Byzantine Empire and the occupation and sacking of Constantinople in that year by the Serenissima and a Crusader army.
189 PINCUS, 1992, 101–114.
190 TAFURI, 2014 (1993), 181.
191 TAFURI, 1989 (1986), 112.
192 Ibidem, 113–114.

193 Ibidem, 166.
194 TAFURI, 2006 (1992), XXVIII.
195 TAFURI & FOSCARI, 1983, 7.
196 Ibidem, 8.
197 TAFURI, 1990 (1980), 2.
198 Ibidem, 8.
199 TAFURI, 1994, 18.
200 TAFURI, 1989 (1986), 170.
201 TAFURI, 1998, 29.
202 Ibidem, 41.
203 Ibidem, 43.
204 Ibidem.
205 LACHMANN et al., 1988–1989, 115–152.
206 TAFURI, 1998, 50.
207 TAFURI, 2006 (1992), 159.
208 Ibidem, 11.
209 DELEUZE, 1968; DERRIDA, 1967; VATTIMO, 1980.
210 Fuori means "out there" in English.
211 VATTIMO, 1993, 2.
212 TAFURI, 1989, 198.
213 TAFURI, 1990 (1980), 2.
214 TAFURI, 1989 (1986), 199.
215 RELLA, 1994 (1978), 18. a.t.
216 Ibidem, 16.
217 Ibidem, 42.
218 TAFURI, 1989 (1986), 150.
219 Ibidem 200.
220 TAFURI, 1989 (1986), 13.
221 Ibidem.
222 TAFURI & FOSCARI, 1983, 41.
223 TAFURI, 1989 (1986), 74.
224 TAFURI, 2006 (1992), 221.
225 Ibidem, 220.
226 TAFURI & FOSCARI, 1983, 42.
227 TAFURI, 1989 (1986), 4.
228 PASSERINI, op. cit., 48.
229 TAFURI & FOSCARI, 1983, 78.
230 TAFURI, 1989 (1986), 2.
231 TAFURI, 2014 (1993), 27.
232 TAFURI, 1989 (1986), 193.
233 TAFURI, 2014 (1993), 27.
234 VV.AA., 2004.
235 MARRAMAO, 2012 (1992), 164.
236 CACCIARI, 1996, 41.
237 MARRAMAO, 2012 (1992), 166.
238 TAFURI, 2014, 176.
239 Ibidem, 179.
240 TAFURI, 1989 (1986), 150.
241 Ibidem, 190.
242 Ibidem, 199–200.
243 TAFURI, 1990 (1980), 5.
244 CACCIARI, 2009, 199.
245 TAFURI, 1990 (1980), 5.

246 TAFURI, 2006 (1992), 197.
247 Ibidem, 220.
248 CACCIARI, 1996, 17.
249 Ibidem, 28.
250 Ibidem, 29.
251 TAFURI, 2014, 180.
252 CACCIARI, 2016, 13.
253 CACCIARI, 2016, 22.
254 TAFURI, 2006 (1992), 21.
255 Ibidem, 21–22.
256 TAFURI, 2014, 173.
257 TAFURI, 1992 (2006), 219.
258 As an example, it is interesting to note that in the mentioned interview of Ana Luiza Nobre of 1993, to the question about the significance he could attribute to Brazil at that moment, Tafuri responded: "I see Brazil as a mix of ingenuity and courage, which intrigues me. I don't have much information on Latin America in general, but it is probable that new things come from countries with less complex implications than those from European countries". From NOBRE, 1993.

4 Essay 3: Orientalism and Modern Architecture

The Debate on the Flat Roof[*]

In one of the most influential biographies of Ludwig Mies van der Rohe, Franz Schulze reproduces the famous photomontage of Weissenhof Siedlung in Stuttgart in which instead of the lonely couple looking toward the camera in the original photo, the site is inhabited by people with dark complexion dressed in typical Middle Eastern dishdashas and keffiyehs. So that there are no doubts about the place the authors of the photomontage suggest that the construction should be found, a camel is in the foreground, contemplated by two lions from a patio in one of the houses. In the caption, Schulze says it is a pseudo "Arab village", a tricked-up anonymous photograph of the Weissenhof housing project dated 1934.[1] Schulze adds that two of the most recognized leaders of architectural culture in Stuttgart – Paul Bonatz and Paul Schmitthenner – considered this new architecture as "a heap of flat cubes, arranged in manifold horizontal terraces (…) that bear resemblance to a suburb of Jerusalem".[2] The author understands that this identification was inappropriate, and an attack on Mies who, instead, would have only been trying to reduce the buildings to "cubic masses (…) as a purification of architectural form". According to Schulze, for Mies, this search was based on profound philosophical, technical, and economic reasons and had nothing to do with the topic of places outside of Europe, as the anonymous photomontage insinuated.

This interpretation is commonplace in the historiography of modern architecture. It should be noted that, despite their obvious political differences, Schulze, as well as Bonatz and Schmitthenner, agree that this identification of Weissenhof Siedlung would imply a disqualification of its author. More generally, it assumes a presumed purity of its European foundations (or at most Euro-American) that even today is maintained, insisting that

> the architecture of the modern movement – which is Bauhaus architecture, or that of the great experts in rationalism of the twenties – is an international architecture, abstract. On the contrary, the notion of "Mediterraneity" is an attitude towards architecture that emerged as a reaction against this.[3]

In the opposite direction to this affirmation, in the lines that follow I will try to show that the interpretation of Bonatz and Schmitthenner was correct; that is, the

DOI: 10.4324/9781003452263-4

Figure 4.1 Stuttgart, Weissenhofsiedlung, Araberdorf, photomontage by Kunstverlag Hans Boetticher Stuttgart, 1934, postcard, 1940. (SESAM-Mediathek Stadtmedienzentrum Stuttgart. https://sesam.lmz-bw.de/details/512245.)

reference to Middle Eastern vernacular architecture – Mediterranean and originating in North Africa – constituted one of the components of modern architecture as formulated in the sphere of German-speaking Europe. It is understood that I do not intend to deny other reasons that gave rise to that architecture. My purpose instead is to show that this case constitutes additional proof of the way in which cross-fertilization processes constitute the dynamic basis of the construction of modern architecture (as they are for human creativity, in general) and that they accelerated with the expansion of capitalism across the world. Only the hegemony of a provincial vision of history (self-centered in the North Atlantic) explains why this inevitable global interweaving of modernization processes has been ignored until now.

Nothing but a Horrible Mass of Houses Built with Earth

Since the Treaty of Küçük Kaynarca of 1774, the main Western powers began their expansion into territories hitherto controlled by the Ottoman Empire. With this expansion, Europeans intensified their interest in the magnificent monuments of these great civilizations and in the history of those territories. Of course, since the publication of *The History of Ancient Art among the Greeks* by Johann Joachim Winckelmann ten years earlier, architects and archaeologists had been advancing the study of classical Greece. But it was after the Napoleonic invasion of Egypt that a "new antiquity" emerged as a field of study in the most advanced European academic circles. According to Bruce Trigger, we can say that

The achievements of ancient Near Eastern civilizations were appropriated for western Europe by claiming that western Europeans, rather than the people who lived in the Near East today, were their true spiritual heirs. British archaeologists also stressed that Britain was located where several streams of cultural influence from the Near East had converged.[4]

The importance of ancient monuments and their archaeological studies grew especially in the second half of the 19th century. Until that time the main source of knowledge of non-classical antiquity had been the Bible, but after the unearthing of the palaces of Assyrian kings in the 1840s by the British and the French, studies of these civilizations grew in both countries. With the creation of its own empire, Germany launched an expansive policy in those regions by consolidating its alliance with the Ottoman Empire. With the support of government policies, new institutions and structures were created to organize this new field of knowledge. In 1899 the Deutsche Orient Gesellschaft (German Asia Society) began its work in Babylon, and after 1903 excavations continued along the Tigris toward Assyria.

Suzanne Marchand observed that:

While [the] English, French, and Dutch orientalists of this generation [19th century] made a career of the Orient by going there as officials or travelers, the German orientalists in this period made the Orient a career by becoming academics (...) it is in the study of ancient Orient that Germany made its orientalist fame.[5]

She indicates that studies of "Zoroastrian Persia, the esoteric depths of Ancient India, and the early innovations of the Assyrians and Sumerians"[6] gave rise to a powerful attack on ancient traditional knowledge based on Greek and Biblical texts. And it was mainly in Mitteleuropa where the results of that impact were most convincing. However, despite the growing interest in the cultures and history of these regions, and despite the recognition of the values and implications of Eastern artistic and architectural monuments, at the beginning of the 19th century the Western mentality was not in a position to attribute aesthetic values to the cubic and austere houses that contemporaries inhabited in those same regions. On the contrary, these constructions were considered regrettable products of barbarism and cultural backwardness. In the first report about the recently "discovered" city of Timbuktu, the Frenchman René Caillié wrote in 1830: "I had a totally different idea of the grandeur and wealth of Timbuktu. The city presented, at first view, nothing but a horrible mass of houses built with earth".[7]

Nineteenth-century travel literature is crossed by numerous examples of this initial rejection. In 1853 Chanony described the village of Fondouk (Khemis el Khechna) in Oran as "built 'à la moresque, windowless single-story houses, looking more like a graveyard than rooms".[8] In the same way, Lamartine considered that in Beirut "the houses of the city were grouped in a confused way, and the roofs of some served as terraces for the others".[9] With the expansion of tourism, Jerusalem, a paradigmatic Middle Eastern city, became accessible to an ever-widening

Figure 4.2 "Vue d'une partie de la ville de Temboctou …" (View of a Part of the City of Timbuktu …), from *Illustrations de Voyage à Temboctou et à Jenné, dans l'Afrique Centrale* …, by René Caillié, Couché fils, graveurs, Paris, 1830 (Bibliothèque Nationale de France, Gallica).

European public. Regarding the city Leon Dhéralde wrote in 1881 that its houses "are closed to the street and receive the day only through narrow and infrequent barred openings, or through interior patios; most have terraces in stone or ceramic tiles".[10] On the contrary, having been in conflict with the Ottoman Empire for several centuries, the inhabitants of the main European regions of the Mediterranean basin – southern Italy, Spain, Portugal, Greece, Dalmatia – and in particular their "lower sectors" were not considered as part of "Western civilization". Referring to participants in a celebration in St. Peter's Basilica in Rome, Stendhal wrote that the peasants arrived "accompanied by their families, no less savage than themselves".[11] And similar characteristics are described in the travel accounts of John Eustace,[12] or Hans Gadow who paints the village of Llanaves as "unparalleled in its misery, squalor and dreariness".[13]

For most of these observers, the existence of this scenario in European territory was due to the "pernicious" and long-standing Arab influence in those regions. David Roberts's opinion was that "splendid cities, once teeming with a busy population and embellished with temples and edifices, the wonder of the world, were now deserted and lonely, or reduced by the mismanagement and barbarism of the Muslim creed".[14] Ernest Renan wrote in relation to Sicily: "It is above all Africa. (…) Crossing the villages of the extreme west, towards Alkamo, one even has the impression of being in the Barbary Coast (Maghreb)".[15] In the first descriptions of modern Egypt Edward William Lane argued that

> The dwellings of the lower orders, particularly those of the peasants, are of a very mean description: they are mostly built of unbaked bricks, cemented together with mud. Some of them are mere hovels. (…) In many villages, large pigeon-houses, of a square form but with the walls slightly inclining inwards (like many of the ancient Egyptian buildings), or of the form of a sugar cube, are constructed upon the roofs of the huts, with crude brick, pottery, and mud.[16]

Considering the efforts that were being made at the same time to build a common foundation of the idea of Europe based on ancient Greece, it was probably even more problematic to take over the poor and somewhat "strange" people who inhabited contemporary Greece. At the beginning of the 19th century, travelers had two main representations of Greece, that of antiquity or that of a modern Turkish province proposed by Chateaubriand, who had written: "In vain, in Greece, one tries to free oneself from illusions: the sad truth remains. Lodges of dry mud, more appropriate to serve as shelter for animals than for people".[17] For Henry Belle, first secretary of the French Embassy in the Kingdom of Greece between 1861 and 1863, the Greek peasants "resembled Bedouin tribesmen". Belle considered that "Greece, like Arabia and Africa, reproduced an exotic topos".[18] According to Z. Duckett Ferriman, "the Greek is racially and geographically European, but he is not Western [sic] (…). He is Asian in a hundred ways, but his Orientalism is not Asiatic. He is a bridge between the East and West".[19] Of course, this appreciation of the "lower qualities" of their way of life was similar to the opinions about Spain or Italy. Jean Giraudeau de Saint-Gervais declared that in Agrigento (of Greek origin) "the lower sectors, as mendicant as that of Catania and all of Sicily, still present here a greater degree of neglect and misery".[20]

Nobody Is Immune to a Walk under the Palm Trees[21]

The contemptuous attitude in relation to vernacular constructions in some territories of southern Europe and northern Africa was based on clear divisions between low and high culture and on what Tzvetan Todorov called Herodotus' paradigm.[22] For Todorov, this paradigm is adopted when the "Other" is considered as "barbarian" or inferior, as those who concentrate on the traits opposed to those that define "us". Todorov has shown that there is another way of looking at the "Other", what he calls the Homeric paradigm. In this case we consider the "Other" as the inverted mirror of ourselves. In Homer's paradigm our vices are transformed into the virtues of the Other, and our mutual traits are reversed. During the 19th century, the second paradigm was represented by the romantic gaze, by the search for authenticity in the primitive, for the realm of feelings as opposed to the domain of reason, for nature against artificiality, for the nobility of "culture" against the vulgarity of "civilization". The idea of "Orientalism" developed by Edward Said has been exceptionally productive and has prompted a significant amount of new critical studies on these topics. From the point of view we are considering, Said's concept of "Orientalism" encompasses both variants of Todorov's paradigms. The romantic gaze is part of Homer's approach. Travelers, artists, politicians, anthropologists, archaeologists, historians, philologists, and growing masses of common people visited the "Orient" directly or in their imagination. From this contact, novel approaches emerged, new representations were built, and new values were put into circulation.

Typical manifestation of the changes produced by experiences in situ is the famous phrase of Eugène Delacroix after his first encounter with Morocco (July 5, 1832). Addressing his compatriots, the painter exclaimed: "Well done! You fight and conspire, but how extraordinarily ridiculous you are! Go to the Maghreb and learn what patience and philosophy are". In relation to our subject, the Middle Eastern villages or cities were represented as background in his epic paintings such as *The Sultan of Morocco and his Entourage* or *The Convulsionists of Tangier* (1838). Sometimes the white urban configurations of these towns reached European viewers with the low-intensity backgrounds of landscape paintings as in Edward Lear's *View of Beirut* (c.1861), in *Tangier: The White City* (1893) by John Lavery, or in *View of Fez* by Asouau Mammeri. Jerusalem was one of the most attractive centers

Figure 4.3 Eugène Delacroix, *Convulsionists of Tangier*, 1838 (Minneapolis Institute of Art).

Figure 4.4 William Holman Hunt, *Nazareth*, 1905, New York, The Macmillan Company London, Macmillan & Co., Ltd. (New York Public Library).

for Western visitors, and the trip to the Holy Land was one of the most successful itineraries of nascent tourism companies.

In the previous section we have mentioned negative appreciations, but, armed with the painter's romantic view, the citizens of London, Paris, or Berlin could also appreciate the beauty and nobility of these austere urban scenes, thanks to the particular interpretation proposed by works such as *Bethlehem from the North* (1892), *Nazareth*, or *The Dome of the Rock, Jerusalem, during Ramadan* (1854–1855) by William Holman Hunt, or in *Jerusalem, Looking to Mount Scopus* (1925) by David Bomberg.

The flat roofs, the terraces, the absence of axial symmetry, the clear geometric volumes, and the absence of decorative additions seem to have been increasingly attracting Western observers, and these characteristics are presented in *The Casbah of Algiers* (1874) by Alphonse Asselber, in *The Drought near Briska* (1885) and *Laghouat in the Algerian Sahara* (1879) by Gustave Gillaumet, in *A Street in El-Aghouat* (1853) and *People of Algeria* (1853) by Eugene Fromentin, or even, already at the beginning of the 20th century, in *Assouan, Morning* and *A Street, Sidi-Bou-Said* (1923) by Albert Marquet. But, in addition, the luminous quality of the spaces and the texture of the architecture were also exposed in close-ups as the central object of the painting on numerous occasions, such as in the case of *Une Rue d'Algier* (1875) by Jean Seignemartin and Alfred Dehodencq's *Interior of a Moroccan Courtyard* (1860), and would continue to be present later in Jacques Majorelle's *The White Wall* (1930).

Of course, toward the turn of the century, under the philosophical, economic, and aesthetic conditions that were determining the emergence of Cubism, these architectural and urban configurations were more consciously observed by many artists as models, precedents, or preferential objects of representation. This was the approach to our subject by painters such as Kees van Dongen, Marquet, Kandinsky, and Klee, as we will discuss later. But it was not only through the painters that these images became frequent for the European public. Countless postcards, daguerreotypes, and photo albums recorded, reproduced, and widely distributed the features of these Middle Eastern vernacular constructions. A few examples are the Jerusalem Photographic Album (1865) prepared by Sergeant James McDonald, following the Ordinance Survey established by the authorities of the British occupation of Palestine, or the work of photographers such as Louis de Clercq in Tripoli (1859), Auguste Salzmann in Jerusalem and Bethlehem (1854), Henri Duveyrier or James Robertson, among many others.

There were many reasons and ways to romanticize the approach to this culture. Referring to Arabs, Wilfred Scaven Blunt was outraged by "the contrast between their noble pastoral life on the one hand, with their herds of camels and horses (…), and (…) the ignoble squalor of the French settlers, with their wine shops and swine".[23] Blunt respected Arabs as equals, as fellow aristocratic "knights of the desert".[24] From the romantic approach, Arab realities were observed with perplexity and in contradictory ways. Thackeray raved about the multiple dimensions of cities, where "there is a fortune to be made by painters in Cairo. (…) I never saw such variety of architecture, of life, of picturesqueness, of brilliant colors, light, and shadow".[25]

And in relation to Jerusalem, despite referring to its sordid aspects, Edward Lear also stressed that the exterior of the city was "full of melancholic glory and exquisite beauty". According to Charles M. Doughtly, they lived in "clay-built spacious houses, mostly with an upper floor; the windows are open casements for the light and air, their flooring of beaten earth, the crude doors of palm wood, as in all the oases", and when arriving at Boreyda at dusk after crossing the Nefûd dunes he acknowledged finding himself before "a dream-like spectacle – a great clay town built in this waste of sand enclosed by walls and towers and streets and houses".[26] For Luisa Villa, Wilfrid Blunt idealized "the Arabs (the Bedouin tribes, but also the Mahdist warriors) as representatives of a chivalric tradition threatened by encroaching 'progress'" and, in the face of the real Egypt that sought to modernize, he vindicated that what he deemed essential was

> not at all a picturesque place of sexual indulgence, sloth, cruelty, despotism and perpetual political immaturity, not a timeless repository of ancient lore, but a site of austere simplicity and learning, where opinions were debated and where, apart from traditional religious concerns, new and progressive policies could be shaped quite independently of European tutelage, British or otherwise.[27]

For the reasons described above, the sympathetic approximation to the Arab world was particularly remarkable in Wilhelmine Germany, and many institutions dedicated to these topics were created there during the 19th century. The magazine *Morgen*

Ländische Alterhümer was published in 1820, in 1845 the Deutsche Morgenländische Gesellschaft was founded, in 1887 the Orientalische Bibliographie in Berlin, and in 1896 the Vorderasiatische Gesellschaft in the same city. Two years later Wilhelm II traveled throughout the Ottoman Empire invited by the sultan Abdülhamid II.

> His new policy (Neuer Kurs) seemed to respond to the intentions of those who wanted to make Asia Minor the "India of the Germans". (…) Since the beginning of the 19th century they had little by little appropriated the Orient on an intellectual plane. The new means of dissemination such as the illustrated press and photography had contributed to vulgarizing the Orient that, from the 1900s, would become a true fashion.[28]

It is true that many German travelers also complained about the "dirt" and "disorder" that did not seem to gel with an idyllic image of the "Orient". But there were other voices. After his trip to the region, Count Adalbert Sternberg wrote:

> The savages are not the Arabs but us. I wonder then: who are the barbarians? Those who build an urban way of life where there are no police or secret services or those who have an agent of order on every corner because otherwise people would be openly killed or robbed in the streets? I ask: who are the barbarians? Those who leave their merchandise unprotected and for that reason nothing is missing, or those who shield their shops with bars, who have to equip themselves with bells, electric lighting, and night guards to protect themselves? (…) And I ask: who are the barbarians? Those who have to send their children to school under threat of reprisals, or those Arabs who in each village maintain their schools and their teachers at their own expense?[29]

Visitors were impressed by the unity between urban and natural landscapes. For example, in his report on Fez in 1887 Ludwig Pietsch wrote that

> especially during a beautiful day without rain and with a deep blue sky and strong sunlight, in which the Sea (…) shines (…) like a delicate and bluish Turkish silk, these white surfaces of the exterior walls of the houses provide an unimaginable background for the colored figures that stand or squat against them.[30]

The Adoption of the Flat Roof in Mitteleuropa

One of the constitutional characteristics of Western architecture has been the relationship between theories and preexisting built examples as a form of verification of those theories. In this sense, until the first decades of the 19th century, the traditional intellectual framework of architects was not prepared to legitimize the examples we are referring to here. For the institution of architecture, the modest settlements of Middle Eastern peasants began to acquire a certain conceptual visibility with the emergence of romantic ideals.

Herder's book *Reflections on the Philosophy of the History of Mankind* can be considered as the first justification of the theoretical dignity of vernacular production, a justification that, as is known, is synthesized in the concept of "Volkgeist" ("folk spirit"). Following Goethe, we will see later that in the case of architecture, romantic traces can be found in the early work of Karl Friedrich Schinkel. But it was through John Ruskin's writings that the ideas we refer to reach a systematic form in architectural discourse. Indeed, it was in his *The Poetry of Architecture* (1837), that the rooms of the "lower sectors" of society began to be considered for their aesthetic ideas. In that text Ruskin defined the Italian cottage with the traits of "simplicity of form"[31] and "clarity" but identified these traits as part of the typical decadent character of Italy, a country of "desolation", "glorious in its death". Despite the aesthetic values that he found in the Italian cottage, Ruskin understood that these constructions were determined by the "decadence", "indolence", and "abject poverty" of the Italian people.[32]

Other great intellectual contributions were necessary to understand that these constructions could also be considered as sources of inspiration for modern architects. The first one came from the concept of "typology" elaborated by Gottfried Semper, for whom types were "primitive forms, prescribed by necessity, but modified after the first materials which were used for their embodiment".[33] The introduction of the Semperian concept of "type" to the architectural debate is important for the development of our argument because the notion of repetition of form is implicit in it, a notion that was to acquire a vital role in the debate about modern "reproducibility". For Semper "architecture too is based on certain normal forms that – conditioned by an original idea – permit in constant reappearance an infinite variety depending on special purposes and on further determining circumstances".[34] Semper's idea of repetition of forms implied the possibility of considering popular and anonymous domestic architecture as a kind of "natural" product of human "needs", always in force over time. These ideas gave staunch support to the rescue of that anonymous architecture from the spaces of "death" and "decay" where Ruskin had situated them. However, he himself did not address the settlements we are considering here.

Although in this case our topic was not directly alluded to, the interest in pure, simple, and clear forms cannot be left aside when it comes to understanding the theoretical shifts that made it possible and necessary to observe and assess the examples that we are considering. From Adolf Hildebrand to Wilhelm Worringer via Adolf Riegl, the value of "crystalline" or cubic conformations was increasing in the German-speaking world. On the contrary, we know very well that this interest did not only come from this area, as evidenced by the studies on the so-called enlightenment architecture. With the theoretical possibilities of valuing an architecture of simple cubic masses open, it was still necessary to establish the aesthetic legitimacy of popular productions or, even more so, of "uncivilized" extra-European popular productions. For these to become reference models, the rupture of the centrality and univocity of the Western naturalistic classical system and the recognition of different approaches – but of no less cultural consistency – was decisive, a recognition for which Wolfflin's studies or those of the same authors just cited were of fundamental importance.

However, this was not enough to also admit the possibility and necessity of appropriating or adopting some examples that, as we have seen, had until then been considered in most cases as examples of barbarism, poverty, or decadence. It was the feeling of "decadence" of Western civilization, growing from the 1880s, which would be expressed in books such as *Degeneration* by Max Nordau (1892) or after World War I, in the successful *Decline of the West* by Oswald Spengler. This is what opened the doors to the search for new forces in the world of "primitives", topics extensively studied from different perspectives by art historians but scarcely considered in the canonic historiography of modern architecture.

As a product of these many and varied transformations, at the end of the 19th century, vernacular constructions of Mediterranean and Middle Eastern origin began to be taken into consideration by architects seeking a renewal of the discipline. Thus, in his letters from Rome to his friend Josef Hoffmann, Josef Olbrich said that he was not attracted by the "erudite styles" that he found in the city, while he recognized his fascination with the simple and stereometric constructions of Capri, "where the first traces of a spontaneous Eastern architecture can be found".[35] Indeed, later on, he continued his journey toward that "oriental architecture" visiting North Africa before his return to Vienna.

Olbrich's path to "spontaneous Eastern architecture" was paved just a year later by another Rome scholarship winner, his friend Josef Hoffman. Again, it was not the Renaissance or Baroque buildings that fascinated the young architect, but the vernacular constructions, and especially those that Olbrich had discovered in Capri and Anacapri.[36] The admiration of Olbrich and Hoffman for this type of construction had its antecedent in the discovery that Karl Friedrich Schinkel had made during his trip to Italy in 1803. The precedent is important, but the anti-Roman attitude of both disciples of Otto Wagner was not limited to fin-de-siècle Vienna. Suzanne Marchand[37] studied what she called the "attack on Rome" from the German-speaking countries, thereby implying an attack on France's cultural hegemony in Europe. This attitude was common among those who contrasted the weakness and degeneration of the late Roman Empire with the primitive energy of the Germanic tribes and the unflappable stability of the East. Although it is obvious, it should be added that the multiethnic composition of the Austro-Hungarian Empire and its particular location between East and West helped to consolidate this point of view. As part of this cultural context, in 1902 the figure of Josef Strzygowski emerged with his book *The Orient or Rome*. Until his death in 1943 Strzygowski "ceaselessly campaigned for the appreciation of the intrinsic beauties of Near Eastern and völkisch [folk] forms" and exerted a major influence on Austrian historians, artists, and architects.[38]

The first modernist construction in which the flat roof was used was Adolf Loos's Scheu House in Vienna. We will come back to this topic, but let us now remember that when that house was completed in 1912 "weekend strollers reacted allergically and complained that it looked Algerian".[39] Loos acknowledged this affinity but denied any reference to that house and its terrace to Algeria. The fact is, however, that he had indeed visited both that country and Morocco in March 1910, during the construction of his famous Michaelerplatz building. It was in the village

Figure 4.5 Adolf Loos, 1912–1913, Wien, Larochegasse 3, Haus Scheu.

of Ain Snara where, after having searched in many other places, he finally found the marble stone he wanted for that building. The impact of the place on him must have been important because he visited it again in December of the same year on a vacation trip with his wife. Furthermore, for Loos "for four centuries, the flat roof was the dream of the construction artist",[40] except that until the 19th century a technique had not been discovered that would allow the use of "the flat roof terraces [which] have been used in the Orient for centuries (…) in regions free of frost".[41] Middle Eastern architecture continued to attract him throughout his life. He visited the region on other occasions and the impact of the buildings he saw can be seen in other aspects of his work, such as in the Müller House, where according to Christian Kühn he would have applied the room layout and spatial distribution system common in Islamic houses in Cairo.[42]

It was within this Viennese cultural context that Bernard Rudofsky decided to focus his dissertation on the vernacular building systems on the island of Santorini, thus initiating Ariadne's thread that would guide his research presented decades later as his *Architecture without Architects*, one of the most influential architectural theses of the 20th century. Rudofsky studied at the Technische Hochschule in Vienna in the 1920s under the influence of Josef Frank, Oscar Strand, Oskar Wlach, and Walter Sobotka. Strand had traveled to Italy before his graduation in 1906, and there he developed his dissertation on "The Principle of Decoration in Early Christian Art", under Karl König. Wlach had also traveled to Italy in 1905 to prepare his dissertation on the early period of the Renaissance. Frank's, and later Rudofsky's, proposals "derived in large part from an abiding interest in Eastern philosophy, art, lifestyles, and domestic cultures".[43] As can be documented in Frank's case, behind his interest was his education in Oriental and Asian studies at the Wiener Schule der Kunstgeschichte, especially under the direction of Josef Strzygowski at the Wiener Kunsthistorisches Institut. According to Maria Welzig, "Rudofsky and Rainer maintained an interest in anonymous architecture, and the lifestyle, housing, and urban culture of the Middle and Far East" where they traveled starting in 1925.[44] In 1929 Rudofsky spent a long time in Santorini, an island that had been part of the Ottoman Empire for more than two centuries from 1579 to 1821. In 1932 Rudofsky traveled to Capri, Naples, Procida, Positano, and finally Milan.

Le Corbusier's relationship with the vernacular "Orient" has already been thoroughly treated by numerous scholars. Professor Zeynep Çelik maintains, for example, that "already in his writings from 1915 there are references to Islamic architecture and urban forms. (…) Several of his early houses, such as the Jeanneret-Perret (1912), the Favre-Jacot (1912) and the Schwob (1916) are inspired by Ottoman houses".[45] The one mentioned last is a well-known example, usually identified by the inhabitants of La Chaux de Fonds precisely as the "Turkish Villa". But, in reality, his relationship with the world of these constructions could go back further than the famous "Voyage d'Orient" of 1911, at least to the time of his work in Auguste Perret's office and his meeting with Charles Garnier, around 1907–1908.

Figure 4.6 Tony Garnier, Houses at the *Cité Industrielle*. From the book with the same name and the same author, Vol. 2, Massin & Cie., Paris, 1932, p. 24 (Bibliothèque Municipale de Lyon).

When Le Corbusier was a draftsperson for the Perret brothers in Paris, the atelier was tackling the construction of the Cathedral of Oran (Algeria), and Perret's relationship with that city dates back at least to 1902, the date of his project for the theatre in the same city. The Perret brothers would continue their professional work in the Middle East in the following decades through the design and construction of numerous buildings in Egypt, Morocco, and Algeria. For his part, inspired by the previous reconstructions of Delphi by Tournaire (1894) and of Bergamo by Pontremoli (1895), Garnier had exhibited his famous survey for the reconstruction of the Roman city of Tusculum in 1904,[46] in an event where the architect also exhibited his project for the Cité Industrielle. The reconstruction of the domestic architecture of Tusculum was obviously inspired by the contemporary vernacular constructions that he was able to discover through the trips he made not only in Italy during his stay at the Villa Medici but also in Greece and in the Middle East. These reconstructions served as precedents to the flat-roof houses and buildings characteristic of the utopian city that he would publish in 1917.

Of course, it is not possible to establish a clear knowledge of Le Corbusier about these precedents during the time he was linked to both masters, but it is also not possible to deny the close links between his first flat-roof projects for Maison Citröhan and the use of a similar flat-roof type in previous ones by Perret and Garnier.

In any case, it was not in France but in Germany where the connection between the new architecture and the vernacular constructions of the Middle East reached its greatest intensity. It is necessary to remember that the interest in the "new antiquity" was strongly determined by the search for alternative models in relation to the rules and cultural hegemony generated in the Latin world and particularly in France from the 17th century onward. That interest was stimulated by the numerous direct contacts of architects from Germany and Northern Europe with the monuments of Egypt and Mesopotamia in the late 19th century. Wolfgang Pehnt's classic book[47] on the architecture of expressionism is extraordinarily rich in mentions of the works of Hans Poelzig, Walter Gropius, Hugo Häring, Otto Kohtz, and Hermann Billing, among others, that were inspired by the ancient monuments of the Middle East. Following the Hanging Gardens of Babylon, Poelzig's 1916 project for the House of Friendship in Istanbul clearly stated the architect's fascination with oriental terraces and the use of flat roofing. And many of Poelzig's colleagues and artists from Germany, Austria, the Czech Republic, and the Netherlands used this new knowledge as a means to "break down old prejudices and norms".[48]

In the Netherlands, the fascination with ancient Eastern esotericism gave rise to the theosophical interpretation of art and architecture in the writings of J.L.M. Lauweriks and K.P.C. de Bazel. The interest in the Far and Near East determined that *Wendingen*, one of the most influential journals in the Netherlands, devoted a large space to these cultures, and in relation to our topic, in particular, it should be remembered that Lauweriks illustrated his article "The Titanic Work of Art" with a drawing of the small town of Izdighast in Persia.[49] Also from 1912, the Villa Allegonda in Katwijk aan Zee is another early example of the modernist use of the flat roof. The house was built with the intervention of J.J.P. Oud, who would become one of the main figures of modern architecture, and one of the leaders of the De

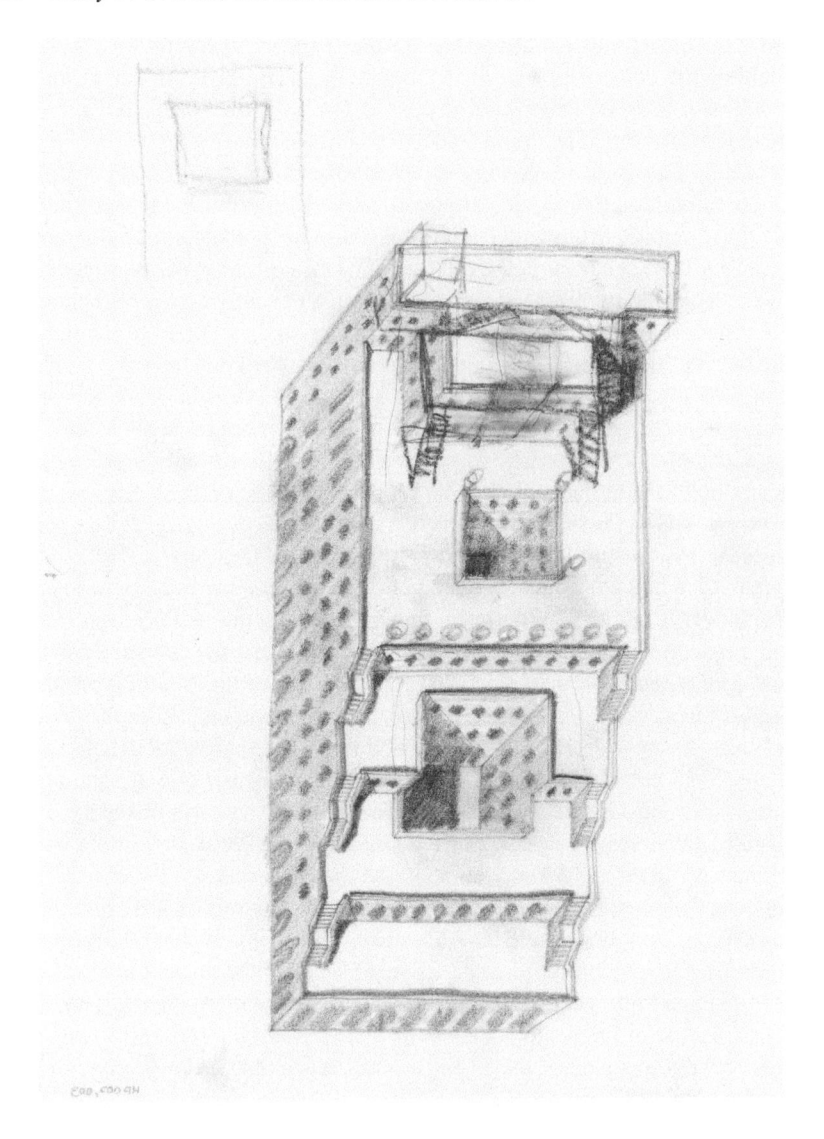

Figure 4.7 Hans Poelzig, House of Friendship, Istanbul, Perspective view, Technische Universität Berlin, Architecture Museum, Inv. Nr. HP 007,005.

Stijl group, together with Piet Mondrian and Theo Van Doesburg. We know about the importance of theosophy for the theory and practice of that group. Despite the differences between Lauweriks and Oud, both shared the same "Orientalizing" cultural climate of the late 19th century, a climate stimulated in the Netherlands by research and studies developed especially at Leiden University. The conception of the house was not Oud himself but the painter Menso Kamerlingh Onnes. Being a young student at the time the project was launched, Oud was invited to build the

Figure 4.8 Villa Allegonda J.P. Oud, c. 1918, Photographer unknown. Instituut Collectie Nederland (inv.nr. AB5055). Katwijk aan Zee.

house following the ideas proposed by Kamerlingh Onnes. The painter was the brother of the Nobel Prize laureate in Physics Heike Kamerlingh Onnes, the *pater familiae* of one of the most prominent and active families in the cultural circles of Leiden University. In the case of this Villa on the beach, it was Menso who promoted its construction as a good opportunity to recreate the images that he had collected during his trips to North Africa.

Lauweriks, Oud, and later Mies van der Rohe were in turn part of the circle gathered around the figure of the German industrialist Karl Ernst Osthaus, a prominent member of the Deutscher Werkbund and one of the most sophisticated protagonists of modern German culture. In 1910 Osthaus was planning to build an "Artists' Colony" in Hohenhagen, in connection with which he recalled: "How much Europe can learn from the Islamic Orient!", adding "I don't remember ever having had a strong impression of domestic peace [Wohnfrieden] than in those little alleys, removed from the world and enclosed in high houses and walls".[50]

Osthaus's lifelong interest in the Middle East must be highlighted because his was one of the many cultural circles where new ideas were expressed and disseminated until they reached their maximum synthesis and public status in the

Essay 3: Orientalism and Modern Architecture

Bauhaus school around which the most intense confrontations took place. Different studies have analyzed the reasons that placed the "flat roof" at the center of these debates, transforming what was initially only a technical debate into a kind of "Kulturkampf", a culture war. Especially since its use in the Fagus factory by Walter Gropius in 1911, the adoption of this type of cover became a hot field of contention between the traditionalist and modernist sectors. The relationship with Middle Eastern precedents was sometimes denied or sustained, both to attack and to defend the use of this resource. Immediately after World War I the expressionist circles within architectural culture felt particularly attracted to the "Orient", and in those years it was difficult to distinguish a radical separation between the distinct groups within those circles, since their participants changed their relative positions continuously. It is equally difficult to distinguish clearly between the appreciation of "high" cultural expressions and the interest in "vernacular" constructions.

Under the leadership of Herwarth Walden, the circle of the "Der Sturm" was permeated with "Oriental" curiosity. Walden was married to the poet Else Lasker-Schüller, and, in fact, she had a special interest in Palestine, having published *The Nights of Tino of Baghdad* in 1907, *The Prince of Thebes* in 1914, and the *Hebrew Ballads* in 1913. Walden's Café des Westens used to bring together figures such as Carl Einstein, Alfred Kerr, Karl Kraus, Adolf Loos, Alfred Döblin, and Kokoschka, among others. Among Paul Scheerbart's books on this subject are his 1897 novels *Tarub, Baghdad's Famous Cook* and *Der Tod der Barmekiden: Arabischer Harenmsroman*.[51] Walter Gropius was also linked to this group, and many scholars have identified this phase of his career as "romantic", at least until 1923–1924.[52]

However, considering his project for the Sommerfeld House in 1921, during these years Gropius seems not to have been too convinced about the programmatic value of the flat roof. No one can deny the importance of the constructivist exhibition of 1922 in Berlin or the arrival in that city of Lazlo Moholy-Nagy and Theo Van Doesburg in that same year and their subsequent incorporation into the Bauhaus. These facts stimulated the adoption of the flat roof as an expression of abstract architecture. Although these ideas came from the artistic field, it is no less true that the white cube volumes and flat surfaces were also elusive yet effective representations of standardized and industrial architecture.

But it should also be noted that flat roofs were not the most appropriate forms of these European regions, in relation to the actual development of construction technologies and the requirements of the local climate at that moment. Indeed, although traditionalists' arguments were associated with nationalism and racism, their most powerful point against the use of the flat roof was technical. The flat roof was considered appropriate for the dry climates of North Africa but not for the cold, rainy, and snowy climate of Northern Europe.[53] Even a supporter, albeit moderate, of the new architecture such as Werner Hegemann warned that Schultze-Naumburg knew the subject perfectly from a technical point of view, since he had used it on the terraces of his own buildings and thought that the relationship that he proposed with the Arab peoples was "convincing at first sight".[54]

The hypothesis that we are trying to demonstrate starts from recognizing that the adoption of the flat roof by German-speaking architects and more generally by modernist architects was above all a consequence of the drive toward abstraction that characterized modern culture. It was, in other words, a proposal with a cultural aesthetic origin and not a consequence of a pragmatic requirement per se. Even more it had to be developed against the grain of basic technical and economic conveniences. If such an illogical solution attained a significant role in central Europe, this was due to the pivotal presence of artists in the main centers of architectural renewal. In other words, despite the "technological" preaching of almost all its protagonists, the revolution in architectural culture did not have its main mobilizing core in the profession itself but in the contacts of some of these architects with a cultural avant-garde that had nothing to do with architecture's conservative building practice.

We have already seen the importance that the expressionists gave to the relationship with the "Orient". The other decisive artistic current in the adoption of the flat roof was, as is known, Cubism. This argument has been thoroughly touched upon in the studies of modern culture, and it is not our purpose to insist on it here. Once the principle of a cubic and even abstract aggregation of volumes was accepted as a starting point for modern architecture, it became evident that the Middle Eastern town and its vernacular architecture was the best example to observe and use as a precedent that would confirm the spatial and urban advantage of such idea. And there was then a solid theoretical framework that made this claim possible.

The bridge between pictorial visions, Middle Eastern precedents, and the formation of the latest ideas in architecture was possible by the presence of two leading figures of that period, Wassily Kandinsky and Paul Klee, who were fascinated by the built landscape they had the opportunity to personally encounter in North Africa before World War I. Kandinsky and Gabriele Münter traveled to Africa in December 1904. Studies of the former, such as "Tunis, Street" or "Arab City", were carried out during their visit to Tunis. Both artists collected numerous sketches, drawings, and photographs of landscapes in El-Ariana and Sidi Bou Said and of architectural details in Booten and Kairouan. Even after the trip, Kandinsky continued to draw colored representations of Tunisian motifs. The artist recalled that "once I painted a landscape 'from my memories' better than directly from nature. So, I painted 'Old Town' and later made many Dutch and Arabic drawings".[55] This was even the case in 1909 "when in 'Improvisation 6 (African)' Kandinsky again resorted to the 'oriental' memories of his trip to Tunis".[56] Paul Klee visited Tunisia, particularly Kairouan in 1914 with August Macke and Louis Moillet. In the book on this trip that Wilhelm Hausenstein published in 1921, the author maintained that the painters were looking for an "encounter of the Latin with the world of Hannibal and the Saracens".[57] With this trip, Klee sought a "compromise of the West with the East via the Venetian, the Adriatic, perhaps even the Byzantine with Asia Minor, with Palestine and with North Africa".[58] A month before the publication of the book in November 1921, Klee was invited by Walter Gropius to join the Bauhaus school, and it is well known that, from then on, his teaching role in the school would have increasing importance.

It can be argued that the dispute over the flat roof began in 1922, when it was being used increasingly frequently by German modernist architects. Mies van der Rohe did so in the cases of the Peterman, Lessing, and Eliat houses in 1922–1923. In 1922, in "Mitteilungen des Deutschen Werkbundes", Theodor Heuss echoed the fierce opposition that this trait generated, warning that "the Association for the Protection of the Fatherland has announced the need to unleash a protest against the 'flat and eastern' roof".[59] From the Bauhaus Exhibition in Weimar that took place in 1923, the use of the flat roof began to be assumed as a modernist flag. Exhibited at the event were Georg Muche's House on the Hill (Haus am Horn) and the plan for a Bauhaus housing complex in Dessau, by Hungarian artist Fred Forbat. This plan was not built but was made up of a group of cubic houses on a hill, similar enough to what would later be Mies's project, not to ignore it as a precedent of the Weissenhof in Stuttgart. The house, on the contrary, was a very controversial construction. Although it has often been attributed to Walter Gropius, it was actually carried out against the ideas of the school director, as a result of a vote that took place between students and teachers on different projects, in which Gropius's proposal was rejected. The symmetrical composition of Muche's project is usually attributed to some affinity with the classical world, as well as to a relationship with Roman precedents due to its organization around a central atrium. But Muche was a member of the Expressionist movement and a young but leading figure in "Der Sturm" circle. Considering his active membership in the pre-Islamic Persian cult of Mazdaznan along with Johannes Itten, other references for the house should not be ruled out. On the one hand, with its flat roofs and pyramidal shape, it does not look so much like a Roman house but like a ziggurat; on the other, its square floor plan with rooms surrounding a courtyard was one of the typical forms of the Iraqi houses that were known in the Berlin environment at the time, thanks to the studies and publication of Oscar Reuther's *Das Wohnhaus in Bagdad und anderen Städten des Irak* (1910) or Felix Langenegger's *Die Baukunst des Irak* (1911), among others.

But there is another, more problematic example of the use of the flat roof in 1923 that needs to be taken into consideration. I am referring to the famous project by Mies van der Rohe for the Concrete Country House. Two issues must be analyzed here. The first is the drastic change that Mies's architecture underwent in that period. It has been argued that in this case his use of the flat roof had the precedent of his project for the Kröller Müller Villa, from 1914, a project whose apparently flat roof must obviously be related to the precedents of his teacher Peter Behrens and to the architecture by Karl Friedrich Schinkel. However, between Kröller Müller and the Country House, that line suffered an interruption. After the 1914 project, Mies used traditional sloping roofs for all his buildings and never returned to the flat roof throughout the almost ten years that passed until the work on the Country House. It is well known that this house is part of a series of projects in which its author experimented with varied materials, postulating a radical rejection of traditions but also the need to prioritize construction and matter in architecture. Precisely in open opposition to the artistic inclinations of many of his colleagues, Mies thereby rejected any kind of "aesthetic" justification for the new architecture.

As was acutely observed by Detlef Martins, Mies's sudden passage from tradition to avant-garde in the early twenties can be explained by his perception of being rejected by the most advanced circles in Berlin.[60] This change was expressed in his subsequent approach to the Dada group. Mies's explicit constructive postulate and, consequently, his experiments with varied materials (concrete, glass, brick) should not be confused with the real problems he had to solve, much less with his aesthetic preferences. From the point of view of the aesthetic debates in which he was immersed at that time, the Concrete Country House is a hybrid between the architectural principles derived from "Cubism" and those derived from "Neoplasticism". The adoption of the flat roof is not an exclusive result of its "constructive" postulates but, on the one hand, must be understood by the need to find a clear roof solution to the contorted composition of the floor plan (a composition that would have determined a complicated solution if employing pitched roofs), and on the other, more importantly, must have also been conditioned by his adherence to an abstract, non-figurative aesthetic.

In addition to his relations with the German avant-garde groups, Mies was strongly linked to the Dutch groups. It is not a random coincidence that he "Dutchified" his name precisely in those years. However, in the Netherlands the inclination toward a "cubist" or "neoplastic" approach to architecture was a matter of debate. Van Doesburg had worked closely with J.J.P. Oud until both artists broke off their relationship because the former believed in the possibility of a neoplastic architecture, while the latter believed that, in relation to painting, architecture was a more complex activity that could not be "reduced" to neoplastic postulates. On the contrary, Oud was convinced that the attention of architecture should be directed toward Cubism as a more appropriate source of inspiration. In 1918 the magazine De Stijl published a project for a house with a flat roof, the work of Jan Wills,[61] in 1919 a flat roof version of Robert van't Hoff's Bush House (Huis ter Heide),[62] and in the same year two sculptures by Vantongerloo that constituted stimulating attempts at the articulation between cubism, neo-plasticism, and architecture. Starting from his unsought relationship with the vernacular "Cubist" architecture of the Middle East in the Villa Allegonda, Oud continued his "Cubist" investigations in small house projects, but his most important proposal after that experience was the project of a factory in Purmerend from 1919 and a warehouse and distillery in 1920.[63] If we compare the Oud factory with Theo van Doesburg's Maison d'Artistes exhibited in 1925, it is possible to observe that, while the former was anchored to the earth, the latter was ideally supposed to float in an infinite non-gravitational space. In the eyes of architects, it was tectonic determination that separated Cubism from Neoplasticism.

Mies's project for the Concrete Country House is "Cubist" because of its general tectonics and its grip on the floor. However, the horizontal windows that interrupt the continuity of the corners, along with the cantilevered entrance canopy, were neoplastic features, aimed at achieving a combination of elements "in the air". As is evident in his writings about this project, Mies was aware of the risky and problematic construction solution that he had to invent for the flat roof, not only because of the special thermal insulation that the use of concrete made necessary but also

126 *Essay 3: Orientalism and Modern Architecture*

Figure 4.9 Concrete country house. Mies van der Rohe. As presented in *Mies in Berlin*, the catalogue of the exhibition with this name curated by Terence Riley and Barry Bergdoll, The Museum of Modern Art, New York, 2002, p. 191.

because of his determination to generate continuity between the wall and the roof to make the volumes more abstract, which forced him to bring the water toward the center of the surfaces, which as any builder knows, only in distant appearance or in concept can they be considered absolutely flat in wet weather.[64] On the contrary, in 1923 it was already clear that, if it was a matter of responding to the nature of the material, the best applications of reinforced concrete led to the creation of continuous membranes and not discontinuous associations of beams, columns, and vertical and/or horizontal flat surfaces. The works of Hennebique and Perret were too well known for Mies to be unaware of their existence. That the project in reinforced concrete constituted for Mies a problem that was not satisfactorily resolved in the Country House is shown by the fact that although he tried to use it in a series of his houses from the 1920s (albeit hybridized with brick), in practice, he returned to using that material only nearly three decades later. It would be the use of steel that would allow him an adequate relationship between his constructive and aesthetic ideas. Hence his project for the "Weissenhof Siedlung" represents his farewell to cubism: in the following year of 1929, with the Barcelona pavilion, Mies would find the synthesis that he had been so intensely searching for.

During 1923 another house with a flat roof was built, this time with a more direct relationship with the Middle East. Indeed, the Sternefeld House was the first in which Erich Mendelsohn applied this resource, abandoning his previous commitment to curvilinear and organic forms, as he had expressed in his Einstein Tower of 1921, although paradoxically it was also inaugurated in 1923. Jewish militant who throughout his life manifested a deep commitment to his Middle Eastern roots, in that same year Mendelsohn visited Egypt and Palestine in the company of Hendrikus Theodorus Wijdeveld. Mendelsohn summed up his East–West integration program in the preface to his enthusiastic book *Amerika*.

The debate about the non-European relevance of the flat roof reached its most explicit expression as a result of an initiative by Walter Gropius. In 1926 the director of the Bauhaus decided to take the discussion outside of Germany, aiming at the internationalization of the problem. The flat roof should thus lose its local characterization as a typically Middle Eastern resource to become a universal and idiosyncratic feature of modern architecture. For this Gropius presented the topic in the magazine *Die Bauwelt*, proposing a five-point questionnaire. Alluding to the examples that he had presented in his book *International Architecture* the previous year, Gropius defended the flat roof as an aesthetic resource that should belong to all the architects of the world and not be reduced to a single region. In his article Gropius clearly stated his demand for a cubic shape and a flat roof as a requirement that could achieve a good technical resolution, and it was this technical justification that he sought with his questionnaire. Faced with those who, according to him, argued that "this eastern shape roof did not correspond to the Nordic area", he maintained that numerous "practical experiences have shown, however, that these assumptions have no validity".[65]

The opinions collected by the Gropius questionnaire were published in a special issue of *Das Neue Frankfurt* (The New Frankfurt: a monthly magazine for the problems of metropolitan construction) with the title "The flat roof", in 1927. The "crème de la crème" of modern architects participated in the issue, most of them trying to justify the adoption of this appeal through technical, economic, and functional arguments. Le Corbusier was among the few who recognized that the use of reinforced concrete made it possible to build "an oriental garden full of powerful beauty".[66] André Lurçat was the only one who admitted the importance of the "oriental influence" in the preference for the flat roof in modern architecture. Even more in his presentation he attributed to "nationalist" (European) prejudices the resistance to admitting such influence. For Lurçat it was necessary to recognize the "oriental configuration" of the flat roof, but in his opinion

> with these new means of our technique we are returning to an ancient tradition, and in this way we are unconsciously returning to the sources, to

Figure 4.10 Magazine cover. "Das neue Frankfurt: internationale Monatsschrift für die Probleme kultureller Neugestaltung", 1.1926/1927. Special Issue: "The Flat Roof". Published by Englert und Schlosser, Frankfurt (Universitätsbibliothek Heidelberg).

the land itself. (…) Our best useful configurations, which bring us closer to the eternal meaning of architecture, – he admitted – have taken us naturally towards the East, where the path of our civilization comes from, and from whose eternal forms we come.[67]

Who Owns the Mediterranean?

In the preceding paragraphs we have been able to observe that certain extra-European cultural experiences and images must be considered to understand the dense web of philosophical, technical, political, social, and economic considerations that explain the emergence of one of the constitutive features of modern architecture. These experiences and images were given different names: Saracen, Oriental, Arab, Algerian, Islamic, Ottoman, Persian, Moroccan, and even Italian or Spanish. We also saw that these designations were preferred in German-speaking countries, seeking in them the basis for an alternative position to the Latin heritage identified with the cultural hegemony of France in European culture until well into the 19th century. In parallel or rather as the flip side of that search, an alternative formulation was created. This alternative was, and continues to be, the concept of "Mediterranean" (Mediterranée) as a countercultural offensive in relation to Mitteleuropa, of German origin, as an attempt to establish itself at the center of modern times. Starting from the idea of "Mediterranean", the local diversity and the multiple and complex manifestations along the coast of that sea were unified as belonging to a single essential unit. Under this unifying conceptual umbrella, the discussion would later shift toward the determination of the most appropriate character of that synthesis.

However, the idea of this possible "Mediterranean" unity is currently being contested by many anthropologists such as João de Pina-Cabral, who rhetorically wonders: "Are the Algarve mountaineers more like Moroccans than like minhotos? Are Andalusians more like Tunisians than like Gallegos? Are the Pisticcesi more like Libyans than like Piedmontese? Are Greeks more like Egyptians than other Balkan peoples?"[68] For Michael Herzfeld "those who sell the images of this [Mediterranean] quintessence to Western European and North American tourists have rarely hesitated to exploit the uniformly romanticized image of a 'Mediterranean culture'".[69] Herzfeld argues that "the creation of this stereotype (…), also serves the interest of the industrialized nations who patronize the Mediterranean lands".[70] Of course, it is not by chance that the construction of the idea of the "Mediterranée" begins with the disappearance of the Ottoman Empire and the occupation of the Middle East by Western powers. Following Anne Ruel, we can say that "the invention of the Mediterranean" took place throughout the 19th century, transforming into a noun that until then had been used as an adjective.[71]

In the construction phase of a Mitteleuropa alternative to the Latin/rational/French hegemony in European culture, it was Friedrich Nietzsche who installed the Mediterranean as an exceptional civilizational core. However, according to Georg Stauth and Marcus Otto, Nietzsche reinvented classical Greek culture as a perfect expression of the Mediterranean articulation of East and West. For these scholars "Nietzsche located the Dionysian principle on the 'eastern' side of the Mediterranean, to distance this principle from its specific Greek gestation".[72] Nietzsche's continual appeal to "the light of the south" is well known, especially in relation to music. It is enough to remember his exaltation of Bizet in "The Case of Wagner": "Il faut méditerraniser la musique!"[73] But it should not be forgotten that Nietzsche's was a European project. In *Beyond Good and Evil* he praised Bizet for having discovered "a piece of the South in music". And in the following aphorism he imagines "a super-Germanic music, (…) a super-European music which holds its own even in the presence of the brown sunsets of the desert, whose soul is akin to the palm tree and can be at home and can roam with great and beautiful, lonely beasts".[74]

Ruel has called it "an invention of geographers" and has explained how this invention was initially applied by Conrad Malte-Brun.[75] From the point of view of French scientific geography, it was only after 1876 when the Mediterranean was recognized as that great mediator "that moderates the climates of all the coastal areas to which it facilitates access".[76] In 1908 Elisée Reclus[77] was the *first* "geographer who consecrated the Mediterranean as an autonomous object of study", even conceiving it as "a historical, economic and cultural space".[78] In his detailed study, Ruel uses a quote from Pignaud that allows him to synthesize his idea of "Mediterraneity" as a historical and therefore variable construction, a myth:

> The Mediterranean, in other times, meant balance, measure, harmony; it is enough to open a newspaper to see that today it means discord. (…) Reflecting on the Mediterranean, analyzing this vague and seductive concept, whose prestige is all the stronger the more its content is questioned, means questioning the relationships between real and imaginary, between a desired existence and a lived existence. (…) The Mediterranean, finally, is nothing more than the image that we make of it.[79]

In 1902 the renewed French expression "la Mediterranée" acquired what is considered its most accurate representation in Aristide Maillol's sculpture of a woman, called precisely "la Mediterranée". For writers such as Robert Rey or Octave Mirabeau, the qualities of that woman would be strength, serenity, and health.

After World War I and the defeat of Germany, the rejection of the "Nordic" components as causes and symptoms of decadence expanded under the influence of thinkers such as Charles Maurras. For him

> Latins were represented as a people shaped by the land, unified by the sunlight they shared. (…) Instead of race and other restrictive categorizations, Latinists offered a dedication to the particularity and externality, to the forms of nature and the objects and spaces of daily life.[80]

It is important to remember that this contrast between the Germanic world, experienced in the immediate post-war period as "decadence" and the strength of the "luminous south", was equally decisive in what would be one of the greatest versions of the Mediterranean as a whole. We are referring of course to the work of Fernand Braudel. He himself acknowledged that he "could have been a historian of Germany. (…) But I did my military service in the occupation troops of the Rhineland, and I had a certain disillusionment with Germany (…) and in the end I stayed with the Mediterranean".[81] And it was in Algeria, immediately after that German experience, that Braudel "discovered" the Mediterranean in the early 1920s, stationed there as a professor after graduating. As Giuliana Gemelli has keenly observed "Braudel was nothing more than a man from the north enchanted by the Mediterranean, (…) The Mediterranean was not a space for him, but above all a homeland that could shelter his 'many roots'".[82] Many studies have been carried out on the "Mediterranean" components and impulses in Le Corbusier's architecture, and there is no doubt about his identification, in the late twenties, with the idea of a Mediterranean/Greek/Latin/French architecture as opposed to a cold "Germanism" in step with the ideas of Maurras.

With subtle differences that same interpretation was assumed by leading figures in Italy. Michelangelo Sabatino demonstrated the importance that several of them, such as Virgilio Marchi and Fortunato Lepero, gave to the vernacular constructions of Capri since the early twenties, paradoxically as inspiration for Futurist projects. In 1931 Carlo Enrico Rava introduced an "imperial" approach to the same topic. For him it was nonsense to copy the classical Roman or Moorish architecture in the Italian colonies, where the local architecture was perfectly modern and appropriate to its climatic and technical conditions, and where, in addition, the vernacular houses were, in his opinion, "a reinterpretation of the Roman domus".[83] Paradoxically, the fact that the Italians used these North African vernacular constructions as a reference, with their classical plan and central courtyard, was nothing more than a return to their own sources.[84] Taking a humanist/populist point of view, Giuseppe Pagano for his part introduced in 1935 a different interpretation of vernacular architecture. For Pagano, it was the problem of reproducibility or industrial repetition that should have prompted modern architects to look at those constructions that he considered truly modern, like the "type objects" promoted as examples by Le Corbusier.[85]

There was also a Jewish "Mediterranean". And this is the one that Erich Mendelsohn favored against the conception of Jewish architects in Palestine who, like Arieh Sharon or Julius Posener, wanting to represent Israel as a modern nation, adopted the "international style", and rejected any kind of "Oriental" references because they were linked to Arab nationalism. "Posener quickly dismissed the Arab village as a model for Jewish settlers in Palestine, dismissing Palestinian Arabs as having any authoritative knowledge of architecture".[86] In the opposite direction, Mendelsohn sought to transfer his Zionist conceptions derived from Martin Buber to his architectural ideas. In the words of Alona Nitzan-Shiftan, "Buber professed that the 'great spiritual traditions' of the Orient would act as a balance to the materialistic excesses of the West and suggested that Jews were the mediating agents of that mission".[87]

Between 1931 and 1934 Mendelsohn was involved together with Wijdeveld and Amedée Ozenfant in the creation of the Académie Européenne Mediterranée (AEM) (Mediterranean European Academy) to counterbalance a "classical" approach to what they judged to be an excessively technical evolution of the Bauhaus in Berlin. Mendelsohn was by then disenchanted with regard to the possibilities of a technologically oriented modernism. "Technology – he lamented – established the predominance of a materialistic conception of life, which puts the question of the purpose of life over life itself".[88] The AEM settled in Cavaliere, in a building conceived by Wijdeveld, but it was destroyed by fire and in 1933 Mendelsohn was forced to flee Germany. From that moment onward he turned his attention to Palestine, reinforcing his belief in the possibility of recovering the modern project through the search for its roots in the Eastern side of the sea. In this new phase of his career, the alternative should be based on "villages untouched by civilization" and he sought such "eternal" laws in the architecture of antiquity and the vernacular architecture of the Mediterranean basin. This architecture, he believed, embodied fundamental principles rather than academic rules. As a Jewish Palestine, he thought this would be the perfect blending of the material achievements of the West with the eternal truths of the East.

And there was also, of course, a Spanish appropriation of the Mediterranean. This version was generated within the GATCPAC group. In the report on Ibiza published in the sixth issue of their magazine AC, the editors suggested a relationship between the façades of the J.J.P. Oud project at Weissenhof Siedlung in Stuttgart and the fishermen's houses of Sant Pol and proposed the latter as a model to follow. In his study of this topic, Antonio Piza observed that the editors "do not talk about the interior or the (hygienic) problems, nor about the particular functions that are fulfilled there". For AC "the popular Mediterranean architecture has (…) a series of constants that are repeated throughout all the Mediterranean countries, (…) countries all derived from a single civilization".[89] Finally, underlining the common characteristics of this architecture with modern architecture in another article titled "Mediterranean Roots of Modern Architecture", the magazine wondered "why has modern architecture been called Germanic?" and put forward the topic of constant characteristics that would continue to be repeated to this day, namely, "modern architecture, technically, is largely a discovery of the Nordic countries, but spiritually it is Mediterranean architecture the one that inspires this new architecture".[90]

Despite the many interpretations and cultural controversies since the beginning of the 19th century, in the late twenties and early thirties, under the leadership of Le Corbusier, not only did the idea of "Mediterranée" take root as an original reference for true modern architecture, crossing out any reference to any debt to the Arab world, but while crossing out this notion, still in force to this day, an idiosyncratic "Latin soul" of that supposed cultural unit was also adopted. The victory of that paradigm was enshrined in 1933 in a well-known international event. After meeting for the third time in Brussels in 1930, the fourth International Congress of Modern Architecture took place precisely on board a ship sailing the Mediterranean. The trip began in Marseille, as a clear demonstration of the effectiveness that this idea had achieved, remaining at the center of the narrative of the history of modern architecture. Paradoxically not this time either, in truth, had it been a natural affinity arising from the "Latin soul". As a result of the most consistent research carried out on the relationship between German and Spanish modernism, Joaquín Medina Warmburg has shown that

> the voyage of the Patris II in the summer of 1933 was not an initiative of Le Corbusier, nor of his disciple Sert, nor from any other member of the Mediterranean group within CIRPAC, but from the German delegate from the Bauhaus, Marcel Breuer. His proposal had a different bias from the one that finally characterized that trip. Breuer had visited Spain at the end of 1931 and had succumbed to the fascination of the "simple and bizarre Spanish towns".[91]

But, as had already happened in the cases already mentioned, the disciple of Gropius also warned that the root of these architectures should be sought further south and later continued his journey to Africa. From there he wrote to Ise Gropius

> In Tetouan I was overcome by the impression of this white city. I admired the faces of the Arabs, their pride, their filth, their laxity. Nothing to the left or right of the road, villages, blacks, nomads, Abd-el Krim's messengers on horseback.[92]

Notes

* This work was first presented at the symposium 'Making Europe: The Global Origins of the Old World' organized by Sven Beckert, Dominic Sachsenmaier, Julia Seibert at the Freiburg Institute for Advanced Studies, Albert-Ludwigs-Universität Freiburg in May 2010, and was published the same year (See Acknowledgments). We reproduce it without modifications because although various subsequent studies related to the topic have been disclosed, the ideas and/or data presented in them do not substantially alter the hypotheses we attempt to sustain.
1 SCHULZE, 1985, 96.
2 Ibidem.
3 SOLA-MORALES Ignasi, "Arquitectura; la especificidad mediterránea", in DUBY, 1997, 464. Author's translation (a.t.)
4 TRIGGER, 1984, 365.
5 MARCHAND, 2001, 466.
6 Ibidem.
7 CAILLIE René, *Journal d'un voyage* à *Temboctou et* à *Jenné, dans l'Afrique centrale ... pendant les années 1824, 1825, 1826, 1827, 1828 ... Avec une carte itinéraire, et des remarques géographiques, par M. Jomard*, Paris, 1830. Cited in VV.AA., 1998, 16.
8 CHANONY, 1853, 319. a.t.
9 DE LAMARTINE, 1861, 83. a.t.
10 DHERALDE, 1881, 100. a.t.
11 BRETTELL, 1986, 161.
12 CHETWODE, 1837.
13 GADOW, 1897, 126.
14 Quoted in BALLANTINE James, *The Life of David Roberts, R.A, Compiled from His Journals and Other Sources*, Edinburgh, 1896; and reproduced in KABBANI, 1994, 32.
15 RENAN, 1878, 88. a.t.
16 LANE, 1837, 18.
17 CHATEAUBRIAND, 1834, 154. a.t.
18 Quoted by PECKHAM Robert Shannan, *The Exoticism of the Familiar and the Familiarity of the Exotic. Fin-de- siècle travelers to Greece*, in DUNCAN & GREGORY, 1999, 164.
19 TODOROVA, 1997, 16.
20 GIRAUDEAU DE SAINT-GERVAIS, 1835, 164. a.t.
21 VON GOETHE, 1809. a.t.
22 TODOROV, 1993
23 BLUNT Wilfrid Scawen, *A Secret History of the English Occupation of Egypt*, New York, Alfred Knopf, 1895, 5.
24 KABBANI, op. cit.
25 THACKERAY William Makepeace, *Cornhill to Cairo*, 1847, quoted in BUGLER, 1984, 28–29.

134 *Essay 3: Orientalism and Modern Architecture*

26 DOUGHTY, 1984, 239.
27 VILLA Luisa, "Modernism, Imperialism and Wilfried Scawen Blunt", in PATEY et al., 2005, 266.
28 ALEXANDRE, 2004, 212. a.t.
29 STERNBERG (t.a.), 1908, 104–105. a.t.
30 PIETSCH, 1878, 160. Cfr. LAZAARE, 1998. a.t.
31 RUSKIN, 1878, 57.
32 Ibidem, 62.
33 MALLGRAVE, 1985, 62.
34 HERRMANN Wolfgang, "Semper und Eduard Vieweg", in BÖRSCH-SUPAN, 1976, 216–217.
35 OLBRICH Josef Maria, "Postcard from Capri", in BORSI & GODOLI, 1986, 178. Olbrich's and Hoffmann's experiences in Capri were treated by GRAVAGNUOLO B., "From Schinkel to Le Corbusier. The Myth of the Mediterranean in Modern Architecture", in LEJEUNE & SABATINO, 2010; and in POZZETTO, 1979. On the interest of architects in Capri's vernacular houses, see also MANGONE, 2004.
36 BORSI & GODOLI, op. cit.
37 MARCHAND, 1994.
38 Ibidem.
39 LOOS Adolf, "Eine neue Hausform: terrassenhaus. Das Grand-hotel Babylon", in *Die Neue Wirtschaft*. Wirn, 1 Jg. 20.12.1923, Spanish translation "El Hotel 'Grand Babylon'" (1923), in LOOS, 1972, 263.
40 Ibidem.
41 Ibidem.
42 KÜHN, 2001, 37. a.t.
43 WELZIG Maria, "Viennese Interactions", in WELZIG, 2007, 82.
44 Ibidem, 89.
45 ÇELIK, 1992, 59.
46 WIEBENSON, 1969.
47 PEHNT Wolfgang, *Die Architektur des Expressionismus*, Arthur Niggli Verlag, Stuttgart, 1973.
48 MARCHAND, 2001, 469.
49 LAUWERIKS, 1919.
50 POMMER & CHRISTIAN, 1991, 40.
51 ALLEN, 1983.
52 PEHNT, 1971.
53 SCHULTZE NAUMBURG Paul; "Mein baukünstlerisches Vermächtins. Das Dach", in BORRMANN, 1989. A description of the story of the "dispute" over the roof plane in Germany in POMMER, 1983.
54 HEGEMANN, 1927.
55 BARNETT, 1996, 36. a.t.
56 BRUCHER, 1999, 200.
57 HAUSENSTEIN, 1921, 113. a.t.
58 Ibidem, 117.
59 HEUSS, 1922, 6–7. a.t.
60 MARTINS Detlef, "Architectures of Becoming: Mies van der Rohe and the Avant-Garde", in RILEY & BERGDOLL, 2001, 106–133.
61 WILLS, 1918.
62 VAN'T HOFF, 1918, 84a. a.t.
63 OUD, 1920, 88a.
64 "Der Nachteil des Eisenbetons ist seine geringe Isolierfähigkeit und seine grosse Schallleitbarkeit"; VAN DER ROHE, 1923, 1. a.t.; also TEGETHOFF, 1981. Muche's house at the Bauhaus exhibition during the same year experimented with a new type of hydraulic

isolation: Tortoleum, created in 1914 by Dr. Eduard Dyckerhoff and made with peat. But in any case the roof needed of a visible slope to quickly remove water.
65 GROPIUS, 1926.
66 LE CORBUSIER, 1927, 169. a.t.
67 LURÇAT, 1927, 175. a.t.
68 DE PINA-CABRAL, 1989, 399.
69 HERZFELD Michael, "'As in Your Own House': Hospitality, Ethnography, and the Stereotype of Mediterranean Society", in GILMORE, 1987, 76.
70 Ibidem.
71 RUEL, 1991, 7–14. a.t.
72 STAUTH & OTTO, 2008, 46. a.t.
73 NIETZSCHE, 2008, 22.
74 NIETSZCHE, 1917, 193. Also SHAPIRO, 2008.
75 MALTE-BRUN Conrad, *Précis de géographie universelle ou description de toutes les parties du monde, un plan nouveau d'après les grandes divisions du globe*, Ed. Buisson, Paris, 1812, in RUEL, 8. a.t.
76 PINGAUD Bernard, "Milieu des terres", in *L'Arc. Cahiers méditerranées*, Winter 1959, in RUEL, op. cit., 13.
77 RECLUS Elysée, "L'homme et la Terre", 6 volumes 1906–1908, in RUEL, op.cit., 8.
78 RUEL, op. cit., 9.
79 PINGAUD, op. cit., in RUEL, op. cit., 12.
80 THOMPSON, 1998, 47.
81 BRAUDEL, 1985, 43. a.t.
82 GEMELLI, 2005, 41. a.t.
83 GRESLERI et al., 1993, 273. a.t.
84 RAVA, 1931; also MCLAREN, 2002.
85 ALBINI et al., 1947.
86 NITZAN-SHIFTAN, 1996, 158.
87 Ibidem, 165.
88 HEINZE-GREENBERG, 2002.
89 ROVIRA, 1997, 60. a.t.
90 ANONYMOUS, 1935, 31.
91 Letters from Marcel Breuer to Ise Gropius (Madrid, November 4, 1931, Barcelona, November 20, 1931, and Algeciras, Winter 1931), BHA, Berlin. MEDINA WARMBURG Joaquín, "Razón y vida. El ideario de Walter Gropius en su red hispanoamericana", in MEDINA WARMBURG, 2018, 46. a.t.
92 Ibidem.

5 Essay 4: The Grand Move

How the Smithsons Contributed to the Restoration of Western Europe's Cultural Centrality (1945–1956)

Introduction

Until 1947, the Congrès Internationaux d'Architecture Moderne (CIAM, the International Congresses of Modern Architecture) mainly comprised European figures. However, after World War II, a significant transformation was necessary. Europe's loss of both cultural and political prominence it previously held during the global capitalist expansion posed the old leaders in front of a paradox: even as their ideas had meanwhile gained global traction, they found themselves contending with three emerging influential entities on the international stage of power – the United States, the Soviet bloc, and the "Third world".

This essay proposes that, stemming from an implicit debate/dialogue with the emerging "Others" of Europe in the post-war era, the young members of CIAM, operating within Team X, showcased a determined effort to reclaim Western Europe's architectural and cultural centrality. The study is divided into two sections: the first section examines the responses of CIAM leaders to the post-war changes, while the second section focuses on the perspectives of Team X. This latter segment particularly emphasizes the contributions of Alison and Peter Smithson, acclaimed for their clear insights into the issue and their influential roles within Team X. Additionally, their perspectives resonated with the prevailing anxiety in British society and culture following the dissolution of its extensive and enduring modern empire. In our view, the British context exemplifies the most compelling manifestation of the European aspiration to restore the dominant position lost due to the war.

The distress stemming from the separation of "Art" and "Life" was a defining characteristic among modern artists.[1] They perceived the closure of the Humanist cycle due to its inability to meet the demands of the modern world and maintain that intrinsic unity. Synthesizing both aspects became a crucial concern shared by the group of modernist architects convened under CIAM.[2] However, given that architecture is intertwined with a vast network of economic and political interests, realizing this ideal necessitated garnering support from governments and public opinion.

On the one end, they were those who argued that a modern, rational, and all-encompassing administration of "Life" would reconfigure the material world.

DOI: 10.4324/9781003452263-5

Advocates of this perspective emphasized establishing ties with political and social institutions. They believed that extensive social programs focusing on housing and services could only be resolved through maximal rationalization. They envisioned a new urban life, architecture, and design emerging from these processes. "Art", they argued, would no longer be confined to separate expressions (painting, sculpture, architecture, etc.) but would rather permeate every facet of the world. This reinforced the necessity for a "Plan" – a cohesive strategy aimed at overseeing the entire world. This group was identified as the "constructive" avant-gardes. Consequently, art and architecture absorbed the ideologies of "planning" that had been proliferating since the early 20th century in the United States and Europe, seeking to regulate the disorderly expansion of capitalism.[3]

Contrary to the dominance of "Life" over "Form", the opposing extreme championed radical autonomy from the rules of the Humanist past and pragmatic demands. This autonomy provided fertile ground for the emergence of a new way of seeing capable of housing and *representing* "Life". Advocates of this position delved into exploring the possibilities unleashed by this formal autonomy, promoting a fresh articulation of architecture with the arts. The main proponents of these ideas were the suprematists, neoplasticists, and expressionists.

Of course, there existed room for ambiguity as well. Prior to the war, the central role granted to artists at Walter Gropius' Bauhaus ran parallel to his pursuit of a "rational construction system". Similarly, Le Corbusier's advocacy for a close relationship with painters, sculptors, and writers in *L'Esprit Nouveau* coexisted with his own involvement in the journal *Plans*. The hypothesis proposed by Sigfried Giedion, an art historian, regarding the influence of Cubism on the construction of modern space, coexisted with his engineering background and interest in "mechanization". Needless to say, the latter figures were the key pre-war leaders within CIAM.

CIAM's Failure to Catch Up with the New Post-World War II Conditions

The outbreak of World War II led to the dispersal of the CIAM members, halting their regular congresses and thinning their contacts in Europe. However, the emigration of key figures to the United States during the 1930s, due to the expansion of totalitarian regimes in their own countries, facilitated the maintenance of their connections.[4]

During the war, the militarization of activities extended into planning and engineering, amplifying the demand for experts capable of efficiently managing the large-scale production, distribution, and utilization of goods across the globe.[5] The war promoted an accelerated industrialization in housing production, rationalization of construction methods, and distribution systems.

Following the conflict, this momentum continued to surge, as new planning structures, administrative frameworks, and technical specializations significantly impacted architecture and town planning.[6] Alessandro De Magistris pinpointed two influential texts: Ludwig von Mises's *Bureaucracy*, published in the United States in 1944, and Friedrich Hayek's *The Road to Serfdom*, released the same year in Britain. In the realm of architecture, he highlighted Henry Russell Hitchcock's "The Architecture of Bureaucracy and the Architecture of Genius", an article in the January 1947 issue of *The Architectural Review*. According to Hitchcock the traditional profile of the creative architect (the "genius") was to be joined by a new form of professional practice: "the architecture of bureaucracy".[7]

The CIAM referents found Hitchcock's dichotomy unacceptable as it portrayed a radical separation, counter to their promotion of a synthesis. In this new context, their pre-war avant-garde profile had to be concealed, while highlighting their experience and knowledge as experts.[8] To address this need, some CIAM members followed Sert, Giedion, and Léger in promoting an architecture that could efficiently accommodate programmatic requirements while also integrating monumental artistic expressions, including sculptures, bas-reliefs, mosaics, and frescoes. The experiences of Mexican muralism and Brazilian tropicalism served as inspiration for this choice.[9] This "New Monumentality" was an alternative to the dichotomy between the two trends – "artistic" and "functional/technicist" – that had been in conflict since the congress's inception in 1928 in La Sarraz.

To present the CIAM as politically and technically neutral on an international scale, they sought to expand the organization from a European focus to a global one. This required involving the United States in the CIAM and incorporating numerous non-European groups.[10]

The exiles in the United States were strategically positioned for this initial task, mainly due to their prominent positions in leading universities and their connections within the US establishment. Leveraging the presence of several members in New York working on pavilions for the 1939 International Fair, steering group meetings were arranged in Phoenixville, Pennsylvania, and New York, coinciding with the fair's opening.

A key initiative was to integrate influential figures from US-American architecture and urban planning. In 1944, US-based members formed a CIAM chapter for Post-War Relief and Planning, likely in connection with the United Nations Relief and Rehabilitation Administration (UNRRA) established earlier in 1943.[11] Moreover, to address the country's vastness and diversity, regional groups (West, Central, East) were proposed, discussing the possibility of engaging major architectural corporations like Skidmore, Owings, and Merrill, or forming an alliance with the American Society of Planners and Architects (ASPA), a group involving Serge Chermayeff, Joseph Hudnut, Josep Lluis Sert, and others, focusing on US housing and urban planning issues. While some anticipated ASPA replacing the AIA, this did not materialize.[12] There were even discussions about postponing a CIAM congress to facilitate American members' participation, as evidenced in the case of Bergamo.[13] However, all these efforts ultimately proved unsuccessful.

Since the official arrival of the "White Gods", the local U.S. sphere has been notably hesitant toward CIAM's proposals.[14] Several reasons underlie this resistance: European unfamiliarity with the long-standing, productive local planning experiences, and the robustness of the ideas and institutions that have emerged from that background; the resilience of traditions and organization within the U.S. building industry and the architectural profession; the recent and impactful planning

Figure 5.1 Second from the left Architect Minnette da Silva (Sri Lanka), the first Asian representative of CIAM. During a session of the World Congress of Intellectuals in Defense of Peace at the Wrocław University of Technology, Poland (August 25 to 28, 1948). To her right Pablo Picasso, to her left Jo Davidson and Mulk Raj Anand.

endeavors conducted under New Deal policies; and, notably, the leadership of figures such as Lewis Mumford and Frank Lloyd Wright and their followers, often at odds with CIAM's postulations.

As a consequence, most American architects and planners either overlooked CIAM's existence or disregarded their planning suggestions as overly "totalitarian", excessively intellectual, and ultimately unrealistic – deeming them as typical European concepts ill-suited to the American context.[15] This reaction is well illustrated in the severe critique of Sert's *Can Our Cities Survive* published by Carl Feiss in the *Journal of the Society of Architectural Historians*.[16]

In a telling example of these obstacles, Sert conveyed to Giedion in 1949:

> We feel there's not much to be done about the American group at the moment, but time seems to be working in our favor, and today many young people are interested in CIAM. One day we will finally have an American group representing the young people of this country. That time has not yet come.[17]

Sert's foresight proved accurate. Indeed, during the 1950s and early 1960s, these principles gained significant traction in the United States. Not by chance. This was made possible by the action of the exiled members who, serving as professors, imparted the CIAM principles to these "young people" in the most prominent architecture schools in the country. However, by then, the dissolution of the Congresses in 1959 became an irreversible reality.

Following the war's conclusion, Eastern Europe emerged as another critical territory that CIAM leaders aimed to address to solidify their leadership. Both the Soviet Union and the "people's democracies" played crucial roles in the tasks of reconstruction, in which these leaders sought to play a significant part.[18]

The historical narrative of CIAM's relationship with Eastern Europe can be delineated into two distinct periods, demarcated by the war. In the initial decades of the 20th century, the Russian and later Soviet artistic and architectural avant-gardes played integral roles in shaping the inception of the new architecture. This involvement created a dense network of connections with Western Europeans, culminating in the organization of the first CIAM meeting in La Sarraz. El Lissitsky was among the early advocates of establishing an international organization for modern architects. However, both he and Moisei Ginsburg were invited to the inaugural Congress, but they were unable to attend as the Swiss government denied them entry visas.

Representatives from nations later incorporated into the Soviet orbit actively participated in the five Congresses held before the outbreak of conflict. These delegates epitomized the advanced architectural discourse in Eastern Europe during this period. Notable participants included Farkas Molnar, Marcel Breuer, and György Masirevich from Hungary; Symon and Helena Syrkus, Roman Piotrowski, and Josef Szanajca from Poland; Jaromir Krejcar, František Kalivoda, and Vladimir Antolic from Czechoslovakia; along with Ernest Weismann and Vladimir Antolic from Yugoslavia.

Moreover, this phase witnessed the direct engagement of several key CIAM figures in the Soviet Union. Le Corbusier's contributions are widely acknowledged, particularly through his work on the Centrosoyuz and his involvement in the Palace of the Soviets competition.[19] Additionally, the organized German architectural brigades led by Ernst May, and the presence of ABC members such as the Swiss Hannes Meyer and Hans Schmidt, enriched this interconnected network.

Nevertheless, as a consequence of Stalin's consolidated leadership, "nationalism" and "socialist realism" were adopted as the official cultural line of the USSR by the Communist Party of the Soviet Union in the early thirties. This led to a division within the CIAM, with those like Meyer and Schmidt advocating for these policies on one side, and those who continued to support abstraction in art while opposing a Marxist approach to urban planning on the other side. Furthermore, in 1932, a resolution by the Central Committee of the Communist Party established the Union of Architects of the USSR as the exclusive representative body for Soviet professionals, barring individual participation in other associations such as CIAM.

According to Marcela Hanáčková,

> at a Soviet conference on Western architecture in January 1934, stressing the differences between himself and Le Corbusier, Lurçat said: "Le Corbusier speaks of authority, I speak of the dictatorship of the proletariat".[20]

Despite this divergence, there was an attempt in 1935 to organize one of the congresses in Moscow. This effort was supported by Lázar Kaganovich, who aimed to sustain Soviet Union support among Western leftist intellectuals.

However, this endeavor failed to secure an agreement with CIAM leaders. The ongoing war and the extension of Soviet influence into the so-called people's democracies halted these discussions and the organization of the Congresses.

Following the war, at the behest of Polish representatives Symon and Helena Syrkus, several CIAM members were enlisted as "experts" to participate in the post-war reconstruction plans for Warsaw.[21] The Syrkus couple, in 1946, journeyed to Denmark, England, and the United States, fostering collaborations for this initiative. In the spirit of the anti-fascist alliance, the Syrkus presented an exhibition of the Warsaw project at the Library of Congress in Washington, DC, advocating solidarity with the "socialist camp" and the new Eastern "people's democracies". Philipp Goodwin and Lewis Mumford organized meetings in their residences with the Syrkus and local left-wing intellectuals, aligning with a strong presence of left-wing organizations in England and the United States, such as the British-Soviet Friendship Association, the American-Soviet Friendship Association, and the French-Soviet Friendship Association. Notably, within the realm of planning in the United Kingdom, the Architecture and Planning Group of the Society for Cultural Relations between the British Commonwealth and the USSR was established in 1945.[22] Additionally, the Architects Committee of the National Council of American-Soviet Friendship emerged in New York in 1943.[23]

However, this amicable atmosphere began to change swiftly, implying shifts within CIAM as well. After succeeding Franklin D. Roosevelt in the presidency of the United States, Harry Truman adopted Winston Churchill's doctrine expressed in his "Iron Curtain" speech during a visit to this country on March 5, 1946, illustrating the inevitable global division into two opposing camps. Concurrently, Andrei Zhdanov declared the existence of "two irreconcilable camps" in his speech to the Congress of European Communist Parties at Szklarska Poreba, Poland. The ascendancy of the Communist Party in China in 1949, following the defeat of the Kuomintang (KMT), further solidified the emergence of the new international climate commonly referred to as the "Cold War".

Due to the increased involvement with the United States that we have previously described, understanding the debate within the CIAM during this period necessitates consideration of this significant shift in the political climate. In 1938, the House Un-American Activities Committee was established in this country. Initially intended as a temporary entity, it became a permanent institution by 1945. Its purpose was to investigate and prosecute alleged subversive activities by individuals or organizations affiliated with the Communist Party of the United States. The function of this committee peaked between 1953 and 1954 with the creation of the Committee on Government Operations under the leadership of Senator Joseph McCarthy, leading to anti-communist persecutions that affected numerous architects, including Paul Revere Williams, Frank Wilkinson, and Gregory Ain. And even a group named Citizens against Socialist Housing successfully halted Richard Neutra's Elysian Park Heights housing development in Los Angeles.[24]

142 *Essay 4: The Grand Move*

For CIAM members in exile in the United States seeking support from other architects in the country, this political context deepened their differences with their Marxist colleagues within the organization.

Tensions were evident at the first post-war Congress in Bridgwater in 1947 after it was decided that it would not be held in Czechoslovakia. Reflecting the growing unrest, Helena Syrkus was appointed vice-president of the Congresses, despite her noticeable absence. During their earlier visit to the United States, she and her husband met Gropius, with Helena, noting that he had "become – in the course of 15 years, an American, not only formally".[25]

The peak of polarization between East and West appeared at the Bergamo Congress. In 1948, a communist regime was installed in Czechoslovakia, the Berlin

Figure 5.2 From left to right: Josep Lluis Sert, Claudius Petit, Sigfried Giedion, and Le Corbusier. VII CIAM, Bergamo, July 22–31, 1949. The CIAM Collection. (CIAM-D005-0002), photographer unknown (courtesy of the Frances Loeb Library, Harvard University Graduate School of Design).

blockade was initiated by communist Germany, and a Peace Congress in Poland united leftist intellectuals and artists worldwide. In Italy, the Christian Democratic Party, backed by the United States, won the first post-war national elections, displacing the Communist Party from its previous government positions. During the Congress in Bergamo, Helena Syrkus advocated for "socialist realism" and a radical change within CIAM, proposing to abandon modernist formalism, recognize the impact of class struggle in cities, and reconstitute the organization as the International Congresses of Social Architecture and Social Planning. The Italian Communist Party mobilized architects and architecture students from all over the country to Bergamo to defend these positions. This attempt for a pro-socialist shift was supported by the left wing of the congresses, including Mart Stam, André Lurçat, Hans Schmidt, Karel Teige, Jaromir Krejcar, and Hannes Meyer, despite his non-participation at the time. Giedion later acknowledged,

> On the hot afternoon of July 29, 1949, the discussion within the city hall also became heated as two different attitudes towards art made themselves evident. It became clear that aesthetic problems are not just personal affairs but part of our attitude towards the world, merging, sometimes tragically, into politics.[26]

As a result of the confrontations in Bergamo, representatives of the "people's democracies" in the CIAM Permanent Council, including Helena Syrkus for Poland, Josef Fischer for Hungary, and Josef Havileck for Czechoslovakia, declined to participate in the subsequent congress in Hoddesdon, England, in 1951.

The task of integrating new groups from territories that would later be recognized as the "third world" achieved some success but paradoxically led to the demise of the CIAM congresses.

The first post-war CIAM in England (Bridgwater, September 1947) included representatives from Canada, Algeria, India-Ceylon (India had declared independence in August), Argentina, and Cuba, alongside European countries that had participated in the pre-war congresses. The VIIth Congress in Bergamo in 1949 lacked significant involvement from non-European figures but showcased projects from Morocco, Brazil, Argentina, Colombia, and Peru by Ecochard, Le Corbusier, and Sert. In the subsequent VIII Hoddesdon Congress in 1951, new groups like those from Colombia and Israel were included. However, the most significant success in CIAM's expansion occurred at the IXth Aix-en-Provence Congress in 1953, boasting an organization of nearly 3,000 followers from 31 countries with an attendance of 250 participants.[27]

Ironically, this numerical success instigated a crisis in hegemony. Jean-Lucien Bonillo suggests that "the diversity of social statuses, cultures, and approaches was one of the reasons (for the) failure of CIAM 9 and the impossible consensus".[28] Similarly, Giedion acknowledged, "The onslaught of the younger generation was sometimes so violent that we were embarrassed to face it".[29]

Faced with the evident crisis in the roles of Le Corbusier, Giedion, Sert, and Gropius in upholding European centrality, the Aix-en-Provence Congress signaled

144   Essay 4: The Grand Move

to the young members of Team X the urgent need to reestablish that centrality through a significant theoretical shift. The lively and carefree presence of the younger generation and the famous striptease at the end of the party on the terrace of the Unité d'Habitation seemed to have unsettled the Dutch delegation.[30] However, there was a deeper reason for this shift: the modernist principles and language of the "founding fathers" had transformed into an "international style". Yet, these principles and language no longer represented societies experiencing the most advanced modernization processes. Instead, cities like Ibadan, Chandigarh, Cape Town, and Rio de Janeiro demonstrated how these principles and language could be enriched in diverse geographical contexts.

In this context, the significance of the Latin American nations demands special attention, particularly due to their substantial role within the emerging international organizations in the immediate post-war years. Apart from India, these countries held a significant number of votes capable of shaping critical decisions in the realm of construction and planning. This was apparent in various positions of authority, such as Colombian Eduardo Zuleta Angel's chairing of the United Nations commission for constructing the organization's headquarters in New York. Notably, it was Zuleta Angel himself who extended the offer to Le Corbusier to design the Plan for Bogotá.[31] Similarly, Mexican Manuel Torres Bodet held the position of secretary general of UNESCO during the construction of its headquarters in Paris.[32] It is probable that Sert's proposal to Gropius in 1949 to hold the next Congress in 1951 in Colombia, Cuba, or Peru was both to solidify his position in the region and because of the vibrant intellectual atmosphere found in Latin America.[33]

When it came to forming the team for the United Nations building, the presence of Latin Americans was crucial. Oscar Niemeyer and Julio Villamajó, representing Brazil and Uruguay respectively, were two of the ten participants involved in this endeavor.[34] During the Bridgwater Congress Wiener observed that

> Most of the educated classes in Latin America were the ruling classes, so that the great many of the earnest young men were now in ministerial positions, and all the young groups consistently worked along CIAM lines. (…) Governments changed rapidly (in Brazil), but dictators or democrats or whatever they were, they all wanted to plan on the right lines.[35]

Additionally, the leaders of the organization recognized the importance of garnering the support of young Latin Americans in their disputes with the younger Western Europeans during the Congresses. In his correspondence with Le Corbusier in preparation for the Bergamo Congress, Sert noted, "Your cooperation and that of ASCORAL will put (the) CIAM back on the right track and get them out of the analytical impasse. All the Latin groups have aligned on your side with the French group".[36]

In his book *A Decade of New Architecture* (1951), Sigfried Giedion summarized the Bridgwater Congress pointing out what he perceived as a regression that had taken place, concealed under the guise of a "humanizing architecture" associated with Swedish production and the British "new empiricism". However, he highlighted that in the USA, in Canada and in South America a young generation (...) will have a decisive influence upon future developments. (...) The contributions that come from the soil of Finland and of Brazil are not frontier enterprises or provincialism, but works of inspiration, of new discovery.[37]

Figure 5.3 A view of the beaches of Rio de Janeiro. Cover of the first issue of *The Architectural Review* dedicated to Brazilian architecture. Vol. 95, No. 567, March 1945.

In reference to the Bergamo Congress, Sert conveyed to Giedion,

> The Latin American groups will be more numerous in the coming congresses. (…) I think we cannot continue to consider central Europe as the main field of interest for CIAM. Explanation of CIAM ideas both to east and west should be the basis for our program.[38]

The star of Latin American architecture was Brazil. After the exhibition organized by MoMA in 1943, its recognition spread worldwide through the special issues devoted to it by publications such as *The Studio* (October 1943), *The Architectural Review* (March 1944), *L'Architecture d'Aujourd'hui* (September 1947 and August 1952), *The Architectural Forum* (November 1947), and many others.[39]

Despite nearly a hundred Latin American architects being associated with CIAM in the early 1950s, prominent figures from Brazil never formally joined the organization. The weakness of CIAM during that period was notably highlighted by the jury formation for Brasilia in 1956. While Niemeyer successfully nominated his US-American friend and CIAM member, Stamo Papadaki, the other proposed CIAM member, Maxwell Fry, was ultimately replaced by William Holford, a significant figure in the London Plan. André Sive, from the Ministère de la Reconstruction et de l'Urbanisme, represented France. Neither Holford nor Sive was a member of the organization.[40]

In the post-war period, the endeavor to expand to "other groups working on these problems" encountered a paradox. As La Sarraz ideas expanded, a multitude of non-European figures adhering to those ideas emerged on the international scene, seeking inclusion in more cosmopolitan and open organizations. The Comité International des Architectes and the Réunions Internationales des Architectes (RIA) were the oldest.[41] In June 1948, the Union International des Architectes (UIA) was established, gathering over 400 architects from 30 countries during its first Congress. UIA quickly gained recognition and delegates at various international institutions, superseding CIAM as a neutral reference for large-scale architectural and urban planning requirements. Notably, the Second UIA Congress in 1951 was held in Rabat, Morocco, showcasing its internationalist spirit with the participation of 21 countries.[42]

The CIAM's ambition to guide post-war reconstruction in the realms of architecture and urban planning is evident in an early memorandum proposed by Richard Neutra and drafted by Paul Lester Wiener, where it was stated that "it is necessary that foreign governments responsible for the reconstruction of Europe recognize and accept the ideas, designs, etc. of CIAM. (…) I propose that a list of American and foreign rulers be drawn up".[43]

Contacts between the CIAM leadership group and UN authorities predated the establishment of UNRRA, its wartime predecessor. Between 1944 and 1947, Ernst Weissmann, a participant in pre-war CIAM meetings representing Yugoslavia, served as the Director of the Industrial Rehabilitation Division of UNRRA. In exile in the United States since 1939, Weissmann had collaborated with José Luis Sert on a housing block project in New York. As the director of Housing, Urban, and

Territorial Planning at the United Nations, Weissmann facilitated the hiring of his former partner, and CIAM president, as the expert designer for the Havana Plan.

Other significant figures linked to CIAM during the founding years of the United Nations included Richard Neutra, Arne van der Goot, Gunnar Myrdal, and his wife, Alva Reimer Myrdal. Neutra participated in the San Francisco Conference of 1945 where the United Nations was established. Van der Goot, a representative of the United Nations at the 1951 CIAM, had strong connections to Gropius and Sert. The Myrdals were acquainted with Sven Markelius, a Swedish CIAM member, and had undertaken a cooperative housing project. Alva succeeded van der Goot, and Gunnar served as the secretary of the UN Economic and Social Council from 1947.[44]

CIAM leaders seized an opportunity to gain international recognition during the construction of the UNESCO headquarters in Paris. UNESCO engaged Walter Gropius and a group from the Congresses to collaborate on a project.[45] In March 1947, Julian Huxley, UNESCO's President, was approached by CIAM authorities to propose forming a UNESCO committee focusing on planning and architecture.[46] Subsequently, UNESCO organized an international conference on this subject in Mexico in November 1947. The influence of CIAM leaders on official architectural education persisted notably in the 1950s and 1960s. As late as 1959, advisors like Sert and Reginald Isaacs were involved in establishing a school of architecture in Puerto Rico.

UNESCO's commitment to fostering global cultural cooperation aligned with the idea of the "integration of the arts", shared by Giedion and other CIAM members. Consequently, CIAM played a pivotal role in the 1952 International Conference on the Arts in Venice.[47] Moreover, CIAM was frequently sought for its expertise, particularly in housing planning and construction. It was consulted as an expert in housing planning by Alva Myrdal for the United Nations in 1950.[48] Additionally, CIAM was invited to prepare an exhibition on urban planning in Geneva in 1952[49] and was called upon by the UN and UNESCO to collaborate in studies on urbanization and housing in New Delhi in 1953.[50] Moreover, members of CIAM met with UN-related officials in Geneva in 1952 to outline a program to improve services for economically weak groups in the eastern Mediterranean and Africa.

Nevertheless, it's important to note that while the CIAM members served as key references for various departments of the United Nations in the years immediately following the war, that role diminished in later years. This decline was largely due to the emergence of other organizations we have referenced, as well as the challenges faced by the old leaders in aligning their artistic ambitions with the organization's primarily technical demands.

The trust of international organizations such as the UN and UNESCO in CIAM, as the most qualified experts in urban planning and architecture, was severely undermined due to the episode involving the UNESCO building. Rather than acting as efficient and "objective" technical professionals, the Congress leaders displayed prima donna-like arbitrariness, vying to imprint their signatures on the project. In a letter dated November 8, 1951, the Secretary General of UNESCO, Manuel Torres Bodet, informed Sert of the appointment of Eugene Beaudoin as the potential architect for the future building.[51] Sert's proposal of Le Corbusier was not accepted, prompting Torres Bodet to suggest forming a commission to supervise the studies and the selection of the architect.

Despite UNESCO consulting the International Union of Architects, the "Panel of 5" was eventually composed of Gropius, Markelius, Rogers, Costa, and Le Corbusier, all CIAM members.[52] As Sert assured Le Corbusier, it was the first time they could work in "real teamwork".[53] The "Panel" ultimately appointed Le Corbusier as the project's architect, a decision deemed unethical by various organizations, including the Royal Institute of British Architects. As an alternative, the "Panel" appointed a team of three architects: Breuer, Zehrfuss, and Nervi, leading to a dispute among CIAM leaders, mainly under Le Corbusier's pressure.[54]

The UNESCO authorities were concerned that these struggles could jeopardize the entire enterprise. Mr. Carneiro, a UNESCO diplomat involved in the headquarters process, informed Sert that "since UNESCO relied on CIAM, this matter is definitely a CIAM matter".[55] Breuer, Zehrfuss, and Nervi eventually completed their work, but tensions within the group escalated to such an extent that Giedion and Sert warned the affair "may be the end of our congresses, a rather painful, regrettable end".[56]

In summary, despite sporadic achievements, the primary post-World War II goal of CIAM, to solidify the organization and its members as the central international reference point for architecture and urbanism, remained unachieved. Ultimately, this failure stemmed mainly from their persistence in striving for a synthesis between individual creativity ("Art") and the "architecture of bureaucracy" ("Life"), a synthesis that clashed with the disenchanted concept of modernization. Furthermore, there was a political naiveté in the CIAM leaders, who, in the post-war period, failed to recognize that competition within international organizations for vital commissions extended beyond disciplinary values, mainly being an expression of the power dynamics in the Cold War.

Acknowledging these weaknesses, the young members of Team X from Western Europe accused the "founding fathers" of failing to comprehend the post-war world and advocated for radical changes within the organization. Nevertheless, it has to be noticed that the differences between these groups were not as radical as perceived: ultimately, neither side abandoned the pursuit of recovering the lost pre-modern "synthesis". At most, the younger generation proposed an alternative means to achieve it. In the end, both the former leaders of CIAM and Team X advocated for architecture and urbanism that preserved the individuality of creators, steering clear of submerging them into an administered world. Additionally, both factions shared the common objective of restoring the centrality of Western Europe within the realm of modern architectural culture.

To establish their own agenda these young architects undertook a multifaceted intellectual program. They needed to find an alternative to the principles and regulations established by CIAM while also coming to terms with what they termed "the modernist brother" or those who had embraced those rules and principles globally. Furthermore, they needed to free themselves from the European inferiority complex, both in terms of the dominating US-American influence vying for leadership in the "West" and the apparent triumph of "Eastern" comprehensive planning.

The Smithsons' Grand Move

Amid the discontent with the post-war recovery's direction, the most radical voices in British culture were anything but optimistic or celebratory of their country and society.[57] One of the most scathing assessments of the period was presented in 1961 under the impactful title *The Stagnant Society*, authored by Michael Shark, where he condemned the poverty concealed by the façade of renovation and comfort.[58] According to Robert Hewison, referencing a similar sentiment, Colin Wilson[59] straightforwardly stated, "I believe that our civilization is in decline, and that Outsiders are a symptom of that decline".[60] Shark and Wilson articulated the paradox of disappointment hidden beneath an acceptable, even desirable, surface, making it harder to overcome. For example, in one of the emblematic manifestos of the "Angry Young Men", filmmaker Lindsay Anderson, upon returning from the continent after attending the Cannes Film Festival, denounced that while great films were produced worldwide, "Britain did not appear in the list. It is six years since a British feature won a prize at Cannes".[61]

The architectural profession was not immune to this context: first, because the profile of the traditional, "creative", architect tended to be replaced by other forms of professional practice (Hitchcock's dilemma); second, because the "democratic" society rejected the forms of monumentalism that were now attributed exclusively to both Fascist and Soviet totalitarian regimes; and third, because the collective imaginary – centered on the structural feats of steel – had to be replaced by the introduction of household appliances and media.

In 1954, to the chagrin of many architects, *The Economist* proposed a brutal diagnosis in this regard. It was argued that

> of the 18,000 registered architects in Britain over half are already in salaried employment. (…) The radical school (…) foresees that more and more work will be done by departments of qualified salaried officials, or by tough "business architects", while private practice shrinks to the hard core of big consulting engineers. (…). It is not for those who appreciate the aesthetic values in architecture, a very comfortable prospect.[62]

The malaise had one of its most outstanding expressions in the Great Meeting that took place at the Royal Institute of British Architects (RIBA) in 1958, in which sectors of the new left led by Cleeve Barr and Anthony Cox launched an attack against what they called, referring to the Institute, a "cozy club for elderly private practitioners".[63] The consequence of this attack was "The architect and his office: a survey of organization", a study presented to the Council of the Royal Institute on February 6, 1962. The profession – it denounced – was then much closer to the social and earth sciences than to the dynamics and artistic fields of creativity.

In short, it became evident that the transformations that were taking place in Great Britain were far from being recognized by the architectural discipline, and especially by its specific modes of organization. One of the voices most concerned about this relative backwardness was that of James Stirling. For him "in the United

States 'functionalism' now means adaptation of the building to industrialized production processes, but in Europe (we maintain) the substantially humanistic method of designing for a specific function".[64] Stirling's analysis of the state of technological – and therefore theoretical – backwardness in which British architecture found itself was manifested in his text on the "New Regionalism", from 1957, where he admitted that

> an average [US] American family can afford a thing built with new methods and new materials. (…) In our country, on the other hand, the decline of technology, particularly in building and civil engineering, is forcing architects to move away from a radical perspective. (…) As a nation, we probably have the architecture we deserve (…) ((Today we) do not belong to the great currents of modern architecture.[65]

"Unfortunately" – he would bitterly recognize in a text the following year – "in the field of private building, quantitatively speaking, the state of architecture (and the status of the architect) has never been worse".[66]

After the war, Americanism in Europe – and in Britain in particular – was a product of the spontaneous reaction of gratitude and admiration by the local population toward the United States, but also of an intense diplomatic and political effort developed with the impulse of the US Government. Just as an example, in relation to the Fulbright exchange programs: "In 1949 alone (its first year of operation in the UK), it was responsible for sending 257 American professors, teachers, and students to Britain, and 237 Britons to the U.S.".[67]

Devastated, the countries of Western Europe needed American help and were even seduced by the "American way of life". But at the same time, they did not cease to resent this new situation, and the traditional European anti-Americanism experienced a new inflection.[68] Moreover, the US-Americans did not limit themselves to expanding their influence in Europe but also interfered in the decolonization movements, which accentuated the weakening of the former powers' dominance in their areas of influence in Africa, Asia, and Latin America. According to Hugh Wilford, in Britain, the work of Graham Green was one of the clearest expressions of this attitude. He points out that not by chance for the British protagonist of Green's *The Quiet American* (1955), the "Americans" are "those (big, boyish, middle-aged and) noisy bastards at the Continental (Hotel)".[69]

Moreover, British anti-Americanism was supported both from the right and the left political wings, something that can explain Peter Smithson's self-identification with the "left" and their controversies with the "communists", as we will see later. According to Hugh Wilford, "conservative intellectuals feared the threat to their own 'minority culture' presented by the democratization of cultural consumption; socialists fretted about the danger to the survival of both local folk traditions and proletarian political consciousness".[70]

In the contradictory context of competition and aid with the United States, a complicated web of feelings, ideas, and positions was woven, where lines of support and rejection often intersected with equal intensity.

Peter Smithson's "discovery of 'America'" is illustrative in this regard. It took place while he was serving in the British Army between 1942 and 1945 in the Queen Victoria's Own Madras Sappers and Miners regiment. Born in the industrial town of Stockton-on-Tees, he had begun his architecture studies in 1939 in Durham (Newcastle) and resumed them on his return from the war. The social climate in which he grew up was as "very left" as he himself characterized it. The rejection of the intricate and dirty urban environment generated by the Industrial Revolution was common, as well as through libraries and popular associations the reading (influenced by Ruskin and Morris) of literature and of the "socialists", from Bernard Shaw's *Complete Works* to texts like *Anarchy & Order* and *Poetry & Anarchism* by Herbert Read. In this context, the examples of Le Corbusier published in *L'Architecture Vivante* and those of the works published by Gropius in *The New Architecture and the Bauhaus* appeared as a worthy and hopeful alternative to the popular habitat.[71]

With the QCOMSM, Smithson went from the harsh and cold environment of Durham to the hot jungles and mountains of India and Burma. It was his first trip outside Britain, and, of course, he was impressed by both the local monumental and popular constructions.[72]

But it was the impression received from the US-Americans that left the main mark on him. Upon his arrival to Rangoon in 1945 with the allied reoccupation troops, he experienced a shocking contrast between the obsolete equipment abandoned by the British during their retreat and the

> American equipment (...) ordinary things like jeeps, trucks, bulldozers. I mean I had never seen a bulldozer before the war. (...) This kind of equipment was new to us (...). They had to be invented during the war, therefore those who were soldiers at that time experienced a kind of technical revolution.[73]

This was a technical and political experience as well. Somehow, what happened in the war showed him that his country had fallen behind in the race for progress and development.

As a result of that experience, he became aware not only of different lifestyles but also, and more decisively, of the new modes of rationalization of production and management that were coming into being. As a British study acknowledged, "a new type of man is emerging in modern communities, neither the landed aristocrat nor the independent, capital-owning entrepreneur, but the manager, the highly skilled technician".[74] And the architectural expression of this "highly skilled technician" was Hitchcock's "architecture of bureaucracy".[75]

Similar to the Smithsons, the young Western European architects of Team X were profoundly struck by the emergence of an "Americanized" world in the post-reconstruction era. Aldo van Eyck eloquently conveyed this sentiment when he observed that "there is no room for the imponderable. (...) Instead of the inconveniences of corruption and confusion, we have now obtained the tedium of hygiene".[76] According to him, buildings had been "transformed the building into

152   Essay 4: The Grand Move

Figure 5.4 "The amazing thing for me was the machinery of war – the Bailey Bridge, the vehicles, the Jeep" (Peter Smithson to Beatriz Colomina. COLOMINA & SMITHSON, 2000, 15). An announcement from the War Office published in the *Picture Post* on March 13, 1954, and held among Peter Smithson's papers in which the demountable bridges reminiscent of those used by the Army Corps of Engineers, from which he was a part during the war, can be seen. The Alison and Peter Smithson Archive. Folder E004 (courtesy of the Frances Loeb Library, Harvard University Graduate School of Design).

an additive sequence of beautiful surfaces (I find it difficult to find words for what I saw in the United States) with nothing but emptiness on either side".[77] Peter Smithson observed that "the situation of architecture in the United States (...) is that there is still a belief in a square, 'rational' architecture. (...) Even when new structural solutions are introduced (...) they are resolved in the old 'International Style' manner".[78] Exceptions, such as those seen in the works of Charles Eames or Louis Kahn, offered an "approximation to the new European way of thinking. However, from their viewpoint across the Atlantic, it seemed as if American architects mostly embraced the existing status quo of social and building types".[79] Jerzy Soltan concluded that the imperative task at hand, stating "the previous generation of CIAM had to fight an enemy outside the movement. Our task is to fight the enemy within, the 'modernist brother'".[80]

The United States also presented other intriguing elements that attracted attention from the very early meetings of the Independent Group, which the Smithsons were part of. Discussions led by Banham focused on the symbolism of Detroit cars, while Alison and Peter Smithson delved into the relationship between American advertising and architecture, and Richard Hamilton explored the styling of mass consumer products. Notably, Los Angeles and other American cities served as exemplars for the Smithsons' considerations on circulation. They advocated the necessity to "approach the American standard of mobility".[81] Jaspar Maase highlighted that "America provided the physical, ideal, and symbolic materials, arguments, and examples that were (and increasingly will continue to be) used in the Old World to articulate and cohere different interests".[82]

It has not been adequately recognized that the aspects which captivated the young British artists were frequently linked to the somewhat "wild" or "primitive" elements of the United States' modernization. In their pursuit of alternatives to established modernism, the English group looked anew at the US-American world, reviving the age-old European notion of its "lack of culture" but this time, not to dismiss it but to consider it a model worth following.

For Peter Smithson,

> the things a European most values from American culture are the throw-away objects, such as the magnificent magazines, advertising, and packages. In the refrigerators and motor cars, as in heavy earth-moving equipment and freight trains, the feeling for American values is communicated through an imagery **created without self-consciousness**. (a.e.)[83]

In reflection, Peter Smithson proposed that while the United States should be admired for its overwhelming technological development, its cultural development had not yet reached the same level to create aesthetic responses. Ironically, their admiration for the United States coexisted with an underlying anti-American sentiment, as highlighted in Guldall's study that addresses "anti-Americanism that attempts to bring about inner unity by representing the United States as Europe's constitutionally different and inferior 'other'".[84] A decade later, the Smithsons continued this thought, explaining the "American deficit" as follows: "Motor cars in general seem nearer to American design truth than buildings. In building there seems too easy an acceptance of outworn European modes, and an evasion of responsibility for creating genuine American organizational and aesthetic techniques".[85]

Nevertheless, while the United States was the most powerful player, there were others in the post-World War II game, starting with the Soviet Union and its expanded "Socialist field".

Hailing from the industrial districts of northern England, Alison and Peter Smithson harbored an authentic empathy for the working-class sectors, which led them to integrate Judith Stephen's studies of East London's neighborhoods into their thinking. Their provincial and working-class origins – external to the empire's capital – also connected them to the circle of the "angry young men". However, their unique background led to an ambivalent stance toward left-wing ideologies.

As Reyner Banham noted in 1964, this ambiguity was mirrored in his own positions during the prior decade, where his zeal for Pop clashed with his political views. His advocacy for New Brutalism was a response to "Communist doctrine" and Pevsner's viewpoints.[86] One might argue that the populist avant-gardism embodied in the Pop aesthetic clashed with the "New Humanism" inspired by Swedish labor reformism, not to mention the "realism" supported by pro-Soviet communists, similar to the Smithsons' conundrum. The Smithsons found Le Corbusier's Unité d'Habitation in Marseilles as a synthesis, combining a "progressive" high-density approach and an aesthetic that transcended the conventional modernist norms advocated by the "modernist brothers" at the Institute of Contemporary Art (ICA.) Within the London County Council, they, along with a group including Colin St. John Wilson, James Stirling, Alan Colquhoun, Peter Carter, Bill Howell, John Killick, and Gillian Sarsen, aligned themselves with the "hard" "non-Marxist" faction challenging the "softs" of the traditional left consisting of socialists and communists.[87]

Notably, following the events of 1948 mentioned earlier, a less severe version of American McCarthyism began to take root in the UK, resulting in heightened discrimination against Soviet sympathizers in key civil service positions. Stephen V. Ward's study reveals that the London County Council was filled with such sympathizers. For instance, in 1951, Monica Felton was dismissed from her position as Chairman of the Stevenage Development Corporation by Hugh Dalton, the Minister of Local Government and Planning, after her return from a visit to a prison camp in North Korea.

In their quest to foster a new European architectural avant-garde, the Smithsons championed the need to eliminate the representative structures that had gradually inflated the CIAM's size. Instead, they advocated for a more direct and "familiar" mode of understanding, which tended to involve just a limited number of Western European participants. Jerzy Soltan, a member of the Polish ASP Group (Akademia Sztuk Pięknych) with Oskar Hansen, shared numerous urban and architectural concepts akin to those held by Team X members. He was part of four of the group's 17 meetings. In addition to Soltan and Hansen from Poland, the only other Eastern European participant in Team X meetings was Károly Polónyi from

Hungary.[88] Despite their differences, Soltan and Hansen responded vehemently to Alison Smithson's "authoritarian" manner during the Bagnols-sur-Cèze Team X meeting in 1960. Hansen argued for a more democratic approach, saying, "Let us cast off the 'general's uniform' and listen to each one of us. Even should one who has the opportunity to speak remain silent, he has spoken in the opinion of all".[89] Similarly, Kisho Kurokawa, present at two Team 10 meetings, observed a destructive tendency within the group, stating, "It tends to alienate members, in some cases it drives out all but one single member".[90]

The challenges encountered by young architects in Poland prompted Soltan to seek international support and question the "conservative" stance of Helena Syrkus. However, the "sectarianism" among the principal members of Team X resulted in a sudden break with the CIAM leaders and prompted Soltan to emphasize the necessity of forming a broader alliance with the "periphery" of the Congresses. "A steady exchange of thought in the CIAM spirit", he contended, "if now just less necessary for the architects of Western Europe and the Americas, begins only to have a real importance for the architects of eastern [sic] Europe, the Middle East, India, and so on".[91] The Team X members' commitment to the "open form" deepened the divisions with the authoritarian and centralized planning of the "East", as notably observed during the Bergamo Congress. Statements such as "union movements are out of date as we approach the period of you and me" or "the open form, unlike closed difference, treats the potential energy of self-determination as a basic element, organic and inseparable" could only be entertained within a political and social context that conflicted with the ideologies of the Eastern Communist regimes.[92]

Conversely, upon assuming the role of First Secretary of the Communist Party of the Soviet Union, Nikita Khrushchev criticized "socialist realism" and actively promoted modern architecture starting from 1954, notably advocating for the extensive construction of prefabricated housing. This movement prompted a surge of "modernist brothers" to join the expanded domain of the "bureaucratic interpretation of modernism", a stance that the "angry young men" in Western Europe had set out to defeat.

The third player was the "third world".

As previously highlighted, the pursuit of total "Integration of Arts" was conceived by the leaders of the CIAM as a means to bridge the gap between "Form" and "Life" created by modernization processes. The experiences in Latin America further reinforced that belief.

However, for the young European radicals, the approach was quite the contrary. It wasn't about seeking an articulation between "experts" and "artists" but about discovering a new form of synthesis. Aldo van Eyck expressed this during the CIAM congress in Dubrovnik: "The wonderful thing about architecture is that it is an art: simply that. (…) For almost half a century, architects have been meddling with the principle of art, squeezing it into the waistcoat of semi-science".[93]

As per Peter Smithson,

between 1939 and 1949 there was no new architecture in Europe; building ceased because of the war. To see a new building that had been built during those ten years, you had to go to Scandinavia, or South America. The whole Brazilian thing occurred during the wartime period, but it was so far away.[94]

Following its exhibition in New York and various other museums in the United States, the Museum of Modern Art's "Brazil Builds" exhibition was displayed in London amid the war, sparking considerable impact and initiating a process of widespread recognition that extended for more than ten years. The RIBA, upon its inauguration, acknowledged that "in some ways this recent modern building in Brazil is even more significant than the pre-war modern building in Switzerland, Czechoslovakia or Sweden".[95]

The materials unveiled in the exhibition were the subject of an issue of The Architectural Review the following year, completely dedicated to "Brazil". The editorial comment in this issue underscored the relationship between the "canon" and Power, suggesting that the high quality of these works was due to their origination from an equally potent country. According to *The Architectural Review*

> there is no doubt that this war is going to prove (…) a rearrangement of the Balance of Power. One of the new forces to be reckoned with could be Brazil, the third largest political entity in the Western Hemisphere.[96]

While Europe was experiencing destruction and catastrophe due to the war, some saw new potential forces among the allies, including distant Latin America. Brazil, termed a "Europe in another soil and another climate", represented the search for the future beyond Europe. Brazil (as well as Mexico) expressed "mysterious" forces "because they are so rich subjects of speculation that we can always think about them, without ever reaching the end of their possibilities, past and future".[97]

Ten years after the initial exhibition, in July 1953, a new Brazilian Exhibition was presented in London, this time at the Building Center. It was another moment of acknowledgment and celebration as Brazil, "a non-industrial country (which) has blossomed out into a vigorous modern architecture (… with) strong national and climatic characteristics that are entirely its own (… and with) a refreshing absence of modernist drawing-board clichés".[98]

> To the European architect – editorialized The Architectural Review – (…) could any glass tower of medieval imagination appear as improbable as skyscrapers which are reported to have been withdrawn [there] to the vertical by hydraulic jacks resting on refrigerated quicksand.[99]

Moreover, as most colonial territories and substantial sections of Latin America were situated in tropical or subtropical zones, the functional principles were tailored to create unprecedented formal solutions. These regions naturally lent themselves to the modernist concept of transparency and fluidity between interior and exterior spaces, owing to their warm climate. In contrast, in colder or temperate areas, the extensive use of glass was essential to retain solar heat during winter.

As pointed out by Clive Entwistle, in the immediate post-war period, the brise-soleil device allowed for the true internationalization of modernist principles for the first time. This device was not just about addressing the ubiquity of modernist architecture but also opened up new plastic possibilities.[100]

The figurative sobriety of the Labor Party's public post-war architecture programs inspired by the achievements of Swedish social democracy was not welcomed by many "outsiders". Like John Boynton Priestley, they encouraged a more committed radicalism in creative activities.

Thus, when in 1955 for the first time in London Maxwell Fry presented at the RIBA the architectural results that were being achieved with the construction of public buildings in a provincial capital of the former "jewel" of the Crown such as Chandigarh, several of the commentators of the lecture remained perplexed, and not without a hint of elegant envy. One of them criticized himself by recognizing the "poor" British contribution to the solution of urban and architectural problems. Highlighting "the incredible achievement of this city of Chandigarh" he added: "Chandigarh has been built in three years, at three times the speed at which our own new towns are being built".[101] The judgment of Jane Drew about the modest architecture of the "tidy communal flats" would be terminating: will be final: "The slightly attractive, but detailed, Scandinavian prescription provides a friendly domestic feeling that scarcely it hides the underlying monotony, although this is justified by the greater lack of inspiration".[102]

Fry welcomed the contribution of a new architecture that would overcome this monotony, recognizing that it could come not only from the different conditions of climate in tropical territories but also from the contact with different cultures. Cultures that, in the new political climate of decolonization, were presented as models, not so much for the qualities of some of their objects but, as a whole, for constituting an alternative to the "western malaise". In this text, Fry was strongly critical of the architecture of the "machinist society", something that he exemplifies with the housing project of Kensal House in North Kensington (London), insofar as they were products "driven out by the nineteenth-century way of looking at the things still dominant with us, by analysis, factualism, specialization and the perpetual warfare of commerce". On the contrary, he sees in Africa, through the example of the constructions of the AmaNdebele in Pretoria, a manifestation of an "aristocratic feeling for design", concluding that the products of these people "become Works of art so firm and yet so persuasive that it is now they and not Paxiteles who fertilize the imagination of Henry Moore and Paul Klee and fill the void in our Western culture". For Fry, at the opposite pole to the "harmony" of the AmaNdebele, their environment, and their things was the

> maladjustment, the great sickness of our Western civilization, that fills the mental hospitals and half the normal hospitals, too, that peoples the psychiatrists' couches, creates **outsiders and existentialists** (a.e.) and sets a permanent frown on the brows of city dwellers half our World over.[103]

158   Essay 4: The Grand Move

In the face of such enthusiasm for a "tropical" alternative version of modernism, the Smithsons judged them with critical condescension. According to their perspective, this type of architecture was not only characteristic of hot climates but of backward societies. "The imagery and techniques that tropical countries often propose, such as Brazil, Mexico or Venezuela", they wrote,

> are due to their vitality and glamour and their use of relatively simple technology. But these buildings emerge from a Baroque culture, which still conceives of buildings as isolated monuments, each sufficient in itself, and are still the product of rich communities of old-style capitalism. And it is not right to base the form of a building on climate and environment. A glass box and a solid concrete cave can produce the same conditions of comfort if one is able to provide the corresponding mechanical equipment.[104]

What was the reason for this reaction that replaced fascination with arrogant disregard?[105]

Here is our hypothesis. Until the fifties, the canon of modern architecture was made up of works conceived and built by the West. Given that modernist theories were synthesized in a set of presumably universal design procedures and principles, modern architecture was practiced by following those procedures and principles all over the world. One key point to understanding this version of modernist architecture is that in regard to its constructive aspects, the priority of the most referential European modernists (i.e. Le Corbusier, Mies, Gropius, Oud, Rietveld) was not the literal expression of materials and/or building processes but their *re-presentation*. In this way, the "universalist" conditions of modernist production enabled the emergence of candidates to the canon anywhere on earth. The eventual inclusion of buildings located in peripheral countries like Persia, Brazil, and Palestine in Gropius's canonic *Internationale Architektur* (1925) offers clear proof of the flexibility of this set-of-rules. According to Gropius, it was not the degree of development of the single countries but the capacity of their talented architects to interpret the new "Zeitgeist" that determined the place of their works in that canon. By introducing novel solar control solutions, Brazilian architects paved the way for an articulation between modernist ideas in architecture and tropical conditions, *regardless* of the "backward" status of the society that had generated it.

The reaction of the Smithsons and other members of Team X against this sort of "tropical fever" we were describing can be interpreted as a contribution to block the expansion of modern architecture's canon beyond the limits of the West. To regain the European cultural centrality after the war debacle, Team X, particularly the Smithsons, had to reorganize the principles of the "modern movement" in a new synthesis. In other words, they had to devise a Grand Move.

The solution consisted in recovering the "true" essence of modernist principles, making pure and sincere once again the universe that the "modernist brother" had rendered opaque by accepting bureaucratization and "empty formalism". It was therefore necessary to seek new forms of "transparency" and technological authenticity, and this, as had already happened in the first decades of the century, led to the search for this purity in societies uncontaminated by modernity.

"Architects", argued Aldo van Eyck, "have betrayed society by betraying the essence of contemporary thought. (…) The time has come to merge the old and the new, to rediscover the archaic, that is to say timeless, qualities of human nature".[106]

The artists of the COBRA group and Dubuffet's preaching opened the way to an investigation of the world of children, which was particularly important in van Eyck's work. Dubuffet, with whom the young Dutch architect had a long-standing relationship, had made his own trip to North Africa in the late 1940s. Shortly afterward, the van Eycks made their first trips to the region, an impulse that later led the couple to the Dogon in sub-Saharan Africa, following in the footsteps of Marcel Griaule.[107]

For Jacob Bakema, "(today) a confrontation is taking place between primitive societies (with an integrated habitat, whose members claim a right to be provided with modern techniques), and our society (disintegrated by these same techniques and seeking new disciplines of integration)".[108]

By focusing exclusively on the habitat in "Third World" nations in an "ethnographic" key, beyond history, the Team X members simultaneously denied the contributions of the *contemporary* architecture produced in those same territories to the international debate.

However, this relativist and "ethnographic" position was contradictory: while van Eyck was enthusiastic about the idea that these places "could not have been very different in Ur, 5,000 years ago", these same models were adopted as the basis for "aesthetics of change". In addition, the ways of life that many of those people were trying to transform were considered "eternal". Team X members adopted examples such as the North African cashbas as "open forms"[109], or rather as a structure with independence from the concrete cultural, social, and even political contents that determined them.

As researched by Sarah Williams, Sartrean existentialism significantly influenced certain group members, particularly in their emphasis on "authenticity", a pivotal element in transforming their concept of "truth", leading to the "brutal" presentation of building materials.[110] However, the rejection of the inevitable "life and death" of historical forms and the premise of the "as found" align with conceptions developing during that time, as observed in the works of figures like Levy Strauss, Foucault, and Roland Barthes. As Kristin Ross highlighted, these ideas pointed toward the "Death of Man", evolving parallel to the endeavors and declarations of Third World leaders such as Fanon or Guevara, who were dedicated to the creation of a "New Man".[111]

Through their criticism of the forms of the "international style" for causing the "tedium of hygiene", the new wave of the European avant-garde simultaneously absolved politics of its responsibilities. Hence, in their "sanitized" use of the "primitive" lessons, one might argue, following Kross, that

> after all, the purpose of structuralism was the ordering of objects, not the critique of their function. The idea that society was composed of agentless

structures helped to reinforce people's growing sense that (...) their lives were defined by unchangeable, lifeless, meaningless, bureaucratic structures governed by no one.[112]

In Britain, the anthropological perspective was enriched in those years due to the reversion to the metropolis from the experiences gained in studying other cultures stimulated by the empire and the war. Since 1945, the anthropological approach to studying the working-class population was promoted by the Institute of Community Studies (ICS) in London. In 1954, Michael Young and Peter Willmott began a detailed investigation of the Bethnal Green neighborhood, where the ICS was headquartered. This initiative was conceived in 1947 due to the concerns expressed by participants in the anthropology seminar at the London School of Economics. Critically evaluating the publication, the magazine "Man" acknowledged "our sociologists have recently discovered the English family (...) (and) how little we know of our own society".[113] The ICS, regarded as a descendant of the Mass Observation movement, conducted a form of "popular sociology" in the thirties in Great Britain under Tom Harrison's leadership. Charles Madge, a key figure in that movement, was concurrently the director of the ICS. Significantly, according to colleagues, the ICS shared with Mass Observation "the same attempt to make articulate the inarticulate humanity of Bethnal Green 'Mum' and the suburban housewife on the doorstep".[114]

Harrison represented a "reflux" back to the metropolis, a shift within "anthropology" as it evolved from studying "imperial subjects" before the war to examining the sociology of the British population. His investigation into working-class life followed an expedition to the current Vanuatu and the Melanesian archipelago.

Jeremy McClancy's study notes,

> for those bourgeois intellectuals who ran Mass-Observation and for those members of the middle-class who read their reports, the lives of the working-class, especially the northern working-classes who lived in industrialized towns such as Bolton, were just as exotic and as unknown as the Trobriand Islanders.[115]

This new anthropological approach, originating from studies of the "primitive", paradoxically contributed to crafting a new expression of "Englishness". The Smithsons' "Grand Move" aimed to reestablish Europe's cultural centrality ... *with the United Kingdom at its core.*

According to Alan Sinfield's examination of literature, politics, and culture in post-war Britain,

> one way of thinking of imperialism is as the export of conflict and violence. With the collapse of colonization, much of the violence comes back home. In the British case, many settlers (...) came back, (...) sometimes inured to racism and brutality.[116]

Essay 4: The Grand Move 161

With the decline of British imperial power, Englishness became a sensitive matter.[117]

Many young intellectuals were disinterested in the empire; they largely opposed the Suez invasion, the "independent" nuclear "deterrent", and displayed hostility toward immigrants.[118]

However, they held a distinct sensitivity toward Englishness, viewing modernism as a passing foreign trend. In the 1950s and 1960s, the blending of Englishness with elements of ex-dominion cultures intensified. Bill Schwarz contends that

> the practice of appropriating the attributes of ethnic others was not simply confined to the self-consciously modern partisans of subcultural subversion. It's too easy to think of Englishness as a self-enclosed category magically reproducing a civilization of never-ending insularity. (…) The frontiers of the empire, in their various forms, created the syntax for a particular style of domestic Englishness.[119]

For Alison and Peter Smithson, the recovery of European cultural centrality needed to be connected to the recovery of the lost English leading role. Three alternatives were presented to them: the Swedish "pragmatism", a return to the picturesque nature associated with Englishness, as advocated by Richards and Pevsner, and the "new monumentality" supported by CIAM leaders, particularly Giedion and Sert.

To explore the potential of the "Swedish" alternative, Peter visited Sweden after his graduation. His engagement with Sigurd Lewerentz's ideas and works opened new perspectives on the materiality of the discipline that was previously absent in British interpretations of modern architecture. Overall, the Swedish experience affirmed that "modesty" was not the attribute enabling Europe and Britain, in particular, to regain a leading role in the post-war context.

Rejecting Pevsner's and *The Architectural Review*'s promoted Englishness carried deeper meaning. As evidenced in the criticism received in general by the "little Englanders", from the "angry young men", this path meant an overt recognition of the loss of British centrality in the world, and with it a kind of self-seclusion in the restricted limits of the territory of the British Isles

According to Harriet Atkinson's research on the Festival of Britain (1951),

> An important area of experimentation for Festival architects engaged with reconstructing the place of Britain, after the blitzing and industrial scarring, was with methods for incorporating open space around buildings. Principles of landscaping associated with the eighteenth-century Picturesque, again became operative in the design of Festival exhibition sites and, in turn, in the postwar reconstruction of British cities and New Towns.[120]

The third alternative was tested during the competition for the reconstruction of Coventry Cathedral. This project seems to have been the Smithsons' first opportunity to find a response to pragmatism and picturesque nostalgia.[121]

162 *Essay 4: The Grand Move*

Their solution involved a large sloped concrete roof covering a space where separate cubic chapels were placed at the angles of a square plan. Likely inspired by Rudolf Wittkower's 1949 publication *Architectural Principles in the Age of Humanism*, their classical inclination was evident not only in the square plan but also in the choice of white aggregate marble to cover the roof, alongside references to Renaissance architecture detailed in their project report.[122] What was surprising was the orientation of the sloped surface along the diagonal of the square. In this way the "classical" plan layout on the main floor took on a Gothic resonance in the section, culminating at an upper vertex, seemingly drawing a connection to the old cathedral building. This approach closely resembled the accentuation of the diagonal corner featured in the Ronchamp chapel project found in Le Corbusier's recently published Volume 5 of the *Complete Works* – a significant reference for the Smithsons at the time.[123] The reference to the master's oeuvre was also observed in the axonometric representation of the ground floor (basement), where the interplay of curves and counter-curves, painted in a range of pastel colors (primarily sienna red), echoed the master's lexicon from the 1920s.[124]

The jury critiqued the Smithsons' formal gesture for its radicality. Despite being calculated by a skilled founding member of Ove Arup, Roland Jenkins, the use of a thin and precast concrete surface to cover the vast area was viewed as risky and untested in Britain.[125] The requirement for a considerable glass area to enclose the

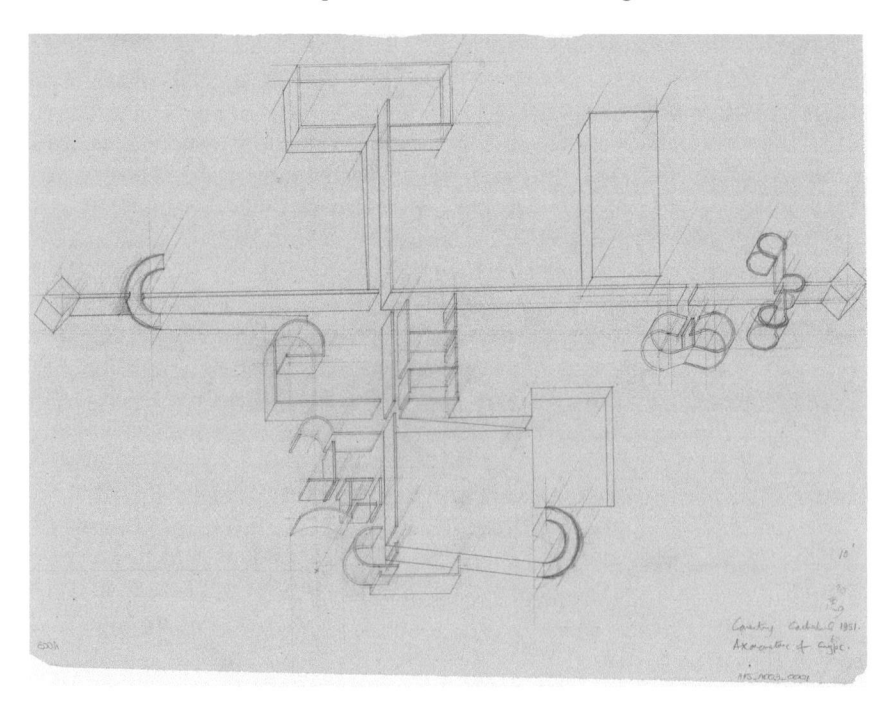

Figure 5.5 Axonometric drawing. Coventry Cathedral, 1951. The Alison and Peter Smithson Archive. Folder A003. (APS_A003_0001) (courtesy of the Frances Loeb Library, Harvard University Graduate School of Design).

volume was another inconvenient aspect of the proposal. Furthermore, inheriting Paxton's Crystal Palace, the submission by Colin St. John Wilson and Peter Carter, covering a similar extensive space with a metallic structure, was considered a suitable modern interpretation of the English tradition.

However, if the Sweden experience taught Alison and Peter Smithson about the inadequacy of "modesty" in characterizing Englishness, the Coventry experience enlightened them about the limits of Giedion's "new monumentality" as well. Their proposal for the Hunstanton School marked the first step toward solving this dilemma.

In 1949, the advanced US-American technological system seemed to have found its aesthetic embodiment in an architecture hitherto almost ignored in Great Britain: Mies van der Rohe's work.[126] As anticipated in the project by St. John Wilson and Carter, it was Mies, not Le Corbusier, who appeared to offer the most promising alternative for British architects seeking liberation from the quandary in which they were ensnared. Mies provided the opportunity to integrate the United States' most advanced techniques with the European cultural tradition, and in particular with the British architectural trend that had been lost in the first half of the 20th century. For the Smithsons, Hunstanton represented a first manifesto, a critique aimed at the provincialism of the "little Englanders". According to them, "only a person familiar with the pathetic figure of English functionalism supported since the war on a crutch of pseudo-science can understand why it was necessary to make such an obvious statement and design such a didactic building".[127]

Moreover, Hunstanton served as a critique of the pervasive vocabulary and syntax that had emerged from the global proliferation of modernism in the preceding

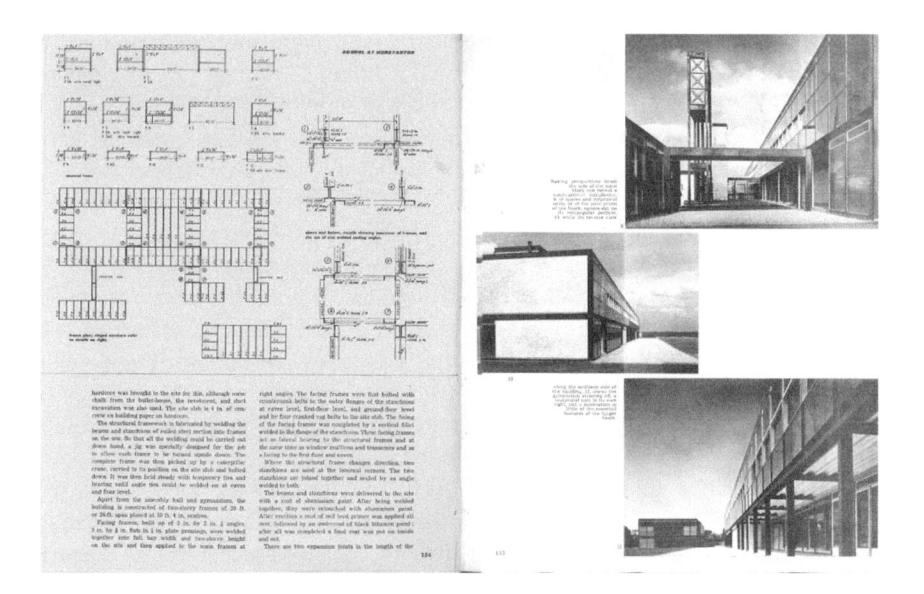

Figure 5.6 Alison and Peter Smithson, The School at Hunstanton Norfolk, as published by The Architectural Review, London, September 1954, pp. 134, 135.

years. In their view the strategy of creating prefabricated systems was a misstep, as it overlooked the pre-existing industrial capacity that had previously positioned Great Britain as a leader in the field. The use of closed systems blocked any attempt to construct an aesthetic system that surpassed singular programs. They argued that "the Hertfordshire County Council has explored the field of prefabricated large module design with (…) limited success. (…) To counteract this tendency, the Hunstanton School (…) rejects the inflexible system of large standard elements and instead assembles existing components".[128]

The "classicist" plan of the school in the Miesian code was envisioned by Peter Smithson to ensure the building's endurance over time. According to him, Hunstanton bore an everyday life at a school,

> and a secret life of pure space, the permanent built Form which will persist when School has given way to Museum or Warehouse, and which will continue to exist as an idea even when the built Form has long disappeared.

This element of their ideas would be reshaped in subsequent years, as the couple discovered that the concept of a building's "permanence" over time aligns more with a conservative, ancient society, whereas an advanced capitalist society should embrace the accelerated obsolescence of its products.

The adoption of a "classicist" plan in an attempt to revive British architecture in the global conversation, akin to a sort of neo-Palladian Englishness, was just one facet of Hunstanton's contributions. The other was the introduction of the concept of "as found" – a notion that, in simplified terms, meant creating by utilizing immediately available resources. In essence, the concept of "as found" shifted the evaluation of architecture from the aesthetic sphere to the moral sphere. Consequently, just as in the British case it was more truthful therefore correct to express their industrial tradition; in other societies, it should be more truthful therefore correct to express their "underdeveloped" condition. Since Hunstanton, the evaluation of modernist works no longer centered around the elegance or creativity demonstrated in the manipulation of modern vocabulary and syntax but rather on whether those works could manifest the "truth" of their production conditions.

The "as found" approach dealt a twofold blow to the potential universalization of the canon. On the one hand, the idea of a modern language, a means of understanding, or a set of valuation norms that transcended local determinations (as was being discovered in other areas of the world) was destroyed or limited to climatic (technical but not cultural) adjustments. On the other hand, a means of differentiation was unveiled for modern architecture, not within a shared code but with a radical characteristic and a political significance.

Curiously, the "as found" also had its origins in a "primitivist" approach, linked to the anthropological shift at the end of the empire that we previously began to discuss. This does not imply that the Smithsons consciously applied the concept to their design process. They won the Hunstanton competition in the summer of 1950, and they claimed the idea was conceived as a consequence of their later participation in the Independent Group, whose initial meetings occurred in the winter of 1951.[129]

In fact, the concept emerged from the interaction between the Smithsons, Eduardo Paolozzi, and Henderson's wife, Judith Stephen. Henderson and Paolozzi shared an interest in procedures or a "primitivist" attitude observed among the artists they encountered during their stays in Paris. As a student at the Slade, Paolozzi was captivated by the Ethnography Department galleries at the British Museum. By 1945, he had begun sketching African sculptures in the Pitt-Rivers Museum in Oxford. Paolozzi remarked,

> The neglect of the primitive was, I feel, part of the wider English insularity. (…) You also see that strange English imperviousness to other influences in the almost frightening way some very strong exhibitions come and go. I remember a superb exhibition in London in the 1950s on Mexican folk art. (…) A Mexican exhibition of that sort seems to me to be much more powerful than, for example, one of the very influential exhibitions of New York Abstract Expressionism.[130]

An interest in "primitive" art wasn't unfamiliar to other Independent Group artists (evident in William Turnbull's sculptures), but Paolozzi's curiosity extended beyond the production of tribes less "contaminated" by Western culture. He was drawn to the attitude of *current* inhabitants of those territories toward things, as they, faced with severe shortages, had to resolve their needs by utilizing all available resources, forming a material culture of bricolage. According to Mc Leod,

> he has a constant preoccupation with re-creation, with trying to establish areas of constancy and transformation. Whereas many artists have taken fragments from exotic cultures to incorporate in their own work, Paolozzi is also interested in seeing these societies as dynamic, evolving cultures.[131]

Paolozzi was progressing toward a novel approach to the so-called "primitive" mentality that anthropology was beginning to unveil, particularly in the works of Claude Lévi-Strauss. Instead of perceiving "primitive" people as using a rudimentary thought system, Lévi-Strauss postulated that it was simply a different approach to reality, parallel to Western scientific modality.

As per the Smithsons, "The 'as found', where the art is in the picking up, turning over and putting with. (…) (T)he 'as found' was a new seeing of the ordinary, an openness as to how prosaic 'things' could re-energize our inventive activity".[132]

According to McLeod,

> To Paolozzi, one of the great strengths of makers in the societies of Africa and the Pacific is their use of simple materials and tools. They, he feels, are still able to grasp the essentials of creation and work directly on the commonest materials to transform them by using only the simplest of tools.[133]

Essay 4: The Grand Move

In *La Pensée Sauvage*, published in France in 1962, Lévi-Strauss would define this procedure as that of the bricoleur.

> The bricoleur – he wrote – is capable of executing a large number of diversified tasks; but, unlike the engineer, he does not subordinate any of them to the obtaining of raw materials and instruments conceived and obtained to suit his project (remember the criticism of A&PS to the specially designed prefabrication systems of schools): his instrumental universe is closed, and the rule of his game is always to make do with "whatever one has", that is, a set, at each finite moment, of instruments and materials.[134]

Upon the opening of the Festival of Britain in May 1951, the limitations of the concepts criticized by the Smithsons became evident in the constructions on the south bank of the Thames. Moreover, in February of the same year, North Korean troops captured Seoul. Due to the lack of steel resulting from the British participation in the United Nations contingent facing the communist attack, the works on the Hunstanton building were disrupted. The school could only be inaugurated in 1954, unintentionally revealing the fragility of the premises guiding its conception.

If the "end of empire" led British anthropology toward the discovery of its own "natives", it also began a form of flattening of differences. What was once a clear distinction of ranks – political, economic, social, and cultural – between "colonizers" and "colonized" was transformed into a form of cultural ecumenism. The production of "savages" moved from exotic collections, scientific cabinets, or avant-garde artists' studios to become a part of "human culture" as a whole.

This neutralization of differences also brought a shift in protagonists in Great Britain's relationship with what is now known as the "British Commonwealth Community of Nations". The 1951 Festival of Britain aimed to solidify this shift in the imaginations of the British and international opinion. As Gavin and Lowe have argued, "the rapidly approaching 'end of empire' produced as reflex a change in the nature of the pioneer, the explorers and discovers of 1951 were scientists, doctors, and technicians – in other words, members of the new class of experts".[135]

The initiative to open British culture to the culture of the "primitive" people, shaping the new nations, began with the organization of the 40,000 Years of Modern Art exhibition. This exhibit, aimed at the general public, elevated the production of these peoples to "high culture", attributing equal merits to Greco-Roman culture in constructing Modern Art.

Some critics of the exhibition lamented the emphasis placed on its surrealist approach" and observed that the experimental art of the modern schools seemed to suffer in "the experimental art of the modern schools suffer severely in the comparison with Negro or Melanesian art for reason of the apparent lack of any informing conviction comparable to the religious sanctions behind the primitive sculptures".[136]

In general, the European environment connected with the visual arts amplified its interest in the creations of non-European "primitive" people in the post-war period. In the British realm, the noteworthy sequence of exhibitions unfolded: first in 1949 with the grand exhibition, followed by the 1952 exhibition organized by the University and the Museum Manchester at the Whitworth Gallery; the 1953 extensive exhibition organized by the Mexican government that toured Europe and the United States, alongside The Webster Plass Collection of African Art at the British Museum, and, in 1954, Cave Drawings: Copies by Abbé Breuil at the Arts Council Gallery.

The fusion between art and anthropology and the concept of an increasingly homogeneous "human culture" received a remarkable international impetus from the exhibition The Family of Man, organized in 1955 by Edward Steichen, then director of photography at the MoMA.[137]

The exhibition displayed scenes captured by numerous photographers from 68 countries, categorized based on shared human characteristics: laughter, birth, work, death, and so on. While some considered this a step forward in solidarity and cultural tolerance, others saw it as a new mystification. In his critique of the exhibition during its presentation in France, titled The Great Family of Man, Roland Barthes wrote:

This myth works in two phases: first, the differences in human morphologies are affirmed, they insist on the exoticism (…), after this pluralism a unit is extracted. Man is born, works, laughs, and dies everywhere in the same way. (…) Everything (in the exhibition) aims to suppress the determining weight of History (… without) penetrating into that further zone of human

Figure 5.7 An image of the exhibition The Family of Man at the Museum of Modern Art, New York, as published in the catalog by Edward Steichen. Edited by the MoMA with the Maco Magazine Corp., c. 1955.

168   *Essay 4: The Grand Move*

behavior where historical alienation introduces those some "differences" (…) that here which we will call much more simply here quite simply call "injustices".[138]

This form of cultural ecumenism was aligned with several post-War initiatives aimed at creating a "better humanity", including the establishment of UNESCO in 1946. Notably, the institution saw significant activity in London from institutions like the Council for International Civic Instruction and the British Association for the Advancement of Science. Its first president was Sir Julian Huxley, a key figure in British neo-Darwinism, who maintained a broadcast program on the BBC during the War.[139] For Huxley, humans represented the pinnacle of evolution as their reason enabled them to manage their evolution and decide the future. However, the accelerated population growth, unaccompanied by food production capability, cast doubt on the possibility of keeping up with the pace of human evolution. The emphasis was placed on world organizations to control these variables.

The concept of the "human family" signaled a growing understanding of global issues in light of the increasing autonomy of peoples formerly under imperial or colonial rule. Arturo Escobar cautioned that it was in this context that the idea of "underdevelopment" emerged. As of 1948, "two thirds of the world's peoples were transformed into poor subjects (…) when the World Bank defined as poor those countries with an annual per capita income below U\$S 100".[140] Thus, with this resolution, the "primitive" inhabitants of a pre-war "archaic world" became the "underprivileged" contemporaries of the post-war era.

The first meaningful manifestation of the neutralization of differences in the values of Form in direct relation to our argument was the realization of the exhibition Parallel of Life and Art (POLAA) in 1953, in which Paolozzi, Henderson, and the Smithsons worked together.[141]

As is known, POLAA consisted of the exhibition of 100 photographs, in which motifs from science, everyday life, anthropology, and art were mixed, shown at different scales, as general views or as details. The exhibition was designed by Alison and Peter who arranged the panels occupying the entire space in vertical, horizontal, and oblique positions.

The interest in this jumble that heralded a radical change in modernist assessment scales was not confined to the United Kingdom. In the field of the arts, the most important and influential operation was carried out by André Malraux with his Museum without Walls.[142] For Malraux, the expanded capacity of reproductions of works of art meant that the entire world could be transformed into a museum. He thought that photography and books encouraged the construction of a new cultural group in which the most diverse manifestations came into dialogue with each other. Photography also allowed works to be cut or reduced, presenting them from new points of view and with new values, enriching each other. The influence of Malraux's ideas was decisive for the realization of POLAA.

In 1947, the year that Henderson visited Paolozzi in Paris, Malraux had published his essay "Le Musée Imaginaire", subsequently reprinted in 1951 in

Figure 5.8 Alison and Peter Smithson, Installation of Parallel of Life and Art, photos by Nigel Henderson, as published in The Charged Void. Architecture by Alison and Peter Smithson, The Monacelli Press, New York, 2001, p. 123.

Les Voix du Silence. (…) For Henderson and Paolozzi, who had spent much of their student days visiting ethnographic and scientific collections in Paris and London, Malraux's essay vindicated their interest in objects and artifacts beyond the confines of traditional Western art and the teaching of the Slade.

> The extent to which they revered and embraced Malraux's ideas was perhaps best demonstrated by the fact that they invited him to open "Parallel of Life and Art".[143]

However, it should be noted that the equalization proposed by the Imaginary Museum was only apparent. In reality, Malraux never ceases to consider Western culture, and particularly European culture, as the highest level of artistic production. Faced with the production of "savage arts", such as ritual masks, he wonders "how to admire them and at the same time admire Poussin and Michelangelo?"[144] and it is answered that although in both cases what attracts us is the accent or what the work momentarily introduces into our appreciation system, in reality: "the mask and Poussin do not play the same role in our culture".[145] Moreover, for Malraux there was no doubt about the centrality and dominant role of Western culture in the organization of "universal" material:

> It is time to realize – he wrote – that the world has not produced, for three hundred years, a single work of art comparable to the highest of the West. What is questioned in our culture is questioned in the past of others: as if this conquering and confused culture wanted to destroy its humanist heritage only to achieve a global humanism, and to annex at the same time what apparently resembles the more to his art, and what is most profoundly foreign to him.[146]

The importance of POLAA in the Smithsons' trajectory lies in the fact that the "as-found" procedure was here carried out without the classicist ties that characterized Hunstanton's project. In POLAA, the obligatory bric-a-brac that characterized the everyday practices of the British people during the war was articulated with the admired practices of the "primitive" peoples and with surrealist procedures, giving rise to a new aesthetic experience. Alex Kitnick has noted that in Henderson and Paolozzi's first project the exhibition was organized along two parallel surfaces. In this case the form of the exhibition literally coincided with its title. But in the space created by the architects, "Art" mixed with "Life", erasing difference. As David Sylvester observed in his review, the exhibition included

> news photos, aerial photos, Victorian photos, X-ray photos, kinetic photos, photo-finishes, photomontages, photograms, photographic illustrations from manufacturers' catalogues; and photographs of antique sculpture, Japanese scripts, Leonardo drawings, Blaue Reiter drawings, children's drawings, classical temples, figures from text-books ancient and modern of botany, geology, mechanics, and anatomy. All of this led to a "consummate inconsequentiality".[147]

Certainly, the apparently chaotic arrangement of the images in space that characterized the exhibition was a fundamental resource to suggest the flattening of difference. However, that wasn't the most important point.

The main support for this in-difference was the absence of words. As in a display of recent archaeological finds from an unknown civilization (or as in the Salon des Refusés of 1863, the first exhibition of modern art), the images were there without a title that would allow the visitors to understand their context, their intention, or their provenance. POLAA seems to have been Smithson's initial step addressed to disregard the problem of Form, giving the illusion (at least in the imagination), of a world of equality in which, by coexisting without values, the differences that separated "art" from "life" or human beings among themselves seemed to be able to disappear.

POLAA can be viewed as a forerunner in the Smithsons' journey, marking a departure from the confines of established aesthetics and a move toward a visually egalitarian expression. It demonstrated their early inclination toward an aesthetic that blended the mundane, the modern, and the so-called "primitive", setting the stage for their future architectural endeavors characterized by a blend of diverse influences and a penchant for inclusivity.

For the British, 1956 was an "Annus horribilis". Two years after the end of rationing was declared in Great Britain, in the months in which the United States detonated the first Hydrogen bomb, and when the "End of Empire" was painfully exposed in the Suez Crisis, the Smithsons built two of their most controversial interventions: the House of the Future (HOF) within the annual exhibition on the ideal house organized by the *Daily Mail* newspaper[148], and the installation Patio and Pavilion (P&P) as part of the exhibition This Is Tomorrow organized by the Independent Group. The future, as can be seen, was the main protagonist in both cases, and it is noteworthy that the construction of this "futurist" discourse takes place in a still relatively backward post-war Britain, confirming the thesis of Perry Anderson. According to him, a "Modernist" avant-garde in the visual arts was a phenomenon of relatively rearguard countries. On the contrary, and for the same reason, neither the United States nor England played any significant role in the artistic revolution of the early decades of the 20th century.[149]

It is true that the country was experiencing a revolution in the transition from old-fashioned pre-war construction industries to the new electronics and sophisticated post-war industries. However, it is no less true that the policy of those years was remarkably forward-leaning, engaged in "futuristic" projects that many considered senseless intentions. A report from the Department of Management of the University of Manchester recognized the propagandistic role of this tension:

> the UK has continued to spend more on defense and prestige projects than on the technologies which matter most for industrial competitiveness. (...) (Moreover) most of (these projects) have been those in which the US has a major presence. The greater financial resources of the latter and its much larger domestic market would appear to constitute almost insurmountable obstacles to the effective implementation of a "high tech" R&D strategy.[150]

In relation to the Tory celebration of the future, the role of HOF was ambiguous: it was part of two main historical series. To begin with, the construction was a new version of a tendency to imagine the future that went back to the books by Mercier (*L'An 2440*) and Madden (*Memoirs of the Twentieth Century*) in the 18th century, and that expanded throughout the 19th century in numerous literary works that included domestic futurism, such as those of Jules Verne, Edward Bellamy, or H.G. Wells, to which must be added the predictions of engineers such as Nicola Tesla or Thomas Edison.[151] In 1900, John Elfreth Watkins Jr. published a widely circulated article in the *Ladies' Home Journal* titled "What May Happen in the Next Hundred Years", in which he predicted changes in cooking and communication. Kasimir Malevich had proposed a House of the Future for Leningrad in 1927, and the following year another House of the Future was designed by S. Rowland Pierce and R.A. Duncan, which was also featured as part of the *Daily Mail* exhibition of Ideal Homes. These early *Daily Mail* HOF had a conventional "modern" appearance (cubic and without applied decoration) and already highlighted the possible "revolutionary" changes in domestic life as a result of the application of new technologies. In a similar context (trying to contribute a leap forward to emerge from a context of crisis), in 1933 in the United States, the exhibition A Century of Progress was promoted, including the Home of Tomorrow by Gilbert Rohde with Herman Miller.[152]

Therefore, it can be said that, in terms of its program and the type of technological changes presented, the Smithsons' HOF of 1956 wasn't particularly novel. What set HOF apart was the material with which it was built and, consequently, its form.

In the mid-1950s, the plastics industry in Great Britain was trying to catch up with advances in the use of these products in the United States, where the Society of Plastic Industries had already been created almost two decades before (1937). Consequently, the issue of "plastics" flooded advertising in newspapers and especially in magazines aimed at the female population.[153] But not only that. V.E. Yarsley and E.G. Couzens, and the design historian John Gloag published books about plastics under the popular Penguin Books or Pelican imprint: *Plastics* (1941), and *Plastics in the Service of Man* (1956). According to Tom Fisher, *Plastics* ended

> with a eulogy to plastic, or more precisely to the human being living in a world where plastics are the characteristic material of his environment. This "Plastic Man", living in the "plastic age" inhabits a "world of color and bright shining surfaces", his plasticized life completed by being laid to rest sealed in a plastic coffin.[154]

The use of plastics in HOF was a response to the "as found" logic. On August 11, 1955, the Smithsons were tasked with designing a House of the Future,[155] and in 1956, the new artificial plastic products were the "stars" of the supposed future building materials. In this sense, HOF revealed the same building logic as Hunstanton.

The topological continuity of the surfaces of its plastic shell owes a debt to the aesthetics of automobiles promoted by Alison and Peter's friend Richard Hamilton and, even more so, to that of the interiors of submarines, which were subordinated to the modeling of metal plates. Buckminster Fuller's Dymaxion metal bathroom was likely another source, and we should not dismiss the inspiring curvilinear continuity of plastic surfaces applied for the first time worldwide to the interior design of the English airplanes Vickers Viscount that started flying in 1953. However, when observing the drawings of the HOF, made with freehand lines, its non-technological character of simulacrum becomes evident. Nothing is more alien to the precision habits of advanced industrial production than this means of expression.

By embracing this new "material" condition, the Smithsons took a leap forward in their pursuit of finding a new solution to the modern crack between "Art" and "Life". Unlike the obligatory assembly of diverse materials that until then characterized the construction and equipment of the buildings, with its consequent discontinuities, they realized that the use of plastic allowed them to resolve almost all the functions of the house in a topological way.[156] As Roland Barthes pointed out in those same years, plastics were a material in infinite transformation and "less a thing than a trace of a movement".[157] With the use of plastic in the manner of HOF, life itself generated form.

HOF entered into a dialogue with the plastic house crafted by Dietz, Heger, and McGarry for Monsanto in 1957, and the plastic hotel cabin envisioned by architects Schein, Couton, and Magnant for the Camus company in September 1956. However, a notable distinction set HOF apart from these other plastic designs. With its handmade construction, HOF stood in stark contrast to its contemporary counterparts, conceived as genuine industrial prototypes.

Presented in an exhibition attended by women, and families eager to enjoy the latest inventions and household fads, HOF seems at first glance just a clever and flashy game of futurology. Nevertheless, if you analyze it more carefully, it reveals disturbing aspects.

To begin with, Peter Smithson later admitted that the plastic house was only prefab in appearance. Actually,

> It wasn't real. It was made in plywood. It was like an early airplane, where you make a series of forms, then you run the skin over them. The house was made in ten days. It was not a prototype. It was like the design for a masque, like theatre.[158]

And, indeed, HOF was a theatrical scenography to be seen from above by the visitors of the exhibition (this is the reason it lacked a roof).

According to Barry Curtis, HOF seems to have played in the British culture of the fifties a similar role to that of James Bond. "The images of domesticity which marched with the 'post-scarcity' mood of the 1960s seem to parallel the imaginative world of James Bond in a mélange of gadgetry, heraldry, libidinal promise, and international know-how".[159] And even the ambiguous relation of A&PS with the United States is very similar to the one that Fleming attributed to Bond. In the words of Sergio Di Nucci,

> the elegant 007 was the imaginary compensation that the British, and Anglophiles nostalgic for imperial power and the bevels of their taste, could

Figure 5.9 Caves of Les Baux de Provence, near St. Remy, 1953. Photographer Peter Smithson. The Alison and Peter Smithson Archive. Folder BA038 (courtesy of the Frances Loeb Library, Harvard University Graduate School of Design).

greedily consume in the face of the loss of real political prominence. (…) In the whole series, which was to flourish just after Suez, Bond (…) always had to collaborate with the CIA, that in the series was embodied by the agent Felix Leiter. This relationship (…) reflected the way in which Great Britain liked to mythologize its relationship with the United States. The English Bond knew how to dress, was educated without exhibitionism, with an infallible taste and rich in resources; the American Leiter only he had much more means and had more money, and he was clumsy, hasty, and fundamentalist.[160]

The concept of the House of the Future can be viewed in divergent ways. On the one hand, it embodies an optimistic outlook toward the future by applying scientific principles to cater to human needs, reminiscent of the perspective advocated by thinkers like Arthur C. Clarke in his popular science fiction works.[161] However, on a deeper level, as Beatriz Colomina has suggested, it can be seen as a refuge – a response to the prevailing climate of atomic fear during that era.[162]

The notion of refuge is underlined by several features of the HOF.[163] It serves as the epitome of artificial living, eliminating the need for external contact and independent of external air. Water collection is showcased through a conspicuous gargoyle and pitcher system in the courtyard. Additionally, residents have a designated space for creating their clothing, enhancing their self-sufficiency. This autonomy is accentuated by the ambiguous "urban" nature of the house. Despite its ability to connect with similar units around a central patio, the lack of public spaces in these streets paints a bleak picture far from optimism.

Some draw parallels between HOF and Aldous Huxley's *Brave New World*. However, it's crucial to realize that in Huxley's dystopian vision, despite being artificially "produced", children were essential to ensure the continuity of the species. In contrast, the "city" envisioned by the Smithsons seems to lack the presence of children entirely, reflecting the absence of human expectation for the future. The desolate urban images suggested by these drawings are located at the antipodes of the vital atmosphere hinted at by Henderson's widely publicized photographs of the streets of Bethnal Green.[164] This echoes Huxley's cautionary message: "This, I take it, was the message of Brave New World (HOF) – This (future) is possible: for heaven's sake, be careful about it".[165]

The topological aesthetics of the HOF correspond to the modeling of materials like plaster, mud, or soft stones. This aesthetic aligns with works such as Finsterlin's plaster models (1920), Mendelsohn's Einstein Tower (1921), and Frederik Kiesler's Space-House (1933, published in *Architectural Record* in 1939), later developed into his Endless-House.

In applying this aesthetic direction to the domestic unit, the architects essentially echoed one of the oldest traditions of human habitation: troglodyte dwellings, much like the caves of Les Baux-en-Provence they had visited in 1953. Alison and Peter kept color copies of the photographs taken during that trip, and these images resonate in the topological continuity of the HOF's surfaces, particularly in the resolution of furniture as gaps or protuberances in the walls.

In the project's description, it is stated that

> the house is arranged around the patio garden. It is heated throughout, and the rooms flow into one another freely like the compartments of a cave, and

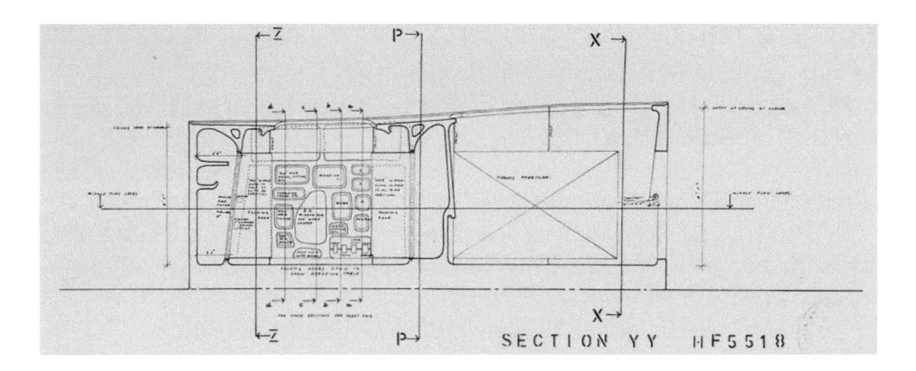

Figure 5.10 House of the Future, Section YY HF5518 in which one can see the molding of the walls to store the house's equipment. The Alison and Peter Smithson Archive. Folder A019 (courtesy of the Frances Loeb Library, Harvard University Graduate School of Design).

176   Essay 4: The Grand Move

OF THE FUTURE

his year's Ideal Home Exhibition, which opens at Olympia, London, on March 6, is a forecast by Alison and 1, A./A.R.I.B.A. of house design in the 1980's.

n of the House of the
o present a probable design
ars from now. The organ-
concensus of opinion among
sulted was that this period
duce as many revolutionary
past 100 years; changes not
ty of life, but also in the
niques of building the home
ll live.
m house. It has only one
e basic design can, of course,
irger family houses.
  arranged around the patio
heated and air-conditioned
the rooms flow freely into
te the compartments of a
ive, too, the skewed passage
  compartment to another
tains privacy.
tment differs in size, shape
eight, to suit its particular
highest room is the living-
orth side of the house and
ross the patio; the lowest,
in the opposite side. The

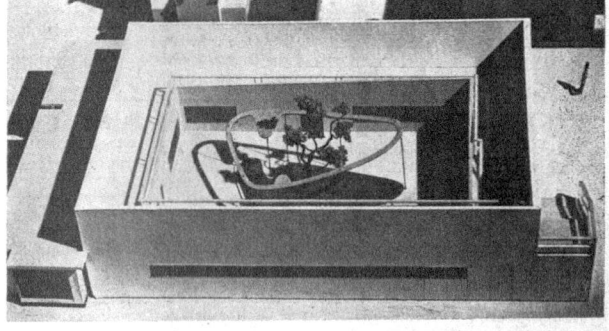

Model of the exhibition house

Figure 5.11   Alison and Peter Smithson, House of the Future. Photography of the model. See a view of the "theatrical" installation featuring an elevated perimeter catwalk, from where the audience observes actors representing future life. From *The Municipal Journal* (currently "The MJ"), March 2, 1956.

like in a cave, the skewed passage that joins one compartment to another effectively maintains privacy.[166]

Years later, in a reflective turn from her earlier design principles, Alison proposed a vision advocating "a change of attitudes toward our use of the Earth: a use of things without excess of enjoyment in a less wasteful way".[167] The examples she referred to, prompting a reconsideration of the subject of human habitation, were those found in the representations of Saint Jerome by Renaissance artists. In the depictions of Saint Jerome in his studio, she saw a depiction of an urban world perfectly harmonized with the inhabitant, while those showing Saint Jerome in the desert illustrated a necessary connection with nature. Most notably, she dedicates the final paragraph of this text to Saint Jerome in the "Grotto".[168]

Particularly evident in Mantegna's version of Saint Jerome in Bethlehem, the adaptation of rock shapes and their transformation into furniture can be observed in the accessories of the refuge. These elements serve as places where the inhabitant rests, leans, or safeguards and arranges their few possessions.

HOF embodied that grotto. As a "cave", the HOF design responded to the model that, according to the tradition of Western architecture, represents one of the two primary versions of the myth of dwelling.

The "other" version, the "hut", would be presented a few months later with the Patio and Pavilion "house".

The Smithsons' P&P formed part of the 12 installations within the This Is Tomorrow exhibition, curated by Theo Crosby, holding a renewed significance within the ongoing discourse.[169] The event was envisioned as an alternative to a proposal formulated by the London section of Groupe Espace, organized according to the

Figure 5.12 Alison and Peter Smithson, Photo of *Patio and Pavilion* at the exhibition This Is Tomorrow, by Nigel Henderson, as published in *The Charged Void*. Architecture by Alison and Peter Smithson, The Monacelli Press, New York, 2001, p. 150.

principles of CIAM. For this reason, P&P can be interpreted as part of the internal controversy within CIAM. Its occurrence coincided with the rise of Team X during the Dubrovnik Congress in August 1956, eventually leading to CIAM's dissolution in Otterlo in 1959.

The Groupe Espace, considered a continuation of De Stijl and the Bauhaus, was founded by André Bloc in Paris in 1951. In 1953, Paule Vézelay (born Marjorie Watson-Williams) initiated a section of Groupe Espace in London, aiming to integrate architecture and the arts, aligning with the objectives of Leger, Sert, and Giedion since the previous decade. This integration of architects and artists was a pivotal aspect of the group's formation.

The Groupe Espace included architect Carlos Villanueva, who in 1952 extended invitations to several members to participate in creating the Ciudad Universitaria in Caracas, a building site arguably considered one of the most universally acclaimed examples of "integration of the arts". Additionally, in 1954, Groupe Espace organized a large exhibition in Biot, France, partly financed by Villanueva.[170]

After a complex process, by early 1955, the London section of Groupe Espace was joined by three architects – Bernard Grimshaw, Vivien Pilley, and F.D.H. Catleugh – along with designer Jerzy Faczynski, painters Bertram Eaton, Charles Howard, and Ithel Colquhoun, and sculptors Victor Anton, Peter Stroud, and Geoffrey Clarke. Assisted by Leslie Martin, the group secured the ceremonial foyer of the Royal Festival Hall for a group exhibition in October and November that year.

Eminent international figures from the Groupe, including Bloc himself, Jean Arp, Sonia Delaunay, Etienne Beothy, Walter Gropius, and Day Schnabel, also

Figure 5.13 Andrea Mantegna, *Saint Jerome in the Desert* (1448–1451). Sao Paulo Museum of Art (MASP).

participated in the show. Vézelay proposed the inclusion of Independent Group artists to Colin St. John Wilson and Theo Crosby, though the idea was rejected. Wilson and Crosby later acknowledged that the concept of This Is Tomorrow originated from that debate. According to Alan Fowler, the architect Peter Smithson, (…) later recounted that the idea for this Whitechapel show originated with discussions with Vézelay, adding that, so far as Groupe Espace itself was concerned, "everybody said no, we don't want that, we want to do our own thing".[171]

As Lawrence Alloway acknowledged in the catalog's Introduction, This Is Tomorrow "wanted to experiment in various channels without submitting to the idea of synthesis in which the separate contributions are sympathetically bound together".[172] Participants were stimulated "to compete as well as to complement each other, just as (…) the members of antagonistic cooperative groups compete".[173] Indeed, the exhibition brought together 12 groups of artists and architects in competition, but it was only two of them that rejected the logic of internal cooperation (the architects designing the continent and the artists providing the content): numbers two and eight. Without them, This Is Tomorrow would hardly have played the watershed role that art history has recognized. Both proposals broke with the isolation of art from life that the Institute of Contemporary Art criticized.

In Hamilton, McHale, and Voelcker's proposal, the "re-union" was apparent not only in the celebrated initial emergence of pop art "Just what is it that makes today's homes so different, so appealing" by Hamilton but also in the amplified image of Marilyn Monroe and a giant bottle of beer in its exterior, and notably in the exit of the Robot Robbie from the stand and his immersion as one more among the exhibition audience.

Group six in the exhibition catalog, comprising Henderson, Paolozzi, and the Smithsons, explicitly stated that their pavilion

> represents the fundamental necessities of the human habitat in a series of symbols. The first necessity is for a piece of the World, the patio; the second necessity is for an enclosed space, the pavilion. These two spaces are furnished with symbols for all human needs.[174]

Their arrangement of the P&P elements was described as an "ironic transformation of Gottfried Semper's primitive hut", as suggested by Sarah Goldhagen.[175] Julian Myers' study further reveals that P&P proposed a sharp criticism of the "future" by reducing the habitat to rudimentary components and defining the landscape as "underdevelopment". According to Myers, the

> collapse of the "modern" into the primordial and the futuristic culminates in (…) P&P. This environment articulated, simultaneously, a primitive, pre-technological wasteland inscribed by hands that have barely begun to use tools, and the scene of a technological apocalypse.[176]

The installation's elements were provided by Henderson and Paolozzi. Paolozzi's contribution, a large stone inscribed with primordial signs reminiscent of an

180   *Essay 4: The Grand Move*

archaeological find, was paired with an image of the Taos pueblos in the catalog. Henderson's Head of a Man was

> constructed of amorphously cut, nearly unrecognizable shards of photographs (…) The resulting man stares, wide-eyed and snack-jawed, at the ruination of the World around him, features blurred and chest heaving. His catastrophic habitat was, to be sure, a humorless parody of Britain's "aesthetic of scarcity", of the poor war-weary city of London in the late 1940s. (…) In other ways, it represents, as David Melior suggests, the apocalyptic fantasy of "Tory futurism"; that is, the fantasy of nuclear annihilation that excused martial nationalism and reactionary technophilia.[177]

This pessimistic viewpoint was shared by group two. The presence of Robot Robbie as a central figure in the film *Forbidden Planet* holds significant relevance. Contrary to the celebration of technology that might be assumed at first glance, the film actually presents a familiar call for the necessity of maintaining "humanistic" control over the newly accessible spaces unveiled by the rapid advancements in science. The creatures encountered by the stranded travelers on the "forbidden planet" were, in essence, manifestations of the darker aspects of the human psyche.

It was the film's lead scientist, at the cost of his own life, who had unearthed a method to manipulate this darker side of humanity.

The somber atmosphere portrayed in the film and related themes must be understood in connection to the prevailing direction of contemporary British society at that time. This wasn't solely due to the Suez affair; it was a period when broader anti-nuclear sentiments were pronounced. On July 9, 1955, the Russell-Einstein Manifesto was issued in London, reflecting a widespread anti-nuclear consciousness. This anxiety reached its peak in the same city in February 1958 with the initial significant mobilization of the Campaign for Nuclear Disarmament.

Given that HOF and P&P referred to the future and that, moreover, both cases were carried out in the same year separated by a brief interval, it is evident that to grasp their meaning we should consider them together. Furthermore, the two constructions work like both sides of a coin in terms of their shape and in terms of their materials: HOF is a house with an interior patio, P&P is a pavilion within a patio; HOF is made with advanced technology material, P&P with precarious materials. We have also seen that in HOF and P&P the application of the concept of "as found" is verified and that both cases share a veiled pessimistic criticism of the British present.

However, is it not strange that the future was represented by both a technologically advanced artifact and a precarious construction? And, furthermore, if in both cases it was a matter of discussing the idea of Integration of the Arts defended by the CIAM referents: to what extent did the same line of response preside over the two projects? Lastly, and in relation to the first considerations of this essay: what position do HOF and P&P share regarding the bureaucratization of the profession, and regarding the proposals that came from the other side of the "iron curtain", issues that, as we saw, Alison and Peter Smithson were not indifferent to?.

The most convenient answer to the first question seems to be that the couple used the two projects not so much as futuristic divinations, but rather as a *second manifesto*, addressed not so much to imagine what a house would be like in the future, but rather to propose a future path for Architecture: *Vers une Architecture*. In this light, in a "modernist" way HOF celebrated the innovative capacity provided by the incorporation of the new materials that were appearing, while P&P warned, also in a "modernist" way, about the need to keep your eyes open (*ouvrir les yeux*!) to the simplest anonymous solutions.

In HOF, the dominance of "life" imprinting itself onto the new material became manifest. Similarly, despite presenting itself as an integrated effort between architects and artists, P&P did not actually embody any synthesis. A&PS deliberately confined their involvement to producing the project sketch. During the construction, the couple traveled to Dubrovnik for their participation in CIAM X, allowing the artists to occupy the space, simulating the spontaneity of everyday living.

The use of innovative and lightweight plastic material for constructing houses in HOF served as a response to the dominance of heavy prefabrication advocated by the Soviet bloc. Additionally, the (populist) spontaneity seen in Bethnal Green's backyards, which inspired P&P, countered the authoritarian imposition of Form by the Soviet Plans. On the other front, it became evident that neither HOF nor P&P fit within the framework of the "architecture of the bureaucracy" since that neutrality had drained it of "art".

As previously mentioned, the young Europeans of Team X, who were responsible for interrupting the continuation of the Congresses in 1959, were also avoiding the acknowledgment of the dislocation of values as a consequence of modernization. Seeking genuine art and architecture within the streets and aligning with the popular preferences of consumer society was another attempt to retrace the path back to a harmonious intellectual practice. In a letter dated August 29, 1959, Giedion acknowledged the decline of CIAM, admitting, "CIAM as an institution of the 'avant-garde' also lost its meaning. There is not and cannot be an avant-garde. This time is over".[178] The position of the young Europeans appears nostalgic in relation to Giedion's lucid recognition.

However, deep down, Alison and Peter never ceased to be the most distinguished disciples of their respected mentors. Their Grand Move was extraordinarily successful: in the following years, Europe, and Britain in particular, effectively recovered a predominant role in the construction of 20th-century architectural culture. Like Prince Salina, the famous character in Lampedusa's work, they managed to "change everything so that everything could remain".

Notes

1 Sokratis Georgiadis proposed a very clear description of this problem in his *Siegfried Giedion. Eine Intellektuelle Biographie*, GTA/AMMANN, Zurich, 1989, p. 13: "the 19th century (was) (…), according to Giedion, a deeply divided century; the economic, technical, scientific achievements that it brought forth surprised people's emotions and could not be absorbed by them. The unity of culture was thus menacingly undermined" (translated by author [t.a]). Giedion himself wrote: "John Dewey, in his 'Art as

182 Essay 4: The Grand Move

Experience', points out that 'compartmentalization of occupation and interests brings about separation of that mode of activity commonly called "practice" from insight, of imagination from executive doing, of significant purpose from work, of emotion from thought and doing' ", in GIEDION, 1941, 12. The topic started to be examined in the second half of the 19th century in the writings of John Ruskin and Friedrich Nietzsche (CAME, 2014). The division between "Art" and "Life" as a determinant topic for the emergence of modern art and architecture has been treated by an extensive bibliography (LEE, 1906; STURGE MOORE, 1910; KRISHNA, 1940; KAPROW, 2013).
2 The most relevant studies on the CIAM regarding our approach are STEINMAN, 1979; ADAMS, 1987; MUMFORD, 2000, 2009; BALLENT, 1995.
3 On the creation and adoption of the planning theories in this period: KEYNES, 2004; HOFSTADTER, 1955; ROTHBARD, 1991. On the differentiation between "destructive" and "constructive" avant-garde groups cfr. TAFURI, 1969. On the "destructive" positions: OESTERREICHER-MOLLWO, 1979.
4 Cfr. MOHOLY-NAGY, 1965, 24–26; KENTGENS-CRAIG, 1999, 170–203.
5 KUMAR SARKAR, 1943, 161–190; KIRKPATRICK, 1990, 17–21; COHEN, 2011.
6 COHEN, 1998; DE MAGISTRIS, 1984.
7 DE MAGISTRIS, 1984, 184.
8 KOHLRAUSCH, 2019, 57–96.
9 GIEDION et al., 1958, 4852.
10 Not by chance Le Corbusier focused his post-WWII reflections on giving his proposals a "scientific" basis, as he did with the creation of the Modulor, his proposals for the sunshade system or his systematization of transit structures.
11 UNITED NATIONS RELIEF AND REHABILITATION ADMINISTRATION, 1948; FRYDRYŠKOVÁ, 2008.
12 MUMFORD, 2000, 147.
13 Giedion to Sert, 9.2.49. Giedion's letter to Sert of 9.2.49. Special Collections, Harvard Graduate School of Design, The Alison and Peter Smithson Archive (SCHUGSD TAPSA), C6.
14 "White Gods" is an expression used by Tom Wolfe to designate the Bauhaus exiles in the United States: WOLFE, 2009.
15 KENTGENS-CRAIG, 2001, 170–183.
16 MUMFORD, 2001, 140.
17 Ibid.
18 Among many others, REID & CROWLEY, 2000; BLAKESLEY & REOID, 2007; BYKOV/GUBKINA, 2019; UDIVICKI-SELB, 2020; LODDER, 1985, 2013, 2018.
19 STARR, 1980, 209–221; CIUCCI, 1972, 171–194.
20 HANÁČKOVÁ (2019, 212).
21 The Polish CIRPAC delegates were Syrkus (member of the initial CIRPAC) and Szanajca (replaced in 1933 by Piotrowski), albeit Syrkus exerted by far the strongest influence. On the cold war political tensions and modern architecture cfr. KOHLRAUSCH, 2019, 235–280.
22 MALICH, 2023.
23 NEMZER, 1949, 265–284.
24 MASTERS, 2012.
25 HANÁČKOVÁ, 2019, 159.
26 GIEDION, 1958, 79.
27 Bonillo argues that "G. Candilis advances the undoubtedly very exaggerated figure of 500 participants (Architecture d'Aujourd'hui n°49, Oct. 1953). For the figure of 250, we refer to a press article based on the message of M. Servan, director of the Ecole des Arts et Métiers (Le Provençal, 28/07/1953)". BONILLO, 2006, 88–89.
28 *Architecture d'Aujourd'hui – USA, Contributions américaines*, n°50/51, Dec. 1953, article by Siegfried Giedion, "Aspects de l'Architecture aux Etats-Unis en 1953", pp. 7–9. In BONILLO, Ibid.

29 BONILLO, Ibid.
30 BONILLO, Ibidem.
31 Cfr. TARACHÓPULOS, 2006.
32 On Torres Bodet's participation in this event: TORRES BODET, 1969, 1970, 1971. On the UNESCO building PEARSON, 2010; POROS, 2023, 74–101.
33 Sert to Gropius, SCHUGSD 21.6.49.
34 PHIPPS, 1998; STOLLER& LOEFFLER, 1999.
35 "CIAM. Arts Council, Bridgwater", 1947.
36 Fondation Le Corbusier (FLC). Leter from J.L. Sert to Le Corbusier, 13/09/194.
37 GIEDION, 1951, 3.
38 Jose Luis Sert to Giedion November 11, 1947, SCHUGSD folder C4.JLS, in MUMFORD, 2000,185.
39 CAPELLO, 2011.
40 HOLFORD, 1962, 1.
41 VISCHER, 1954. On the role of Pierre Vago cfr. the special issue of *L'Architecture d'aujourd'hui, "Soixante années d'AA 1930-1990"*, December 1990
42 KÖHRING, Alexandra, "'Friendly Atmospheres'? The Union Internationale des Architectes between East and West in the 1950s", in BAZIN et al., 2016, 297–310; ZUBOVICH, 2016.
43 SCHUGSD CIAM archive 2.6.44.
44 BARBER, 2008. After this initial period, Alva Myrdal developed a distinguished career centered in nuclear disarmament. She was awarded the Nobel Peace Prize in 1982.
45 SCHWARZ, 2016.
46 SCHUGSD 6.3.47.
47 *The Artist in Modern Society* (…), 1954.
48 Myrdal to Sert, SCHUGSD 6.6.50.
49 Sert to Giedion, SCHUGSD 12.6.52.
50 Giedion to Keenleyside (UN official) SCHUGSD 3.9.53. Giedion refers to the CIAM members linked to the program as "our best experts".
51 Torres Bodet to Sert, SCHUGSD 8.11.51.
52 Gropius to Sert, SCHUGSD 11.9.52.
53 Sert to Torres Bodet, SCHUGSD 8.11.51.
54 Sert asks Panel members to include Corbu in SCHUGSD 5.11.52.
55 Giedion to Rogers, SCHUGSD 17.6.53.
56 Giedion to Rogers, SCHUGSD 18.6.53.
57 For a survey on the architectural debates in Britain during this period cfr. BULLOCK, 2002; HIGGOTT, 2006. See also: LACHMAN, "The Angry Young Man", in LACHMAN, 2016, 7–28.
58 SHANK, 1972; JEFFREYS, 1997, 110–130.
59 WILSON, 2014.
60 HEWISON, 1981, 136.
61 ANDERSON et al., 1958, 156.
62 "The Architect's Dilemma", in *The Economist* 25.7.53. Reproduced in JRIBA, April 1954.
63 ESHER, 1981, 65.
64 STIRLING 1956, 41.
65 STIRLING , 1957, 53..
66 STIRLING 1958, 61.
67 WILFORD Hugh, "Britain: In Between", in STEPHAN, 2007, 26.
68 Anti-americanism has a long tradition where it was frequent to refer to "the rowdy, uncultured Yankees, which we have encountered regularly since Trollope and Dickens", in GULDDAL, 2011, 148.
69 Ibidem, 146.
70 STEPHAN, 2007, 23.

71 "A Conversation between Peter Smithson and Wouter Vanstiphout", in SPEAKS & HADDERS, 1999.
72 SPELLMAN & UNGLAUB, 2005.
73 Ibidem. Cfr. also COLOMINA & SMITHSON, 2000, 3–30. The main action of the allies in Burma was the construction of the Ledo Road, an extraordinary engineer's project to transport supplies for the Chinese Army.
74 WALTERS, 1945, 257
75 DE MAGISTRIS, op. cit.
76 VAN EYCK Aldo, "Discussion", *Architectural Design*, November 1958: in SMITHSON, 1966, 39.
77 Ibidem.
78 Ibidem.
79 Ibidem.
80 Soltan, Jerzy, *Architectural Design*, May 1960, in SMITHSON, 1966, 17.
81 SMITHSON A&P, 1956, 34
82 MAASE, 1999, 11.
83 SMITHSON A&P, 1970, 139. (author's emphasis).
84 If it is true that each nationalism (…) begins with a real or fabricated common enemy, then the current image of America in Europe may well become the beginning of a new pan – European nationalism", ARENDT, 1954, 416. Cf. MARKOVITS Andrei, *Uncouth Nation. Why Europe Dislikes America*, Princeton University Press, Princeton, 2007, pp. 201–23. GULDALL, 2011, 7.
85 SMITHSON A&P, 1970, 139.
86 BANHAM, 1966. In this regard cfr. GROAZ Silvia, "The New Brutalism: Ethic vs. Marxism? Ideological Collisions in Post-War English Architecture", in JANNIÈRE & SCRIVANO, 2021.
87 KITE Stephen, "Softs and Hards: Colin St. John Wilson and the Contested *Vision of 1950s London*", in CRINSON & ZIMMERMAN, 2010; WARD, 2012, 499–524.
88 MORAVANSZKY, 2017, 662–688.
89 Ibidem.
90 ESCHER, 2014, 102.
91 Ibidem.
92 HANSEN Carre Bleu, 1961, in SMITHSON, 1966, 35.
93 VAN EYCK Aldo, "Meeting at Oterloo", in SMITHSON, 1967, 39.
94 SMITHSON, 2005, 16.
95 GOODWIN Philip, "Review of *Brazil Builds*", *JRIBA*, May 1943, p. 155.
96 Ibidem.
97 Ibidem.
98 "Brazilian Architecture", *JRIBA*, July 1953, p. 351.
99 "Report on Brazil", *The Architectural Review*, London, October 1954, vol. 116, p. 694.
100 BARKER, 2017.
101 Lionel Brett Intervention at FRY, 1955. Not by chance Nehru did *politically* hire the French Le Corbusier as the leader for the design of the city, instead of his first choice for a British planner.
102 "Editor's Foreword", *Architects' Year Book*, 4, 1951.
103 FRY, 1955 (author's emphasis).
104 SMITHSON A&P, 1970, 173.
105 I refer to "Report on Brazil", the previously mentioned dossier published by *Architectural Review* with the testimonies of some of the participants in the first Sao Paulo Architecture Biennial.
106 VAN EYCK, Aldo at the CIAM in Oterloo, in SMITHSON, 1967, 4.
107 VAN BEEK, 1991.
108 BAKEMA, "Carré Bleu", 1961, in SMITHSON, 1967, 8.

109 The interest on the "open" form was part of the post-war "un-formalism" questioning of the "high" classic (and early modernist) great Form. JAY, 1983, 61–73.
110 GOLHAGEN Sarah, "Freedom's Domiciles: Three Projects by Alison and Peter Smithson", in GOLDHAGEN & LEGAULT, 2001.
111 KROSS, 1999.
112 KROSS, 1999, 176.
113 BANTON Michael, 1958, 34–35.
114 HASLEY, 1961, 796.
115 MCCLANCY, 1995, 508.
116 SINFIELD, 2004, 125.
117 WHITTLE, 2016, 109–144.
118 SINFIELD, 2004.
119 SCHWARZ Bill, "Reveries of Race. The Closing of the Imperial Moment", in CONEKIN et al., 1999, 119.
120 ATKINSON, 2012, 65. Also TURNER, 2011. On the Picturesque debate in the fifties, BANHAM Reyner, "Revenge of the Picturesque: English Architectural Polemics, 1945-65", in VV.AA, 1968, 267.
121 CAMPBELL, 1992, 219.
122 Ibidem, 220. In the presentation of their project A&PS wrote: "it would shine out white like the Florence Baptistery in the cathedral at Coventry" (ibidem, 218), and later "Modern Architecture is heir to this great tradition and has at its disposal means of expression which would have sent Brunelleschi wild with joy" (ibidem, 221).
123 The accentuation of the diagonal was not frequent in Le Corbusier's oeuvre. He previously used a square plan divided by the diagonal in his serial houses for craftsmen in 1924.
124 See image 4.5.
125 HOBBS, 1985.
126 "On Tyneside I was surrounded by brick that industry continued to dirty. For me, the steel sections seen had been the abandoned shipyards of the 1930s; they were the porches of the shipyards; riveted or welded, the skeletons of ships. The final object was the clad ship, a product of the plant where it was designed and where I used to get admission; where, on the enormous tables, were the gigantic templates of boxwood curves used to draw the profiles of the ship, understandably within the same tradition of how the equinus of the Doric capital was decided". Alison Smithson, December 1985 and April/May, 1986, in SMITHSON A&P, 1994, 42.
127 Footnote in the Competition Report for Hunstanton, in SMITHSON A&P, 2001, 67.
128 SMITHSON A&P, "Hunstanton Secondary Modern School", in SMITHSON A&P, 2001 (1953), 41.
129 ROBBINS, 1990, 61.
130 PAOLOZZI Eduardo, "Primitive Art, Paris and London", in PAOLOZZI, 1985, 11.
131 MC LEOD Malcolm, "Introduction", in PAOLOZZI, 1985, 17.
132 SMITHSON A&P, "The 'As Found' and the 'Found'", in ROBBINS, 1990, 201.
133 MC LEOD Malcolm, Ibidem.
134 LEVI STRAUSS, *Wild Thought* (Mehlman J., Leavitt J. trans.), The University of Chicago Press, Chicago and London, 2021, 21.
135 CONEKIN, 2003, 57.
136 FAGG, 1949, 9.
137 SANDEEN, 1995; TĪFENTĀLE, 2018.
138 BARTHES, 1972, 100.
139 SWETLITZ, 1995, 181–217; HUXLEY, 1993, 607–620.
140 ESCOBAR, 1994, 24.
141 Like the attempt of Dubuffet's 1949 *Art Brut* exhibition where 63 artist's work where mixed with other 137 works were of "the mad and the criminal", POLAA was an intent

186 *Essay 4: The Grand Move*

to "ignore" the problem of "form". The topic in relation to POLAA was developed in WHITELEY, 1990, 188–221.
142 MALRAUX André, "Museum without Walls", in MALRAUX, 1978, 13–130.
143 WALSH, 2001, 137.
144 MALRAUX, 1978, 556.
145 Ibidem.
146 Ibidem, 591.
147 SYLVESTER David, "Round the London Art Galleries", *The Listener*, September 24, 1953, cited in KITNICK, 2011, 78.
148 WHITELEY, 2012, 50–52; COLOMINA Beatriz, "Unbreathed Air 1956", in VAN DEN HEUVEL & RISSELADA, 2004, 12–29; RYAN, 1997; OWEN, 2001, 18–21. There was a US-American version in the competition *Design of a house for Cheerful Living* (1945), organized by *Pencil Points*; see GALVÁN et al., 2015, 75–86.
149 ANDERSON, 1984, 96–113.
150 ANCHOR, 1986.
151 ALKON, 1987.
152 An early survey on the "Houses of the Future" was published in SCIENTIFIC AMERICAN, 1932, 228–229.
153 MEIKLE, 1992, 173–182; FISHER, 2013, 285–303.
154 FISHER, 2013, 288.
155 Official letter from The Daily Mail Ideal Home Exhibition organization confirming the commission. SCHUGSD TAPSA BA008.
156 The only discordant aspect that the passage of time makes evident is the intersection between the supposedly "topological" aesthetics of the shell and the still dominant aesthetics of boxes in post-war British artifacts.
157 BARTHES, 1972, 97.
158 COLOMINA & SMITHSON, 2000, 24. For the theatrical condition cfr. also COLOMINA, "Unbreathed …", op. cit., 39–42.
159 CURTIS, 1998, 266. On the meaning of Bond's gadgets in British society MILLARD, 2018.
160 DI NUCCI, 2006.
161 MCALEER, 2013.
162 COLOMINA, "Unbreathed …", op. cit.
163 On this pessimistic context cfr. SCHEIBACH, 2021, 1–11; HIGHMORE B., "Memories of Catastrophes Yet to Come: New Brutalism and Thing-Memory", in SMELIK & PLATE, 2013, 75–91.
164 In the General Statement of the project, the Smithsons appear to have acknowledged *ex post* this evident objection to HOF. They clarified that "the tiny garden is obviously inadequate for the play of bigger children, so you must imagine a block of houses such as these, with garages and workshops, next to houses where necessary, interspersed with small paved play areas and with great swathes of parkland running through the residential areas". SCHUGSD TAPSA BAOO7.
165 Aldous Huxley in BLOOM, 2011, 13. On the "nuclear" war fear on the fifties HERMANN (chapter 4), 2015, 70–104.
166 SCHUGSD TAPSA BAOO7.
167 SMITHSON Alison, "The Desert … The Study", in VAN DEN HEUVEL & RISSELADA, 2004, 225.
168 Ibidem, 227.
169 PEZOLET, 2009, 44–49; HIGHMORE, 2006, 269–290; SMITHSON A&P, 2002, 37–44.
170 GAY, 2017, 5.
171 FOWLER, 2007, 178. It's worth noting that at the Groupe Espace Royal Festival Hall Exhibition in 1955, Clarke's sculpture, consisting of a transparent (plastic?) sphere, was exhibited under the title "House of the Future". Of course, this doesn't necessarily mean that there was a direct connection with the Smithsons' HOF.

172 ALLOWAY, "Introduction", VV.AA, 1956.
173 Ibidem.
174 "Group 6", VV.AA, 1956.
175 GOLHAGEN Sarah, "Freedom's …", op. cit.
176 MYERS, 2000, 81.
177 Ibidem, 83.
178 Giedion to Bakema, SCHUGSD 29.8.59 H.

Bibliography

ACKERMAN James, "In Memoriam: Manfredo Tafuri, 1935-1994", *Journal of the Society of Architectural Historians*, Vol. 53, No. 2, June 1994, pp. 137–138.
ACTON Mary, *Learning to Look at Modern Art*, Routledge, London, NY, 2004.
ADAMS Constance M., (Doctoral dissertation) *The architecture of revolution : the C.I.A.M. and the social production of art*, Harvard University, Cambridge Mass.,1987.
ALBINI F., PALANTI G., CASTELLI A., *Giuseppe Pagano Pogatsching*, Editoriale Domus, Milan, 1947.
ALEXANDRE Philippe, "La Deutsche Orient-Gesellschaft. Enjeux nationaux, culturels et scientifiques de l'arcvhéologie allemande au Proche et Moyen-Orient à l'époque de Guillaume II", *L'Orient dans la culture allemande aux XVIII et XIX siècles*. Actes du colloque organisé par le Centre d'Etudes Germaniques et Scandinaves (LIRA) de l'Université Nancy 2, 9 et 10 décembre 2004.
ALKON Paul K., *Origins of Futuristic Fiction*, University of Georgia Press, Athens, 1987.
ALLEN Roy F. *Literary Life in German Expressionism, and the Berlin Circles*, Umi Research Press, Ann Arbor, MI, 1983.
ANCHOR J. R., "The historical development of Government innovation policy in the UK", *Occasional paper No. 8601*. Dept. of Management Sciences, Uni, Manchester, Manchester 1986.
ANCHOR J.R. "The Historical Development of Government Innovation Policy in the UK", *Occasional Paper*, No. 8601. Department of Management Sciences, University of Manchester, Manchester, 1986.
ANDERS Leslie, "Engineer Reconnaissance in Forbidden North Burma", *Military Affairs*, Vol. 20, No. 3, Autumn 1956, pp. 129–138.
ANDERSON L., HOLROYD S., HOPKINS B., LESSING D., TYNAN C., WILSON C., *Declaration*, MacGibbon & Kee, New York, 1958.
ANDERSON Perry, "Modernity and Revolution", *New Left Review*, Vol. I, March–April, 1984, p. 144.
ANONYMOUS, "Mediterranean Roots of Modern Architecture", in *AC*, No. 18, Barcelona, 1935.
ARENDT Hannah, "Dream and Nightmare", in *Essays in Understanding*, Schocken, New York, 1954 (1994), pp. 409–417.
ARGAN Giulio Carlo, FAGIOLO M., *Guida a la storia dell'arte*, Sansoni, G.C., Firenze, 1974.
ARROJO Rosemary, "Translation, Transference, and the Attraction to Otherness: Borges, Menard, Whitman", *Diacritics*, Vol. 34, No. 3/4, Autumn–Winter 2004, pp. 31–53.

ATKINSON Harriet, *The Festival of Britain: A Land and Its People*, I.B.Tauris, London, 2012.

AURELI Pier Vittorio, *The Project of Autonomy: Politics and Architecture within and against Capitalism*, Columbia University y Princeton Achitectural Press, New York, 2008.

AVERMAETE T., KARAKAYALI S., VON OSTEN M., eds., *Colonial Modern Aesthetics of the Past—Rebellions for the Future*, Black Dog Publishing, London, 2010.

BAKHTIN Mikhail, *The Dialogic Imagination: Four Essays*. M. Holquist, ed. Texas University Press, Austin, 1981.

BALLENT Anahí, *El diálogo de los antípodas. Los CIAM y América Latina: Refundación de lo moderno y nuevo internacionalismo en la posguerra,* Serie Difusión No. 10, FADU/UBA, Buenos Aires.

BANHAM Reyner, "Revenge of the Picturesque: English Architectural Polemics, 1945-65", in *Concerning Architecture: Essays on Architectural Writers and Writing Presented to Nikolaus Pevsner,* Allen Lane, London, 1968, pp. 265–373.

BANHAM Reyner, *The New Brutalism: Ethic or Aesthetic?*, Architectural Press, London, 1966.

BANHAM Reyner, *Theory and Design in the First Machine Age*, Praeger, Westport, 1960.

BANNER Louis, *Intertwinned Lives: Margaret Mead, Ruth Benedict and their circle*, New York, Knopf, 2003.

BANTON Michael, "Two Studies of Kinship in London", *Man*, Vol. 58, No. 58, February 1958, pp. 34–35.

BARBER William J., *Gunnar Myrdal, An intellectual biography* Palgrave Macmillan, London, 2008.

BARKER Arthur, "Modern Movement Mediations: Brazilian Modernism and the Identity of Post-War Architecture in Pretoria, South Africa", *Dossiê Brasil-África do Sul| Paranoá*, No. 18, 2017. https://doi.org/10.18830/issn.1679-0944.n18.2017.03.

BARNETT Vivian Endicott, *Das bunte Leben. Wassily Kandinsky im Lenbachhaus*, Dumont Köln, München, 1996.

BAROCCHI Paola, "Commento Secolare" to the edition of the "Vite" by Studio per Edizioni Scelte, Florence, 1997.

BARTHES Roland, "The Great Family of Man", in *Mythologies*, Hill and Wang, New York, 1972, pp. 100–102.

BARTHES Roland, *La mort de l'auteur, Le Bruissement de la langue*, Seuil, Paris, 1984 [BARTHES Roland, "La mort de l'auteur", *Manteia*, No. 5, 1968].

BATES Thomas R., "Gramsci and the Theory of Hegemony", *Journal of the History of Ideas*, Vol. 36, No. 2, April–June 1975, pp. 351–366.

BEDESCHI G. *La parabola del marxismo in Italia 1945-1983*, Laterza, Bari, 1983.

BENEVOLO Leonardo, *Storia dell'architettura moderna*, Laterza, Bari, 1960.

BERNAL Martin, *Black Athena the Afroasiatic Roots of Classical Civilization, Vol. I, The Fabrication of Ancient Greece 1785–1985*, Rutgers University Press, London, 1987.

BIRAGHI Marco, *Progetto di crisi: Manfredo Tafuri e l'architettura contemporanea*, Christian Marinotti Edizioni, Milan, 2005 [English translation: *Project of Crisis. Manfredo Tafuri and Contemporary Architecture*, MIT Press, Cambridge, 2013].

BLAKESLEY R. & REOID S. (Eds.), *Russian art and the west. A century of dialogue in painting, architecture, and the decorative arts*, Nothern Illinois University Press, Dekalb, 2007.

BLANC Jan, "Winckelmann et l'invention de la Grèce", in Cahiers "Mondes anciens" Histoire et anthropologie des mondes anciens, 11, 2018.

BLOOM Harold, *Brave New World*, Chelsea House Publications, New edición, London, 2011.
BLOOM Harold, *Genius. A Mosaic of One Hundred Exemplary Creative Minds*, Warner Books, New York, 2002.
BLOOM Harold, *The Anxiety of Influence, Is Unavoidable. A Theory of Poetry*, Oxford University Press, Oxford and New York, 2007.
BLOOM Harold, *The Western Canon. The School and Books of All Times*, Epublibre (digital edition), 2017.
BLUNT Wilfrid Scawen, *A Secret History of the English Occupation of Egypt*, Alfred Knopf, New York, 1895.
BOLLMAN Stefan, *Monte Verità.1900. Der Traum vom alternativen Leben beginnt*, Deutsche Verlags-Anstalt, Munich, 2017.
BONIFACIO P., PACE S., ROSSO M., SCRIVANO P., eds., *Tra guerra e pace. Societa, cultura e archittura nel secondo dopoguerra*, Hoelpi, Milano, 1998.
BONILLO Jean-Lucien, "La modernité en héritage Le CIAM 9 d'Aix-en-Provence et la crise générationnelle du Mouvement Moderne", in *Rives méditarréennes*, 24/2006, https://journals.openedition.org/rives/561?lang=en#tex
Book Review, "Comment on Brazil Builds", *Journal of the Royal Institute of British Architects*, May 1943.
BORRMANN Norbert, *Paul Schultze-Naumburg. 1869-1949. Maler. Publizist. Architekt. Vom Kulturreformer der Jahrhundertwende zum Kulturpolitiker im Dritten Reich*, Bacht, Essen, 1989.
BÖRSCH-SUPAN Eva et al. *Gottfried Semper und die Mitte des 19.Jahrhunderts*, Birkhäuser, Basel, 1976.
BORSI F., GODOLI E., *Vienna 1900. Architecture and Design*, Rizzoli International Publications Inc., New York, 1986.
BOUCHARD D.F. ed., *Language, Counter-Memory, Practice. Selected Essays and Interviews*, Cornell University Press, Ithaca, NY, 1977.
BOWNESS Alan, *Modern European Art*, Thames and Hudson, London, 1972.
BRAUDEL Fernand (EWALD F., BROCHIER, J.J. interviewers), "Mares y tiempos de la Historia" , *Vuelta*, Vol.9, No. 103, 1985, spanish translation from Ibidem, "Une vie pour l'histoire", *Magazine littéraire*, No. 212, November 1984, pp. 43–46.
BRETTELL Caroline B., "Nineteenth Century Travelers' Accounts of the Mediterranean Peasant", *Ethnohistory*, Vol. 33, No. 2, Spring 1986, pp. 159–173.
BRIGGS Asa, "Great Britain: the cultural environment in 1945", *The Unesco Courier,* October 1985.
BRUCHER Günter, *Wassily Kandinsky. Wege zur Abstraktion*, Prestel, München, London and New York, 1999.
BRUNO Giordano, *De l'nfinito, universo e mondi*, John Charlewoods's Press, London, 1584.
BRUSCHI Arnaldo, *Bramante*, Laterza, Bari, 1969.
BUGLER Caroline, "Innocents Abroad: Nineteenth Century Artists and Travelers in the Near East and North Africa", in STEVENS Mary Ann (Ed.), *The Orientalists: Delacroix to Matisse*, Royal Academy of Arts, London, 1984, pp. 27–31.
BULLOCK Nicholas, *Building the Post-War World: Modern Architecture and Reconstruction in Britain,* Routledge, London, 2002.
BURKHARDT Rukschcio, ROLAND Schachel, *Adolf Loos: Leben u. Werk*, Residenz Verlag, Salzburg, 1982.
BYKOV A. & GUBKINA I., *Soviet Modernism. Brutalism. Post-Modernism. Buildings and Structures in Ukraine 1955-1991*, Osnovy Publishing, Kyiv, 2019.

192 Bibliography

CACCIARI M., RELLA F., TAFURI M., TEYSSOT G., *Il Dispositivo Foucault*, CLUVA, Venice, 1977.

CACCIARI Massimo (RAKANATSKY Marc Ed., SARTARELLI Stephen trans.), "Loosian Dialectics", in *Architecture and Nihilism: On the Philosophy of Modern Architecture*, Yale University Press, New Haven, CT, 1993 [CACCIARI Massimo, *Oikos da Loos a Wittgenstgein*, Officina Edizoni, Rome, 1975], pp. 101–119.

CACCIARI Massimo, "Qualche scritto su guerriglia e imperialismo", *Contropiano*, No. 1, 1968, pp. 201–206.

CACCIARI Massimo, "The Geophilosophy of Europe" in *The Unpolitical* [Chapter 9] Fordham University Press, New York, 2009.

CACCIARI Massimo, *Dallo Steinhof. Prospettive viennesi del primo Novecento*, Adelphi, Milano, 2005.

CACCIARI Massimo, *Europe and Empire: On the Political Forms of Globalization,* Fordham University Press, New York, 2016.

CACCIARI Massimo. *L'arcipelago*, Adelphi, Milano, 1996.

CAME Daniel (Ed.), *Nietzsche on Art and Life*, Oxford University Press, Oxford, 2014

CAMPBELL Louise, "Towards a New Cathedral: The Competition for Coventry Cathedral 1950-51", *Architectural History*, Vol. 35, 1992, pp. 208–234.

CAMPORESSI Piero, *Il pane selvaggio*, Il Saggiatore, Milan, 1980.

CAPELLO Maria Beatriz, "Recepção e difusão da arquitetura moderna brasileira nos números especiais das revistas especializadas européias (1940-1960)", *9° seminário docomomo brasil interdisciplinaridade e experiências em documentação e preservação do patrimônio recenté*, Brasília, June 2011, www.docomomobsb.or

CARAMUEL Y LOBKOWITZ Juan, *Straight and Oblique Civil Architecture*, Vol. II, Camilo Corrado, Vigevano, 1687.

ÇELIK Zeynep, "Le Corbusier, Orientalism, Colonialism", *Assemblage*, No. 17, April 1992, pp. 58–77.

CESARIANO Cesare, *Vitruvius. Di Lucio Vitruvio Pollione. De Architectura LIbri Dece*, Gotardus Da Ponte, Como, 1521.

CHANONY, *Mémoire d'un voyage en Algérie, et retour par l'Espagne*, C. Hingray, Paris, 1853.

CHATEAUBRIAND François-René de, *Itinéraire de Paris à Jérusalem*, Chez Léfaivre Libraire, Paris, 1834.

CHETWODE EUSTACE John, *A Classical Tour through Italy*, Baudry's European Library, Paris, 1837.

CHIESA Lorenzo, TOSCANO Alberto, eds., *The Italian Difference: Between Nihilism and Biopolitics*, Re-Press, Melbourne, 2009.

CIAM, Arts Council, Bridgwater, *The Architect and Building News*, September 19, 1947.

CIPOLLA Carlo, *Chi ruppe i rastrelli a Montelupo?*, Il Mulino, Bologna, 1977.

CIUCCI Giorgio, "Le Corbusier e Wright in URSS," 171-194, in Manfredo Tafuri (ed.), *Socialismo, città, architettura URSS,1917-1937: il contributo degli architetti europei*, Officina, Rome, 2nd ed., 1972.

CIUCCI Giorgio, "Gli anni della formazione", *Casabella*, No. 619–620, 1995, pp. 12–27.

CLAYTON Peter, *The Seven Wonders of the Ancient World*, Routledge, London and New York, 1988.

COHEN Jean-Louis, "La coupure entre architects et intellectuels, ou les enseignements de l'italophilie", *In Extenso. Recherches à l'Ecole d'Achitecture Paris-Villemin*, In Extenso. Recherches, Paris, 1984.

COHEN Jean-Louis, *Architecture in Uniform: Designing and Building for the Second World War,* Editions Hasan, Paris, 2011.

COHEN Jean-Louis, *L'Architecture au futur depuis 1889*, Phaidon, Paris, 2012.
COHEN Jean-Louis; "Avant l'Apres-guerre. Seconde conflit mondial et internationalization de la condition du projet" in BONIFACIO, PACE, ROSSO, SCRIVANO (eds.), *Tra guerra e pace. Societa, cultura e archittura nel secondo dopoguerra*, Franco Angeli, Milan, 1998.
COLLETTI Lucio, *From Rousseau to Lennin: Studies in Ideology and Society*, Monthly Review Press, New York, 1974, p. 3.
COLOMINA B., SMITHSON P., "Friends of the Future: A Conversation with Peter Smithson", *October*, Vol. 94, Autumn 2000, pp. 3–30.
COLOMINA Beatriz, "Sex, Lügen und Dekoration: Adolf Loos und Gustav Klimt", in the exhibition catalog *Adolf Loos: Our Contemporary, Unser Zeitgenosse, Nosso Contemporaneo*, curator Yehuda E. Safran, GSAPP, Columbia University, New York, 2012.
COLOMINA Beatriz, "Unbreathed Air 1956", in VAN DEN HEUVEL Dirk & RISSELADA Max, (Eds.), *Alison and Peter Smithson-from te House of the Future to a house of today"* 010 Publishers, Rotterdam, 2004, pp. 30–49.
CONEKIN B., MORT F., WATERS C., eds., *Moments of Modernity. Reconstructing Britain 1945-1964*, Rivers Oram Press, London, 1999.
CONEKIN Becky, *The Autobiography of a Nation. The 1951 Festival of Britain*, Manchester University Press, New York, 2003.
CONNORS Joseph, "Poussin detrattore di Borromini", in FROMMEL Christoph L., SLADEK Elisabeth (eds.), *Francesco Borromini, Atti del convegno internazionale* (Rome 13–15 Gennaio 2000), Electa, Milan, 2000, pp. 191–204.
COSPITO Giuseppe, "Egemonia/egemonico nei "Quaderni del carcere" (e prima)", *International Gramsci Journal*, Vol. 2, No. 1, 2016.
COTTINGTON David, *Modern Art. A Very Short Introduction*, Oxford University Press, Oxford and New York, 2008.
CRINSON M., ZIMMERMAN C., eds., *Neo Avant-Garde and Postmodern. Postwar Architecture in Britain and Beyond*, YC British Art, London, 2010.
CURTIS Barry, "Review of RYAN, Deborah, *The Ideal Home through the 20th Century*, Hazar, London, 1997", *Journal of Design History*, Vol. 11, No. 3, 1998, pp. 266–268.
CURTIS William, "Modern Architecture [by] Manfredo Tafuri, Francesco Dal Co", *Journal of the Society of Architectural Historians*, Vol. 40, No. 2, May 1981, pp. 168–170.
CURTIS William, *Modern Architecture since 1900*, Prentice Hall, Upper Saddle River, NJ, 1983.
DAMISCH Hubert, "L'Autre "Ich", L'Autriche- Austria, or the Desire for the Void: Toward a Tomb for Adolf Loos", *Gray Room*, Vol. 1, 2000, pp. 26–41.
DAPÍA Silvia G., "Pierre Menard in Context", *Borges Variations*, No. 2, 1996, pp. 100–113.
DAY Gail, "Manfredo Tafuri, Frederic Jameson and the Contestations of Political Memory", *Historical Materialism*, Vol. 20, No. 1, 2012, pp. 31–77.
DE LAMARTINE Alphonse, *Voyage en Orient*, Baumgärtner Buchhandlung, Leipzig, 1861.
DE MAGISTRIS Alessandro; "Burocrazie, strategie,apparati. Un'introduzione", in BONIFACIO, PACE, ROSS, SCRIVANO, (eds.), *Tra guerra e pace. Societa, cultura e archittura nel secondo dopoguerra*, Franco Angeli, Milan, 1998, pp. 183–190.
DE PINA-CABRAL João, "The Mediterranean as a Category of Regional Comparison. A Critical View", *Current Anthropology*, Vol. 30, No. 3, June 1989, pp. 399–406.
DELEUZE Gilles (LESTER Mark trans., BOUNDAS Constantin V. ed.), *The Logic of Sense*, The Athlone Press, London, 1990 [DELEUZE Gilles, *Loguique du Sens*, Les Editions du Minuit, Paris, 1969].
DELEUZE Gilles, *Différence et répétition*, Presses Universitaires de France, Paris, 1968.

DEMPSEY Charles, "The Carracci Postille to Vasari's Lives", *The Art Bulletin*, Vol. 68, No. 1, March 1986, pp. 72–76.
DERRIDA Jacques, *L'écriture et la différence*, Éditions du Seuil, Paris, 1967.
DERRIDA Jacques, *Le monolinguisme de l'autre ou la prothèse d'origine*, Galilée, Paris, 1996.
DHÉRALDE Leon, *Voyage en Orient, Jérusalem et la Palestine*, F. F. Ardant frères, Paris, 1881.
DI BIAGIO Anna, "Egemonia leninista, egemonia gramsciana", *Passato e presente: revista di storia contemporánea*, No. 74, 2008, pp. 29–54.
DI NATALE Maria Concetta, GUTTILLA Mariny, eds., "Argan e l'insegnamento universitario gli anni palermitani 1955-1959", *Atti del Convegno nazionale di studi*, Palermo, Palazzo Chiaromonte (Steri), January 28, 2011.
DI NUCCI Sergio, "Recordando a los iracundos", *Radar (Pagina 12)*, 2006.
DOUGHTY Charles M., *Passages from Arabia Deserta*, selected by GARNETT Edward, Penguin Books, Harmondsworth, 1984 (1931). Originally published in *Travels in Arabia Deserta*, The Cambridge University Press, London, 1888.
DREYFUS Hubert, "Heidegger on the Connection between Nihiulism, Art, Technology and Politics", in Charles Guignon, ed., *The Cambridge Companion to Heidegger*, Cambridge University Press, Cambridge & New York, 1993, pp. 345–372.
DUBY Georges, ed., *Los ideales del mediterráneo. Historia, filosofía y literatura en la ciudad europea*, Icaria Editorial, Barcelona, 1997.
DUDLEY George, *A Workshop for Peace: Designing the United Nations Headquarters*, Cambridge, Mass., 1994.
DUNCAN James S., GREGORY Derek, eds., *Rites of Passage: Reading Travel Writing*, Routledge, London, 1999.
Editorial Comment, "Brazilian Preview", *The Architectural Review*, Vol. 114, No. 679, July 1953, pp. 10–15.
ELIOT T.S. (CUDA Anthony and SCHUCHARD Ronald eds.), *The Complete Prose of T. S. Eliot. The Critical Edition*, Vol.2 "The Perfect Critic", 1919–1926, Johns Hopkins University Press, Baltimore, MD/Faber & Faber, London, 2014.
ESCHER Cornelia, "Between Ciam and Team 10: The "East" and the Peripheries Of Ciam", in *Team 10 East: Revisionist Architecture in Real Existing Modernism*, Museum of Modern Art in Warsaw, Warsaw, 2014, pp. 101–106.
ESCOBAR Arturo, *Encountering Development. The Making and Unmaking of the Third World*, Princeton University Press, Princeton, NJ, 1994.
ESHER Lionel, *A Broken Wave: The Rebuilding of England, 1940-1980*, Allen Lane, London, 1981.
FAGG William, "Primitive and Modern Art in London", *Man*, No. 2–4, January 1949, p. 9.
FELIBIEN André, *Des principes de l'architecture, de la sculpture, de la painting, et des autres arts qui en dépendent: Avec un dictionnaire des termes propres à chacun de ces arts*. chez la Veuve & Jean-Baptiste Coignard, fils. Avec privilege de sa Majesté, Paris, 1697.
FELIBIEN André, *Entretiens sur les vies et sur les ouvrages des plus excellents peintres anciens et modernes*. Chez Pierre Le Petit, Imprimeur & Libraite ordinaire du Roy, rué S. Jacques , à la Croix d'Or, 10 Avec Privilege de Sa Majesté, Paris. 1666.
FELTRINELLI Giangiacomo, *Contro l'imperialismo e la colalizione delle destre*, Feltrinelli Ebook, Milan, 2012.
FENOULHET Jane, GILBERT Lesley, eds., *Narratives of Low Countries History and Culture Book*, Reframing the Past Book, UCL Press, 2016.

FERNANDEZ Macedonio (OBIETA A. de ed.), *Papeles de recienvenido y la continuación de la nada*, Corregidor, Buenos Aires, 1989.

FILIPPINI Michele, "Tra scienza e senso comune. Dell'ideologia in Gramsci", *Scienza & Politica*, vol. XXV, No. 47, 2012, pp. 89–106.

FISHER Tom, "A World of Colour and Bright Shining Surfaces: Experiences of Plastics after the Second World War", *Journal of Design History*, Vol. 26, No. 3, Special Issue: Shininess, 2013, pp. 285–303.

FISTETTI Francesco, "La crise du marxisme en Italie: 1980-2005. Esquisse d'une histoire des intellectuels", *Cités*, Vol. 4, No.32, pp.159-183, 2007.

FOUCAULT Michel (MISKOWIEC Jan trans.), "Of Other Spaces", *Diacritics*, Vol. 16, No. 1, Spring 1986, pp. 22–27.

FOUCAULT Michel, "Des espaces autres" (conference delivered at Cercle d'ètudes architecturales on March 14, 1967), in *Architecture/Mouvement/Continuité*, October, 1984], pp. 46–49.

FOWLER Alan, "A Forgotten British Constructivist Group: The London Branch of Groupe Espace, 1953-59", *The Burlington Magazine*, Vol. 149, No. 1248, (British Art) March, 2007, pp. 173–179.

FRAMPTON Kenneth, *Modern Architecture. A Critical History*, Thames & Hudson, London, 1980.

FRANGENBERG Thomas, "Abraham Bosse in Context: French Responses to Leonardo's Treatise on Painting in the Seventeenth Century", *Journal of the Warburg and Courtauld Institutes*, Vol. 75, 2012, pp. 223–260.

FREUD Sigmund, "Analysis terminable and interminable" (1937), in *The Standard Edition of the Complete Psychological Works of Sigmund Freud. Translated from the German under the General Editorship of James Strachey*, Vol. XXIII, The Hogarth Press and the Institute of Psyco-Analysis, 1964.

FRY Maxwel, "Chandigarh: The Capital of the Punjab", Lecture at RIBA 4.1.55 published January 1955.

FRYDRYŠKOVÁ, J., "UNRRA and Support for Science", *Acta polytechnica* Prague, Vol.48, 2008, pp. 38–39.

FUSARO Diego, in https://www.youtube.com/watch?v=9fIwgvkWIvU [Accessed April 25, 2016].

GADOW Hans Friedrich, *In Northern Spain*, Adam and Charles Black, London, 1897.

GALVÁN Desvaux N., CARAZO LEFORT E., TORDESILLAS A., "Casas para un mundo feliz", *RA, Revista de Arquitectura*, Vol. 17, 2015, pp. 65–76.

GARTH Todd S., *The Self of the City Macedonio Fernández, the Argentine Avant-Garde, and Modernity in Buenos Aires*, Bucknell University Press, Cranbury, NJ, 2005.

GAY Diana, Fernand Léger et le groupe Espace à Biot. Un terrain d'expérimentation pour une modernité, 2017.

GAZDA Elaine K., ed., *The Ancient Art of Emulation. Studies in Artistic Originality and Tradition from the Present to Classical Antiquity*, The University of Michigan Press, Ann Arbor, 2002.

GEMELLI Giuliana, *Fernand Braudel*, Universidad de Valencia, Valencia, 2005.

GIEDION Sigfried, *A decade of New Architecture*, Girsberger, Zürich, 1951.

GIEDION Sigfried, *Architecture You and Me. The Diary of a Development*, Harvard University Press, Cambridge MA, 1958.

GIEDION Sigfried, *Space, Time and Architecture*, Harvard University Press, Cambridge Mass., 1982 [1941].

196 Bibliography

GIEDION, S., LEGER, F., SERT, J.L., "Nine Points on Monumentality" (1943), in *Architektur und Gemei*nschaft, Rowohlt, Hamburg, 1956. English version in *Architecture, you and me*, Harvard University Press, Cambridge MA, 1958, pp. 25–40.

GILMORE David D., ed., *Honor and Shame and the Unity of the Mediterranean*, American Anthropological Association, Washington, DC, 1987.

GINSBURGH Victor, WEYERS Sheila, "On the Formation of Canons: The Dynamics of Narratives in Art History", *Empirical Studies of the Arts*, Vol. 28(1), 2010, pp. 37–72.

GINSBURGH Victor, WEYERS Sheila, "Persistence and Fashion in Art Italian Renaissance from Vasari to Berenson and Beyond", *Poetics*, Vol. 34, 2006, pp. 22–44.

GINZBURG Carlo, CASTELNUOVO Enrico Castelnuovo, "Centro e Periferia", in Giovanni Previtali Ed., *Storia dell'arte italiana*, Part I, Vol. I, Einaudi, Turín, 1979, pp. 285–352.

GINZBURG Carlo, *Il formaggio e i vermi. Il cosmo di un mugnaio del '500*, Adelphi, Milan, 1976.

GIRAUDEAU DE SAINT-GERVAIS Jean, *L'Italie, la Sicile, Malte, la Grèce, l'Archipel, les îles Ioniennes et la Turquie : souvenirs de voyage historiques et anecdotiques*, Delaunay Libraire, Paris, 1835.

GLANCEY Jonathan, *20th Century Architecture: The Structures That Shaped the Century*, Carlton, London, 1998.

GOLDHAGEN Sarah Williams & LEGAULT Réjean, *Anxious Modernisms. Experimentation in Postwar Architectural Culture,* MIT Press, Cambridge, Mass., 2001.

GOMBRICH Ernst, *Ideals and Idols*, Phaidon, Amsterdam, 1979.

GOMPERTZ Will, *What Are You Looking at? The Surprising, Shocking, and Sometimes Strange Story of 150 Years of Modern Art*, Penguin Books, New York, 2012.

GORAK Jan, *The Making of the Modern Canon. Genesis and Crisis of a Literary Idea*, Bloomsbury Academic, New York, 2014.

GRACIA Jorge J.E., "Borges's "Pierre Menard": Philosophy or Literature?", *The Journal of Aesthetics and Art Criticism*, Vol. 59, No. 1, Winter 2001, pp. 45–57.

GRAMSCI Antonio (FUBINI Elsa, ed.), *La costruzione del partito comunista. 1923-1926*, Torino, Einaudi, 1971.

GRESLERI G., MASSARETTI P.G., ZAGNONI F., *Architettura italiana d'oltremare: 1870-1940*, Marsilio, Venezia, 1993.

GRISKO Michael, ed., *Freikörperkultur und Lebenswelt. Studien zur Vor- und Frühgeschichte der Freikörperkultur in Deutschland*, Kassel University Press, Kassel, 1999.

GROAZ Silvia, "The New Brutalism: Ethic vs. Marxism? Ideological Collisions in Post-War English Architecture", in JANNIÈRE Hélène & SCRIVANO Paolo (eds.) "Committed, Politicized, or Operative : Figures of Engagement in Criticism from 1945 to Today", *Histories of Postwar Architecture*, No 7 , September 3, 2021, pp. 104–123.

GROPIUS Walter, "Das flache dach. Internationale Umfrage" "Die Bauwelt. Zeitschrift fur das gesamte Bauwesen", *Heft*, Vol. 8, No. 17, February 25, 1926, pp. 162–168.

GUETZKOW J., LAMONT M., MALLARD G., "What Is Originality in the Humanities and the Social Sciences?", *American Sociological Review*, Vol. 69, April 2004, pp. 190–212.

GUIBAULT Serge (Goldhammer A. trans.), *How New York Stole the Idea of Modern Art*, University of Chicago Press, Chicago, IL, 1985.

GUILLORY John, *Cultural Capital: The Problem of Literary Canon Formation*. E-book, The University of Chicago Press, Chicago, IL, 1993.

GULDDAL Jesper, *Anti-Americanism in European Literature*, Palgrave Macmillan, London, 2011.

HABERMAS Jürgen (LAWRENCE Frederick trans.), *The Philosophical Discourse of Modernity.* Twelve Lectures, Polity Press, Cambridge, 1998 [HABERMAS Jürgen, *Der philosophische Diskurs der Moderne: Zwölf Vorlesungen*, Suhrkamp Verlag, Frankfurt-am-Main, 1985].

HAN Byung-Chul, *The Expulsion of the Other*, Polity Press, Medford, MA and Cambridge, 2018.

HANÁČKOVÁ Marcela, *CIAM and the Cold War. Helena Syrkus between Modernism and Socialist Realism*, Doctoral Thesis, ETH Zurich, 2019.

HARE David, "The Myth of Originality in Contemporary Art", *Art Journal*, Vol. 24, No. 2, Winter 1964–1965, pp. 139–142.

HASLEY A.H., "Review of Family and Class in a London Suburb", *American Sociological Review*, Vol. 26, No. 5, October 1961, pp. 169–177.

HAUSENSTEIN Wilhelm, *Kairuan. Eine Geschichte vom Maler Klee*, Kurt Wolf, München, 1921.

HEGEMANN Werner, "Schräges oder flache Dach?", *Wasmuths Monatshefte fur Baukunst*, 11 jg, 1927.

HEIDEGGER Martin, *Der Feldweg*, Vittorio Klostermann GmbH, Frankfurt am Main, 1989 [Translated by Bret Davis to English as *Country Path Conversations* (Bloomington: Indiana University Press, 2010)].

HEIDEGGER Martin, *Gelassenheit*, Verlag Günther Neske, Pfullingen, 1959 [Translated to English as *Discourse On Thinking,* by John Anderson and Hans Freund (New York: Harper & Row, 1966)].

HEINZE-GREENBERG Ita, "An Artistic European Utopia at the Abyss of Time: The Mediterranean Academy Project, 1931-34", *Architectural History*, Vol. 45, 2002, pp. 441–482.

HERMANN Martin, *A History of Fear. British Apocalyptic Fiction, 1895−2011*, Epubli, Berlin, 2015.

HERNÁNDEZ Silvia, "Figuras de Alteridad: Ensayos a partir de Borges y Chesterton", *Andamios*, Vol. 8, No. 16, May–August 2011, pp. 91–112.

HEUSS Theodor, Mitteliungen des Deutschen Werkbundes, 22 July 1922.

HEWISON Robert, *In Anger. Culture in the Cold War. 1945-1960*, Oxford University Press, London, 1981.

HEYNEN Hilde, "The Venice School, or the Diagnosis of Negative Thought", in *Architecture and Modernity. A Critique*, MIT Press, Cambridge, MA, 1999, pp. 128–147.

HIGGOTT Andrew. *Mediating Modernism: Architectural Cultures in Britain*, Routledge, London, 2006.

HIGHMORE B., "Memories of Catastrophes Yet to Come: New Brutalism and Thing Memory", in SMELIK Anneke & Plate, LIEDEKE (Eds.), *Performing Memory in Art and Popular Culture*, Routledge, Oxford and New York, 2013, pp. 75–91.

HIGHMORE Ben, "Rough Poetry: 'Patio and Pavilion' Revisited", *Oxford Art Journal*, Vol. 29, No. 2, 2006.

HIGHMORE Ben, "Rough Poetry: "Patio and Pavilion" Revisited", *Oxford Art Journal*, Vol. 29, No. 2, 2006, pp. 269–290.

HITCHCOCK Henry-Russell, "The International Style Twenty Years After", *The Architectural Record*, August 1951.

HITCHCOCK Henry-Russell, JOHNSON Philip, *The International Style: Architecture since 1922*, Norton, New York, 1932.

HOBBS Roland, "Ronald Stewart Jenkins: Engineer and Mathematician", *The Arup Journal*, Vol. 20, No. 2, Summer 1985, pp. 9–13.

HOEKSTRA Titia Rixt, Building versus Bildung. Manfredo Tafuri and the Construction of a Historical Discipline, Doctoral Dissertation, Rijksuniversiteit Groningen, 2005.
HOFSTADTER Richard, *The Age of Reform: From Bryan to F.D.R.,* Knopf Doubleday Publishing Group, New York, 1960.
HOLFORD William, "Brasília: The Federal Capital of Brazil", *The Geographical Journal*, Vol. 128, No. 1, March 1962, pp. 134–136.
HOLQUIST Michael, *Dialogism. Bakhtin and His World*, Routledge, London and New York, (1990) 2002.
HUDSON HICK D., SCHMÜCKER R., eds., *The Aesthetics and Ethics of Copying*, Boombsbury, London, 2016.
HUXLEY Julian, "Julian Huxley on Population and Human Destiny", *Population and Development Review*, Vol. 19, No. 3, 1993, pp. 607–620.
HUXLEY Thomas Henry, *Man's place in nature,* Appleton, New York,1899.
Introduction *The Architectural Review*, Vol. 95, No. 567, March 1944.
IVARS Lorena Ángela, *Borges en Sur*, Emecé, Buenos Aires, 1999.
JAMES Julie, "1964 or 1974: Which Is "The Other?"", *Borges Variations*, No. 8, 1999, pp. 142–152.
JANNIÈRE H., SCRIVANO P., eds., *Histories of Postwar Architecture*, Committed, Policized, or Operative: Figures of Engagement in Criticism from 1945 to Today, No. 7, September 3, 2021.
JAUSS Hans Robert, *Toward an Aesthetic of Reception*, University of Minnesota Press, Minneapolis, MN, (1982) 2005.
JAY Martin, "Modernism and the Retreat from Form" (Chapter 11), in *Force Fields*, Routledge, London, 1983, pp. 147–148.
JEFFREYS K., "The Stagnant Society: Modernising Britain", in *Retreat from New Jerusalem. British Policy 1951-1964*, Palgrave Macmillan, London, 1997, pp. 110–130.
JOSEPH Jonathan, *Hegemony. A Realist Analysis*, Routledge, London and New York, 2002.
KABBANI Rana, *Imperial Fictions: Europe's Myths of Orient*, Pandora, London, 1994.
KAPROW Alan, *Essays on the Blurring of Art and Life*, University of California Press, Berkeley, Los Angeles, London, 1993.
KENTGENS-CRAIG Margret, *Bauhaus And America. The Bauhaus First Contacts 1919 1936*, The Mit Press, Cambridge, MA, 1999
KEYNES John Maynard, *The End of Laissez-Faire: The Economic Consequences of the Peace*, Prometheus Books, New York, 2004 [1919].
KING Anthony, *The Bungalow: The Production of a Global Culture*, Oxford University Press, Oxford and New York, 1995.
KIRKPATRICK Charles E., "Strategic Planning for World War II The Victory Plan in Context", *Army History* , No. 16, Fall 1990, pp. 17–21.
KISS Sándor, "L'interférence du centre et de la périphérie (Illustrée par des exemples de diachronie romane)", *Écho des études romanes. Revue semestrielle de linguistique et littératures romanes*, Vol. VI, No. 1–2, 2010, pp. 69–76.
KITE Stephen, "Softs and Hards: Colin St. John Wilson and the Contested *Vision of 1950s London",* in CRIMSON Mark & ZIMMERMAN Claire (Eds.), *Neo Avant-Garde and Postmodern. Postwar Architecture in Britain and Beyond*, YC British Art, London, 2010, pp. 55–77.
KITNICK Alex, "The Brutalism of Life and Art", *October*, Vol. 136, Spring 2011, pp. 63–86.
KLAWITER Randolph J., "Peter Altenberg and Das Junge Wien", *Modern Austrian Literature*, Vol. 1, No. 4, Winter 1968, pp. 1–55.

KOCOUREK Rostislav, "De la perspective centro-périphérique en linguistique", *Écho des études romanes. Revue semestrielle de linguistique et littératures romanes*, Vol. VI, No. 1–2, 2010, pp. 21–31.

KOHLRAUSCH Martin, "Architects as Experts of the Social: A new Type entering the European Scene", in *Brokers of Modernity: East Central Europe and the Rise of Modernist Architects, 1910-1950*, Leuven University Press, Leuven, 2019, pp. 57–96.

KOHLRAUSCH Martin, Chapter 6, "Under Pressure: Modernist Architects and the Rise of Political Extremes", in *Brokers of Modernity: East Central Europe and the Rise of Modernist Architects, 1910-1950*, Leuven University Press, Leuven, 2019, pp. 235–280.

KÖHRING Alexandra, "'Friendly Atmospheres'? The Union Internationale des Architectes between East and West in the 1950s", in BAZIN, J., DUBOURG GLATIGNY, P., PIOTROWSKI, P. (Eds.), *Art beyond Borders. Artistic Exchange in Communist Europe (1945-1989)*, Central European University Press, Budapest, 2016.

KRAUS Karl, *Sprüche und Widersprüche*, Suhrkamp, Frankfurt, 1965.

KRAUSS Rosalind, *The Originality of the Avant-Garde and Other Modernist Myths*, MIT Press, Cambridge, 1985.

KRISHNA Roop and Mary, *Art and Life*, Rama Krishna and Sons Anarkali, Lahore, 1940.

KRISTEVA Julia (ROUDIEZ Leon trans.), *Strangers to Ourselves*, Columbia University Press, New York, 1991 [KRISTEVA Julia, *Etrangers a nous-memes*, Librairie Artheme Fayard, Paris, 1988].

KROSS Christine, *Fast Cars, Clean Bodies*, MIT Press, Cambridge, MA, 1999.

KÜHN Christian, *Das schöne, das wahre und das richtige: Adolf Loos und das Haus Müller in Prag*, Birkhäuser, Berlin, 2001.

KUMAR SARKAR Benoy, "World-Politics and Post-War Economic Planning", *The Indian Journal of Political Science*, October-December, Vol. 5, No. 2, 1943, pp. 161–190.

LACAN Jacques, "The Self in Freud's Theory / Class 19. Introduction to the Great Other", *The Seminars of Jacques Lacan / Seminar 2*, May 25, 1955.

LACHMAN Gary, "The Angry Young Man" in *Beyond of Robot. The Life and Work of Colin Wilson*, Penguin Random House, New York, 2016, pp. 7–44.

LACHMANN Renate, ESHELMAN Raoul, DAVIS Mark, "Bakhtin and Carnival: Culture as Counter-Culture", in *Cultural Critique*, No. 11 (Winter, 1988–1989).

LANE Edward William, *An Account of the Manners and Customs of the Modern Egyptians*, Ward, Lock and Co., London, 1837.

LANGFELD Gregor, "The Canon in Art History: Concepts and Approaches", *Journal of Art Historiography*, No. 19, December 2018, pp. 1–18.

LANGHOLM Sivert, "On the Concepts of Center and Periphery", *Journal of Peace Research*, Vol. 8, No. 3/4, 1971, pp. 273–278.

LAPLANCHE Jean, *Essays on Otherness*, Routledge, London and New York, 1999.

LAU Kwok-Ying, CHEUNG Chan-Fai, KWAN Tze-Wan, eds., *Identity and Alterity. Phenomenology and Cultural Traditions*, Verlag Konigshausen & Neumann, Würzburg, 2010.

LAUWERIKS J.L.M., "Het Titanischein De Kunst Door", *Wendingen*, No. 4, April 1919, pp. 3–6.

LAZAARE Khalid Lazaare, *Marokko in deutschen Reisebereichen des 19. Und beginnenden 20. Jahrhunderts: Vorstudien zur deutschen Wahrnehmung einer islamischen Region*, P. Lang, Frankfurt am Main and New York, 1998.

LE BLANC Aleca, "Palmeiras and Pilotis", *Third Text*, Vol. 26, No. 1, 2012, pp. 103–116.

LE CORBUSIER, "Die Eroberung des flaches Daches", *Das Neue Frankfurt. Internationale Monatsschrift für die Probleme kultureller Neugestaltung*, No 7, October–December 1927, pp. 167–169.

LEACH Andrew, Choosing History. A Study of Manfredo Tafuri's Theorisation of Architectural History and Architectural History Research, Doctoral Dissertation, Faculteit Ingenieurswetenschappen, Universiteit Gent, 2005–2006.
LEE Vernon (born PAGE Violet), *Laurus Nobilis. Chapters on Art and Life*, John Lane, London, New York, 1909.
LEJEUNE J.-F., SABATINO M., eds., *Modern Architecture and the Mediterranean*, Routledge, London and New York, 2010.
LEVI Giovanni, *L'eredità immateriale*, Il Saggiatore, Milan, 1985.
LEVINAS Emmanuel, "La Huella del Otro" in *La huella del Otro,* Taurus, Mexico, 2000, pp.45–74. English versión "The Trace of the Other", (LINGIN A. trans.) in TAYLOR Mark C., ed., *Deconstruction in Context. Literature and Philosophy*, The University of Chicago Press, Chicago, IL and London, 1986. From "La Trace de l'Autre", in *En découvrant l'existence avec Husserl et* Heidegger, Vrie, 1967.
LÉVINAS Emmanuel, *Humanisme de l'autre homme*, Fata Morgana, Montpellier, 1972.
LIGUORI Guido, "'Senso comune' e 'buon senso' nei quaderni del carcere", relazione per il *Seminario sul lessico dei quaderni*, International Gramsci Society, Rome, 13 May 2005, pp. 1–23.
LIJSTER Thijs, *Benjamin and Adorno on Art and Art Criticism*, Amsterdam University Press, Amsterdam, 2017.
LINELL Per, *Rethinking Language, Mind, and World Dialogically Interactional and Contextual Theories of Human Sense-Making*, Information Age Publishing Inc., Charlotte, 2009.
LLORENS Tomas, "Manfredo Tafuri: Neo-Avant-Garde and History", *Architectural Design*, Vol. 51, Nrs.6/7, 1981, pp. 83–95.
LOCHER Hubert *Daidalos*, "'Genug der Originalgenies! Wiederholen wir uns unaufhörlich selbst!' ("'Enough of the Original Geniuses! Let Us Repeat Ourselves Unceasingly!)'", in *Daidalos*, "Das Neue/What's New", No. 52, June 15, 1994, pp. 72–75.
LODDER Christina, *Russian Constructivism*; *Russian Suprematism*, Uale University Press, New Haven, 1985.
LODDER Christina, *The Ghost in the Machine: The Modernist Architectural Utopia under Stalin, in Utopian Reality*, Brill, Leiden, 2013.
LOOS Adolf, 'Architektur', in *Sämtliche Schriften*, Herold, Wien, München, 1962, pp. 302–318 [*On Architecture: Studies in Austrian Literature, Culture and Thought*, Ariadne Press, Riverside, 2007.]
LOOS Adolf, "Heimatkunst", in *Sämtliche Schriften*, Herold, Wien, München, 1962, pp. 331–341.
LOOS Adolf, *Adolf Loos: Ornamento y Delito y Otros Escritos*, Gustavo Gili, Barcelona 302-318 see change in text, 1972.
LUCAS-FIORATO C., DUBUS P., *La reception des Vite de Giorgio Vasari dans l'Europe des XVIe-XVIIIe si è cles*, Droz, Genève, 2017.
LURÇAT André, "Der Weg zur Terrasse", *Das Neue Frankfurt. Internationale Monatsschrift für die Probleme kultureller Neugestaltung*, No. 7, October–December, 1927, pp. 173–175.
LYOTARD Jean-Francois (Geoff Bennington and Brian Massumi trans.), *The Postmodern Condition: A Report on Knowledge*, University of Minnesota Press, Minneapolis, 1984 [LYOTARD Jean-François, *La condition postmoderne. Rapport sur le savoir*, Editions du Minuit, Paris, 1979].
MAASE Jaspar, "'Americanization', 'Americanness' and 'Americanisms'. Time for a Change in Perspective?", in *The American Impact on Western Europe; Americanization*

and Westernization in Transatlantic Perspective (Lecture, 25–27.3.99), Conference at the German Historical Institute, Washington, DC, March 25–27, 1999, in *Conference Papers on the Web*.

MAASE Jaspar, "'Americanization', 'Americanness' and 'Americanisms'. Time for a Change in Perspective?", in *The American impact on Western Europe; Americanization and Westernization in Transatlantic Perspective*, (Lecture, 25-27.3.99), Conference at the German Historical Institute, Washington, D.C., March 25–27, 1999, in *Conference Papers on the Web*, pp. 1–15.

MACFARLANE Robert, *Original Copy Plagiarism and Originality in Nineteenth-Century Literature*, Oxford University Press, Oxford, 2007.

MACHICAO Y PROEMER A., NOLDA A., SIOUPI A., eds., *Zwischen Kern und Peripherie. Untersuchungen zu Randbereichen*, De Gruyter, Berlin, 2014.

MADONNA Maria Luisa, "'Septem Mundi Miracula' come Templi della Virtù: Pirro Ligorio e l'interpretazione Cinquecentesca delle Meraviglie del Mondo", *Psicon*, Vol. 7, No. 3, 1976, pp. 25–63.

MALICH Ksenia, "Kind Regards in These Difficult Times: Anglo–Soviet Architectural Relations during the Second World War", *Arts*, Vol. 12, No. 158, July 13, 2023. https://doi.org/10.3390/ arts12040158.

MALICH Ksenia, "Kind Regards in These Difficult Times: Anglo–Soviet Architectural Relations during the Second World War", *Arts* 12: 158. https://doi.org/10.3390/arts12040158

MALLGRAVE Harry Francis, "London Lecture of December 1853: On the Origin of Some Architectural Styles" (Gottfried Semper), *RES: Anthropology and Aesthetics*, No. 9, Spring 1985, pp. 53–60.

MALRAUX André (GILBERT Stuart trans.), "Museum Without Walls" (Le musée imaginaire), in *The Voices of Silence*, Princeton University Press, Princeton, NJ, 1978, pp. 13–130.

MANDARINI Matteo, "Beyond Nihilism: notes towards a critique of left-heideggerianism in Italian philosophy of the 1970s" in CHIESA Lorenzo & TOSCANO Alberto, *The Italian Difference. Between nihilism and biopolitics*, re.press, Melbourne, 2009, pp. 55–80.

MANGONE Fabio, *Capri e gli architetti*, Massa, Naples, 2004.

MARCHAND Suzanne L., "The Rhetoric of Artifacts and the Decline of Classical Humanism: The Case of Josef Strykowski", *History and Theory*, Vol. 33, No. 4 (Theme Issue 33: Proof and Persuasion in History), December 1994, pp. 106–130.

MARCHAND Suzanne, "German Orientalism and the Decline of the West", *Proceedings of the American Philosophical Society*, Vol. 145, December 2001, pp. 465–473.

MARFÈ Luigi, "Estética de la repetición en la ficción de Jorge Luis Borges", *HYBRIS. Philosophy Magazine*, Vol. 8, September 2017, pp. 227–239.

MARRAMAO Giacomo, "Universalism and Politics of Differfence: Democracy as a Paradoxical Community", *The Passage West: Philosophy After the Age of the Nation State*, Verso, London, 2012. [Marramao, Giacomo, "Paradossi dell'universalismo", in *Le idee della sinistra,* Editori Riuniti, Roma, 1992]

MARX K., ENGELS F., *Marx & Engels on Literature and Art: A Selection of Writings*, Telos Press, St. Louis, 1973.

MARX Karl, *Grundrisse: Foundations of the Critique of Political Economy*. Trad. Martin Nicolaus, Penguin Books, London, 1993.

MASTERS Nathan, "Chavez Ravine: Community to Controversial Real Estate", in *KCET*, September 13, 2012.

MAXWELL Robert, ed., *Stirling. Scritti di architettura*, Skira Editori, Milan, 1998.

MAY Reinhard, *Heidegger's Hidden Sources. East Asian Influences on His Work*, Routledge, London, 1996.

MC LEOD Malcom, *Introduction* to PAOLOZZI Eduardo, *Lost Magic Kingdoms and Six Paper Moons from Nahuatl*. An Exhibition at the Museum of Mankind, British Museum Publications, London, 1985, pp. 15–60.

MCALEER Neil, *Sir Arthur C. Clarke: Odyssey of a Visionary*, RosettaBooks LLC, New York, 2013.

MCCARTHY Conor, *The Cambridge Introduction to Edward Said*, Cambridge University Press, Cambridge et al., 2010.

MCCLANCY Jeremy, "Brief Encounter: The Meeting, in Mass-Observation, of British Surrealism and Popular Anthropology", *The Journal of the Royal Anthropology Institute*, Vol. 1, No. 3, September 1995, pp. 495–507.

MCFARLAND Thomas, "The Originality Paradox", *New Literary History*, Vol. 5, No. 3, Spring 1974, pp. 447–476.

MCLAREN Brian, "The Italian Colonial Appropriation of Indigenous North African Architecture in the 1930's", *Muqarnas*, Vol. 19, 2002, pp. 164–192.

MEDINA WARMBURG Joaquín, *Walter Gropius, proclamas de modernidad. Escritos y conferencias, 1908-1934*, Editorial Reverté, Barcelona, 2018.

MEECHAM Pam, ed., *A Companion to Modern Art*, John Wiley & Sons, Hoboken, NJ, 2018.

MEIKLE Jeffrey L., "Into the Fourth Kingdom: Representations of Plastic Materials, 1920-1950", *Journal of Design History*, 1992, Vol. 5, No. 3, pp. 173–182.

MELMAN Charles, *D'un Autre à l'autre, deuxième tour... sur le séminaire 1968-1969 de Jacques Lacan*, Edition de l'Association Lacanienne Internationale, Paris, 2007.

MENDELSOHN Erich, *Amerika: Bilderbuch eines Architekten*, Rudolf Mosse Buchverlag, Berlin, 1928.

MILLARD André, *Equipping James Bond. Guns, Gadgets, and Technological Enthusiasm*, Johns Hopkins University Press, Baltimore, MD, 2018.

MOHOLY-NAGY Sibyl, "The Diaspora", *Journal of the Society of Architectural Historians*, March, 1965, Vol. 24, No. 1., in particular chapter 4 "Controversies Surrounding Bauhaus Architecture", pp.170-203.

MOMETTI Felice, "Ideologia come architettura. Manfredo Tafuri e la storia critica", *Scienza & Politica*, Vol. XXV, No. 47, 2012, pp. 107–133.

MORAVANSKY Akos, "Peripheral modernism: Charles Polónyi and the Lessons of the Village", *The Journal of Architecture*, Vol. 22, No. 4, May 2017, pp. 662–688.

MOUFFE Chantal, "Hegemony and Ideology in Gramsci", in *Gramsci and Marxist Theory*, Routledge, London and New York, 1979, pp. 168–203.

MUALEM Shlomy, "Borges and Levinas Face-to-Face: Writing and the Riddle of Subjectivity", *Philosophy and Literature*, Vol. 41, No. 1A, July 2017, pp. 315–343.

MUMFORD Eric, *The CIAM discourse on Urbanism, 1928-1960*, MIT Press, Cambridge Mass.; 2000.

MYERS Julian, "The Future as Fetish", *October*, Vol. 94, Autumn 2000, pp. 62–88.

MYHRA David, "Rexford Guy Tugwell: initiator of America's Greenbelt New Towns, 1935 to 1936", In *Journal of the American Institute of Planners,* May, 1974, pp. 176–188.

NAMORATO Michael V., *Rexford G. Tugwell: a biography*, Bloomsbury Academic New York, 1988.

NEMZER Louis, "The Soviet Friendship Societies",*The Public Opinion Quarterly*, Vol. 13, No. 2, Summer, 1949, pp. 265–284.

NIETSZCHE Friedrich (ZIMMERN Helen trans.), *Beyond Good and Evil*, Modern Library Publishers, New York, 1917.

NIETZSCHE Friedrich, *The Case of Wagner, Nietzsche Contra Wagner, and Selected Aphorisms*, The Project Gutenberg EBook, April 7, 2008 [Ebook 25012].

NISBET Robert A., "Genius & Milieu", *Proceedings of the American Philosophical Society*, Vol. 126, No. 6, December 17, 1982, pp. 441–451.

NITZAN-SHIFTAN Alona, "Contested Zionism -- Alternative Modernism: Erich Mendelsohn and the Tel Aviv Chug in Mandate Palestine", *Architectural History*, Vol. 39, 1996, pp. 147–180.

NOBRE Ana Luisa, "Entrevista a Manfredo Tafuri", in *Urbanismo* No. 48, Jun/Jul 1993, Sao Paulo.

OSBORNE Peter, ed., *Socialism and the Limits of Liberalism*, Verso, New York, 1991.

OSTERREICHER-MOLLWO Marianne, *Surrealism and Dadaism*, Phaidon, London, 1979.

OTTO Christian (review of TAFURI, DAL CO, 1979), "'Modern Architecture' by Manfredo Tafuri, Francesco Dal Co, Robert Erich Wolf; 'Architecture and Its Interpretation: A Study of Expressive Systems in Architecture' by Juan Pablo Bonta; 'The Aesthetics of Architecture' by Roger Scruton", *Art Journal*, Vol. 40 "Modernism, Revisionism, Plurism, and Post-Modernism", No. 1/2, Fall–Winter 1980, pp. 423–427.

OUD J.J.P., "Ontwerp voor een entrepôt met stokeri", *De Stijl*, Vol. 3, No. 10, 1920, p. 89.

OWEN Gwendolyn, "Alison and Peter Smithson's 1956 "House of the Future"", *Gastronomica*, Vol. 1, No. 1, Winter 2001, pp. 18–21.

ÖZYETIŞ Emre, Re-visiting the Political Context of Manfredo Tafuri's 'Toward a Critique of Architectural Ideology': 'Having Corpses in Our Mouths', Master's Dissertation, School of Architecture and Design, Design and Social Context Portfolio, March 2013.

PANZIERI Raniero, *La crisi del movimento operaio: Scritti interventi lettere, 1956-1970*, Lampugnani Nigri, Milan, 1973.

PAOLOZZI Eduardo, *Lost Magic Kingdoms and Six Paper Moons from Nahuatl*. An Exhibition at the Museum of Mankind, British Museum Publications, London, 1985.

PASSERINI Luisa, "History as Project: An Interview with Manfredo Tafuri", *ANY: Architecture New York*, No. 25/26, 2000, pp. 10–70.

PATEY C., CIANCI G., CUOJATI F., eds., *Anglo-American Modernity and the Mediterranean*, Università degli Studi di Milano. Facoltà di Lettere e Filosofia, Milan, 29–30 September 2005.

PATTERSON David, "Bakhtin on Word and Spirit: The Religiosity of Responsibility", *Cross Currents*, Vol. 41, No. 1, Spring 1991, pp. 33–51.

PEARSON Christopher E.M., *Designing UNESCO: Art, Architecture and International Politics at Mid-century*, Routledge, London, 2010.

PEHNT Wolfgang, "Gropius the Romantic", *The Art Bulletin*, Vol. 53, No. 3, September 1971, pp. 379–392.

PEHNT Wolfgang, *Die Architektur des Expressionismus*, Arthur Niggli Verlag, Stuttgart, 1973.

PEREZ ESCOLANO Victor, PLAZA Carlos, "Escritos de Manfredo Tafuri (1959-1994 (2014)", in PEREZ ESCOLANO V., PLAZA C. (dir. and coord.), *Manfredo Tafuri desde España. Apendices*, Junta de Andalucìa. Consejería de Cultura y Patrimonio Histórico. Patronato de la Alhambra y Generalife, Granada, 2020, pp. 11–40.

PEVSNER Nikolaus, "Originality", *The Architectural Review*, June 1954, pp. 367–369.

PEVSNER Nikolaus, *Pioneers of Modern Design. From William Morris to Walter Gropius*, Penguin Books, Thetford, [1936] 1977.

PEVSNER Nikolaus, *Pioneers of the Modern Movement from William Morris to Walter Gropius*, Faber & Faber, London, 1936.

PEVSNER Nikolaus, *The Sources of Modern Architecture and Design*, Thames & Hudson, London, 1968.

PEZOLET Nicola, "'Signs of Inhabitation': The Critical Legacies of Patio and Pavilion", *Thresholds*, 2009, No. 35, pp. 44–49.

PHIPPS Linda Sue, *Constructing the United Nations headquarters: modern architecture as public diplomacy* (Ph.D. dissertation), GSD, Harvard, 1998.

PIETSCH Ludwig, *Marokko. Briefe von den deutschen Gesandtschaftreise nach Fez im Frühjar 1877*, Brodhaus, Leipzig, 1878.

PINCUS Debra, "Venice and the Two Romes: Byzantium and Rome as a Double Heritage in Venetian Cultural Politics", in *Artibus et Historiae*, Vol.13, No. 26, 1992, pp. 101–114.

PINTO A., KŇAKAL J., GIRVAN Ch., "The Centre-Periphery System Twenty Years Later", *Social and Economic Studies*, Vol. 22, No. 1, 1973, pp 34–89.

POMMER Richard, "The Flat Roof: A Modernist Controversy in Germany", *Art Journal*, Vol. 43, No. 2, Revising Modernist History: The Architecture of the 1920s and 1930s, Summer 1983, pp. 158–169.

POMMER Richard, CHRISTIAN F. Otto, *Weissenhof 1927 and the Modern Movement in Architecture*, The University of Chicago Press, Chicago, IL and London, 1991.

POROS John, "The UNESCO Headquarters: The Beginning", in *Marcel Breuer. Shaping Architecture in the Post-War Era*, Routledge, London, 2023, pp. 74–101.

POSADAS J., "El congreso cultural de La Habana, El desarrollo mundial de la revolución socialista y la construcción de los estados obreros", *Lucha Obrera*, May 15, 1959, p. 7.

POZZETTO Marco, *La Scuola di Wagner 1894-1912. Idee. Premi. Concorsi*, Comune di Tireste, Trieste, 1979.

PURDY Daniel, "The Cosmopolitan Geography of Adolf Loos", *New German Critique*, No. 99, Autumn 2006, pp. 41–62.

RAJAGOPALAN Kanavillil, "Aesthetics vs. Ideology: The Case of Canon Formation", *British Journal of Aesthetics*, Vol. 37, No. 1, January 1997, pp. 75–83.

RAVA Carlo Enrico, "Panorama del Razionalismo, di un'architettura coloniale moderna", *Domus*, 1931, pp. 163–166.

REID S.E. & CROWLEY D. (Eds.), *Modernity and Material Culture in Post-War Eastern Europe*, Berg, Oxford, 2000.

REILL Peter Hanns, SZELÉNYI, eds., *Cores, Peripheries and Globalization*, CEU Press, Budapest and New York, 2011.

RELLA Franco, *Il mito dell'altro: Lacan, Deleuze, Foucault*, Feltrinelli, Milano, 1978.

RENAN Ernest (t.a.), *Mélanges d'histoire et de voyages*, Calmann, Levy Editeurs, Paris, 1878.

RICOEUR Paul, *Soi-même comme un autre*, Editions du Seuil, Paris, 1990.

RIECKMANN Jens, "'Jung Wie' – Prägung und Rezeption in den neunziger Jahren", *Modern Austrian Literature*, Vol. 18, No. 1, 1985, pp. 39–49.

RILEY Terence, BERGDOLL Barry, eds., *Mies in Berlin*, MoMA, New York, 2001.

ROBBINS David, ed., *The Independent Group: Postwar Britain and the Aesthetics of Plenty*, The MIT Press, Cambridge, MA, 1990.

RODRÍGUEZ MARTÍN María del Carmen, "A través del Espejo. Doble y Alteridad en Borges", *Anuario de Estudios Americanos*, Vol. 65, No. 1, January–June 2008, pp. 277–291.

RODRIGUEZ-MOYA I., MÍNGUEZ V., *The Seven Ancient Wonders in the Early Modern World*, Routledge, London, 2018.

ROTHBARD Murray N., *The Progressive Era*, Mises Institute, Auburn, 2017.

ROVIRA Josep, "Arquitectura, el mediterráneo es su cuna", in PIZZA Antonio (ed.), *Josep Lluís Sert y el Mediterráneo*, Barcelona, 1997 [ROVIRA Josep, "Architecture, the Mediterranean and Is Its Cradle", in PIZZA Antonio (ed.), *Josep Louis Sert and the Mediterranean*, Barcelona, 1997], pp. 46–79.

ROWLAND Ingrid D., CHARNEY Noah, *The Collector of Lives: Giorgio Vasari and the Invention of Art*, WW. Norton & Company, New York, 2017.

RUEL Anne, "L'invention de la Méditerranée", *Vingtième Siècle. Revue d'histoire*, No. 32, Special Issue: *La Méditerranée. Affrontements et dialogues*, October–December 1991, pp. 7–14.

RUSKIN John, *The Poetry of Architecture*, George Allen, London, 1878.

RYAN Deborah S., *Daily Mail Ideal Home Exhibition*, Hazar Publishing, London, 1997.

SAID Edward, *The World, the Text, and the Critic*, Harvard University Press, Cambridge, MA, 1983.

SAMMUT Adam, "Maarten van Heemskerck's Eight Wonders of the Ancient World: Contesting the Image in an Age of Iconoclasm", *Dutch Crossing*, Vol. 46, No. 2022, pp. 1–23.

SANDEEN Eric J., *Picturing an Exhibition: The Family of Man and 1950s America*, University of New Mexico Press, Albuquerque, 1995.

SAUDRAIS Anthony, "Félibien, critique d'art? Esthétique du « regard Félibien » dans l'oeuvre de Raphaël et de Michel-Ange", *Nouvelle revue d'esthétique*, Vol. I, No. 27, 2021/1, pp. 13–20.

SCALVINI María Luisa, SANDRI María Grazia, *L'immagine storiografica dell'architettura contemporanea da Platz a Giedion*, Officina, Roma, 1984.

SCALZONE Oreste, *Biennio Rosso. Figure e pasagi di una stagione*, SugarCo, Milan, 1988.

SCHEIBACH Michael, "Faith, Fallout, and the Future: Post-Apocalyptic Science Fiction in the Early Postwar Era", *Religions*, Vol. 12, No. 520, 2021, pp. 1–11.

SCHULZE Franz, *Mies van der Rohe. A Critical Biography*, University of Chicago Press, Chicago, IL, 1985.

SCHWARTZ Hillel, *The Culture of the Copy Striking Likenesses, Unreasonable Facsimiles*, Zonebooks, New York, 1996.

SCHWARZ Bill, "Reveries of Race. The Closing of the imperial moment", in CONEKIN B., MORT F., WATERS C., eds., *Moments of Modernity. Reconstructing Britain 1945-1964*, Rivers Oram Press, London, 1999, pp. 189–207.

SCHWARZ Katrin, *Bauen für die Weltgemeinschaft : die CIAM und das UNESCO-Gebäude in Paris*, De Gruyter, Berlin, 2016.

SCILIRONI Carlo, "Momenti dell'irrazionalismo contemporáneo", *Idee*, No.18, 1991, pp. 119–126.

SHANK Michael, *The Stagnant Society*, Penguin, Harmondsworth, 1972 (1961).

SHAPIRO Gary, "Nietzsche's Geophilosophy and the Direction of the Earth", *Journal of Nietzsche Studies*, Vol. I, No. 35/36, Autumn 2008, pp. 9–27.

SHERER Daniel, "Progetto and Ricerca. Manfredo Tafuri as Critic and Historian", *Zodiac*, Vol. 15, 1996, pp. 32–56.

SICCA Cinzia Maria, "Vasari's Vite and Italian Artists in Sixteenth-Century England", *Journal of Art Historiography*, No. 9, December 2013, pp. 1–18.

SINFIELD, Alan, *Literature, Politics, and Culture in Postwar Britain*, Continuum, London and New York, 2004.

SITWELL Scheverell, "The Brazilian Style", *The Architectural Review*, Vol. 95, No. 567, March 1944, pp. 65–77.

SMELIK Anneke, PLATE Liedeke, eds., *Performing Memory in Art and Popular Culture*, Routledge, Oxford and New York, 2013.

SMITHSON A. & P., "'Patio and Pavilion' Reconstructed", *AA Files*, No. 47, Summer 2002, pp. 37–44.

SMITHSON A. & P., "Hunstanton *Secundary* Modern School", in *The Charged Void*, The Monacelli Press, New York, 2001, pp. 40–45.

SMITHSON A. & P., *Changing the Art of Inhabitation*, Princeton Architectural Press, Princeton, NJ, 1994.

SMITHSON A. & P., *The Charged Void. Architecture*, The Monacelli Press, New York, 2001.

SMITHSON Alison & Peter, "Leter to America", *Architectural Design*, March, 1958, quoted in SMITHSON Alison, ed., *Team X Manual*, Ediciones Nueva Vision, Buenos Aires, 1966 (London, 1962).

SMITHSON Alison, *The nature of Identity*, 1976. A Paper to be read at Ramsar, October 1976. The Smithson Collection Special Collections Graduate School of Design Harvard University.

SMITHSON Alison & Peter, in *Architectural Design*, July, 1956, quoted in SMITHSON Alison, ed., *Team X Manual*, Ediciones Nueva Vision, Buenos Aires, 1966 (London, 1962).

SMITHSON Peter (CATHERINE Spellman and KART Unglaub eds.), *Conversations with Students. A Space for Our Generation*, Princeton Architectural Press, New York, 2005.

SMITHSON Alison and Peter, "Mobility" in *Ordinariness and Light: Urban Theories 1952-1960 and Their Application in a Building Project 1963-1970*, MIT Press, Cambridge, 1970, pp. 144–153.

SOLL Ivan, "The Re-Invention of the Wheel: Quixotic Reflections on Repetition and Creativity" (Spanish version), *Politeia: Magazine of the Faculty of Law, Political and Social Sciences*, No. 25, 2000, pp. 43–54.

SOLTAN Jerzy, *Architectural Design*, May 1960, in SMITHSON Alison, ed., *Team X Manual*, Ediciones Nueva Vision, Buenos Aires, 1966 (London, 1962), pp. 16–17.

SORENSEN Diana, ed., *Territories & Trajectories. Cultures in Circulation*, Duke University Press, Durham and London, 2018.

SPEAKS M., HADDERS G., *Crimson. Mart Stam's Trousers: Stories from Behind the Scenes of Dutch Moral Modernism*, 010 Publishers, Rotterdam, 1999.

SPELLMAN C., UNGLAUB K., eds., *Peter Smithson. Conversations with Students*, Princeton Architectural Press, New York, 2005.

STARR Frederick, "Le Corbusier and the USSR: New Documentation", Cahiers *du Monde russe et soviétique* , Apr. - Jun., Vol. 21, No. 2, 1980, pp. 209–221.

STAUTH G., OTTO M., *Méditerranée. Skizzen zu Mittelmeer, Islam und Theorie der Moderne*, Kadmos, Berlin, 2008.

STEINER George, *Grammars of Creation*, Faber and Faber, London, 2002.

STEINMAN Martin, (Doctoral dissertation), *Congres Internationaux D'architecture Moderne / Internationale Kongresse fuer Neues Bauen Dokumente 1928-1939*, Eidgenössischen Technischen Hochschule, Zürich, 1979.

STEPHAN Alexander, ed., *The Americanization of Europe. Culture, Diplomacy, and Anti-Americanism after 1945*, Berghahn, Oxford and New York, 2007.

STERNBERG Graf Adalbert, *Die Barbaren von Marokko*, Wiener Verlag, Vienna, 1908.

STEWART Janet, *Fashioning Vienna Adolf Loos's Cultural Criticism*, Routledge, London and New York, 2000.

STIRLING James, "A personal point of view on the current situation", *Architectural Design*, June 1958, (trans. auth), from Maxwell, Robert (ed.), *Stirling. Scritti di architettura*, Skira Editori, Milan, 1998, pp. 61–64.

STIRLING James, "Regionalism and modern architecture", *Architects' Year Book,* No.8, 1957, pp. 51–60 (trans. auth), from Maxwell, Robert (ed.), *Stirling. Scritti di architettura,* Skira, Editori, Milan, 1998.

STIRLING James, "Ronchamp. Le Corbusier's chapel and the crisis of rationalism", *Architectural Review*, March 1956, trans. auth), from Maxwell, Robert (ed.), *Stirling. Scritti di architettura*, Skira Editori, Milan, 1998, pp. 41–50.

STOLLER E. & LOEFFLER, J. (Photographs by), *The United Nations*; Princeton Architectural Press, Cambridge, Mass., 1999.

STRAUSS Levi, *El Pensamiento Salvaje,* Fondo de Cultura Económica, Mexico, 1964 (1st Spanish ed. from French *La pensée sauvage,* Plon, Paris, 1962)

STURGE MOORE Thomas, *Art and Life*, Methuen & Co, London, 1910

SWETLITZ Marc, "Julian Huxley and the End of Evolution", *Journal of the History of Biology*, Vol. 28, No. 2, 1995, pp. 181–217.

SYMES Colin, "The Paradox of the Canon: Edward W. Said and Musical Transgression", *Australia Discourse: Studies in the Cultural Politics of Education*, Vol. 27, No. 3, September 2006, pp. 309–324.

TAFURI M. & DAL CO F., *Architettura contemporanea*, Electa Editrice, Milan, 1976.

TAFURI M., DAL CO F., *Modern Architecture*, WOLF R.E. (trans.), Harry N. Abrams, New York, 1979 [*Architettura Contemporanea*, Electa Editrice, Milan, 1976].

TAFURI M., SOPRANI L., "Problemi di Critica e problemi di datazione in due monumentI taorminesi: il palazzo dei duchi di S. Stefano e la Badia Vecchia", *Quaderni dell'Istituto di Storia dell'Architettura*, No. 511, 1962, pp. 1–13.

TAFURI Manfredo (by Pellegrino d'Acierno and Robert Connolly trans.), *The Sphere and the Labyrinth*, MIT Press, Cambridge, 1990 [*La Sfera e il Labirinto*, Giulio Einaudi Editori, Torino, 1980].

TAFURI Manfredo (D'ACIERNO Pellegrino and CONNOLLY Robert trans.), *The Sphere and the Labyrinth, Avant-Gardes and Architecture from Piranesi to the, 1970s*, MIT Press, Cambridge, 1990 [TAFURI Manfredo, *La Sfera e il Labirinto. Avanguardie e architettura da Piranesi agli anni '70*, Giulio Einaudi Edi tori, Torino, 1980].

TAFURI Manfredo (LEVINE Jesica trans.), *History of Italian Architecture, 1944-1985*, MIT Press, Cambridge, MA, 1989 [*Storia dell'Architettura Italiana 1944-1985*, Piccola Biblioteca Einaudi, Turin, 1986 (1st ed. 1982)].

TAFURI Manfredo (SHERER Daniel trans.), *Interpreting the Renaissance: Princes, Cities, Architects*, Yale University Press, New Haven, CT, 2006 [TAFURI Manfredo, *Ricerca del Rinascimento*, Giulio Einaudi Editore, Turin, 1992].

TAFURI Manfredo (text); DIERNA S., SOPRANI L., TAFURI M., TESTA G., URBANI A. (surveys); "L' ampliamento barocco del Comune di S. Gregorio da Sassola", in *Quaderni dell'Istituto di Storia dell'Architettura* (Università degli Studi di Roma La Sapienza, Dipartimento di Storia dell'Architettura, Restauro e Conservazione dei Beni Architettonici), 1961, pp. 31–48.

TAFURI Manfredo (VERRECHIA Giorgio trans.), *Theories and History of Architecture*, Granada Publishing Limited, St. Albans, 1980.

TAFURI Manfredo and FOSCARI Antonio, *L'Armonia e i Conflitti. La Chiesa di San Francesco della Vigna nella Venezia del '500*, G. Einaudi, Torino, 1983.

TAFURI Manfredo, "Austromarxismo e città: 'Das rote Wien'", *Contropiano*, No. 2, 1971, pp. 259–311.

TAFURI Manfredo, "La vicenda architettonica romana 1945-1961", *Superfici*, April 1962, pp. 20–42.

TAFURI Manfredo, "Lavoro intellettuale e sviluppo capitalistico", *Contropiano*, No. 2, 1970 (C) [Also published in English in TAFURI Manfredo, *Architecture and Utopia: Design and Capitalist Development*, MIT Press, Cambridge, 1994 (1st ed.)], pp. 241–281.

TAFURI Manfredo, "Les bijoux indiscrets", in *Five Architects NY*, Officina Edizioni, Roma, 1976, pp. 7–33.

TAFURI Manfredo, "Order and Disorder: The Dialectic of Modern Architecture", The Hans Vetter Memorial Lecture, Carnegie Mellon University, Pittsburgh, April 7, 1976, Mimeo.

TAFURI Manfredo, "Per una critica dell'ideologia architettonica", in *Contropiano*, No. 1, 1969 (C) [Translated to English: "Toward a Critique of Architectural Ideology", in HAYS Michael K. (ed.), *Architecture Theory since 1968*, MIT, Cambridge, 1998], pp. 31–80.

TAFURI Manfredo, "Retorica e Sperimentalismo: Guarino Guarini e la Tradizione Manierista", in *Guarino Guarini e l'internazionalita del barocco: atti del convegno internazionale*, Vol. 1, Accademia delle Scienze di Torino, Turin, 30 September–5 October, 1968, pp. 667–704.

TAFURI Manfredo, "Socialdemocrazia e città nella reppublica di Weimar", *Contropiano*, No. 1, 1971, pp. 207–223.

TAFURI Manfredo, "The Disenchanted Mountain", in Ciucci G., Dal Co F., Manieri-Elia M., Tafuri M. (eds.), *The American City: From the Civil War to the New Deal*, Granada, London, 1980 (CA) ["La montagna disincantata", in Ciucci G., Dal Co F., Manieri Elia M., Tafuri M. (eds.), *La Cittá Americana: de la guerra civile al "New Deal"*, Laterza, Bari, 1973 [Translated to English by Barbara Luigia Le Penta].

TAFURI Manfredo, "The Historical Project", introduction to *The Sphere and the Labyrinth* (MIT Press: Cambridge, 1990) [*La Sfera e il Labirinto*, Giulio Einaudi Editori: Torino 1980, pp. 1–24. English translation by Pellegrino d'Acierno and Robert Connolly].

TAFURI Manfredo, FROMMEL Christoph Luitpold and RAY Stefano Ray, *Raffaello architetto,* Electa, Milano, 1984 [Catalog of exhibition held at Palazzo dei Conservatori,

TAFURI Manfredo, *Jacopo Sansovino e l'architettura del '500 a Venezia*, Marsilio, Venice, 1969.

TAFURI Manfredo, *L'architettura del Manierismo nel cinquecento europeo*, Officina Edizioni, Roma, 1966.

TAFURI Manfredo, *L'Architettura moderna in Giappone*, Capelli Editore, Roma, 1964 (G) [TAFURI Manfredo (MOSTAFAVI Mohsen ed.), *Modern Architecture In Japan*, Mack Books, London, 2022].

TAFURI Manfredo, *La Dignità dell'Attimo, Trascrizione multimediale di Le Frme del Tempo. Venezia e la modernità., una lezione di Manfredo Tafuri*, Università IUAV, Venice, 1994.

TAFURI Manfredo, *Ludovico Quaroni e lo sviluppo dell'architettura moderna in Italia (LQ)*, Edizioni di Comunità, Milan, 1964.

TAFURI Manfredo, *Materiali per il Corso di Storia dell'Architettura IIa A*, IUAV, CLUVA, Venice, 1979.

TAFURI Manfredo, PEREZ ESCOLANO Victor, trans., *La Arquitectura del Humanismo*, Xarait Ediciones, Madrid, 1978 [TAFURI Manfredo, *L'Architettura dell'Umanesimo*, Laterza, Bari, 1969].

TAFURI Manfredo, *Progetto e utopia. Architettura e sviluppo capitalistico*, Laterza, Bari, 1973.

TAFURI Manfredo, *Storia dell'ideologia antiurbana*, Istituto Universitario di Architettura di Venezia, Course "Storia dell'architettura 1A/2A", Academic year 1972–1973, IUAV, Venice.

TAFURI Manfredo, *Theories and History of Architecture*, Granada Publishing, London, 1980 [*Teorie e Storia dell'architettura*, Laterza, Bari, 1970. Translated to English by Dennis Sharp].
TAFURI Manfredo, *Vittorio Gregotti, progetti e architetture*, Electa, Milan, 1982.
TARCHÓPULOS, D. "Las huellas del plan para Bogotá de Le Corbusier, Sert y Wiener". *Scripta Nova. Revista electrónica de geografía y ciencias sociales*. Barcelona: Universidad de Barcelona, 1 de agosto de 2006, vol. X, núm. 218 (86). [ISSN: 1138-9788]
TEGETHOFF Wolf, *Mies van der Rohe. Die Villen und Landhausprojekte*, Bacht, Essen, 1981.
TEYSSOT G., HENNINGER P., "One Portrait of Tafuri: An Interview with Georges Teyssot", *ANY: Architecture New York*, No. 25/26, 2000, pp. 10–16.
THOENES Christof, "Architectural Orders: Rebirth or Invention?", *Art in Translation*, Vol. 9, No. 3, 2017, pp. 296–311.
THOMPSON David, "Making No Portraits. T.S. Eliot, Mimesis and the Politics of Mediterranean Classicism", *Comparative Literature*, Vol. 50, No. 1, Winter 1998, pp. 32–56.
TĪFENTĀLE Alise, "The Family of Man: The Photography Exhibition That Everybody Loves to Hate", *FK*, 2 July 2018, https://fkmagazine.lv/category/text/essay/.
TODOROV Tzvetan, *On human diversity: nationalism, racism, and exoticism in French thought*, Harvard University Press, Cambridge, MA, 1993.
TODOROVA Maria, *Imagining the Balkans*, Oxford University Press, New York, 1997.
TORRES BODET Jaime, *Memorias*, Vol. *El desierto internacional*, Porrúa, Mexico, 1971.
TORRES BODET Jaime, *Memorias*, Vol. *La victoria sin alas*, Porrúa, Mexico, 1970,
TORRES BODET Jaime, *Memoriqs*, Vol. Años contra el tiempo, Porrúa, Mexico, 1969.
TRIGGER Bruce G., "Alternative Archaeologies: Nationalist, Colonialist, Imperialist", *Man, New Series*, Vol. 19, No. 3, September 1984, pp. 355–370.
TRONTI M., ACCORNERO A., CACCIARI M., *Operaismo e centralità operaia*, Editori Riuniti, Roma, 1978.
TRONTI Mario, "Classe, partito, classe", *Classe operaia*, No. 3, March 1967, pp. 221–226.
TRONTI Mario, "Marx ieri e oggi", in *Operai e Capitale*, Giulio Einaudi Editore, Torino, 1966 (Italian edition), pp. 31–38 [Translated to English as TRONTI Mario, "Marx Yesterday and Today"].
TURNER Barry, *Beacon for Change. How the 1951 Festival of Britain Helped to Shape a New Age*, Aurum Press, London, 2011.
TZARA Tristan, Dada Manifesto, published in No. 3 of the Zurich *DADA Magazine*, May 1918.
UDIVICKI-SELB Danilo, *Soviet Architectural Avant-Gardes. Architecture And Stalin's Revolution From Above, 1928-1938*, Bloomsbury Publishing Plc, London, 2020.
UNITED NATIONS RELIEF AND REHABILITATION ADMINISTRATION, *The story of UNRRA*, UNRRA, Office of Public Information, Washington, D.C., 1948.
Unkown Author (UA) "The architect's Dilemma", in *The Economist* 25.7.53. Reproduced in RIBA, April 1954.
VAN BEEK Walter E.A., "Dogon Restudied: A Field Evaluation of the Work of Marcel Griaule", *Current Anthropology*, Vol. 32, No. 2, April 1991, pp. 139–167.
VAN DEN HEUVEL, D., RISSELADA, M., eds., *Alison and Peter Smithson-from te House of the Future to a House of Today*, 010 Publishers, Rotterdam, 2004.
VAN DER ROHE Ludwig Mies, "Bauen", *G*, No. 2, September 1923, p. 1.
VAN EYCK Aldo, "Discussion", *Architectural Design*, November, 1958. Quoted in SMITHSON Alison (ed.), *Team X Manual*, Buenos Aires, 1966; (London, 1962).

210 Bibliography

VAN MANDER Karel, *Le livre des peintres*, Les Belles Lettres, Paris, 2001 [1604].

VAN PEER Willie, "Canon Formation: Ideology or Aesthetic Quality?", *British Journal of Aesthetics*, Vol. 36, No. 2, April 1996, pp. 97–108.

VAN'T HOFF Robert, "Huis ter Heide", *De Stijl*, Vol. 2, No. 7, 1918, pp. 30–32.

VASARI Giorgio (CONWAY BONDANELLA Julia and BONDANELLA Peter trans.), *The Lives of the Artists*, Oxford University Press, Oxford and New York, 1991.

VATTIMO Gianni, *Le avventure della differenza,* Garzanti, MIlan, 1980 [Translated as *The Adventure of Difference: Philosophy after Nietzsche and Heidegger*, Baltimore, MD, John Hopkins University Press, 1993].

VERDURA Carlos Enriquez, *Tesis de licenciatura en relaciones internacionales, Jaime-Torres Bodet y la UNESCO. Los Limites de la cooperación internacional*, Colegio de Mexico, Mexico, 1997.

VINKEN Barbara, "Auf Leben und Tod: Vasaris Kanon", in Renate von Heydebrand (ed.), *Kanon Macht Kultur. Theoretische, historische und sozial Aspekte ästhetischer Kanonbildungen*, Verlag JB Metzler, Stuttgart and Weimar, 1998, pp. 201–214.

VISCHER Paul; "Les relations internationales entre les Architectes", *UIA Bulletin*, May 1954, pp. 7–12.

VON GOETHE Johann Wolfgang, *Die Wahlverwandtschaften*, II, VII, J.G. Cottaischen Buchhandlung, Tübingen, 1809.

VON HEYDEBRAND Renate, ed., *Kanon, Macht, Kultur. Theoretische, historische und sozial Aspekte ästhetischer Kanonbildungen*, Verlag JB Metzler, Stuttgart and Weimar, 1998.

VON HUMBOLDT Wilhelm (COWAN M. trans.), *An Anthology of the Writings of Wilhelm von Humboldt: Humanist without Portfolio*, Wayne State University Press, Detroit, 1963 [VON HUMBOLDT Wilhelm, *Wilhelm von Humboldts gesammelte Schriften*, Leitzmann and Gebhardt, Berlin, 1903, vol. 3].

VON SCHLOSSER Julius, *Die Kunstliteratur, ein Handbuch zur Quellenkunde der neueren Kunstgeschichte*, Kunstverlag Anton Schroll & Co., Vienna, 1924.

VON STADEN Heinrich, "Nietzsche and Marx on Greek Art and Literature: Case Studies in Reception", *Daedalus*, Vol. 105, No. 1, Winter 1976, pp. 79–96.

VON THÜNEN Johann Heinrich, "Der isolirte Staat in Beziehung auf Landwirtschaft und Nationalökonomie", Rostock, 1850.

VOSWINCKEL Ulrike, *Freie Liebe und Anarchie. Schwabing-Monte Verita, Entwürfe gegen das etablierte Leben*, Alitera Verlag, Munich, 2009.

VVAA. "Progetti di Architetti Italiani", Casabella, N0 289, July 1964, pp. 9–11

VV.AA, "Conversación con Manfredo Tafuri" (Buenos Aires, Agosto de 1981) in *Materiales*, Buenos Aires, March 1982. Reproduced in VV.AA, *Tafuri en Argentina*, ARQ ediciones, Santiago de Chile, 2019.

VV.AA, *Concerning Architecture: Essays on Architectural Writers and Writing Presented to Nikolaus Pevsner*, Allen Lane, London, 1968.

VV.AA, *Hommage à Jean Hyppolite*, Presses Universitaires de France, Paris, 1971.

VV.AA, *Images of the Orient. Nineteenth Century European Travelers to Muslim Lands*, Council on Islamic Education, National Center for History in the Schools, University of California, Los Angeles, 1998.

VV.AA, *Socialismo, città, architettura, URSS 1917-1937. Il contributo degli architetti europei*, Officina Editori, Rome, 1972.

VV.AA, Special Issue "Imperialismo e Rivoluzione in America Latina", *Quaderni Piaccentini*, No. 31, 31th July 1967, pp. 1–259.

VV.AA, *The Art of Diplomacy. Brazilian Modernism Painted for War*, Embassy of Brazil in London, April–June, 2018.

VV.AA. "Houses of the Future", *Scientific American*, Vol. 147, No. 4, October 1932, pp. 228–229.

VV.AA., "Gli ultimi CIAM", Gregotti Vittorio Ed., special issue of *Rassegna*, 52/4, 1992.

VV.AA., *"Soixante années d'AA 1930-1990"*, *L'Architecture d'aujourd'hui,* special issue, No.172, December 1990.

WALLERSTEIN Immanuel, *The Modern World-System. I. Capitalist Agriculture and the Origins of the European World-Economy in the Sixteenth Century*, Academic Press Inc., New York, 1974.

WALSH Victoria, *Nigel Henderson. Parallel of Life and Art*, Thames and Hudson, London, 2001.

WALTERS F.P., *Building Peace Out of War. Studies in International Reconstruction*, International Affairs, Volume 21, Issue 2, April 1945, p. 257.

WARD Stephen V., "Soviet Communism and the British Planning Movement: Rational Learning or Utopian Imagining?", *Planning Perspectives*, Vol. 27, No. 4, October, 2012, pp. 1–26.

WEDEMEYER-KOLWE Bernd, *Der neue Mensch. Körperkultur im Kaiserreich und in der Weimarer Republik*, Königshausen & Neumann, Würzburg, 2004.

WEISS Peter (SKELTON Geoffrey trans.), *The Persecution and Assassination of Jean-Paul Marat as Performed by the Inmates of the Asylum of Charenton under the Direction of the Marquis de Sade*, Atheneum, New York, 1965 [WEISS Peter, *Die Verfolgung und Ermordung Jean Paul Marats dargestellt durch die Schauspielgruppe des Hospizes zu Charenton unter Anleitung des Herrn de Sade*, Suhrkamp Verlag, Frankfurt am Main, 1964].

WELZIG Maria, *Lessons from Bernard Rudofsky. Life as a Voyage*, Birkhäuser in cooperation with AzW, Basel, 2007.

WESTPHAL Merold, "The Canon as Flexible, Normative Fact", *The Monist*, Vol. 76, No. 4, 1993, pp. 436–449.

WHITELEY Nigel, "Banham and 'Otherness': Reyner Banham (1922–1988) and His Quest for an Architecture Autre", *Architectural History*, Vol. 33, 1990, pp. 188–221.

WHITELEY Nigel, "This Is Tomorrow, 1956", in *Art and Pluralism. Lawrence Alloway's Cultural Criticism,* Liverpool University Press, Liverpool, 2012, pp. 50–52.

WHITFIELD Clovis, review of "L'Architettura del Manierismo nel Cinquecento Europeo", *The Burlington Magazine*, Vol. 110, No. 784, July 1968.

WHITTLE Matthew, "Englishness in Transition: Moving from the Imperial to the National", in *Post-War British Literature and the "End of Empire"*, Part II, Chapter 4, Pallgrave Macmillan, London, 2016. Editor is indicated. pp. 109–144.

WIEBENSON Dora, *Tony Garnier: The Cité industrielle.* George Braziller, New York. 1969.

WILFORD Hugh, "Britain: In Between", in Stephan, Alexander (ed.), *The Americanization of Europe. Culture, Diplomacy, and Anti-Americanism after 1945*, Berghahn, Oxford/ New York, 2007, pp. 23–43.

WILLIAMS Gwyn A., "The Concept of 'Egemonia' in the Thought of Antonio Gramsci: Some Notes on Interpretation", *Journal of the History of Ideas*, Vol. 21, No. 4, October–December, 1960, pp. 586–599.

WILLIAMS Raymond, *The Politics of Modernism*, Verso, London and New York, 1994.

WILLS Jan, "Moderne Bouwkunst bij noodwoningen in gewapend beton", *De Stijl*, Vol. 1, No. 8, 1918, pp. 48–49.

WILSON C., OSBORNE J., WAIN J., TYNAN K., HOPKINS B., ANDERSON L., HOLROYD S., LESSING D., *Declaration,* MacGibbon & Kee, New York, 1958.
WILSON Colin, *The Outsider*, Diversion Books, London, 2014 (1956).
WOLFE Tom, *From Bauhaus to Our House*, Pan Macmillan, Stuttgart, 2009.
WRIGHT Steve, *Storming Heaven. Class Composition and Struggle in Italian Autonomist Marxism*, Pluto Press, London, 2002.
ZAPPEN James P., *The Rebirth of Dialogue Bakhtin, Socrates, and the Rhetorical Tradition*, State University of New York Press, Albany, 2004.
ZEVI Bruno, *Storia dell'architettura moderna*, Giulio Einaudi, Turin, 1950.
ZUBOVICH Katherine, "Debating 'Democracy': The International Union of Architects and the Cold War Politics of Expertise", *Room One Thousand*, No 4, 2016, pp. 104–116.
ZUCKERT Catherine, "Nietzsche on the Origin & Development of the Distinctively Human", *Polity*, Vol. 16, No. 1, Autumn 1983, pp. 48–71.

Index

40,000 Years of Modern Art exhibition 166

A Century of Progress exhibition 172
ABC Group 140
Abdülhamid II, Sultan of the Ottoman Empire 114, 118
Académie Européenne Mediterranée (Mediterranean European Academy) 131
Académie Royale 12
Ackerman, James S. 40
Actividad Contemporánea magazine 132
Adalbert Sternberg, Count Graf 114
Adorno, Theodor 17
Aeschylus 98
aesthetic cycle 41
aesthetic of scarcity 180
Africa 7, 52, 56, 93, 110–165
Aglionby, William 14
Agnadello (Italy) 84–85
Agrest, Diana 62
Agrigento (Italy) 110
Aïn Smara (Algeria) 117
Ain, Gregory Samuel 141
Aix-en-Provence 143
Albania 93
Alberti, Leon Battista 71–82
Alexander, Christopher 9
Alexandria (Egypt) 94
Algeria 116, 119, 143
Algerian Revolution 47
Alhambra (Spain) 96, 98
Alighieri, Dante 83
Alkamo (Italy) 110
Alloway, Lawrence 179
Altenberg, Peter 20, 21
Altieri, Charles 15

AmaNdebele 157
American Society of Planners and Architects (ASPA) 138
American-Soviet Friendship Association 141
American way of life 150
Americanism 150, 153
Amsterdam (The Netherlands) 49, 85
Anacapri (Italy) 116
Anderson, Francis (Perry) 171
Anderson, Lindsay 149
angry young men 149–161
Antolic, Vladimir 140
Anton, Victor 177
Antwerp (Belgium) 12
Architecture and Planning Group of the Society for Cultural Relations between the British Commonwealth and the U.S.S.R. 141
architecture of bureaucracy 138–148
Argan, Giulio Carlo 41–54
Argentina 93, 143
Arizona (USA) 8
Arp, Jean 177
Arsenale di Venezia (Venetian Arsenal) 78, 85, 93
Arts Council Gallery 167
Arup, Ove 162
as found logic 159–180
Asia 6, 52, 56, 93, 114, 150
Asian Tigers 93
ASP Group (Akademia Sztuk Pięknych) 154
Asselbergs, Alphonse 112
Assemblee de Constructeurs pour une Renovation Architecturale (ASCORAL) 144

Assennato, Marco 79
Association for the Protection of the Fatherland 124
Assyria 108
Atelier 5 9
Atkinson, Harriet 161
Atomic fear 174
Aurigemma, Maria Giulia 43
Australia 7
Austria 20, 119
Austro-Hungarian Empire 116
authenticity 26, 110, 159
avant-garde 20–171

Babylon (Mesopotamia) 108
Bach, Johann Sebastian 16
Badia Vecchia 43
Bagnols-sur-Céze (France) 155
Bakema, Jacob Berend (Jaap) 159
Bakhtin, Mikhail 25, 30, 87
Bandinelli, Baccio 12
Banham, Reyner 153–154
Barbaro, Daniele 77
Barbaro, Marcantonio 85
Barbary Coast 110
Barcelona 7, 65
Baroque 4, 44–49, 116, 158
Barr, Cleeve 149
Barthes, Roland 33, 159–173
Bauhaus 106, 122–137
Bawa, Geoffrey 5
Beaudoin, Eugene 147
Bedeschi, Giuseppe 55–56
Behrens, Peter 124
Beirut (Lebanon) 108
Bellamy, Edward 172
Belle, Henry 110
Bellori, Giovanni Pietro 12
Benevolo, Leonardo 9, 54, 74
Bengal 6
Benjamin, Walter 17–85
Benthal Green (London) 160, 175, 181
Beothy, Etienne 177
Bergamo (Italy) 119, 138–155
Berlin (Germany) 112–131
Bethlehem 113, 176
Bhahba, Homi K. 19
Billing, Hermann 119
Biot (France) 177
Biraghi, Marco 55
Bizet, Georges 129
Blanc, Jan 26
Bloc, André 177
Bloom, Harold 15, 17

Blunt, Wilfrid 113
Bo Bardi, Lina 5, 19
Boccaccio, Giovanni 87
Bolton (United Kingdom) 160
Bomberg, David 112
Bonatz, Paul 106
Bond, James 173–174
Bonillo, Jean-Lucien 143
Booten (Liberia) 123
Bordone, Benedetto 84
Boreyda (Saudi Arabia) 113
Borges, Jorge Luis 24–32
Borromini, Francesco 33–51
Bosnia 93
Boyd, Robin 7
Boynton Priestley, John 157
Bramante, Donato 33, 83, 87
Brasilia (Brazil) 39, 146
Braudel, Fernand 130
Brazil 39, 143–158
Brazil Builds Exhibition 7, 156
Breuer, Marcel 132, 140, 148
Breuil, Henri (Abbé) 167
Bridgwater (UK) 142–144
Brindisi (Italy) 93
British Association for the Advancement of Science 168
British Broadcasting Corporation (BBC) 168
British Commonwealth of Nations 7, 166
British Museum 165, 167
British neo-Darwinism 168
British-Soviet Friendship Association 141
Brunelleschi, Filippo 1, 42–43, 71–77
Bruni, Francesco 50
Bruno, Giordano 39, 96
Brussels (Belgium) 132
Buber, Martin 131
Buckeridge, Bainbrigg 14
Buckminster Fuller, Richard 172
Buenos Aires (Argentina) 9, 69, 76–84
Bureaucratization 158, 168, 180
Burke, Peter 98
Burma (Myanmar) 151
Busoni, Ferruccio 16

Cacciari, Massimo 22, 24, 54–98
Café des Westens 122
Caillié, René 108
Cairo (Egypt) 117
California (USA) 6
Cambridge (USA) 24
Campaign for Nuclear Disarmament 180
Camporesi, Piero 67

Camus Company 173
Canada 143, 145
Candela, Félix 39
Candilis, Georges 8
Canella, Guido 54
Cannes Film Festival 149
Canon 2–41, 156–164
Cape Town (South Africa) 144
capitalism 2–7, 55–79, 107, 137, 158
Capri (Italy) 116, 118, 131
Caramuel y Lobkowitz, Juan 15
Carducho, Vicente 14
Caritas di Roma 93
Carnegie Mellon 62
Carneiro, Paolo 148
Carracci, Annibale 12
Carrera, Alessandro 97
Carter, Peter 154, 163
Casabella 67, 74
Casbah 8
Cassiodorus 15
Cassirer, Ernst Alfred 50
Castiglione, Baldassare (Count of Casatico) 87
Castro, Fidel 57
Catania (Italy) 110
Catleugh, F.D.H. 177
Cavalaire-sur-Mer (France) 131
Cavalcanti, Alberto 39
Çelik, Zeynep 118
Cellini, Benvenuto 12
center/periphery 9, 42–95
Central Committee of the Communist Party 140
Cervantes, Miguel de 28, 87
Césaire, Aimé 56
Cesariano, Cesare di Lorenzo 15
Ceylon (Sri Lanka) 143
Chandigarh (India) 144, 157
Chanony 108
Charles V, Holy Roman Emperor 83, 98
Chateaubriand, François-René Vicomte de 110
Chermayeff, Serge 138
China 56, 93, 141
Choisy, Auguste 19
Christianity 117, 143
Churchill, Winston 141
CIAM Chapter for Post-War Relief and Planning (CAPP) 138
Cicero, Marcus Tullius 87
Cipolla, Carlo Maria 67
Citizens Against Socialist Housing (CASH) 141

Ciucci, Giorgio 48
Ciudad Universitaria de Caracas 177
Clarke, Arthur C. 174
Clarke, Geoffrey 177
Classe e Partito Journal 58
Classe Operaia 55, 57
classicism 12, 50, 51
COBRA Group 159
Cohen, Jean-Louis 60
Cold War 8, 141, 148
Colletti, Lucio 55
Colombia 143, 144
Colomina, Beatriz 152, 174
Colquhoun, Alan Harold 154
Colquhoun, Ithel 177
Comité international pour la résolution des problèmes de l'architecture contemporaine (CIRPAC) 132
Comité International des Architectes 146
Common Sense 5, 31
Communist Party of the Soviet Union 140, 155
Communist Party of the United States 141
Conference of Tropical Architecture 7
Congrès Internationaux d'Architecture Moderne (CIAM) 7, 10, 132–181
Congreso de la cultura 56
Congress of European Communist Parties 141
Constantinople (Istanbul) 84, 94, 119
Contropiano journal 53–59
Cortázar, Julio 56
Cortese, Giovanni Andrea (Abbot of San Benedetto) 87
Costa, Lucio 39, 148
Council for International Civic Instruction 168
Couzens, E. G. 172
Coventry Cathedral 161–163
Cox Wakefield, Sir Anthony 149
creation 22–42, 74, 87, 165
Croce, Benedetto 41
Crosby, Theo 176, 178
Cuba 56, 143, 144
Cubbit, James 7
Cubism 5, 8, 112–137
cultural ecumenism 166, 168
Curtis, Barry 173
Curtis, William 40
Cusa, Nicholas of 97
Czech Republic 119
Czechoslovakia 140, 142, 143, 156

216 *Index*

Dada Group 125
Dagnino, Tomas 40
Daily Mail Newspaper 171, 172
Dal Co, Francesco 39, 61, 64
Dalmatia (Croatia) 109
Dalton, Hugh 154
Damascus (Syria) 94
Das Neue Frankfurt magazine 127
Dasein 80
Davidson, Jo 142
de Bazel, K.P.C. 119
de Clercq, Louis 113
de l'Orme, Philibert 50
de Lamartine, Alphonse 108
De Magistris, Alessandro 137
De Michelis, Marco 55
de Saussure, Ferdinand 89
de Silva, Minette 5, 19, 142
De Stijl 120–125
Debray, Jules Regis 57
Dehodencq, Alfred 112
Delacroix, Eugène 111
Delaunay, Sonia 177
Deleuze, Gilles 69, 88
Della Volpe, Galvano 55
Dellavolpism 56
Delphi (Greece) 119
Denmark 141
Der Sturm 122, 124
Derrida, Jacques 30, 63, 76, 88
Dessau (Germany) 124
Detroit (USA) 153
Deutsche Morgenländische Gesellschaft 114
Deutsche Orient Gesellchaft (German Asia Society) 108
Deutscher Werkbund 121
Dhéralde, Leon 109
di Gattinara, Mercurino 83
Di Nucci, Sergio 173
dialectic synthesis 59
dialogical 5, 9, 24, 30, 84, 97
Die Bauwelt magazine 127
Dietz, Albert G. H. 173
Döblin, Bruno Alfred 122
Dogon (Mali) 8, 159
Dolce, Lodovico 12
Domènech i Montaner, Lluís 65
domesticity 173
domination 5, 15–31, 69–90, 136, 170
Don Quixote 28, 32
Donà, Doge Leonardo 92, 93
Dorner, Alexander 52
Doughtly, Charles M. 113

Drew, Jane 7, 19, 157
Dreyfus, Hubert 81
Dubrovnik (Croatia) 155, 177, 181
Dubuffet, Jean 159
Duncan, R.A. 172
Durand, Jean-Nicolas-Louis 19
Dürer, Albrecht 43
Durham (Newcastle) 151
Duveyrier, Henri 113
Dymaxion 172

Eames, Charles 153
Eaton, Bertram 177
Écochard, Michel 143
Edison, Thomas 172
Egypt 14, 106–127
Einstein, Carl 122
Eisenman, Peter 62, 63
El-Ariana (Tunisia) 123
el-Krim, Abd 132
electronics 171
Elfreth Watkins, John Jr. 172
Elysian Park Heights 141
End of Empire 166–171
Englishness 160–164
Entwistle, Clive 157
Enzensberger, Hans Magnus 56
Erasmus, Desiderius 87
Erlach, Johann Bernhard Fischer von 18, 19
Ermolaeva, Vera 5
Escobar, Arturo 168
Euripides 76
Europe 1, 12, 29, 41–65, 90–137, 150–161, 167, 181
European Coal and Steel Community 66
Eustace, John 109

Facoltà di Architettura di Napoli 63
Faczynski, Jerzy 177
Fair of Venice 80
Fanon, Frantz 47, 159
Fascism 45
Fathy, Hassan 5
Feiss, Carl 139
Felibien, André 12
Felton, Monica 154
Feltrinelli, Giangiacomo 58
Fergusson, James 19
Fernandez, Macedonio 32
Ferriman, Z. Duckett 110
Festival of Britain 161, 166
Fez (Morocco) 114
FIAT 66
Finland 145

Finsterlin, Hermann 175
Fischer, Josef 143
Fisher, Tom 172
Fistetti, Francesco 79
Five Architects NY exhibition 63
Flat Roof 7, 10, 112–128
Fletcher, Sir Banister 19
Florence (Italy) 12, 25, 50, 85
Fondouk (Algeria) 108
Forbat, Alfréd (Fred) 124
Formalism 64, 143, 158
Foscarini, Jacopo 85
Foucault, Michel 6, 26, 69–81, 159
Fouquet, Jean 43
Fowler, Alan 178
France 12, 19, 51, 60, 116–167
Frank, Josef 117, 118
French-Soviet Friendship Association 141
Freud, Sigmund 24, 79, 82
Frobenius, Leo 7
Fromentin, Eugène 112
Frommel, Christoph 49
Fronte Unitario Omosessuale Rivoluzionario Italiano (FUORI) 88
Fry, Maxwell 7, 146, 157
functionalism 150, 163
Fusaro, Diego 79
Futurism 172, 180

Gadow, Hans Friedrich 109
Galilei, Galileo 44
Galle, Philips 12, 14
Gandelsonas, Mario 62
Garnier, Charles 118, 119
Gaudí, Antoni 7
Gavin, Owen 166
Gelassenheit 80, 86
Gemelli, Giuliana 130
Geneva (Switzerland) 24, 147
Genoa (Italy) 85
Germany 19, 64, 65, 108–143
Gestell 79, 81
Giedion, Sigfried 137–139, 143–148, 161–181
Gillaumet, Gustave Achille 112
Ginsburg, Moisei 140
Ginsburgh, Victor 17
Ginzburg, Carlo 67, 82
Giocondo, Fra Giovanni 92
Giraudeau de Saint-Gervais, Jean 110
Giussano, Giovanni Pietro (Cardinal Archbishop of Milan) 51
Gloag, John 172
Goethe, Johann Wolfgang von 115

Goldhagen, Sarah 179
Gombrich, Ernst 15, 16
Goodhart-Rendel, Harry Stuart 25
Goodwin, Philipp 141
Gothic 33–52, 162
Gramsci, Antonio 5, 31
Granada (Spain) 96, 98
Gray, Eileen 6, 19
Greco, Dominico (El Greco) 14
Greece 14–28, 107–119
Green, Graham Henry 150
Greene, Beverly Lorraine 19
Gregotti, Vittorio 54, 61
Griaule, Marcel 159
Grimshaw, Bernard 177
Gritti, Doge Andrea 84, 90
Gropius, Ise 133
Gropius, Walter 19, 52, 119–158, 177
Group Espace 177–179
Grup d'Arquitectes i Tècnics Catalans per al Progrés de l'Arquitectura Contemporània (GATCPAC) 132
Guarini, Camillo Guarino 71, 98
Guattari, Félix 69
Guevara, Ernesto (Che) 56, 57, 159
Guillory, John 15, 16
Guldall, Jesper 153
Gunder Frank, Andre 57

Habermas, Jürgen 26
Hadid, Zaha 5
Hamilton, Richard 153, 172, 179
Han, Byung-Chul 4, 30
Hanáčková, Marcela 140
Hansaviertel (Berlin) 46
Hansen, Oskar 154, 155
Häring, Hugo 119
Harrison, Thomas (Tom) 160
Hausenstein, Wilhelm 123
Havana (Cuba) 9, 56
Havana Plan 147
Havileck, Josef 143
Hawksmoor, Nicholas 51
Heemskerck van Veen, Maarten Jacobsz 12–15, 19
Hegel, Friederich 1
Hegemann, Werner 122
hegemony 7–10, 30–31, 83–143
Heger, Frank J. 173
Heidegger, Martin 48, 76–93
Henderson, Nigel 167–180
Hennebique, François 126
Henry VIII 51
Herder, Johann Gottfried 115

Index

Hernández, Silvia 24
Herodotus 110
Hertfordshire County Council 164
Hertziana Library 49, 82
Herzfeld, Michael 129
Heterotopia 69, 70
Heuss, Theodor 124
Hewison, Robert 149
Hildebrand, Adolf von 115
Hiroshima Peace Memorial 46
Hitchcock, Henry Russel 138–151
Hobsbawm, Eric 56
Hoddesdon (UK) 143
Hoffmann, Josef 116
Hohenhagen (Germany) 121
Holford, William 146
Holman Hunt, William 112
Home of tomorrow 172
Homer 29, 110, 111
House of the future (HOF) 171–181
House Un-American Activities Committee (HUAC) 141
Howard Houghton, Charles 177
Howell, William (Bill) 154
Hudnut, Joseph F. 138
humanism 1, 29–42, 90, 154, 170
Humboldt, Wilhelm von 26
Hungary 47, 54, 140, 143, 155
Hunstanton School 163–172
Husserl, Edmund 46, 48
Huxley, Aldous Leonard 175
Huxley, Julian 147, 168

Ibadan (Nigeria) 144
Ibiza (Spain) 132
Imaginary Museum 170
immanent critique 17
imperialism 2, 56–57, 160
Independent Group 153, 165, 171, 178
India 93, 108, 143–144, 151–155
Industrial Revolution 151
influence 9, 17, 30–33, 74
Institute for Architecture and Urban Studies 62
Institute of Community Studies (ICS) 160
Institute of Contemporary Art (ICA) 154, 179
integration of the arts 147, 177, 180
International Conference on the Arts 147
International Congresses of Social Architecture and Social Planning 143
international style 131, 144, 153, 159
Iraq 14

iron curtain 141, 180
Isaacs, Reginald 147
Israel 131, 143
Istituto Universitario di Architettura di Venezia (IUAV) 54, 61–67, 80
Italian Christian Democratic Party 143
Italian Communist Party 56–57, 60–67, 80–88, 143
Italian Miracle 50, 55
Italy 12, 14, 44–67, 87–143
Itten, Johannes 124
Izdighast (Iran) 119

Japan 44–52
Jauss, Hans Robert 19, 31
Jenkins, Roland 162
Jerusalem 106–113
Journal of the Society of Architectural Historians 40, 139
Julius II (Pope) 15, 83

Kaganovich, Lázar 141
Kahn, Louis 7, 153
Kairouan (Tunisia) 123
Kalivoda, František 140
Kamerlingh Onnes, Heike 121
Kamerlingh Onnes, Menso 120, 121
Kandinsky, Wassily 113, 123
Katwijk aan Zee (The Netherlands) 119
Kenya 7
Kerr, Alfred 122
Khrushchev, Nikita 155
Kiesler, Frederik 175
Killick, John 154
King, Anthony 6
Kircher, Athanasius 19
Kirchner, Ernst Ludwig 21
Kitnick, Alex 170
Klee, Paul 48, 113, 123, 157
Klein, Robert 85
Kohtz, Otto 119
Kokoschka, Oskar 21, 122
König, Karl 117
Kosik, Karl 31
Kraus, Karl 20, 122
Krauss, Rosalind 26
Krejcar, Jaromir 140, 143
Kristeva, Julia 24, 30
Kross, Matthias 159
Kühn, Christian 117
Kuomintang party 141
Kurokawa, Kisho 155

Index 219

La Chaux de Fonds 118
La Sarraz (Switzerland) 138–146
Labor Party 157
Lacan, Jacques 30
Lampedusa, Giuseppe Tomasi di 181
Lancaster Fleming, Ian 173
Lane, Edward William 110
Langenegger, Felix 124
Langfeld, Georg 15
Lasker-Schüller, Elisabeth (Else) 122
Latin America 39, 56–57, 144–156
Lauweriks, Johannes Ludovicus Mathieu (J.L.M) 119–121
Lavery, John 111
Le Corbusier 5–8, 30, 64–163
Lear, Edward 111, 113
Léger, Fernand 138, 177
Legrand, Jacques-Guillaume 19
Leiden University 120, 121
Leiter, Felix 174
Lenin, Vladimir 57, 58, 63
Leningrad (Russia) 172
Lepero, Fortunato 131
Levi, Giovanni 67, 82
Lévi-Strauss, Claude 159, 165, 166
Levinas, Emmanuel 25, 30, 94
Levitt, Theodore 93
Lewerentz, Sigurd 161
Lijster, Thijs 17
Lisbon (Portugal) 98
Lissitsky, Lázar Márkovich (El Lissitsky) 140
Llanaves (Spain) 109
Lloyd Wright, Frank 30, 52, 139
Llull, Ramon 97
local/universal 3–7
London (UK) 85, 112, 156–180
London County Council 154
London School of Economics (LSE) 160
Loos, Adolf 20–24, 116–122
Los Angeles (USA) 141, 153
Lotz, Wolfgang 71
Lowe, Andy 166
Lurçat, André 127, 140, 143
Lyotard, Jean-François 67

Maase, Jaspar 153
Machado, Rodolfo 62
Macke, August Robert Ludwig 123
Madden, Samuel 172
Madge, Charles 160
Madrid (Spain) 85
Maestrovic, Matko 60

Maghreb 94, 111
Magnant, Yves 173
Mahler, Gustav 24
Maillol, Aristide 130
Majorelle, Jacques 112
Makepeace Thackeray, William 113
Maldonado, Tomás 39
Malevich, Kasimir 172
Malraux, André Georges 168–170
Malte-Brun, Conrad 130
Malvasia, Carlo Cesare 12
Mammeri, Asouau 111
Manchester (UK) 167, 171
Mandarini, Matteo 59, 79
Manieri-Elia, Mario 75
Mannerism 41–51, 71
Mannheim, Karl 59
Mantegna, Andrea 176
Marchand, Suzanne 108, 116
Marchi, Virgilio 131
Markelius, Sven 147, 148
Marquet, Albert 112, 113
Marramao, Giacomo 94
Marseille (France) 132, 154
Martin, Leslie 177
Martínez, Jusepe 14
Marx, Karl 16, 54–58, 76
Marxism 16, 40–79, 140–142
Masaccio 43
Masirevich, György Jr 140
Mass Observation Movement 160
Maurras, Charles 130
May, Ernst 7, 140
Maynard Keynes, John 59
McCarthy, Conor 32
McCarthy, Joseph Raymond 141
McCarthyism 154
McClancy, Jeremy 160
McDonald, James (Sergeant) 113
McGarry, Frederick J. 173
McHale, John 179
McLeod, Malom 165
Medina Warmburg, Joaquín 132
Mediterraneity 107–132
Melior, David 180
Melograni, Carlo 74
Mendelsohn, Erich 127, 131, 175
Mercier, Sébastien 172
Mertins, Detlef 125
Mesopotamia 119
Mexico 39, 93, 147–158
Meyer, Hans Emil (Hannes) 140, 143
Michelangelo 12, 33, 49, 170

microhistory 67, 82
Middleton, Robin 64
Mies van der Rohe, Ludwig 7, 30, 106, 121–127, 158, 163
Milan (Italy) 85, 118
Miliban, Ralph 56
Miller, Herman 172
Ministère de la Reconstruction et de l'Urbanisme 146
Mirabeau, Octave 130
Mises, Ludwig von 137
Mitteleuropa 108, 114, 129
modern movement 1, 45–52, 74–86, 106, 158
modernity 1–5, 26–28, 67–94, 159
Moholy-Nagy, Lazlo 122
Moillet, Louis 123
Molnár, Farkas 140
Mondrian, Piet 120
Monroe, Marilyn 179
Monsanto Company 173
Montano, Giovanni Battista 71
Monte Verità (Switzerland) 21
monumentality 138, 161–163
Moore, Henry 157
More, Thomas 84
Morgen Ländische Alterhümer magazine 114
Moro, Aldo (Prime Minister of Italy) 67
Morocco 111, 116, 119, 143
Morris, William 25, 75, 151
Moscow (Russia) 141
Muche, Georg 124
Mumford, Lewis 139, 141
Münter, Gabriele 123
Muralism 138
Muratori, Saverio 48
Museum of Modern Art (MoMA) 7, 146, 167, 169
Museum without Walls 168
Myers, Julian 179
Myrdal, Alva 147
Myrdal, Gunnar 147

Naples (Italy) 118
National Council of American-Soviet Friendship 141
Negri, Antonio (Toni) 54, 59, 79
Neoplasticism 125
Nervi, Pier Luigi 64, 148
Netherlands 119, 120, 125
Neutra, Richard 7, 141–147
New Brutalism 154

New Deal 139
New Delhi (India) 147
New Economic Policy 63
New York 138–156
Nicholas V (Pope) 78
Niemeyer, Oscar 39, 144, 146
Nietzsche, Friedrich 27, 76, 95, 129
Nihilism 77, 89
Nitzan-Shiftan, Alona 131
Nordau, Max 116
Nordic Rollwerk 71
North Korea 154

Oceania 93
Olbrich, Josef 116
Operai e Capitale 57
Oppositions Journal 62, 70
Oran (Algeria) 108, 119
Organization of Contemporary Architects 63
Orient 48–52, 84–131
Orientalische Bibliographie 114
Orientalism 3, 10, 110, 111
originality 6, 9, 25–33
Osborne, Peter 16, 20
Osthaus, Karl Ernst 7, 121
otherness/other 5–12, 20–24, 76–97
Otterlo (The Netherlands) 177
Otto, Christian F. 66
Otto, Marcus 129
Ottoman Empire 108, 114, 129
Oud, Jacobus Johannes Pieter (J.J.P.) 119, 120–125, 132, 158
Oxford (UK) 165
Ozenfant, Amedée 131

Paci, Enzo 48
Pagano, Giuseppe 131
Pakistan 7
Palace of the Soviets competition 140
Palestine 113, 122–131, 158
Palladio, Andrea 78
Pani, Mario 39
Panzieri, Raniero 55–56
Paolozzi, Edoardo 165–169, 179
Papadaki, Stamo 146
Parallel of Life and Art (POLAA) Exhibition 168–171
Paris 85, 112, 147, 165–177
Partito Socialista Italiano di Unitá Operaia (PSIUP) 54, 56
Pasolini, Pier Paolo 88
Passerini, Luisa 48, 54, 76

Patio and Pavilion (P&P) 171–181
Patris II (ship) 132
Patterson, David 25
Paxiteles 157
Paxton, Joseph 163
Pehnt, Wolfgang 119
Pelli, César 39
Pennsylvania (USA) 138
Pérez Escolano, Victor 60
Perret, Auguste 118, 119, 126
Perriand, Charlotte 6
Persia 108, 158
Persico, Edoardo 45
Peru 9, 143, 144
Peruzzi, Baldassare Tommaso 71, 82
Petit, Claudius 139
Pevsner, Nikolaus 25, 74, 154, 161
Phoenixville (USA) 138
Picasso, Pablo 5, 142
Pico della Mirandola, Giovanni 88
picturesque 113, 161
Pietsch, Ludwig 114
Pignaud, Bernard 130
Pilley, Vivien 177
Pina-Cabral, João de 129
Piotrowski, Roman 140
Piranesi, Giovanni Battista 72, 73
Pitt-Rivers Museum 165
Pittsburgh 61
Piza, Antonio 132
Plan for Bogotá 144
plastics 157–181
Plato 28
Poelzig, Hans 119
Poland 140, 143, 154, 155
Polirone (Italy) 87
Politecnico di Milano 49
Polónyi, Károly 154
Pontremoli (Italy) 119
Portinho, Carmen 5
Portoghesi, Paolo 49, 95
Portugal 109
Posener, Julius 131
Positano (Italy) 118
Postcolonial 2, 3, 18, 19
Poussin, Nicolas 12, 10
Prague Linguistic Circle 41, 42, 95
Pretoria (South Africa) 157
PREVI 9
primitivism 52
Princeton University 62
Procida (Italy) 118
Prometheus 78

provincialism 145, 163
Prussia 16
Puerto Marghera (Italy) 54
Puerto Rico 147
Purmerend (The Netherlands) 125

Quaderni Piacentini 56
Quaderni Rossi 54, 55
Quaroni, Ludovico 44, 45, 46
Queen Victoria's Own Madras Sappers and Miners regiment (QCOMSM) 151
Quetglas, José 60

Rabat (Morocco) 146
Rabelais, François 87
Rainer, Roland 118
Raj Anand, Mulk 142
Rangoon (Myanmar) 151
Raphael 12, 49, 82–86
Rapisarda, Giusi 62
Rava, Carlo Enrico 131
Read, Herbert 151
Reclus, Jacques Elisée 130
Red Brigades 67
Regional Plan of New York 61
regionalism 3, 4, 150
Reidy, Affonso Eduardo 39
Rella, Franco 30, 67, 89
Renaissance 19, 43, 49–77
Renan, Joseph Ernest 110
Réunions Internationales des Architectes (RIA) 146
Reuther, Oscar 124
Rey, Robert 130
Reynolds, Joshua 33
Richards, J.M. 161
Ricoeur, Paul 30
Riegl, Alois 115
Rietveld, Gerrit 158
Rinascita Journal 80
Rio de Janeiro (Brazil) 144, 145
Roberts, David 109
Robertson, James 113
Robot Robbie 179, 180
Rockefeller Center 61
Rogers, Ernesto Nathan 49, 148
Rohde, Gilbert 172
Romania 93
Romano, Giulio 49, 71, 77, 86, 87
romanticism 1, 26
Rome 15, 28, 45–54, 80–116
Roosevelt, Franklin D. 141
Ross, Kristin 159

Rossanda, Rossana 56
Rossi, Aldo 54, 70
Rostow, Walt 58
Rowland Pierce, Stephen 172
Royal Festival Hall 177
Royal Institute of British Architects (RIBA) 148–157
Rudofsky, Bernard 8, 117, 118
Ruel, Anne 129, 130
Ruskin, John 115, 151
Russia 63, 93
Russian Revolution 57

Sabatino, Michelangelo 131
Said, Edward 3, 10–32, 111
Salon des Refusés 171
Salutati, Coluccio 50
Salzmann, Auguste 113
Sambricio, Carlos 60
Samonà, Giuseppe 54
San Gregorio da Sassola (Italy) 44
Sansovino, Jacopo 53, 90
Sant Pol de Mar (Catalonia) 132
Santorini (Greece) 117, 118
Sarajevo (Bosnia and Herzegovina) 94
Sarsen, Gillian 154
Sartre, Jean-Paul 46–48
Scalvini, Maria Luisa 75
Scardeone, Bernardino 12
Scheerbart, Paul 122
Schein, Ionel 173
Schinkel, Karl Friedrich 115, 116, 124
Schlosser, Julius von 12
Schmidt, Johannes (Hans) 140, 143
Schmitthenner, Paul 106
Schnabel, Day 177
School of Fontainebleau 71
Schultze-Naumburg, Paul 122
Schulze, Franz 106
Schumpeter, Joseph 59
Schwarz, Bill 161
Scilironi, Carlo 79
Sedlmayr, Hans 85
Seidler, Harry 7
Seignemartin, Jean 112
Semerani, Giuliano 54
Semiotics 54
Semper, Gottfried 115, 179
Semprun, Jorge 56
Seoul (South Korea) 166
Serlio, Sebastiano 50, 51, 90
Sert, Josep Lluís 7, 8, 132–177
Shakespeare, William 87

Shark, Michael 149
Sharon, Arieh 131
Shaw, George Bernard 151
Sicily (Italy) 43, 110
Sidi Bou Said (Tunisia) 123
signification 25
Silvetti, Jorge 62
Simmel, Georg 86, 95
simulacrum 28, 173
Sinfield, Alan 160
Singapore 94
Sive, André 146
Skidmore, Owings and Merril (SOM) 138
Smeraldi, Smeraldo 71
Smithson, Peter & Alison 8, 10, 136–181
Sobotka, Walter 117
Socialist Party 54
Socialist realism 140–155
Society for Cultural Relations between the British Commonwealth and the USSR 141
Society of Plastic Industries 172
Socrates 76
Soll, Ivan 28
Soltan, Jerzy 153, 154, 155
Soviet Union (USSR) 39, 56–64, 93, 136–154
Spain 14, 19, 60, 96–110
Spengler, Oswald 116
St. John Wilson, Colin 154, 163, 178
St. Petersburg (Rusia) 58
Stalin, Joseph 140
Stam, Mart 143
Stauth, Georg 129
Stearns Eliot, Thomas 29
Steichen, Edward 167, 169
Steiner, George 27
Stendhal 109
Stephens, Judith 154, 165
Stevenage Development Corporation 154
Stewart, Janet 20
Stirling, James 9, 149–154
Stockton-on-Tees (UK) 151
Strand, Oscar 117
Strategy of Contaminatio 87
Stroud, Peter 177
structuralism 54, 159
Strzygowski, Josef 116, 118
Stuttgart (Germany) 106, 124, 132
sub-Saharan Africa 159
Suez Invasion 161, 171, 174, 180
Sullivan, Louis 75
Sweden 156, 161

Switzerland 65, 156
Sylvester, David 170
Symes, Colin 16, 29
Syrkus, Helena 140–143, 155
Syrkus, Symon 140, 141
Szanajca, Josef 140
Szklarska Poreba (Poland) 141

Tafuri, Manfredo 1, 9, 26–99
Tange, Kenzō 5, 46, 49
Taormina (Italy) 43, 44
Team X 7, 8, 136–177
technique 62–94, 127
Technische Hochschule 117
Teige, Karel 143
Tempesta, Antonio 19
Tesla, Nicola 172
Tetouan (Morocco) 133
Teyssot, Georges 67
The Architectural Review 7, 25, 138–163
The Chicago Tribune 22
The Economist Magazine 149
The Family of Man exhibition 167–169
The Great Family of Man exhibition 167
The Historical Project 67–95
Third World 8, 41–65, 94, 136, 143, 155, 159
This is Tomorrow Exhibition 171–179
Thompson, Edward Palmer 67
Tigris 108
Timbuktu (Mali) 108
Todorov, Tzvetan 110, 111
Torino (Italy) 71
Torres Bodet, Manuel 144, 147, 148
Tournaire, Joseph Albert 119
Tours, Gregory of (Saint) 15
Tricontinental Conference 56, 57, 94
Tricontinental Journal 56
Trigger, Bruce Graham 107
Tripoli (Libya) 113
Tronti, Mario 54, 55, 58, 59
Tropicalism 138
Truman, Harry S. 141
Tunis (Tunisia) 123
Turkey 14
Turnbull, William 165
Turner, John F.C. 9
Tusculum (Italy) 119

underdevelopment 8, 58, 89, 168, 179
UNESCO 144–148, 168
Union International des Architectes (UIA) 9, 146, 148

Union of Architects of the USSR 140
United Kingdom 14, 19, 58, 108, 138–181
United Nations 144, 146, 147, 166
United Nations Relief and Rehabilitation Administration (UNRRA) 138, 146
United States 1, 3, 19, 61–174
University of Palermo 43
University of Rome 43, 45
Urfa (Turkey) 94
Uruguay 144
Utopia 9, 53–63, 82–84

van del Weyden, Rogier 43
van der Goot, Arne 147
Van Doesburg, Theo 120, 122, 125
van Dongen, Kees 113
van Eyck, Aldo 8, 9, 151–159
Van Eyck, Jan 43
van Mander, Karel 12
van't Hoff, Robert 125
Vanbrough, John 51
Vantongerloo, Georges 125
Vanuatu 160
Varchi, Benedetto 12
Vasari, Giorgio 12–19, 33
Vattimo, Gianteresio (Gianni) 80, 88
Venezuela 158
Venice (Italy) 76–98, 147
Vernacular 8, 107–132
Verne, Jules 172
Vézelay, Paule 177–179
Vico, Giambattista 28, 29, 41
Vienna (Austria) 24, 64, 98, 116, 117
Vietnam 56–58
Villa, Luisa 113
Villamajó, Julio 144
Villanueva, Carlos Raúl 39, 177
Vinken, Barbara 15, 17, 20
Virgil 1
Vitruvius 15
Voelcker, John 179
Volkgeist 115
Von Hayek, Friedrich 137
Vorderasiatische Gesellschaft 114

Wagner, Otto 116
Walden, Herwarth 122
Wallerstein, Immanuel 95, 96
Ward, Stephen V. 154
Warsaw (Poland) 141
Washington DC (USA) 141
Watkin, David 64
Weber, Maximilian (Max) 59